Clinical Social Work

CLINICAL
SOCIAL WORK

by
HELEN NORTHEN

New York   Columbia University Press

Columbia University Press
New York   Guildford, Surrey

Library of Congress Cataloging in Publication Data
Northen, Helen.
Clinical social work.

Bibliography: p.
Includes index.
1. Social service.   2. Social case work.   3. Medical
social work.   I. Title.
HV31.N67   361.3'2   81-10235
ISBN 0-231-03800-3   AACR2

10 9 8 7 6 5 4 3 2

*Clothbound editions of Columbia University Press books
are Smyth-sewn and printed on permanent
and durable acid-free paper.*

Dedicated To
two great social workers,
Arlien Johnson and Gertrude Wilson,
whose inspiration led me to pursue a lifelong
interest in the development of practice theory

CONTENTS

PREFACE

Almost forty years ago, Bertha Reynolds, a famous social work educator, challenged the profession of social work with the proposition that there is a generic social work that is basic to all forms of practice and that is not divisible into casework, group work, and community organization. Since then, other leaders in the profession have anticipated the eventual development of a method of social work that would encompass services to individuals, families, and nonfamily groups. The idea of a common method has fascinated me all of my professional life. I have searched persistently for both the similarities and differences in work with individuals and work with groups. More recently, I have become convinced that there is indeed a method which can be applied to helping people singly or in their associations with other people. Social workers can and should become competent in using individual and group processes in accordance with the needs and characteristics of their clients. It is to be remembered, however, that the application of any theory is always specific to the particular persons and social situations involved.

In this book, I offer a theoretical orientation to a common method of practice for clinical social work. Clinical social work is a term that designates professional services to and in behalf of clients when the purpose is to maintain and enhance the psychosocial functioning of individuals, families, and small groups. It is a term, however, that is not universally acceptable, because some practitioners still equate it with treatment of diagnosed pathology in psychiatric settings. As used in this book, clinical social work does not focus on pathology. It encompasses the functions of development, prevention, and therapy. It is concerned with maximizing the availability of intrapersonal, interpersonal, and environmental resources for the benefit of clients. This usage is consonant with the National Association of Social Worker's recent definition of clinical social work.

An ecological systems perspective on people and their environments undergirds the descriptions of values, knowledge, skills, and processes. Within this broad viewpoint, the social worker uses knowledge from multiple scientific sources that contributes to understanding the interdependence of biological, psychological, social, and cultural forces that influence the behavior of clients and the practitioner's interventions in the helping process. The theoretical approach is an extension and elaboration of psychosocial theories of practice. It emphasizes more fully the sociocultural aspects of the relationships among people and between people and their environments. It might be called a psychosocial-systems theory of practice.

The literature on social work practice has exploded since 1970, and there are exciting ideas therein. There is also a vast repository of important contributions from earlier times. In addition to drawing on the most recent literature, I have included many of the important contributions from the past. When possible, I have reported on major findings from research on the concepts, principles, and processes of practice that are relevant to this theoretical approach. I recognize that all knowledge is tentative and subject to further explication and testing through appropriate research designs.

In the first five chapters of the book, the philosophical, scientific, and technical foundations of the emerging theory are described and explained. In the remaining chapters, the social work process is traced from the beginning to the end. The generic concepts have been illustrated with excerpts from records of work with different client systems in varied settings.

The writing of this book is simply a way-station on a route to the development of an integrated practice theory that can meet the needs of clients to achieve greater satisfaction in social living and to cope with their problems in psychosocial functioning. The adventure began many years ago when, as a college student, I studied biology, philosophy, psychology, and sociology. In spite of the compartmentalization of these academic disciplines, I perceived no conflict among them. Indeed, each seemed to provide particular pieces of values and knowledge that ought to be interrelated to explain the multi-faceted gestalt of human behavior in social environments. When I decided to become a social worker, it was natural to select a school, the University of Pittsburgh, that offered an opportunity to study the application of theories about human development and psychosocial behavior to casework, group work, and community organization. Other experiences as a practitioner, field instructor, doctoral student, and faculty member enhanced my knowledge about and competence in practice with individuals, groups, and communities. When Arlien Johnson, Dean of the School of Social Work at the University of Southern California, recruited me for a position on the faculty, I was given special responsibility to work toward better integration of the knowledge and skills of social group work into the total curriculum. In 1964, the faculty decided to develop a generic curriculum that would prepare students for the flexible use of individual, family, and group modalities. The task of conceptualizing learning, and teaching integrated practice has been, and still is, a complex and challenging one. There is much work still to be done: it is hoped that this book will make a contribution to that endeavor.

The book has been written primarily for clinical social workers and students in schools of social work. In order to understand the theory and practice, the student should have adequate grounding in the behavioral science foundation, usually obtained in undergraduate education and courses in the sequence of Human Behavior and the Social Environment. It will be used most appropriately after the student has had an introduction to social work practice, developed some skills in interviewing and in facilitating group processes, and has an opportunity to apply the content to the field.

As indicated in the dedication, Arlien Johnson and Gertrude Wilson contributed greatly to my interest in integrated practice theory. In my efforts to develop such theory, I have been stimulated, supported, and challenged as a participant in a group of educators who were committed to the goal of preparing students for effective practice. Many of my colleagues at the University of Southern California participated in the early and ongoing development of the curriculum on integrated practice, particularly June Brown, Josephine Di Paola, Frances Feldman, Rose Green, Margaret Hartford, Elizabeth Mc-

Broom, John Milner, Howard Parad, Alice Overton, Robert Roberts, Carl Shafer, and Barbara Solomon. Many students in the master's and doctoral programs have evaluated my teaching, shared their experiences in practice with me, and contributed valuable papers and records of practice. Ruth Britton, social work librarian, has provided excellent service and support.

Authors require evaluations of their work from trusted friends and colleagues who are willing to read and criticize the manuscript. I am particularly grateful to Phyllis Caroff and Roselle Kurland of the Hunter College School of Social Work and to Philip Ringstrom, Carl Shafer, and Marie Weil of the University of Southern California who read the manuscript. They generously offered constructive suggestions for revisions and wholehearted support for the endeavor. I feel especially honored that Dorothy M. Swart of Columbia University Press, who was responsible for motivating me to write my first book, was assigned the important task of editing the manuscript. John D. Moore, now Director of the Press, has shown infinite patience and provided the encouragement that was necessary for me to complete the task.

My sincere thanks to all these people.

Helen Northen
University of Southern California
April, 1981

Clinical Social Work

CHAPTER ONE

Perspectives on Social Work Practice

Social work is a multifaceted profession. Its practitioners have assumed responsibility for a wide range of services to deal with problems in the realm of the interaction between people and their environments. They practice in varied fields, with diverse populations, and utilize different theories of practice. They provide direct services to people and they plan, organize, and administer services. They intervene in individual, group, community, and organizational systems. Within this diversity, they have striven to develop a profession with a recognized set of values, purposes, scientific knowledge, and technical competence. The search for a common base for a unified profession has been long and arduous and has not yet been fully achieved.

Within the broad domain of the profession, progress has been made in developing a common base of values, purposes, knowledge, and skills for integrating individual, family, and group modalities of practice. In this book, the task is to develop an integrated theoretical approach to practice for one important part of the profession—direct service to individuals, families, and other small groups toward the general purpose of enhanced psychosocial functioning. The domain includes work in the community in behalf of clients as an integral part of direct service practice. It encompasses the functions of enhancement, prevention, and remediation. The primary theoretical orientation is a social systems one that incorporates understanding of an individual as a biopsychosocial system, interacting with a network of individuals and social systems. It emphasizes the psychosocial relations among persons and the interdependence between people and their environments.

Roots of Integrated Practice

The evolution of theory for social work practice has been characterized by swings of interest between specialized and generalist practice. During the first two decades of the century, practice was generally regarded as specialized by type of agency: charity organization societies, settlements, youth services, child welfare, hospitals, and schools. What were regarded as specializations developed from knowledge of differences in types of organizations, patterns of staffing, and the needs or problems of clients that were of central concern. During this time, however, few distinctions were made on the basis of whether service was rendered to an individual, a family, or a peer group: workers used whatever modality seemed to be practical and helpful.

Specialization by method developed first in social casework, and then in social group work. Mary Richmond, a leader in the charity organization movement, was the major pioneer in developing theory for casework. In *Social Diagnosis,* written in 1917, she specified the knowledge that was basic to understanding clients, their families, and their environments. The process of social diagnosis was presented as the common foundation for all casework practice, regardless of the organization in which it was practiced. The focus of diagnosis and treatment was the family. Casework, however, soon became redefined as work with individuals in a one-to-one relationship. In her second major book, *What Is Social Case Work?,* Richmond said: "Social case work consists of those processes which develop personality through adjustments consciously effected, individual by individual, between men and their social environment."[1] Case work was viewed as only one form of social work, the purpose of which was the development of personality. The other interrelated parts of the profession were group work, social reform, and social research.

The origins of knowledge about work with groups came primarily from practice in settlements, hospitals, and youth organizations. The major contribution to the early literature was probably Grace Coyle's *Social Process in Organized Groups.* Whereas Richmond was associated with the Charity Organization Society, Coyle's experience had been with settlements and the Young Women's Christian Association, in which groups were organized for varied purposes. This book provided a conceptual framework concerning the structure and processes of organized groups that broke ground in a way similar to what Richmond's *Social Diagnosis* had done for casework. Just as social workers interested primarily in work with individuals thought of casework as a specialized method, so too, did this happen in group work.

Along with the primary focus on specialization based on method, the profession was fragmented into specializations by fields of practice. Agencies with common functions had been organized into the Family Welfare Association of America in 1911 and the Child Welfare League of America in 1920. Specialized professional organizations were founded: the American Association of Hospital Social Workers in 1918, the American Association of Visiting Teachers in 1919, and the American Association of Psychiatric Social Workers in 1926.

Challenges to the trend toward specializations occurred, as evidenced by the founding of the American Association of Social Workers in 1921, which sought to unify social workers into one profession. One of the first projects of the new organization was to establish a conference which met at Milford, Pennsylvania. Participants were administrators and board members of national agencies and representatives of the professional organizations. The conference dealt with problems occasioned by the proliferation of specialized forms of casework. Over a period of several years, the participants became convinced that generic social casework was much more substantial in content than were any of its specific emphases. In its published report, the major conclusion was that casework is generic: regardless of agency setting, practitioners require common values, knowledge, and methodology. The generic content was outlined. It was found that "the problems of social case work are fundamentally the same for all fields . . . generic social case work is the common field to which the specific forms of social case work are merely incidental."[2] Although the committee studied only social case work, it concluded that perhaps there is also a generic social work.

At approximately the same time, a study on group work was published, again under the auspices of the American Association of Social Workers. As in the casework study, it was concluded that there was evidence of a growing awareness of common professional ground within group work—a "recognition of a similar philosophy, a convergence of training and technique, some interchange of personnel, and a tendency toward exchange of experience." The purpose of group work was to seek the "development of the individual to his fullest capacity and to encourage more satisfactory relations between the individual and his environment."[3] Note how closely this statement of purpose accords with that of social casework.

As theory for both casework and group work was being explicated and refined, some leaders emphasized the interrelatedness of work with individuals and work with groups. Generic aspects of practice became evident as group workers found it desirable to have personal interviews with members of their groups and as caseworkers added the leadership of groups to their casework services.[4] Agencies were increasingly offering both individual and group services. In writing about developments in the 1930s, Schwartz said that the great depression had much influence on practice: "Thrown together around common problems and a common clientele, caseworkers, group workers, and community organization workers came increasingly to regard themselves as partners in the same enterprise."[5] They were moving toward identification with social work as a profession.

In the late 1930s, Wilson conducted a survey on the relationships between casework and group work, under the auspices of the Family Welfare Association of America. She found that practitioners had many misunderstandings about each other's work. "Vocabulary difficulties, differences in conceptual knowledge, and even differences in fundamental philosophies have blocked progress toward complete and easy cooperation."[6] Mutual understanding was occurring, however, as workers gained experience in referral, coordination, and collaboration. Many clients were receiving a combination of casework and group work services, designed as complementary ways to meet their special needs. She identified a core of values, knowledge, and skills that are generic to both methods. Although there were some important differences also, it was clear that "the poles of thinking are today reaching toward each other."[7]

Increasingly, leaders in the profession questioned whether, in fact, there were separate methods in social work practice. In 1942, for example, Reynolds wrote:

> We can now begin to discern a generic social work that is basic to all forms in which it appears today and that is not sharply divisible into the categories of casework, group work, and community organization. It is all of these and more, because all of these are interrelated as varying aspects of an art of working with people.[8]

Based on a study of trends in professional education for social work in the 1940s, Marion Hathway, who had been the executive director of the American Association of Schools of Social Work, commented that the narrow emphasis on casework had been modified. She said that, although not yet firmly established, trends in the direction of a truly generic preparation for social work practice can easily be identified.[9] Several years later, Arlien Johnson, a leader in community organization and social work education, traced the evolution of casework, group work, and community organization work. She noted that these methods had become independent of specific agencies or fields or practice. They have generic content and are adaptable to many situations and settings. Furthermore, she described a trend toward clarification of the interrelationship between individual and group treatment. She predicted that in the future, all social workers will have basic skills in both individual and group relationships and that the present specializations and designations of methods will disappear in favor of a social work method.[10] Johnson's article was written in 1955, the year that the new National Association of Social Workers was founded in a second attempt to develop a unified professional organization.

An early project of the new organization was to formulate a working definition of social work practice that set forth the common base of practice for work with individuals, groups, and communities.[11] Harriet Bartlett was chairperson of the Commission on Social Work Practice that prepared the report. At the same time, Werner Boehm developed a similar definition for the Council on Social Work Education to guide a curriculum study.[12] Later, Bartlett clarified the interdependency between generic and specific aspects of practice.[13] The term "generic" refers to the values, knowledge, principles, and skills that are common to all forms of practice; there are, however, particular or specific applications and elaborations of the generic base as determined by the needs, problems, and characteristics of clients and by the organizational auspice in which practice takes place.

A reemphasis on social work practice with family units did not emerge until the mid-1950s. Caseworkers became interested in family diagnosis and treatment, as did group workers. There was renewed recognition that the family is a small group system and that concepts concerning the dynamics and structure of small groups are useful in understanding families, taking into account the unique characteristics of the family as a primary group. Work with family units was often one part of a broader plan for service which, depending upon the needs of individuals and the family system, often included individual work, placement of some family members in formed groups, or services to groups of families. These trends hastened the development of knowledge about the common base for practice in direct services to clients, and the differential use of modalities of practice related to their special characteristics and the varied needs of clients.

Evidence that practitioners were giving both individual and group services mounted. Announcements of positions in social agencies increasingly sought social workers who would combine casework and group work and sometimes also community social work activities. Surveys of practitioners indicated that both caseworkers and group workers were serving groups of clients or their relatives, in addition to working with individuals.[14] The applicability of generic concepts and principles to both forms of practice was recognized. Articles and books on integrated practice with individuals and groups were written, as were some on a broader generalist practice that incorporated work with both micro and macro systems.[15] By 1980, a large majority of schools of social work were teaching some form of generic, generalist, or integrated practice.[16]

Rationale for Integrated Practice

Rationales for the development of a generic base for all social work practice have been set forth by many writers. Some social workers are concerned that social work lacks a professional identity and a clear mandate as a profession, with a recognized set of activities that fit together to comprise a unified whole with a common purpose. One consequence of the way social work developed historically was that workers tended to be identified by a particular method, agency function, or field of practice. For example, they were referred to as settlement workers, probation officers, caseworkers, group workers, or even psychiatric group workers or medical caseworkers. These divisions prevented mutual understanding among social workers, thus restricting examination of the common base for social work practice. It has been noted by several authors that, in Siporin's words, "social work is in a state of intense ferment and rapid change."[17] His view is that a professional identity can develop only if there is a shared core of philosophy, purpose, knowledge, and method. In a similar vein, Hartman has stated that a generic reconceptualization of practice can bridge the dichotomies currently fragmenting the profession.[18] Meyer has also noted that there is a need to permeate methodological boundaries so that social work will be able to claim a unitary practice, with specializations restricted to substantive areas and not to methodological ideologies.[19] Before specialization can be viable, said Overton, both the public and the profession must be clear about the general purpose and practice of social work.[20]

Another major rationale for the promotion of a unified approach to practice is that such practice is in harmony with knowledge about human behavior. Artificial segregation of practice by the number of people served at any point of time negates the human condition. The trend in the behavioral sciences is toward a holistic view of people as they interact in a multitude of social networks. Effective functioning requires an adaptive fit between the organism and its environment. In the words of Germain and Gitterman: "Today's environments impose an overwhelming array of adaptive tasks upon people as individuals and within their families and groups. . . . It seems unreasonable to define this need for help with these tasks in terms of a particular practice modality and the restrictive preferences of worker and agency."[21] Such a view of human behavior requires that a social worker be competent to intervene in any part of the person-group-environment gestalt. In social work, as Meyer says, "the blurring of role categories is more consonant with the way people actually live their lives as individuals and as members of families, groups, and communities."[22]

Many social work writers are convinced that the traditional separation of methods is no longer tenable if clients are to receive effective services that are responsive to their needs.[23] The separation of work with individuals from work with groups supports a false dichotomy between persons and their social contexts. It supports a tendency to give services in terms of the practitioner's biases, knowledge, and narrow skills or an agency's outmoded statement of functions, rather than in terms of an assessment of client needs and the particular values inherent in each modality of service. The consequences of possessing knowledge and skill in only one method are fragmentation in assessment and service planning and inappropriate assignment of clients to a mode of service. The fundamental idea behind an integrated approach to practice is that the needs or problems of the client should determine the mode or modes of service. Perlman has cautioned practitioners that the traditional boundaries should not serve as guides for practice, because then treatment is shaped a priori by the particular method to which a worker has allegiance.[24] Schwartz has said it well:

> Any agency should be capable of creating, in each specific instance, that system of client-worker relationships which is most appropriate to its clients' requirements. . . . To describe casework, group work, and community organization as methods simply mistakes the nature of the helping process for the relational system in which it is applied. . . . It seems more accurate to speak of a social work method, practiced in the various systems in which the social worker finds himself or which are established for the purpose of giving service.[25]

Based on an adequate assessment of the individual or family in its situation, the social worker should have the ability to use individual, family, group, and community contexts in a purposeful and planned way. Ron Baker has summarized well the major arguments for a generically oriented and skilled professional social worker. In order to begin where the client is and meet his needs, the perspective is that:

The individual or group that becomes the focus of social work intervention is caught up in a network of relationships, or psychological and social systems, that link the client to his physical and psychological past and present, his family, small groups, neighborhood, and community. When these systems are under excessive strain and in a state of extreme imbalance, social work intervention is likely to be needed. Thus, in his everyday practice, the social worker is faced with a wide range of psychological needs and unhelpful social systems which push him to act at individual, group, or community levels, either at the same time or in rapid succession. If method is to be his servant and not his master, then the social worker needs educating in a wide range of interventive strategies and to be given the opportunities to use them. . . . The human situation is always psychosocial.[26]

Few voices are raised against the trend toward combining work with individuals and work with groups into a division of direct service practice, increasingly referred to as clinical social work. Recent research indicates that social work educators support generic practice, but they define it in different ways: some use the term in relation to direct service practice and others, to practice that encompasses work with communities and larger organizations as well.[27]

Social workers who doubt the desirability of combining casework and group work are concerned about losing the special contributions of each method and the specific skills in relationships that are required in effective work with individuals or groups. They assert that the differences between casework and group work, for example, are so great that they cannot be combined and that it is impossible for a social worker to learn and practice more than one modality.[28] Others take the position that, even if a practitioner should limit his service either to individuals one at a time or to groups, his practice can be relevant only if he has depth of knowledge about social relationships in both dyads and larger systems, and that understanding is enhanced through experience with a range of relationships.

Even when generic or integrated practice is favored, some social workers express concern that depth of skill in individual, family, group, or community services may be sacrificed in favor of breadth of perspective. As efforts to ferret out a theoretical base for practice come to fruition, it may become evident that "a large core of investigative, analytic, and human relations skills cut across system size and will be reinforced rather than diluted by their use in different contexts."[29] In such ways, breadth of knowledge actually contributes to depth. As one perceives the way in which a concept or principle applies in diverse situations, he comes to a deeper understanding of it. As a practitioner attempts, for example, to convey empathy in both individual and family relationships, he becomes more aware of the complexity of the task and of his own feelings and assumptions that interfere with the necessary attitude. As he faces resistance of clients in the one-to-one relationship in various forms, his understanding is increased. When he is also confronted with massive group resistance, he adds to the earlier understanding of the concept.

Development of theories of unified practice, at least in direct services to clients, need not deny the many variations in application of knowledge and methodology to the specific needs of categories of people based on age, sex, ethnicity, social class, and organizational auspice. Nor need it deny that there are differences in the structure of dyads, artificially formed groups, families and their subsystems, and larger aggregates. Some differences in the process and content of assessment and in the use of interactional skills result from structural differences. Social work practice is generic; it is also specific. The common values, knowledge, and skills are applied differentially to specific situations.

Beyond the issue of direct service practice, there is controversy about other forms of specialization in social work. The trend now seems to be toward two major forms of practice: direct services to and in behalf of clients, and services to communities and institutions. As early as 1958, Wilensky and Lebeaux took the position that there should be two models of practice: the skilled social casework or social group work practitioner, and the community organizer and planner.[30] In 1967, Burns argued that the professional objectives of social work education should be to educate a clinician and a social welfare specialist.[31] Over the years, similar proposals for a two-track system of education and practice have been made. Gilbert and Specht, for example, reject a generic or integrated view of social work practice. They assert that the knowledge and skill required of the direct service and social welfare practitioner are different and should be different.

They believe that emphasis on generic or integrated models aims toward "professional unity at the cost of functional relevance."[32]

One argument is that many activities of class advocacy, political action, legislative formulation, and planning and coordination of services have not been carried out in the same agencies that provide direct services to people. Thus, organizational auspice becomes a determiner of specialization. Another argument is that the knowledge required for community organization and planning is essentially different from that required for services to individuals and families. Some social workers, however, have developed models of practice that are inclusive of work with systems of various size and complexity.[33]

Within clinical social work, some community social work activities are as essential as is engagement with clients. One of the characteristics of social work practice that distinguishes it from clinical work by other professionals is concern with the social context. Altering the social situation is one means for achieving objectives. Furthermore, there is responsibility to observe deficiencies in resources or harmful conditions pertaining to clients and to initiate change by making these conditions known to professional and institutional systems. "Thus, clinical social work contributes to the welfare of its clients, but also to the quality of life for people in similar circumstances."[34]

The complexity of social work practice and issues concerning its scope is aggravated by the development of competing theories of practice. By 1950, a diagnostic (later labeled "psychosocial") and a functional theory of practice had been compared and found to be so different that they could not be reconciled.[35] Since then, efforts to develop different theoretical approaches to practice have proliferated in both social work with individuals and social work with groups. Several of the formulations have been applied to work with individuals, families, and small groups; these include the psychosocial, functional, problem-solving, behavior modification, crisis intervention, socialization, and task-centered orientations to practice. In addition, there have been theories developed specifically for work with individuals or work with groups. Comparative analyses of these sets of writings have been made by Simon, Northen and Roberts, and

Turner.[36] The major conclusion has been that there is considerable overlapping among the formulations, but there are also important differences. There are, and probably will continue to be, multiple views of how people can best be helped or multiple models that can be used differentially, dependent upon the needs or problems of clients. The implication is that there is a need to clarify particular approaches to practice that aim to integrate work with individuals, families, and other small groups into a unified whole.

Social work is a profession in flux. There is no one accepted theory of practice around which the profession is united. Each theory incorporates its own constellation of values, purposes, knowledge, and areas of technical competence. As multiple integrated theories are developed and evaluated, their differential usefulness may become apparent. A particular approach may be most appropriate for particular kinds of clients, problems, or organizations. The theorist's ideas about the mission of social work will color what he considers to be the essential ingredients of the theory. In the model of practice herein, the purpose is to effect positive changes in the interactions and transactions among people, more specifically defined as the enhancement of psychosocial functioning and the prevention and treatment of problems in psychosocial relations.

The Purpose of Social Work

Social work has always had concern for individuals in their interpersonal relationships and in encounters with their environment. The term "psychosocial functioning" refers to the characteristic ways that an individual interacts in his personal-social situation. It is influenced by the dynamic interplay of psychological and biological forces within the person and by the outer social and physical characteristics of the situation, including all the persons who are part of that situation. It is influenced by the individual's prior relationships which have hindered or helped him to achieve his potential. Many clients have been deprived of meaningful and satisfying relationships or they have been unable to develop and sustain them: their psychosocial growth has been stunted.

The development of social work as a professional practice grew out of a recognition that the needs for which social services were originally created, such as income maintenance or institutional care, were more than needs for adequate income, food, shelter, or medical care, important as they are. Grace Coyle has said that "the turning point in the development of social work came with the recognition that, accompanying such needs, sometimes as cause and sometimes as effect, were problems in psychosocial relations."[37] The term "psychosocial relations," as used by Coyle, refers not only to the intrapsychic reactions of individuals in their relations with others, but also to the social conditions or situations which contribute to unhappiness or social dysfunctioning. Eileen Younghusband, a prominent British and international social work educator, said that the role of social work

is to help mankind to become more responsible, more civilized, in relation to the weaker members of the community; and in so doing, to help individuals to discover richer and more varied ways of living in society. . . . The social worker is one whose whole professional purpose is to know how to improve the relationships between people. This is a positive concept in that it implies providing opportunities which nurture the individual and for the growth of his total personality, thereby extending his capacity for good relationships and making him more a social being.[38]

Several writers who have been primarily identified with social casework accept the inextricable connection between social relations and social conditions. Early in the history of professional practice, Richmond said that social casework requires skill in discovering the social relationships by which a given personality has been shaped; an ability to get at the central core of the difficulty in these relationships, and power to utilize the direct action of mind upon mind in their adjustment.[39] She emphasized that provision of services and development of relationships go hand in hand.

In a major textbook on social casework, Gordon Hamilton defined the purpose of social work as helping an individual, a family, or a group of persons in their social relationships, and also in improving general social conditions. She thought that social work occupies a peculiarly inclusive position in relation to other professions, since economic and cultural security and individual behavior and social relationships are interwoven. She said:

> It is this integration which consistently has shaped social work and given it its distinguishable if not wholly distinctive pattern; it is this which gives it its complexities, its frustrations, its fascination, and its challenge. Social work is utilized whenever people's capacities to organize their affairs are impaired or they lack satisfaction in ordinary social relationships.[40]

Reynolds viewed the purpose of social work as being to help people to live as social beings: scientific understanding "should bear fruit in better relationships."[41] Similarly, Strean, in an historical study of the purposes of social casework, concluded that the caseworker has a perspective on man and the social environment as a field of interacting forces. The focus on social relationships and social role performance distinguishes and differentiates casework from other helping disciplines.[42] In another reference, he states that he has become convinced that all human beings in distress have been deprived of some crucial interpersonal experience.[43]

Feldman and Scherz, in their concern for family social welfare, came to similar conclusions. They stressed the idea that the part of social work that deals with direct services to people in trouble is vitally concerned with the interpersonal relationships within the family and with other people having significance for them. Other articles and books espouse similar views.[44]

In group work, as in casework, there has continued to be reaffirmation of Coyle's position. Konopka asserted that the practitioner's role is always in the area of human relationships: groups need social workers when individualization is necessary and when members need help with social relationships. Kaiser noted that the essence of social work's credo is the

> sanctity of the individual human being in an interdependent society. . . . Specifically, social group work is concerned with improving the relationships of people by providing and guiding associations and experiences in groups. . . . Many individuals being served in groups are unable to form satisfying relationships with others because of emotional or social maladjustments.[45]

In studying definitions of social group work from the first one in the 1920s to 1964, Hartford concluded that, although there were differences of opinion about the goals of group work, there emerged a consensus that group work aimed to help people who had problems in social relationships and also helped "normal people to grow socially."[46]

The focus on social relationships is a generic one, accepted by writers originally identified with casework, family service, or group work. Interest in relationships is based on knowledge that man and society are inseparable; that people are interdependent on one another for survival and for satisfaction of their needs; that failures in relationships at any point in the life cycle interfere with a person's further healthy development; and that people's conflicts are expressed in their relationships. Social work, as a profession with a major responsibility for the quality of human relations, is concerned with the promotion of opportunities for the enhancement of potentials and for the prevention of problems. It has a responsibility also for the remediation of difficulties and conflicts that have developed.

The Functions of Social Work

Direct services to individuals and families may be developmental, preventive, or remedial in nature. Over the years, there has been controversy around the philosophical issue of whether the mission of social work should be institutional or residual.[47] From an institutional perspective, social work is a permanent and legitimate function in society for helping people to maximize their potentials, leading to the inclusion of, or preference for, developmental and preventive services. From a residual perspective, social work comes into play when society fails to meet human needs, leading to therapeutic or remedial forms of service to people who are at greatest risk. The most prevalent view is that enhancement, prevention, and remediation are all appropriate functions for social work.

Public health and community psychiatry have influenced social work formulations of its functions. These disciplines have identified a continuum of functions from promotion of positive health to remediation. In fact, remediation is viewed as one of three forms of prevention: primary, secondary, and tertiary. Remediation and rehabilitation become synonymous with tertiary prevention.[48] The purpose of primary prevention is to reduce the incidence of disorders through intervention before pathology or malfunctioning occurs. The assumption is that particular conditions or events affect large numbers of people in somewhat similar ways. If people are prepared to face anticipated events, they will be more apt to cope with them adequately and potential problems will be prevented. Secondary prevention occurs after there are warnings of a disastrous event or after symptoms have developed. The aim is to reduce the duration of the disorders which do occur and to prevent disabling aftereffects by early detection and prompt treatment. The purpose of tertiary prevention is to overcome or reduce impairment which has already occurred.

Since systems theory implies multiple influences on a person's functioning at a given time, the public health model requires modification for social work practice. This is because it assumes that a specific determinant causes illness. Parad has noted that since social work deals with complicated systems of multiple causation, "we cannot neatly isolate etiological agents, make easy predictions, and quickly locate and immunize vulnerable clients."[49] Preventive services must take into account the interrelatedness of biological, psychological, and social influences on behavior. The provision of viable preventive services poses formidable obstacles for social work; yet progress has been made in designing and conducting programs that aim to prevent problems in psychosocial functioning.

PRIMARY PREVENTION

Indirect services. Primary prevention is by no means the sole province of the direct service practitioner. Since the early days of the profession, social workers have participated in social investigations to describe social conditions that required change. They try to influence legislation at local and national levels. They note gaps in services, particularly for the poor and ethnic minorities, and argue for planning and legislation to reduce these gaps. They design systems for reaching the people who are most in need of resources. Thus, prevention through social legislation, social action, and community planning and organization has been with the profession since its early days. Direct service workers cannot be expected to eliminate poverty, poor housing, environmental pollution, or racism; but they do influence the policies and procedures of social agencies as these adversely affect the nature and quality of services. They document and disseminate information about the nature and extent of the unmet needs of their clients. They represent their agencies in community efforts to achieve better coordination of services, new programs, or changed policies concerning existing services. They support appropriate legislative proposals and urge that others do so, based on firsthand knowledge of the needs of clients. They participate in projects sponsored by professional organizations and express their social concerns as citizens.

Another preventive activity in which social workers engage is licensing or certification to insure that standards are being met in such diverse facilities as camps, foster homes, family care homes for discharged mental patients, nursing homes, residential treatment facilities, and child care centers. This is a regulatory function that insures that these organizations will provide a physical and social environment conducive to the health and welfare of the clients or residents. If regulation of child care facilities should come to be regarded generally as an essential function of social work, the result could be an "effective application of a socio-legal concept in developing better out-of-home care for children and more farsighted social planning in their behalf."[50] The concept of licensing as prevention has significance for the design and operation of facilities for the aged and other groups, as well as for children.

Licensing is only one means to improve people's living environments. Relative to children, a suitable home is the most crucial milieu. Many dependent, neglected, or abused children are denied the opportunity for growth-producing family relationships because suitable foster and adoptive families are not available. Although there are many good adoptive or foster homes for young children who are white and free from physical or mental handicaps, this is not true for children of minority racial or mixed backgrounds, for older children, or for children with handicaps. If a child is to be prevented from growing up without being a member of a stable family, the deterrents to recruiting foster and adoptive families need to be sought and remedied. When children who need homes are not eligible for adoption, the same careful planning is needed to assure their welfare by preventing inappropriate and multiple placements in foster care or institutions.[51] Foster parents need to be selected with as much care as adoptive parents. If a child becomes eligible for adoption, the foster parents should have priority if they wish to adopt the child and if they have had the child long enough for a caring and nurturing relationship to have developed. The assumption is that if suitable homes can be found for children, their psychosocial development will be furthered and problems prevented. Even more important than placement is reduction in the number of children requiring placement, through provision of economic and psychosocial resources that make possible retention of as many children as possible in their own families, thus helping all members of the family as well as the children.

Children are not the only people who need living environments that provide for satisfying social living. Convalescent and rest homes, board and care homes, and retirement communities can be designed so as to enhance the social functioning of their residents.

Consultation has been described as one means of primary prevention. Its aim is to assist other personnel, who have direct contacts with people, to give more effective services. By working through other individuals or groups, the consultant can make an impact on large numbers of people. According to an agreed-upon purpose and plan, the consultant engages the consultee in a problem-solving process, offering information and suggestions that are sought by the consultee. The focus of the consultation may be a particular case or set of cases or it may be a program or administrative concern. The assumption is that the consultee will be able to give better services or to influence the quality of services given by others, thus preventing potential problems from occurring.

Direct services. Primary prevention, through direct services to client systems, is anticipatory in nature: it is directed toward the future, not the past. Its general purpose is to prevent psychosocial breakdown by enhancing a person's skills and abilities, leading to increased competence in interpersonal relations and a sense of confidence in approaching new life tasks. To keep something from happening, it is necessary to alter certain factors that might contribute to stress. When primary preventive services are provided, the use of the term "problem" can be misleading; "need" is a more appropriate word. This is because services are directed to a defined population which is presumed to need certain services in order to enhance its normal development—not to people with designated problems.

ENHANCEMENT OR DEVELOPMENT

Since prevention implies that there is danger of becoming ill or getting into trouble, some writers prefer to separate a function of development or enhancement from prevention and therapy. Meyer is one of these and says:

> Developmental social services are those that recognize changes in family forms, patterns of child care and socialization, relationships of the aging to the community, modes of health care, and other social responses to the urbanized, post-industrial, technological society. Developmental social services are devised at an institutional rather than a residual level, as a social effort to cope with everyone's personal reality . . . are fashioned after a life model rather than a disease model.[52]

Kahn is another social work educator who argues against classifying promotion of health within a preventive continuum. He suggests that the idea of prevention may be too limiting for social work. Because prevention is tied to pathology, it does not accurately encompass services which enhance social development. Social services should become available as a matter of human right, rather than special eligibility. Status, rather than individual malfunction or inadequacy, should define needs and requirements. Kahn says that prevention and therapy are both necessary, but so are developmental services.[53] Wittman also has emphasized the need for social workers to become more interested in enhancing the well-being of individuals, families, and communities in order to enrich daily living. They should give attention to socially healthy people in order to reinforce ego development and provide help to people at such transition points in their lives as school entrance, marriage, and parenthood.[54]

Services that are designed for helping people who are at critical developmental and transitional points in the life cycle are classified by some authors as primary prevention and by others as developmental or enhancement services. The major purpose of such services is to enhance social competence. Clients are not defined as belonging to a population at risk, nor is it predicted that they will develop problems if they do not receive service. Rather, the assumption is that by anticipating new expectations and preparing to meet them, the ego's coping capacities are enhanced so that new ways can be found to deal with new roles and relationships.

A social form of education is becoming recognized as an essential developmental program in social work. Such programs are designed to enhance the capacity for relating to people in appropriate ways. Services have been offered, for example, to help parents facilitate the successful entry of their children to school. They have been offered to help parents understand and deal with everyday problems in family living. They have been offered to enhance adoptive parents' ability to incorporate the new child into the family. They have been offered to relatives of chronic patients so that they might anticipate and plan for changes in roles that are associated with the illness.

SECONDARY PREVENTION

Early diagnosis and prompt treatment are the hallmarks of secondary prevention. The targets are individuals and families who are already suffering from severe stress of recent origin. Although problems have been identified, such services are considered to be preventive in nature, since the preventive component outweighs the remedial aspects. The aim is to prevent psychosocial stress from becoming debilitative. Unlike primary prevention, the service is given to particular individuals and families, with specified forms of stress.

Crisis intervention is perhaps the best and most fully developed form of secondary prevention. This model of practice has been applied to work with individuals, families, and groups.[55] When a person is in a state of crisis, his steady state is acutely upset as a consequence of exposure to a hazardous event. The precipitating event may be a natural disaster such as flood, fire, or earthquake, or such threatening experiences as rape, attempted suicide, hospitalization, death of a loved one, or separation. The state of crisis is temporary, characterized by signs of confusion or other cognitive disorders and emotional upset which immobilize the ego's problem-solving abilities and interfere with other aspects of daily living. These reactions are responses to stress; they are not pathological. The major goals of crisis intervention are to reduce the immediate effect of stress and to help the clients and others who are influenced by the crisis to mobilize their coping capacities in adaptive ways. The resolution of a crisis involves the individual or family in searching for new ways of coping with the situation and adapting to it. First developed as a service to individuals, crisis intervention is now practiced with family units when there is a collective crisis or when the crisis of one member is upsetting to the others as well. It is also used with formed groups of individuals who share the experience of being in a state of crisis.

REMEDIATION OR THERAPY

Throughout the history of social work practice, the remedial or therapeutic function has had priority. In this type of service, the practitioner helps the client to change those personal and environmental factors which cause breakdown or impairment of psychosocial functioning. Remediation differs from prevention in that help is given to an individual, family, or other group which has already one or more problems in psychosocial functioning. The treatment is based on differential assessment of the person-group-situation configuration; a plan of treatment is developed with the individual or family, and a course of treatment is pursued which is flexibly based on continuous efforts to understand the person or family in the environment. Individual, family, or group modalities of treatment may be used, singly or in combination. The general purpose of remediation is to assist the client to alter the emotions, thought processes, and actions that underlie the difficulty and to alter the factors in the environment that contribute to the problem.

A CONTINUUM OF SERVICES

Developmental, preventive, or therapeutic approaches can be used to meet various needs and problems of people. The selection of the appropriate function is based on whether a problem exists and, if so, the time of onset of the problem. Developmental services do not assume a problem, but rather a common human need for enhancement of social living. Primary prevention precedes the onset of a defined problem; secondary prevention occurs as soon as possible after identification of the problem; and remediation or tertiary prevention occurs when there is an existing problem, acute or chronic, that needs to be resolved or remedied.

In social work practice a service may initially be offered at one level of prevention, followed by services at other levels. During the course of crisis intervention, for example, a problem in the marital relationship may become evident which is not directly related to the crisis. Following the termination of crisis work, the client may be referred to an appropriate service, or a new agreement may be made that the worker and client will work together on the marital problem. This change in focus may also lead to inclusion of the spouse of the client in the treatment endeavor. In treating particular clients, it may be discovered that there are many people who, if they were reached early through an educational approach, might have less chance of developing serious difficulties; a developmental service is offered to the particular population. An acute crisis may occur during the course of another form of treatment, in which case the focus of the service is shifted temporarily to the crisis and its resolution.

Comprehensive programs may be designed to deal with populations having particular needs and problems. One example is that of services to unwed, pregnant adolescents. The girls needed immediate help with their particular problems, decisions concerning their own and the unborn child's future, and the demands of child rearing. It was learned that many of the girls wanted to return to school, but there were obstacles in the form of educational policies which did not permit pregnant girls in regular classes. This led to the establishment of a continuing education program for all pregnant girls in the school system. A variety of individual and group counseling and educational services for the girls, the fathers of the babies, and the girls' families were provided. In this instance, social policy development and social action were combined with direct services of both a preventive and a remedial nature. Although the girls had problems which needed attention, there was a strong component of enhancement and prevention, in terms both of aiding the young mothers to prepare for that role and also to complete high school and thereby acquire basic tools for meaningful employment or higher education. It was anticipated that the girls would be able to rear their infants under more advantageous circumstances than those under which they were reared, thus breaking multigenerational cycles of poverty, dependency, and family pathology.[56]

Developmental, preventive, and therapeutic services together are necessary to assure the effective psychosocial functioning of people. The trend in social work toward developmental and preventive services, in addition to therapeutic or remedial ones, is in line with recent developments in the field of health. A commission on the mental health of children proposed a strategy for mental health in which resources would be deployed in the service of optimizing human development. The commission proposed that social services should be made available to all children and all families as a social utility through a network of comprehensive and systematic services, programs, and policies which would provide every person with the opportunity to develop to maximum potential. Equal priority would be given to comprehensive services to insure the maintenance of physical and mental health, to a broad range of remedial services, and to a system of advocacy to insure effective implementation of the goals.[57] This report was directed to the needs of children and youth, but the same principles are applicable to people throughout the life cycle.

Conclusion

In order to serve people effectively, a model of practice is necessary that integrates values, knowledge, and skills in work with individuals, families, small groups, and environments. The purposes toward which practice is directed lie in the realm of psychosocial relations or social living. The practitioner may intervene with varied client systems at any level of need—enhancement, prevention, or remediation. He may use individual, family, or group modalities of practice at any level of need. Both the modalities of practice and the levels of intervention may be used singly, serially, or in combination. Such flexible practice requires a philosophical perspective and both breadth and depth of knowledge and competence: the challenge is indeed complex.

CHAPTER TWO

Values and Knowledge

Throughout most of the history of social work practice, efforts have been made to understand the person in his situation and thus to provide services that can meet his needs. Helping individuals or families to meet their needs more adequately is based on particularizing the person in his environment, that is, in the network of interlocking social systems of which he is a part. It is a basic principle of practice that the worker individualizes his work with people. Individualization occurs when a person's needs and capacities and the unique qualities of his environment are taken into consideration.

Regardless of whether the early pioneers were most concerned with individuals, groups, or communities, they gradually learned that problems are caused by multiple transactions within a system and between the system and its environment. Jane Addams, that great pioneer in the settlement house movement, wrote dramatically about a lesson learned the hard way. Scientific knowledge of social and political situations had always guided Addams's approach to neighborhood improvement and broader social reform. She insisted that social action should be preceded by carefully ascertained facts. She learned, through trial and error, that this is true for help to individuals as well. In one example, she notified a man that employment was available on a drainage canal and advised him to take the job; otherwise, he could not receive assistance for his family. He went to work, as she recommended, but he died of pneumonia shortly thereafter. In focusing on employment, she had failed to acquire other knowledge about the client and his family. From such experiences she learned that "life cannot be administered by definite rules and regulations . . . the wisdom to deal with a man's difficulties comes only through knowledge of his life and habits as a whole: and to treat isolated episodes is almost sure to invite blundering."[1] She concluded that it is necessary to know people through varying conditions of life. She accepted the need to understand individuals, their families, and their other social relationships as these interconnect with the conditions that affect their lives.

Mary Richmond espoused the idea that social workers need to understand a particular individual in his relationships with others. In social diagnosis, the social worker makes as exact a definition as possible of the situation and the personality, "that is, in relation to other human beings upon whom he in any way depends or who depend upon him, and in relation to the social institutions of the community."[2] To achieve such understanding, scientific knowledge about individuals, families, small groups, and environments is necessary. The emphasis is on the individual in his family and network of social relationships and resources in a community.

Some social workers at different times have espoused either an individual or an environmental causation of a person's difficulties: either the individual has a pathology or a character defect, or he is the victim of environmental circumstances. Most social workers, as was true of Addams and Richmond, have held the idea that man must be understood in relation to his environment. It is not just the problem that is to be understood, but the person-situation or family-situation configuration. All people have basic human needs—for survival, love and satisfying relationships, health, and competence in accordance with their capacities. All people at times have problems in coping with the demands of daily living. There are interconnections between biological, economic, and social-psychological components of human functioning. People can change their own attitudes and behaviors and their environments through individual and group efforts. This biopsychosocial view is now receiving renewed emphasis in social work. Such a view of man and society leads to concern "both with the coping qualities of the person and the qualities of the impinging dyadic, group, organizational, and physical environments."[3] Some writers refer to the theory of practice that is based on this view of man and society as a life model; others, as an ecological approach; and still others, as a systems approach. It is an extension and elaboration of the psychosocial approach to practice with individuals and small groups.[4] The view of man in society is a major philosophical orientation which is consonant with the primary values of social work.

Values

Values are an important determinant of the social worker's selection of knowledge for purposes of assessment and treatment. Values are preferences: they are propositions about what is considered to be desirable. They indicate a "desirable mode of behavior or an end state that has a transcendental quality to it, guiding actions, attitudes, judgments and comparisons across specific objects and situations and beyond immediate goals to some ultimate goals."[5] Values, translated into ethical principles, guide the practice of any profession. They derive from a few fundamental beliefs and attitudes about individuals and society. The ultimate value of social work is that human beings should have opportunities to realize their potentialities for living in ways that are both personally satisfying and socially desirable. Implied in this basic value is simultaneous concern for individual and collective welfare. Implied also is social work's concern with the quality of social relationships and with positive development and prevention, as well as therapy. Two primary values elaborate the meaning of realization of potential.

A primary value is belief in the inherent worth and dignity of the individual. People have worth and dignity simply because they are human beings. About the importance of the value of the worth and dignity of the individual, Younghusband has said, "it is ultimately in this, in the dignity and worth of man, that the philosophy of social work rests."[6] If this belief is accepted, then certain other ideas follow about individuals in relation to society. Each person should be accepted as he is and treated as a whole person in a process of development. He should be treated with respect, in spite of his likenesses or differences in relation to other individuals and population groups. He should have freedom to express himself without fear of negative sanctions. He should have the right to privacy; information given by or about him should be treated with confidence or given to others only with his informed consent.

Social justice is a person's due. Since all people are worthy, social justice is due each one. Everyone should have the right to civil liberties and equality of opportunity without discrimination because of race, ethnicity, social class, religion, age, or sex. A person should have access to resources that are essential to meet his basic needs, not only for survival, but also for the development of his potential. He has a right to make his own decisions and to participate in making group decisions, within the limits imposed by his particular culture and status and with regard to the rights of others. The right to self-determination is not absolute. It needs to be reinterpreted to encompass certain rights of families and other social networks which, in many cultures, take precedence over rights of individuals to make certain decisions. It also needs to be reinterpreted to take into account certain religious beliefs that limit the believer's right to self-determination within certain spheres of life. Religious beliefs may take precedence over individual choice of alternatives. Belief in the worth and dignity of the individual does not obviate belief also in the worth and integrity of the family and extended networks of relationships. There is a delicate balance between individual and group welfare.[7]

The delicate balance between individual and group makes interdependence among people essential to fulfillment of potential. Thus, a second primary value is mutual responsibility. People are not in complete control of their lives; neither are they simply the victims of external circumstances. They are neither dependent nor independent beings. Rather, they are interdependent one upon another for survival and for fulfillment of their needs. They interact with other people and with the social and political institutions of the society in which they live; they both influence and are influenced by others. Mutual responsibility supplants the concept of rugged individualism. A person is and should be an interacting member of society, both giving to, and receiving benefits from, others to the extent of his capacities and the opportunities that are available to him.

Interdependence implies mutuality in relationships among individuals and among groups and organizations. It acknowledges the diversity of groups and cultures that comprise society. American society, as is also true of some other societies, is made up of a network of ethnosystems, each sharing some common values and characteristics and each having some values unique to members of that group.[8] Each individual, family, and group needs to be particularized, so that there can be opportunities for each group in society to maintain its own culture and to make a contribution to the whole. Interdependence is essential to democracy. A democratic philosophy, according to Pray,

> rests upon a deep appreciation of the validity and the value to society as a whole, of these individual differences in human beings. It conceives of social unity and progress as the outcome of the integration, not the suppression or conquest of these differences. Accordingly, it tests all social arrangements and institutions by their impact upon human lives, by their capacity to utilize for the common good the unique potentialities of individual human beings, through relationships that enlist their active and productive participation.[9]

Group as well as individual differences should be accepted and used for the welfare of all.

The ideology of social work from a broad psychosocial perspective is humanistic, scientific, and democratic. It is humanistic in its commitment to the welfare of the client, its concern with client participation and decision-making in the process, its regard for the client as a whole person, and its commitment to the protection of his rights. It is scientific in that it prefers objectivity and factual evidence over personal biases. It emphasizes that the practitioner's judgments and actions are derived from a reasoning process, based on scientific knowledge to the extent that it is available. It embodies the great idea of democracy, not as a political structure, but as a philosophy governing relationships among people, based on reciprocal rights and obligations, and directed toward the welfare of the individual, group, and society.

ETHICS

"Ethics, in effect, is values in operation."[10] Ethical principles derive from values. Professional ethics are a set of moral principles regarding a practitioner's conduct in his relationships with individuals, groups, and organizations. An ethical principle sets forth what a practitioner is obliged to do under certain circumstances. When accepted by a profession, a code of ethics becomes a means of social control of the behavior of practitioners. A code of ethics specifies certain norms or rules that govern behavior. Norms, however, are not rigid; they refer to a range of expectations rather than to specific rules. Thus, no code of ethics can give absolutely clear guidance to a practitioner. There are ambiguities and dilemmas around any ethical issue. A code of ethics alerts practitioners to principles that need to be taken into account in making a choice of plan or action. The major ethical principles are concerned with competence, integrity, propriety, commitment to client welfare, and protection of rights.[11]

A moderate amount of professional competence must be assumed before a practitioner can contend with ethical issues. The resolution of an ethical problem requires that the social worker make a choice and that he has the capacity to do so. The absence of competence is itself an ethical issue. It is unethical to attempt to render a service when one is not competent to do it well. According to Levy, the principle of competence asserts that the worker is ethically accountable for what he does and the way he does it. The worker is expected to be equipped to undertake social work service and to perform the specific function which he undertakes. The new code of ethics of the National Association of Social Workers (NASW) states: "The social worker should strive to become and remain proficient in professional practice and the performance of professional functions." He should retain ultimate responsibility for the nature and quality of the services which he provides.

A second major ethical principle is integrity. According to the NASW code of ethics, the social worker should act in accordance with the highest standards of professional integrity and partiality. He deals with all people with whom he has a professional relationship in a manner that will validate the trust and confidence in him and his profession. He is expected to serve all types of clients on a nondiscriminatory basis. Services are to be given according to the needs of clients, not the social worker's personal preferences and prejudices. The worker does not exploit relationships with clients, colleagues, or significant other persons for personal profit or advantage.

A third major principle is propriety. The social worker should maintain high standards of personal conduct in his identity as a social worker. His private conduct is a personal matter to the same degree as is any other person's, except when his conduct compromises the fulfillment of professional responsibilities. He does not condone or participate in behavior that is fraudulent, deceitful, or otherwise damaging to people. It hardly seems necessary to say that he does not engage in such behavior as drunkenness, sexual intercourse with clients, filthy language, or uncontrolled anger.

Still another principle is that the social worker's primary responsibility is to the welfare of his clients. He protects them from physical or mental harm and unwarranted stress. He assures that services and resources to which they have a right are accessible to them. He is expected to provide the best service of which he is capable and to treat clients with respect, acceptance, and objectivity. Extreme loyalty to clients, however, may result in the neglect of others who may be adversely affected by the client or by what transpires between worker and client. He must often weigh the balance between the welfare of clients and the welfare of others, when these are in conflict. Indeed, when a client is a danger to someone else, the worker has a responsibility to exercise his responsibility to society and take steps to protect a potential victim.

Another interrelated principle is that the social worker protects and safeguards the rights and prerogatives of clients. He makes great efforts to foster maximum self-determination on the part of clients, according to their status and capacity. Self-determination cannot be implemented unless clients participate actively in the process; only through active participation can they engage in making decisions that affect their welfare. Thus, the worker fosters maximum participation of clients in the social work process. He respects the privacy of clients and holds in confidence all information obtained in the course of service. He obtains the clients' informed consent before sharing any confidential information with others. When there are compelling reasons why confidentiality cannot be assured, he informs the clients about the reasons. When there is a clear legal order to divulge information, the worker is bound to offer only the data that is required. Levy sums up the issue by saying, "In one sense, this principle may be summarized as the social worker's obligation to use the client's confidences for him, not against him, and to permit himself to receive confidences from the client only when he may be able to do something constructive with them."[12] When clients are served within their families or other groups, there are special complications in the assurance of confidentiality. The worker, of course, behaves in accordance with the ethical rules, but he has a further responsibility to work with the client system toward the acceptance of a norm of confidentiality among the members.

In addition to obligations to clients, colleagues, and other persons with whom he has a professional relationship, the practitioner is expected to uphold and advance professional values, knowledge, and technology and to promote the general welfare.

Most social workers would probably accept these values and ethical principles as stated in their broad and abstract forms. But when it comes to putting them into operation, the worker's own attitudes and preferences may mitigate against their implementation. The inherent worth, dignity, and respect for clients are violated often by those who espouse them. A frequent example is when a worker has a goal for the client that may be different from the client's goal and that is not shared with, and agreed to, by the client. Another common trap for workers is using certain forms of influence to impose one's own views of desirable choices on the client.

Wide differences in values among clients and among social workers and between clients and social workers pose difficulties. A few examples might clarify the dilemmas. In the field of adoptions, there is controversy concerning the adoptee's right to have information about, or to reestablish relationships with, his biological family and the biological family's right to privacy. In the field of mental health, there is controversy concerning the mentally ill patient's right to refuse treatment and his physician's and family's right and responsibility to support the health and welfare of others in the community. This is an example of belief in the right of people to voluntary help, which may conflict with society's belief that some people need protective services that are involuntary in nature. Another example is one of changing norms that govern sexual behavior as more knowledge is available and there is more open communication about the subject.

There are, however, differences in beliefs about abortion and other forms of birth control, sexual intercourse outside marriage, and acceptable forms of sexual expression. These differences are based on religious beliefs, family or peer group values, and personal convictions. In research, there is the conflict between the subject's right to refuse to participate and the researcher's right to attain valuable knowledge. At a more mundane level is the issue concerning fees for service, whether in agencies or private practice: one of the conflicts is between the need for funds to maintain a service versus discrimination against the poor who cannot afford to pay.

Such conflicts cannot be avoided. The practitioner is obliged to take an informed position on these value dilemmas as well as to understand the views of his clients and the organization which employs him. He is faced with the need to make decisions about how to help clients to deal with these dilemmas. A code of ethics reminds him to follow general moral principles, but he is still left with decisions concerning their implementation.

Knowledge: a Biopsychosocial Systems Perspective

In order to practice according to these values, the social worker needs considerable knowledge about people and their proximate and distal environments. He needs multiple perspectives in order to understand the range of human needs and problems, and the great variety of conditions that hinder or block a client's development. He needs a scheme for interpreting the needs of individuals and families who use social services. Intervention of any kind must be individualized, so that the means employed result in meeting specific needs and thus the achievement of goals. Individualization takes place only when a person's needs and capacities and the qualities of his environment are understood and taken into consideration.

The knowledge that is used as a foundation for a practitioner's activities should be such that it helps a worker to give service to all people in all phases of psychosocial development; to all socioeconomic, racial, religious, and ethnic populations; and to people with varied life styles and those who live under different environmental conditions. The theory should take into account behavior that explains how most people develop and cope with challenges in their lives, as well as taking into account difficulties and deviations in health and behavior. It needs to explain the continuum from very effective functioning to severe malfunctioning. The selected knowledge needs to demonstrate its relevance also for the conditions of life in our society. For many clients, poverty, illness, racism, crime, unemployment, instability, and alienation erode the quality of life. Environmental stress makes it difficult for people to develop their potentialities.

Concepts from the biological, psychological, and social sciences are selected for their pertinence to the effective use of social work in direct services to people for the achievement of goals within the realm of psychosocial functioning. Psychosocial functioning involves a complex gestalt of emotion, cognition, and action within each person as he relates to, and interacts with, other persons in varied situations. Any relationship involves the functioning of two or more persons as mutual need satisfiers. People's problems are viewed as a product of transactions between one system and other systems, as distinguished from viewing them only from either an internal or external causative framework. The integrating idea is the dynamic interplay among person, group, and situation. What is needed is a wide-angle lens.

Within general systems theory, formulations concerning complex adaptive systems in interaction with other systems are clearly useful. Such an ecological systems perspective provides a broad framework to guide the worker in his observations and assessments of a person-group-situation configuration. It is to be noted that the idea of system has been put in a broad context of a network of interacting systems. This newer intersystems network, as it is referred to by Chin, is often called an ecological approach or perspective.[13] Ecology, according to Germain, is a form of general systems theory that is concerned with "the relations among living entities and other aspects of their environment. . . . The perspective is concerned with the growth, development, and potentialities of human beings and with the properties of their environments that support or fail to support the expression of human potential."[14] Its contribution to social work is emphasis on interdependence, transactions, reciprocal roles, and communication. Concepts about systems sensitize the practitioner to the common properties and processes of human units of different sizes and complexities.[15] Systems theory, however, does not provide a sufficient base of knowledge for practice. The theory has limited utility in explaining the development and behavior of individuals, families, and other small groups. Other knowledge needs to be integrated into a systems perspective. These many concepts contained in other bodies of knowledge such as physiology, psychology, social psychology, anthropology, and sociology are consistent with a systems perspective and are complementary to it.

Individuals, families, and groups may be viewed as biopsychosocial systems that are influenced by, and also influence, other systems to which they are related. All of these are complex, adaptive, open systems. Buckley defines a system as "a complex of elements or components directly or indirectly related in a causal network, such that each component is related to some other in a more or less stable way within any particular period of time."[16] More simple definitions are those of Allport, who says it is "a complex of elements in mutual interaction,"[17] and von Bertalanffy, who says it is "a complex of components in interaction."[18] He distinguishes organismic and humanistic theory from a mechanistic systems theory. The essential idea is that a system is a set of elements that are related to each other in such a way that a change in one part results in changes in the others. Hence, a system is comprised of a complex set of interdependent parts related to each other in some fairly stable way. The whole is more than the sum of the parts; the parts are organized and integrated into a whole. Changes in the system occur as consequences of changes within the system interacting with forces in the environment. Human systems are adaptive; they possess the capacity to react to their environments in ways that facilitate the continued operation and growth of the system.

In the literature on general systems theory, there is no one conceptual framework that is generally accepted. There are, however, a number of constructs which have been described frequently in the literature on systems theory and which have also been applied to social work. The constructs which seem to be most applicable to this theory of social work are: boundary, integration or organized complexity, progressive differentiation, social structure, equifinality, steady state, communication, and system-environment interaction.

BOUNDARY

All systems have a semipermeable demarcation line which delimits and defines the components of the system. It distinguishes the system from its component subsystems and from the larger suprasystem of which it is a part—its environment. The environment consists of nature, institutions, man-made things, and a network of social relationships, as these are influenced by the broader culture. The boundary between a system and its environment is partly conceptual and, to that extent, arbitrary. There is greater frequency and intensity of interaction and greater interdependence among the elements within than outside the system. The elements may be thought of as the substantive parts, such as individuals, or as the relational components, such as patterns of affection, roles, and communication. Functionally, the boundary ties together the components into a meaningful whole and serves as a filtering device, admitting certain information into the system and blocking out other inputs.

Systems are more or less open to influences from the environment and more or less able to influence the environment. The more closed is a system, the less likely it is to have the wherewithal to meet its needs, because it cannot benefit from new stimulation that is essential to growth and change. On the other hand, some boundaries are so loose that the identity of the system is weak or lost. Germain cites an example of a disorganized mental patient who is confused about where he leaves off and the environment begins: he does not have a sense of separateness from others.[19] When a systems boundary is too rigid or too loose, the system proceeds toward entropy, the natural and ultimate disintegration. The major tendency in organismic systems, however, is toward a higher order of organization rather than the tendency toward entropy.

INTEGRATION

Organized complexity is characteristic of human systems. An individual is a complex system in which biological, psychological, and sociocultural influences interact and are integrated into the personality. He is in a process of growing and developing in orderly stages throughout the life cycle. There is a need to organize the parts through integration, a process whereby a functional fit is achieved among the components so that they make up an integral whole. The components are health and genetic endowment and personality, with special emphasis on ego functions and social relationships as these interact with sociocultural forces.

Health and endowment. The psychosocial functioning of an individual is greatly influenced by his genetic endowment and by the state of his health, physical fitness, and appearance at a given time.[20] Individuals are genetically different from one another and therefore have different capacities for achieving a positive state of health. But how poorly or well the potentialities are achieved depends upon the psychosocial opportunities that are available to them. Genetic endowment determines certain constitutional strengths and weaknesses which influence the course of development. Endowment determines many aspects of physical abilities and appearance. Sex, skin color, height, and body build are sources of self-esteem and identity, or the opposite. These characteristics also determine expectations that others have for one. An extremely tall young man, for example, is viewed differently from an extremely short one by self and others, and there are different expectations concerning the types of activities in which he will be successful. Differences in skin color, even variations within a given racial group, elicit different feelings on the part of self and others. The dramatic maturational change that occurs at puberty is another example of natural physiological phenomena that stimulate stress on the developing organism and make severe demands on the ego's adaptive capacity. A person's level of intelligence is due, at least partly, to heredity, but it is also influenced by the physical care, nurturance, and opportunities for learning available to him. Feelings concerning the adequacy of intellectual functioning by the person and by others influence a person's self-esteem and identity and the opportunities that will be available to him. Illnesses and physical defects that are in one's heredity or to which a person is predisposed not only threaten life and health, but also tend to carry feelings of inferiority, stigma, anger at parents and other ancestors, guilt, and fear concerning transmission of a defect to others.

The actual state of health, and a person's attitudes toward his health, are important influences on the adequacy of his psychological functioning. When a person feels good about the way his body is functioning, he generally feels good about himself and is able to carry his roles with satisfaction and competence. On the other hand, illness or physical disability is almost always stressful for the patient, his family, and significant others. Adaptive capacities are strained by severe pain and discomfort and by threats to body image and to the security and integrity of the person. Loss of satisfying roles or limitations on activities leads to the need for others to change in order to compensate for the changes in the patient. Some diseases or handicaps which hold little hope for cure or improvement require continual readjustment of the patient and others to a decreasing health status and capacity for assuming life tasks appropriate to the patient's developmental stage. Any surgery is not only life threatening; it is also threatening to the integrity of the body, the more so when there is serious disfigurement or impairment of functioning. Some illnesses and handicaps are accompanied by stigma and feelings of fear, guilt, or shame on the part of others as well as the patient: examples are leprosy, venereal diseases, cancer, and epilepsy. Some somatic illnesses are thought to have psychosocial roots and to be symbolic expressions of inner conflict; these are referred to as psychosomatic illnesses. The physical distress is real, even if there seems to be no organic basis for the disorder. Reactions to illness and disability vary according to the seriousness of the situation, the patient's and family's capacity to cope with stress, and the nature of the available care and resources.

Personality. Freudian psychoanalytic theory has alerted social workers to a number of principles that aid in understanding people in their environments.[21] Behavior is purposeful and goal-directed. There are causal connections and continuities between past and present life experiences. Personality is multifaceted and multiply determined.

Personality patterns are the product of genetic predispositions, past experiences, and current events. They are to be understood in terms of an individual's unique attributes, experiences, interpersonal relationships, perceptions of self in relation to others, and the particular meanings that these phenomena have for him. Preconscious and unconscious forces, as well as conscious ones, motivate feeling, thought, and action. Behavior is shaped by the interplay among a set of interacting processes that have been given the labels of id, ego, and superego. External social requirements, as well as internal needs, must be met to some degree if a person is to function effectively in society.

Ego Functions. Contemporary ego psychology, which developed out of psychoanalytic theory, is essential knowledge for social work practice.[22] According to Boehm, "Since the ego is conceived of as that force in the personality which brings the internal person into relationship with the outside world, it is the particular concept of personality which needs to be stressed in regard to social functioning."[23]

The ego functions to enable an individual to perceive, adapt to, and change his environment and to achieve a satisfactory balance between his own physical and psychological needs and the demands of others. It is a creative force that mediates between a person's diverse internal drives and conflicts, the socially determined values and moral attitudes of the superego, and the demands of external reality. It controls impulses, anxiety, and guilt through the use of such defense mechanisms as repression, regression, denial, rationalization, displacement, and projection. There are areas of the ego which are free of conflict: these include the capacities for perception, motility, thought, memory, and judgment. The ego has a degree of autonomy to function independently of instinctual impulses and drives. It is adaptive, able to adjust harmoniously to the environment. According to Hartmann, "adaptation is primarily a reciprocal relationship between the organism and its environment."[24] Adaptation may be achieved by changes in the psychosocial system of the person, by restructuring and modifying the environment, or both; or by the choice of a new environment. In systems terms, these processes maintain the steady state or enable the system to move toward a changed state. Adaptation is a circular process in that the environment is adapted to the system's needs; the system then adapts to the changed or new environment, and so forth.

The ego has the potential capacity to develop and sustain satisfying object relationships; perceive the self realistically in relation to the environment; engage in mental and language processes; control impulses, anxiety, and guilt; and plan and mobilize for action which requires integration of emotion, cognition, and action skills. It synthesizes various tendencies and functions so that the person is able to feel, think, and act in an integrated manner. In order to function effectively, there needs to be stimulation from what Hartmann calls "average expectable stimulations" that support the development and functioning of the autonomous area of the ego.[25] Adaptive capacities are enhanced or thwarted, depending upon the availability of resources to nourish and support the ego's efforts.

Relationships. Human relatedness is the key to healthy development. Personality is largely formed through relationships with other people in ever widening circles, from the infant's symbiotic relationship to his mother to varied adult object relationships. Changes in personality and in relationships with others are inseparable: an individual's capacity for object relationships is indicative of personality integration. Personality and social relationships are influenced also by the obstacles and opportunities in a person's environment and by the values and norms of the reference groups to which he belongs or with which he identifies.

The most influential system to which most people belong is the family. A family is a group that has assigned functions to carry out and structures to tie the parts together, yet it is always in flux. It changes with the evolution of its members; the development of their abilities to interact with each other and with people outside; additions or losses of members; and stresses, demands, and changes imposed from outside. Families are composed of individuals who are most often related to each other through marriage, blood ties, or adoption. Most families also encompass at least two generations and both sexes.

People belong to many other types of groups during their life spans. Early in his development, a child participates in many informal play and fellowship dyads and larger groups; these affiliations change as he grows older and assumes new roles. People spend many years of their lives in formal or informal educational groups. Many join groups of a supportive, self-help, developmental, or therapeutic nature. Many adults are members of committees and organizations that further their interests or make contributions to the community.

In order to meet their needs, people develop complex patterns of social relationships which are significant to their psychosocial functioning. The compatibility and complementarity among members of a group often determine whether a group will form or whether an existing group, such as a family, will be maintained or disintegrate. When people lack adequate stimulation, there are inadequate new inputs to prevent disintegration. When there is an overload of new inputs into the system, the steady state may also be disrupted. A person's varied emotional responses to others are means toward which he attempts to satisfy his own needs for relationships with others and to avoid threats to himself. According to Schutz, there are three basic interpersonal needs: inclusion, control, and affection.[26] People differ in the extent to which they seek out or desire relationships with others, as contrasted with a preference for being alone. They differ in the extent to which they are included in social networks to which they aspire. They differ in the amount of control and power they have to determine their own destinies. They differ in the amount of control they desire and actually exert over others and in their preferences for being controlled by, independent of, or interdependent with, others. They differ also in their abilities to give and receive love and affection.

The emotional responses of persons toward others and of others toward them may or may not be reciprocated. They are often based on a mixture of conscious and unconscious attitudes. Negative or positive feelings may be based on distortions in perception of reality. A person may have a false perception of another due to ineptness of communication. Words and gestures are not understood. It is common for people to stereotype others according to preconceived ideas about them. Certain distortions in perception of others are connected to mental illness as one aspect of serious problems in the perception of reality. A person may have false perceptions of others, based on transference reactions. Feelings, attitudes, and patterns of responses are transferred from earlier relationships, particularly those with parents. The person misunderstands the present relationship in terms of the past. He tends to relive earlier attitudes with particular people in the present situation. A transference reaction may be functional or dysfunctional to the current relationship. When it is the practitioner who transfers attitudes from his past onto the client, this form of faulty perception is called countertransference.

Relationships are characterized by various positive ties—love, empathy, acceptance, cordiality, and positive identifications; but they are also characterized by such negative ties as hatred, hostility, repulsions, fears, and prejudices. There may or may not be compatibility and complementarity between interpersonal needs. People have different capacities to respond with sensitivity to the feelings of others, and to engage in mutuality of meeting need.

Be it couple, family, or peer group, the specific feelings that members have toward each other and the ways these are exposed differ from one group to another and will vacillate from time to time in any group. Ambivalence is characteristic of all relationships. Feelings shift and change: love may turn into hate or love may deepen, and so forth. There are differences in patterns of feelings, typical of different types of groups. In the family, for example, relationships are continuous, feelings run deeply yet may vacillate extremely from time to time; or they may become stabilized and resistant to change. Within a peer group, on the other hand, there are opportunities to develop new relationships of a more or less intimate nature according to need, choice, and the availability of important persons. Although members of peer groups tend to bring to the group already learned patterns of relating to others and may transfer to others feelings that had their roots in the family, the intimacy of relationships is usually diluted, as contrasted with the intensity of relationships in the family.

PROGRESSIVE DIFFERENTIATION

People develop in fairly orderly phases throughout the life cycle. In Freudian psychoanalytic theory, phases in psychosexual development were formulated, which ego psychologists have later integrated into broader psychosocial formulations. Models of human development assume that there are changes in the state of a system at different times; that the succession of these states indicates that the system is moving in a particular direction; and that there are orderly processes to explain how progression from one state to another occurs. These formulations emphasize the ego's adaptive capacities and its efforts to achieve psychosocial competence. In the words of Freed:

> Because ego psychology involves a longitudinal view of the various stages of human development, from infancy through old age, and treats each of the maturational points and its respective tasks, it is a useful schema for working selectively with people in each of the periods of life. Hence, it is particularly helpful to base diagnosis on developmental theory.[27]

Erikson's formulation of eight stages of psychosocial development opens the personality system to interaction with inner and outer influences, without abandoning the significance of early experiences.[28] In each phase, individuals have new opportunities for psychosocial growth, but the manner in which these opportunities can be used is partially dependent on the individual's success or failure in dealing with the earlier maturational tasks. Erikson's formulation emphasizes capacity for continual growth throughout the life cycle and the influence of relationships and culture on personality development. In each stage, there are issues to be dealt with, needs to be met, tasks to be achieved, and hazards to, and opportunities for, growth. Sociocultural factors interact with physical and psychological ones in determining the adequacy of a person's functioning at a given time. A person needs to achieve the objectives of each phase: the development of trust, autonomy, initiative, industry, identity, intimacy, generativity, and ego integrity. The extent to which a person masters the tasks associated with the earlier phases influences his subsequent development. During each developmental phase, there are normal stresses which contain the potential for crises. Many events in the lives of people are stressful: illness; separations due to hospitalization, death, or divorce; educational challenges; remarriage; step-parenthood; unemployment or retirement; geographical relocation. Undue stress taxes the adaptive capacities of the personality. A person may use adaptive or maladaptive coping mechanisms to deal with the stress. Developmental progress and setbacks proceed in circles that tend to be cumulative in their benign or malignant effects. The sequence of epigenetic phases is thought to be universal, but the typical solutions vary from society to society and by subsystems within a given society. Human maturation cannot be viewed as separate from the social context in which it occurs. For every maturational stage, there always appears "a radius of significant relations" who aid, abet, or hinder the organism's coping with and resolving specific life tasks. Other theorists have formulated somewhat different models for human development, but they share the important idea that the development of the ego incorporates development of morality, cognitive complexity, and capacity for interpersonal relations.[29]

Families have developmental stages that mesh with the development of the individuals who comprise the group.[30] There are phase-specific and transitional tasks that need to be accomplished as the composition of the family, the developmental phases of its members, and the roles of members change. The wide variety of families in our society makes generalization difficult. The most frequent delineation of stages in families assumes that the order is courtship, marriage, couple without children, couple with one child followed by the addition of other children, the leaving of the first child and then of other children, the couple alone, and then a lone person occasioned by the death of a spouse. The significance of such phases is in terms of the changes in the structure and size of the group; the division of responsibilities; the economic and psychosocial stresses at each phase; and the new demands each phase makes on all members of the family. With a few exceptions, these formulations of developmental phases in families do not take into account single-parent families in which the parent never married; those broken by separation, divorce, or early death of one spouse; extended family structures; foster families that include one or more nonrelated children; and reconstituted or blended families composed of combinations of members from two prior families. These formulations do alert workers to changes that occur over time and their significance for family assessment and treatment. There are points of stress which may tax the adaptive capacities of the members. There may be constructive resolution of the problems, regression, or maintenance of chronic difficulties. Each phase requires continual balance between stabilization and change in family structure, relationships, alliances, norms, and role transitions.

Other types of groups, except when the members first come together, have a past history. They change in orderly ways as the members interact with each other and as the group develops patterns of structure and communication. There is an initial phase in which members become related to each other, oriented to the purposes and expectations of the group, engaged in the process, and achieve a working agreement. In one or more intermediate phases, the members explore and test the situation and work through conflicts concerning relationships, roles, norms, and power, leading to an appropriate degree of cohesiveness so that the members' major energies are directed toward working to achieve individual or collective goals, or both. The final stage is one of stabilization of changes made and termination, follow-up, and evaluation.

The principle of progressive differentiation from systems theory asserts that there are developmental sequences characteristic of systems. Development proceeds from a state of relative lack of differentiation to a state of increasing differentiation of the parts from the whole. But human systems are growth-adapting units that strive to maintain themselves through change, so that the differentiated parts are integrated into a functional whole.

SOCIAL STRUCTURE

In any system of two or more people, a structure of statuses and roles develops.[31] Structure makes it possible for social systems to create and distribute responsibilities and privileges and to control individuals in relation to each other. A person's status or position in his family or other social group may be ascribed to him on the basis of such factors as age, sex, ethnicity, physical characteristics, ancestry, marital state, occupation, or reputation. A person's status may also be acquired, based on certain qualities or patterns of behavior.

Every social system, including the dyad, has a structure of roles that accompany a status. There are task or instrumental roles which function to get the work done, and there are expressive or socioemotional roles which function to maintain the system itself. People are expected to behave in certain ways in their roles. The nuclear family has culturally determined or ascribed roles of husband-father, wife-mother, child, and sibling. Often, there are less well-defined roles for relatives and nonrelated persons who are part of a family, and there are many one-parent families which have particular patterns of role expectations. In peer groups, the basic role is friend or member, but there may also be special roles, such as chairperson or committee member. In addition, some roles are acquired through the interaction among the participants: members develop characteristic patterns of behavior, and they are expected to continue to behave in such ways. Examples are the scapegoat, clown, isolate, controller, or sick one. These roles tend to become stereotyped, limiting the range of behavior of the person in the role. A role can be defined only in relation to its complement; for example, the role of husband in relation to wife, or the scapegoat in relation to the scapegoaters.

The major idea about roles is that people in defined social situations behave in patterned ways, with reference to expectations. People tend to organize their behavior so that it conforms to the prevailing expectations. When a person enacts a role, he is responding to a set of expectations that others have for him. He is also, however, adapting the rules that govern the role so that his performance becomes congruent with his own motives and expectations. Individuals differ in the ways in which they interpret their roles, the positive and negative feelings they have about them, the extent to which they perform them satisfactorily, and how they relate to their role partners. An individual's roles are not static but undergo definition and redefinition as the person acts and as other persons respond to his actions. Although there are norms or standards of behavior that govern role expectations, there is usually a range of acceptable behavior. Within each major role there is room for considerable diversity in ways of carrying it out.

Difficulties develop when there is lack of complementarity of roles, ambiguity or conflict about expectations, maldistribution of power and authority, or when role behavior has become rigid. The idea of role emphasizes the importance of relationships between the role partners, whether they be in a one-to-one, family, or group relationship. Complementarity of roles—the harmonious fit of differences—is a synthesis of components that make a whole. Mutuality of meeting a need results in creative adaptability of the members in a family or other group. There are positive identifications and satisfying fits among the participants. There may also be complementary roles which meet the needs of the persons in the role, but which are maladaptive in some way. These roles are often referred to as sadist-masochist, scapegoat-scapegoater, or dominator-submitter. Each partner reinforces the behavior of the other. Thus, complementarity may be either positive or negative in terms of its effect on the psychosocial functioning of the members. It is the interaction among people that needs to be understood, as well as the internal motives and processes of the participants. A well-functioning set of roles in a family or other group is a means for integrating diversity into a functional whole.[32]

EQUIFINALITY

The principle of equifinality is that different initial conditions may lead to similar outcomes and that there may be different developmental routes to the same goal. The achievements of a system are not dependent upon the initial condition. Human systems are constantly in a process of change, as they seek to fulfill individual or group goals. The past is relevant, but it is not causally dominant. "Equifinality replaces the traditional cause-effect analysis by demonstrating its inadequacy to deal with phenomena such as emergence, purpose, goal-seeking, and self-regulation."[33] Equifinality is in harmony with the idea of man as creative and adaptable, not only being changed by, but also changing, circumstances.[34] There is also a complementary principle of multifinality, which states that similar conditions may lead to dissimilar end states. An adaptive goal-seeking system strives to achieve its goals through making internal or external changes, usually both. It can engage in problem-solving processes that consider alternative goals and means to its desired end state. A person or family can, to a large extent, go beyond its initial state. This is achieved through its ability to use new ideas, knowledge, and resources which again can happen only when the boundary is open to such new inputs. People have a certain degree of freedom to determine their own destinies. They act purposefully in relation to their desired objectives. They are influenced not only by their past experiences, they are also influenced by their anticipation of the future and by finding the appropriate means for making and implementing decisions.

STEADY STATE

Although human systems are constantly in a process of change, they also have a tendency to maintain a balance among their parts and between their own internal needs and external demands; this is known as the steady state, sometimes referred to as homeostasis or equilibrium. A steady state is a shifting dynamic balance rather than a static equilibrium. Constancy is maintained in a continuous exchange and flow of matter-energy, in part by the dynamic interplay of subsystems. Unlike equilibrium, the term steady state is used to indicate not only maintenance or return to a prior state, but also movement toward enhancement or change. It maintains the continuity and stability of the system. People need to change if they are to achieve their goals, but they also need to maintain a tolerable level of stability.

Stress and conflict are natural processes that disturb the steady state. Intrapersonal, group, and intergroup conflicts may occur. An individual may experience intrapsychic conflicts, which usually are manifested in their interpersonal relationships. Interpersonal and group conflicts arise out of differences among the participants' goals, values and norms, motivations, unconscious needs, and interests. They may also arise out of differences between the values and norms of the individual or group and those of larger systems in the community. Conflict disrupts the steady state; there is then an increase in stress. Stress may be constructive or destructive to the maintenance and development of a system. The need to reduce unmanageable degrees of stress leads to new adaptations so that a sense of stability and continuity is restored. Under stress, a system operates either to maintain itself, to return to a prior state, or to move toward some new state of being.

A human system has the capacity to adapt to internal stress, stress that impinges upon it from outside, or the complex interaction between internal and external stress. If a system is unable to reduce serious conflict, disintegrating forces take over. Motivation to achieve goals, effective communication within the system and with the environment, and adaptive mechanisms operate to maintain a balance not only sufficient for survival, but often also sufficient to move the system toward its new desired state. It is to be remembered that some stress, however, is essential to motivate the system to new and more desirable levels of functioning. A human system does not continually and only strive for tension reduction or even balance, but also strives for positive changes.

COMMUNICATION

The process by which a steady state is maintained or a new level is reached is communication among people.[35] As systems theory has evolved to take into account the greater complexity of human beings in their organized relationships, it has incorporated knowledge that was developed originally by scholars interested in human communication. Communication is an interactional process by which information is exchanged through a common system of symbols. It deals with the structure and processes through which people exchange information and influence each other. It consists of the verbal, explicit, and intentional transmission of messages between people. It consists also of the nonverbal processes by which people exchange messages.

The basic model of communication is that of a system in which a sender encodes a message that is intended to convey a particular meaning. It is sent along a channel, such as speech or gestures, to a receiver who decodes it, interprets its meaning, and sends a message back to the sender or to another destination. The message sent may not be the one that is received. "Noise" may interfere with and distort the message at any point in the process. Noise, as used by communication theorists, refers to such interferences as actual noise, distractions of various kinds, or faulty perceptions.

A distinctive characteristic of a human being is the ego's capacity for integrating and using input, any information or resource that has been made available to him. Perception involves the capacity to abstract meaning from verbal and nonverbal cues. A person listens and observes selectively according to his knowledge, psychological state, past experiences, the social context of the interchange, and the nature of his relationships with the particular persons in the communicative network. He responds selectively to messages, according to his judgment of the intent and meaning of the message sent. Each message contains both a content and a relationship component. There is "an elaborate set of implicit conventions and rules which govern the origin, flow, and effects of messages."[36] Understanding a message is influenced by the clarity of the message and by its appropriateness to the social context. It is influenced also by certain characteristics of the participants—their past and present experiences with each other and the subject matter, their cognitive capacities, and their language skills.

The result of processing a message is some output. The responses to the output or its consequence are fed back into the system as new input. Some action is taken. The receiver of the message becomes a sender back to the original sender or to another person who decodes the message, interprets it, and responds to it. Feedback is a process that allows a system to check out its effects on its environment through a channel looping back from the output to the input.[37] By this process, a system can maintain its steady state or become motivated to change. It has been defined as "the property of being able to adjust future conduct by past performance."[38] But feedback is not necessarily self-correcting: it can further disrupt the steady state. It can multiply the errors or deviations. One example concerns a student who expresses great anxiety over an examination; the other participants pick up the anxiety and exaggerate further the difficulty and importance of the examination; contagion of anxiety occurs. Energy is directed toward perpetuating the anxiety rather than to preparing for the examination. On the other hand, a different response from a second person might have lessened the anxiety of the first one had he not only recognized and accepted the anxiety, but also put in a corrective idea about the realistic expectations and consequences of the examination. In such ways, feedback can serve to maintain the steady state or initiate changes in the system toward a new state.

In groups, communication becomes quite complicated. The larger the number of participants, the greater are the potential misunderstandings and confusion. A message may be sent to a particular person who does not respond; instead, an unintended recipient decodes the message so that the intended message is not completed, from the viewpoint of the sender. A message may be intended for the group as a whole, but only some members hear and understand it. With those who receive it, each often decodes the message differently; and the one who sends a message back may not represent the feelings or thinking of the group. More than one member may want to send a message at the same time, which results in confusion and inadequate communication.

Essentially, communication is a process of formulating and exchanging meanings. As people communicate with one another, they learn about each other's feelings, hopes, ideas, and values. They exchange feelings, thoughts, and actions. Through verbal and nonverbal communication, there is a reciprocal and cyclical influence of the participants on each other. These transactions may or may not promote positive growth of individuals; they may or may not be constructive for the environment. No system moves toward its goals unless communication is adequate enough to prevent entropy. Without adequate exchanges in quantity and quality, growth and development are limited or distorted; a system needs new inputs in order to move toward a new state.

Communication theory does not explain the factors that bring about a given pattern of behavior in communicating with others. It does give clues concerning what patterns of verbal and nonverbal communication may be perpetuating particular behavior, which can be interrupted through new inputs into the system.[39] Other knowledge, such as ego psychology and sociocultural theories, contributes explanations for the patterns of communication that have evolved.

Systems in Environment

In keeping with a system perspective, the environment is not restricted to what is accessible to immediate perception and open to direct modification; it is not external to an individual and it is not static. Rather, much of the environment has been transmitted to the individual, internalized by him, and transformed by him. The environment is in a process of continuous change. Interacting with biological and psychological forces, the environment affects values, self-image, opportunities to meet needs, and even the way problems are defined. The environment is "a series of concentric circles of influence, all interacting," from the outer edge of society to the most proximate environment.[40] The most influential components of the environment are other people: members of one's family, friends, acquaintances, colleagues, and persons in positions of authority. But the physical environment and resources are also important. The environment offers opportunities and gratifications or it offers obstacles and frustrations. Each person adapts to environmental influences in a different way, because of his unique endowment, experiences, and capacities.

CULTURAL FACTORS

The family and other groups to which a person belongs comprise the context and means for acquiring and changing attitudes, interests, and values. Ego psychology postulates that cultural factors are important determinants of personality formation. A person knows himself not as an idiosyncratic individual, but by his cultural affiliations and heritage. Cultures prescribe the content and methods whereby people are socialized and resocialized. In order to understand people, it is necessary to know their cultural orientations. These are often difficult to determine; for cultures are not static but changing, and people increasingly vary in their own attitudes and behavior from the typical or ideal model. Within the American culture, there are multiple cultures and subcultures, "carried by relatively autonomous groups or strata within the larger society . . . each with its own comparatively distinct value system, its special problems, its distinctive social perspectives."[41] These may be based on combinations of ethnicity, race, and religion, interacting with social class.

The values, norms, language, customs, and traditions of a culture or subculture influence a person's opportunities for effective functioning or they become obstacles to achieving desired goals. An individual's and family's reference groups, based on religion, ethnicity, race, social class, or common interests, serve as a point of reference for self-evaluation and evaluation of others.[42] Some of these reference groups may be mutually sustaining or there may be conflicting purposes, values, and demands made by them on individuals and families. They play an important part in one's sense of identity and self-esteem. The problem of achieving a positive sense of identity may be more serious for persons who are members of ethnic minority groups. Culture conflict often is the outcome when a person is caught between the expectations that various reference groups have for him; for example, family and school, ethnic norms versus predominant group norms, culture transmitted by parents versus that transmitted by peers or teachers, and intergenerational conflict between parents and children.

There are many factors that promote or retard social and economic upward mobility: the size of the ethnic group; the length of time in this country; urban or rural background; facility with English; extent to which discrimination has been encountered; the availability of social and political leadership within the population; the nature and influence of religion; and the extent of deviations from the majority group in fundamental values concerning human relationships, authority, orientation to time, and family structure. Unfortunately, upward mobility tends to be associated with the giving up of certain cultural values, often estranging the upwardly mobile person to some extent from family and other old associations.

There has been a tendency to view minority cultures as negative in their effects on their members, when indeed each culture has many positive characteristics. Many factors promote effective individual and family functioning. As one example, Sotomayor has described elements within the Mexican-American family that have promoted individual integration and group cohesion, including the extended family pattern, respect for the aged, family role patterns, and language.[43] As another example, Locklear has described the attitudes and practices of American Indians which are still valued by them, such as generosity, priority of family and interpersonal relationships, an extended family system, and preference for work that provides inner satisfaction as well as income.[44] Problems are created when these values are not appreciated by other people and when they conflict with those of the predominant culture.

Confusing lower-class status with ethnic values and norms is frequent. There are differences of opinion about the relative importance of social class and ethnicity. Since most immigrants and members of racial minorities have a common plight of economic immobility, Greer asserts that too much emphasis on ethnic differences tends to mask this important fact.[45] But prejudice and discrimination against racial minorities are important contributors to their disproportionate representation among the poor. There is a complex relationship between social class and ethnicity. Understanding social classes and their major differences is necessary because social class status determines, to a large extent, the opportunities available for satisfying and effective social living. It is necessary to be aware of myths about the poor. It is not true, for example, that most poor people have low employment aspirations and lack a work ethic. Furthermore, experts do not agree about the characteristics of social classes beyond the fact that some people have higher incomes, more education, greater access to resources, and more power than others. From a review of the literature, Lieberman concluded that "though differences are believed to exist among different social strata in terms of attitudes and values and they have some relationship to treatability, the evidence is conflicting and controversial."[46] Accurate knowledge is necessary. Overgeneralization about differential characteristics of social classes may distort assessment and provide false criteria for planning. A systems orientation takes into account social class as one interdependent element in human behavior, not as a single causative factor.

An historical perspective on the strengths and difficulties of minority ethnic and racial groups can lead to understanding the particular discriminations and deprivations to which they have been subjected in the past. Some examples are the subjugation of blacks to slavery, relocation of Japanese Americans during World War II, loss of land and other rights of the American Indians, and the extermination of Jews in Germany. These historical events have influenced these people's attitudes toward themselves and others. Substantial differences in values, norms, physical appearance, and language between the members of an ethnic group and the predominant group influence the

extent to which they aspire to and achieve acceptance and full participation in society. Individual racism and institutional racism deter
members of racial minorities from the full exercise of their rights and
from having opportunities for fulfillment for themselves and their
families. Racism implies that one group is superior to another one
and functions to reduce competition of nonwhite groups for desirable
jobs, housing, and political power.[47]

Members of minority ethnic groups have developed varied patterns
of coping with negative stereotyping and discrimination in which
their dignity and worth are demeaned and their rights are violated.
Myths have been perpetuated about minority groups, which are often
rationalizations of members of the predominant group. Even in social
work, it has been noted that "to rationalize their failure to serve,
they [social workers] have projected such negative stereotypes as the
unmotivated client, the lack of communication skills, the inability to
deal with abstractions, the notion that illegitimacy carries no stigma
in minority group communities, and the myth that black people do
not adopt."[48] Other myths can be added, such as the idea that members of minority groups are better served by untrained workers than
by professionally qualified practitioners. The fact is that clients from
these groups can and do make good use of professional service, if
the service is appropriate to their needs and if the workers have the
desire, knowledge, and skills to serve them.

Religious beliefs are an important part of culture, yet social workers have tended to ignore their clients' beliefs and the possible conflict in religious values between the worker and the client.[49] Religious beliefs provide conscious and unconscious norms by which
people judge themselves and others. They may be positive aids in
dealing with problems arising from a sense of uncertainty, powerlessness, and scarcity. They may be used in harmful as well as helpful
ways. Whether helpful or harmful to a client's psychosocial functioning, they define reality for the person. Socialization has been influenced by religious assumptions and values: for example, Protestant-
ism among African Americans, Buddhism among many Asian
Americans, and Catholicism among Latin Americans. Religion interacts with race, ethnicity, and social class in its influence on psychosocial functioning.

It is probably impossible for any social worker to have up-to-date knowledge about all the diverse ethnic, religious, racial, and social class segments of society. But it is possible and necessary to use resources in the form of new experiences, consultation, and literature to develop understanding of the particular clientele one serves. The social worker must have sensitivity and the broad knowledge to distinguish between pathological and sociocultural factors that influence well-being and behavior at a particular time. Recognizing social class and ethnic dimensions of living does not negate the principle that treatment should be individualized. The place of sociocultural analysis in assessment of any client system is an element of a larger whole. It should be seen in this context rather than as a competing explanation.

OTHER ASPECTS OF ENVIRONMENT

The concrete and visible characteristics of the environment are important influences on human development. The physical appearance of the neighborhood in which a person resides and the availability of institutional resources are important, including patterns and quality of housing, availability of health services and transportation, quality of education, sanitation, fire, and police protection. Not only is the actual presence of resources important, but so also are the policies and procedures that govern their use.

The social agency or private office is a social environment for workers and clients. Administrative arrangements, the attractiveness of the physical setting, definitions of roles of client and worker, the nature and quality of staff relationships, the structure and patterns of communication, the nature of the intake process, the functions of the agency, and the relationship of the agency to the community influence greatly the kind of help offered to a client and the way in which it will be accepted or rejected. Other professions with which social work is interdependent often influence the quality of services that can be given. Thus, there is need to assess how the group or private practice setting facilitates or impedes the service given to particular clients and groups of clients.

Germain has identified several categories of modern environments that influence the well-being of people:[50]

1. Modern technology affects health and disease. Examples are newly discovered chemicals that have great potential for both positive and negative outcomes; technological means for prolonging life which create stark moral dilemmas for the patient, family, and the medical profession; other advances that result in pollution and the rise of new environmental diseases; changing technology in employment which creates new opportunities for some, but unemployment and the need for retraining for others.

2. Informational storage systems, increasingly more sophisticated, lead to violations of privacy that may prevent access to credit, employment, or health and life insurance. The explosion of knowledge and the development of new technologies make it difficult for practitioners to be up-to-date in their practice, which is one of their ethical responsibilities.

3. Statutory and regulative aspects of law influence the rights of some people, such as women and patients, and changing laws and regulations concerning such matters as divorce and school desegregation result in rapidly shifting expectations, demands, and opportunities. New statutes and court decisions influence practice in many ways.

4. The economic and political systems often produce inflation, inadequate housing, changes in Social Security, energy, and transportation problems which create hardships for many people.

The environments in which people live are crucial influences on their psychosocial well-being. Many years ago, Towle put it this way: "We know also that unmodifiable adverse social circumstances are decisive and that the tender ministrations of an understanding relationship cannot compensate for basic environmental lacks, meager services, and restrictive agency policies."[51]

Conclusion

An ecological systems perspective which incorporates psychological, social, and cultural knowledge provides a framework for understanding the range of influences on the psychosocial relations of individuals, families, and other groups. It can be overwhelming to practitioners to recognize the vast amount of knowledge that is available about human development, behavior, and the social environment. The very breadth of the perspective requires that knowledge be organized into a framework of a limited number of major constructs that can be applied to practice. Such constructs sensitize the practitioner to the common properties and processes of human systems of different sizes and complexities. Having a generic foundation makes it possible to test out its applicability to new situations and to use the knowledge as it seems appropriate to a particular situation.

Understanding the psychosocial systems perspective has many implications for the practitioner. It influences his attitudes toward his clients. The knowledge base is consistent with the values. It supports an optimistic view of people's capacities to cope with stress and to master situations that confront them. The problems of people are part of the human condition. People are not hopeless; thus, the practitioner can engage himself enthusiastically in building on the positive motivations and capacities of his clientele. The knowledge base infers the need to understand clients, individually and collectively, and the social networks which have an impact on their welfare. Understanding should lead to acceptance of people and an ability to empathize with them and their situations.

The theoretical perspective which has been borrowed and adapted from the biological, psychological, and social sciences underlies the principles of practice that guide practitioners in every phase of the social work process. It is assumed that understanding how, why, and when one should do something contributes to professional competence.

The practitioner needs to have knowledge about people in their environments, as outlined herein. What has been presented, however, is but a conceptual framework; in-depth understanding of the interrelated concepts comes only through study and analysis of the original sources. Knowledge itself is not sufficient. The social worker needs to use that knowledge in working with particular persons and situations. He needs to relate this knowledge to understanding practice itself, its values, purposes, concepts, principles, and processes. How a practitioner makes use of the knowledge that has been summarized in this chapter will be illustrated throughout the book.

Knowledge, organized into a framework for assessing the client-group-situation gestalt, is necessary. Since needs of clients are major influences on the nature of the services to be provided, the basic knowledge is used to assess the needs of all participants in the practice endeavor. Accurate assessment is based on the values and knowledge that have been elaborated and on an understanding of the issues and process of assessment, which is the subject of the next chapter.

CHAPTER THREE

Assessment in Social Work

In medicine, diagnosis is defined as the art and science of identifying a disease or disability. In social work, because of the strong association of diagnosis with illness, the concept of assessment has gradually replaced it.[1] Social workers take into account the individual or family in its environment. They are interested in motivations, capacities, and normal stresses, as well as disease and disability. Early social work leaders translated the term diagnosis to adapt it to the needs of social work. Hamilton, for example, said that,

> Essentially, diagnosis is the worker's professional opinion as to the nature of the need or problem which the client presents. It is not a secret labeling of the client, it is not an uncontrolled adventure into the mysteries of life; it is a realistic, thoughtful, frank, and scientific attempt to understand the client's present need, which is always a person-in-situation formulation, including interpersonal relationships.[2]

Although assessment has become preferred, many writers continue to use the term diagnosis, often interchangeably with assessment.

The purpose of assessment is to understand and evaluate an individual in relation to his family and its environment or to understand a family or other small group in its social context. It is a means of individualizing the person-situation configuration. It is a basis for planning what should be done to enable the system to improve its functioning or to influence changes in its environment. The assessment is flexible and changes as the relationship between a worker and an individual or group develops. It is an ongoing process in which the client participates.

Some social workers have expressed the opinion that emphasis on fact-finding and assessment interferes with the development of dynamic relationships with clients. They fear that if conceptual frameworks for assessment are used, the empathy and art will go out of practice. A systematic approach might restrict spontaneity, depersonalize the client, and interfere with the development of an individualized psychosocial relationship with each person. Bertha Reynolds, a famous practitioner and educator, responded to such concerns in this way:

Penetrating diagnosis and dynamic relationship in social work are not opposed, but complementary. Each stresses something essential, and each, without the other, can be carried to an absurdity. If diagnosis means seeing into or seeing through, that is not possible without a relationship with the client which releases him to be himself, to explore his trouble freely because a helping person is there. . . . On the other hand, a relationship becomes meaningful if it brings to bear on the problem not only the caseworker's warmth, but light which is drawn from scientific training, and from experience in dealing with many such problems. It frees the individual from a sense of being smothered in trouble that is his alone, and lets him draw on experience that is more comprehensive than his, and more free from emotional entanglement. Diagnosis, then, is not imposing the thinking of a stranger with alien interests, but weaving together the threads that both client and caseworker draw from life and work on together.[3]

She further explains that diagnosis can be an imposition "if it ignores the objective reality with which the person is struggling and from which his emotional conflicts are, at least in part, derived."[4] Thus, she urged that diagnosis take into account the interrelationship between internal and external forces. Her subject was casework, but her comments are just as pertinent to work with a client system of any size and type of structure.

In response to concerns that systematic assessment will destroy the humanistic aspects of practice, Simon explained that

The use of a body of theory to organize, systematize, and rationalize a caseworker's knowledge, thinking, and action is ultimately liberating of the personal gifts that mark the artistic practitioner. Having at his command organized and systematic ways of thinking and doing, the caseworker is then free to exercise the empathy and sensitivity, to admit his feelings, to take in the flavor and the uniqueness of the patient and his situation.[5]

Her focus was on work with individuals in medical social work, but the conviction holds as well for other modalities and fields of practice.

Later on, Germain considered the need for social study as a component of practice. She commented that recent research has suggested that drop-outs in the early phase of service may be due, to some extent, to differences in the goals of the social worker and the client. The client seeks immediate help with a presenting problem: the social worker seeks information about the client and his situation in ways that the client may not perceive to be related to his needs. Yet this discrepancy between the worker and client does not mean that the worker should not seek to understand the client's needs and situation. She said:

> It is my conviction that study continues to be an essential element in a scientifically based practice. Indeed, the spirit of scientific inquiry on which study rests is more than ever necessary in the face of the constant change in social needs and conditions that now confront the social worker. Yet it must be study that serves today's demands, not yesterday's ideologies.[6]

It is Germain's view that service becomes more individualized and differentiated when it is particularized for a client with his own needs, in particular situations. This principle of individualization operationalizes the value of belief in the inherent dignity and worth of the individual. In a similar vein, Bartlett takes the position that there needs to be renewed emphasis on the "social worker's responsibility to understand the situation with which he must deal before taking action."[7] She defines professional assessment as a form of logical analysis of a situation. Such an analysis requires expert selection and use of knowledge appropriate to the particular situation.

In social work, the idea of assessment has changed from a period of investigation prior to service to an ongoing process of interaction between the worker and the individual or group. It is not a lengthy phase that precedes any help or service. It is a continuous process that enhances the help that is being given at any time. Within the client-worker interaction, it involves analysis and interpretation of facts as they are presented.

A social worker uses knowledge of networks of social systems first to understand the individuals and groups in situations, and then to plan and guide treatment. Skill in analysis of the situation requires the ability to use a conceptual framework for organizing observations and for planning services. The behavioral science base, as previously described, is used as a guide to determine what the social worker takes into account in formulating his assessment. Even when it is predetermined that individual help will be given, it is important for the practitioner to understand the structure and processes of the client's family—the impact of the family on the individual and his impact on other members and on the functioning of the family system. It is important to assess the influence of his reference groups on his values, goals, and behavior. Likewise, it is important to assess wider environmental influences, regardless of the nature and size of the client system which is to use the service.

A basic assumption underlying the framework for assessment is that human behavior is the product of the transactions between the individual and his environment. Every individual has an interdependent relationship with others; he is a part of a number of interlocking social systems, and certain dimensions of his behavior can be understood only in terms of the structure, function, and development of these networks of interaction and his status and role in them. The worker's assessment is, therefore, related both to individual and social dimensions. At both individual and group levels, the worker is concerned with the nature of stresses from internal and external forces that disrupt the steady state, and the capacity and motivation of the system to withstand strain, cope with change, and find new or modified ways of functioning.

The amount and nature of the data sought vary with the many facets of the service, particularly its purpose and structure. The understanding of the client-group-situation gestalt that is sought cannot include all aspects of the individual's or group's functioning. In accord with the value of the right to privacy, it should be limited to what is essential to achieving agreed-upon goals. If a service is one of primary prevention or enhancement of development, the data obtained are often limited initially to the descriptive characteristics common to the clients, such as phase of development, common experience or status, and certain potential risks to healthy development.

Later, during the process of service, the worker may elicit additional information as it seems particularly relevant, or as individuals who exhibit special problems are identified. If the service is a therapeutic or rehabilitative one, helpful treatment cannot be given unless the worker has adequate understanding of the nature, causative factors, and course of the problematic situation. Such understanding must be combined with understanding of the psychosocial aspects of the problem and the adequacy of the client's current functioning in particular situations.

The structure of the service provides boundaries for exploration concerning people in their situations. For example, when an individual is in a state of crisis, the information sought centers around the precipitating event and the emotional reactions to it. In short-term formed groups, the goals are usually specific to a problem or status shared by members, and the content of the assessment is thus limited to that which is most pertinent to the focus of the group. In work with a family or other natural group, a major focus will be on the adequacy of the structure, composition, communication, and decision-making processes. In work with formed groups, the worker will be alert to cues that help him to understand the patterns of relationships, communication, and problem-solving as these develop; to be aware of sources of conflict among members or between the group and other systems, related to differences in values, goals, role expectations, status, and power; and to evaluate the influence of the composition of the group on its functioning. The need is to begin to work on the particular difficulties as they become evident, and to explore for the feelings, experiences, and information that are essential to the work at hand. The initial assessment may be very limited to what is necessary to make a tentative decision about accepting an applicant for service, or, at least, for accepting a person or family for further study and assessment. Assessment continues, however, throughout the treatment process to guide the worker's interventions at a given time.

Needs and Problems

The presenting request or complaint provides a beginning for the process of assessing client needs. Problems are conditions or situations that are perplexing, difficult, or undesirable. They are barriers to the achievement of goals sought by the client or others in the client's social network. If a person or family decides to apply to a social agency or a private practitioner, each person's views of the need or problem are elicited. In other instances, a client is referred by someone else. In such instances, the initial concern is defined by the referral agent, to whom the client reacts, either confirming or rejecting the idea of the need for help and the nature of the difficulty. Even when the service is a developmental or preventive one, there often is a discrepancy between potential and actual achievement or an awareness of a desire for enhanced opportunities. As the worker explores the nature and scope of the needs with the clients, he seeks their perceptions about who is involved in, or affected by, the problem, when and by whom the problem was first identified, and what feelings and reactions are attached to the problem. He seeks to learn how the problem is experienced by the client, the amount of discomfort, pain, or stress that accompanies it; the extent to which the steady state is disrupted; what efforts have been made to deal with the situation; and ability to cope with the difficulties. As exploration of the difficulty occurs, there may or may not emerge alternative perspectives on the problem. The problem as defined may be quite different from the presenting problem, or a constellation of problems may be identified, one or more of which will be considered appropriate for social work help.

CATEGORIES OF NEEDS AND PROBLEMS

Some typology of needs, conditions, and difficulties aids the worker in securing as complete as possible an understanding of the person-group-situation gestalt. Many practitioners sincerely believe that any classification of problems can do an injustice to the client by providing a worker-oriented rather than a client-focused approach to helping. They think that classifying a client as to type is a first step toward imposing one's own ideas and taking over responsibility for the outcome of help. They assert that any classification denies the uniqueness of a person or group, and violates the ethical principles of individualization and self-determination.[8] A person or group, however, can be understood only if it is perceived in terms of what it has in common with others as well as in its differences from others. Some classification is actually essential to individualization.

A number of social scientists have noted the negative effect of labeling persons as handicapped, mentally retarded, delinquent, psychotic, or terminally ill. They note that the use of labels plays a crucial role in the development and maintenance of deviant behavior: people behave according to the expectations conveyed by the label. The label itself tends to create stereotyped reactions from others. This is probably so, but practitioners can overcome this tendency. In a study of labeling in social work, for example, it was found that social workers did not label clients of low socioeconomic status more negatively than they labeled those with high socioeconomic status; but they did label those with mental problems more negatively than those with other types of problems.[9]

In spite of reservations about the procedure, most scientists argue that some form of categorization is necessary.[10] Allport, for example, has said that the "human mind must think with the aid of categories: we cannot possibly avoid this process. But once formed, generalizations are the basis for normal prejudgment."[11] The problem is that when the categories used are not adapted to new information—when they are used to prejudge a person or a group—they become perpetuated in their initial form. A label then may become an instrument of social control, as when children with handicaps in the use of English are labeled mentally retarded and are progressively denied equal educational opportunities. When individuals are inappropriately labeled, they are stigmatized. A diagnosis, when misused, can become a self-fulfilling prophecy. Thus the way a problem is defined can determine its solution.[12] The problem is further compounded by the fact that classifications are usually imprecise and vague, and often experts do not agree on diagnostic categories, particularly of mental illness. Within any classification, even if accurate, there are innumerable variations among the individuals so labeled. The diagnostic label may be taken for the totality of a person's functioning. Capacities may be overlooked. These objections to classification point to the difficulties involved: they really refer to the misuse of classifications. Some categories are essential to orderly thinking and planning.

A PSYCHOSOCIAL FORMULATION

Since psychosocial functioning is the focus of social work practice, it can be expected that practitioners will be concerned with unfulfilled needs and problems in the realm of human relationships. Each individual and family has its own particular set of needs, but these can be categorized into several major types. These are:

1. *Lack of economic and social resources.*[13] Many clients of social and health agencies face a frustrating array of social problems occasioned by the lack of adequate income, housing, employment, day care facilities, legal aid, and medical resources. Many neighborhoods lack adequate health, recreational, and educational opportunities; aesthetic qualities; and public transportation. In many such situations the problem is created primarily by external factors over which an individual has little control and to which he is responding in normal ways. Deficiencies in tangible means and resources restrict and thwart the ambitions of people and limit their abilities to relate to others. Lack of essential material resources may lead to stress in personal and family functioning and also may deprive people of opportunities to associate with others in mutually enriching ways. In our society, money is highly valued and necessary for fulfilling personal, social, and emotional needs as well as for physical survival. Unemployment or dependency on public welfare often brings stigma and disrespect to the person and his family, leading in turn to loss of self-esteem and self-confidence. Thus, lack of satisfaction in human relationships is often associated with deficiencies in resources.

2. *Lack of knowledge and experience.* Deficiency of knowledge, skills, and experiences influences the nature and quality of social relationships. Lack of opportunities to secure information and to prepare for new or modified roles is a hazard to effective functioning. In many of these instances, socialization has been neglected or inadequate in some important area. Patients may often be exceedingly anxious because they do not have adequate knowledge of the meaning of a medical diagnosis or treatment procedure. Prospective adoptive parents may not have accurate knowledge about the many considerations that ought to go into making an important decision, in terms of their welfare and that of a child who needs a permanent

home. Young adults may not know how to relate to a personnel officer in applying for jobs. Family members may lack skills in communicating with other persons. Clients often lack skills in budgeting and money management. Even though there are resources in a neighborhood, many people do not know about them or do not know how to use them. The lack of use of resources is sometimes striking; for example, an elderly widow did not know that a nutrition program was available to her; a group of mothers living in a public housing project did not know there was an excellent park within walking distance. The social competence of such persons is severely limited by lack of knowledge, curiosity, and experiences that facilitate effective functioning.

3. *Emotional reactions to stress.*[14] One type of stress to which people often react with more than usual emotional upheaval is related to developmental phases. As individuals grow and develop, each phase in the life cycle posits new demands and new opportunities.[15] Stress often accompanies the transition from one phase in the life cycle to the next one. These difficulties may be thought of as typical problems of human growth and development. For example, the young child's need to enter school means separation from his family for increasing periods of time, learning to relate to teachers and other pupils, and mastering academic knowledge and skills. The new demands that face the child create stress for his parents as well. At another end of the life cycle, old age often is accompanied by changes in vital roles, social relationships, and economic resources, about which people have anxiety. These are but two examples of the normal difficulties in mastering the tasks that are specific to each developmental phase, as a person's development meshes with the developmental tasks in the cycle of family life.

A second type, situational stress, includes reactions to hazardous events or circumstances in the life of an individual, family, or group, often of a crisis nature.[16] Events that often precipitate a crisis are medical diagnoses or accidents, natural disasters such as fires or earthquakes, separation or loss, and unemployment or school failure. Especially stressful are such situations when they coincide with maturation to a new developmental phase. The extent to which the new expectations are met or crises resolved depends partially on the availability of material resources and people who can support the person or family through the difficult period of time.

4. *Illness and disability.*[17] Various social, emotional, and economic stresses accompany mental and physical illness and handicaps which, in turn, often threaten interpersonal relationships. Inability to develop and maintain affectional bonds with others is one major difficulty in psychiatric disorders. Whittaker, for example, found that the most severe disturbance in autistic children is the failure to develop satisfactory social relationships. This fact means that such children need social work help, since it is in the area of relationships that the social worker can be most helpful.[18]

In medical and surgical services, the social worker deals primarily with the psychosocial implications of disability, both for the patients and their families. Problems in psychosocial relations often accompany chronic and acute illnesses. There tends to be withdrawal from relationships associated with a crippling condition; feelings of helplessness, loneliness, or degradation related to catastrophic or fatal illnesses; or problems in interpersonal relations for parents and siblings of children with developmental disabilities at various phases of the life cycle.

5. *Loss of relationships.* Separation from some significant relationship or set of relationships with particular others is a source of many difficulties. Separation of children from parents due to death, divorce, incarceration, or foster home placement is a major problem for many clients. Separation of children from one or both parents creates serious psychosocial problems for both the child and the parents. Filial deprivation experienced by parents when children enter foster care is a complement to the more widely studied concept of maternal deprivation.[19] Loss of meaningful relationships with relatives and friends usually accompanies placement of elderly persons in retirement or rest homes, particularly when relocation is not voluntary. Loneliness, a sense of loss, and grief accompany separation from others.

Death of a loved one, of course, is the most devastating form of separation, at whatever phase in the life cycle it occurs. The survivors must cope with intense feelings of loneliness, isolation, guilt, grief, and depression. They must cope with changes in economic and social circumstances. In addition to the emotional reactions to the loss of the deceased person, the survivors experience strains in relationships with other people and difficulties in developing new relationships or deepening existing ones.

6. *Dissatisfactions in social relationships.*[20] Relationships with other people are influenced by intrapsychic problems. People often feel severe dissatisfaction with their relationships. They perceive deficiencies or excesses in their relationships with others. They may fear intimate relationships or be unable to develop intimacy when such a relationship is desired; they may feel concern about the inadequacy of their sexual adjustment. They may suffer from extreme shyness or timidity, leading to deep feelings of loneliness. They may feel that they are unable to be assertive in appropriate ways; that they are too abrasive or overly aggressive; or that they are excessively vulnerable to the criticisms of others. Low self-esteem or a distorted sense of identity may prevent them from entering into and maintaining relationships with desired others. A realistic and positive sense of self-esteem and identity requires the integration of biological and psychosocial factors. Such integration is dependent, to a considerable extent, upon the quality of relationships within a person's family and within his network of relationships in the community.

7. *Interpersonal conflict.*[21] Conflict or dysfunction in central life relationships is frequent, predominantly between marital partners, partners living together outside marriage, parents and one or more children, siblings, or other relatives. Areas of marital conflict are as diverse as patterns of communication, child-rearing practices, sex, money, leisure, relatives, or housekeeping standards. Parent-child dissatisfactions and conflict may revolve around norms of dress, sex, drugs, authority, school performance, money, or choice of friends. There may be conflict in other relationships also, such as those between close friends, pupil and teacher, worker and supervisor, or colleagues.

Conflict may be overt as evidenced in uncontrolled arguments or physical violence. Spouse and child abuse have become major problems with which social workers increasingly are dealing. Various causal dimensions have been identified, including past traumatic experiences of the abusing person; the culturally sanctioned use of physical force; poverty; discrimination; mistaken notions about rights and roles of family members; and mental illness. Conflicts may be covert and expressed through such means as withdrawal from open communication or displacement of hostility onto other people, as when one member of a group becames a scapegoat or rejected isolate. Conflicts may stem from lack of complementarity in basic needs, such as degree of intimacy or distance, love and affection, dependency-independency, and authority and control. They often have their source in conscious or unconscious differences in values, goals, expectations, traditions, and customs. All interpersonal conflicts are difficulties in relationships among people.

8. *Culture conflict*. In our society, there is often conflict among persons and between groups, based on cultural differences, prejudice, or discrimination.[22] Interpersonal dissatisfactions and conflicts are often based, at least in part, on cultural differences. Certain ethnic groups have values which may not be understood by others, creating problems for their members in making choices and adapting effectively to their environments. Differences in values may be expressed in attitudes toward time, material possessions, work, family structure, role expectations, individual versus family decision-making authority, and competition versus cooperation. Members of minority cultures particularly are faced with such decisions as holding to or violating norms regarding food preferences, customs and traditions, family planning, divorce, premarital and extramarital sex, and other personal morals. Adaptation is complicated for persons who have been socialized into one culture whose value system conflicts with the value system of one or more other cultures of which the person is a part. Many people must learn to integrate some aspects of two or more cultures, often made the more difficult because their own culture is devalued by the dominant society.

Members of one culture may become hostile toward the dominant culture when they know that their rights are violated through legal and social inequities and discrimination in housing, employment, education, and health care. Feelings of distrust, suspicion, resentment, and hostility often characterize relationships between members of groups who differ in regard to race, ethnicity, or religion. The result may be negative stereotyping, interpersonal or intergroup tensions, even violence. A person may hold attitudes that restrict his own choices or he may be the victim of the attitudes of others toward him. He may be torn by internal conflict, stemming from differences in values and norms of his various reference groups. A parent's insecurity in his role may be aggravated if his own values and norms are too different from those of the groups which influence the child. Parent-child conflicts develop when children reject their parents' values and expectations, wanting to adapt to the majority culture when the parents are trying to maintain the culture into which they were socialized. Conflict between cultures, then, can result in a variety of intrapersonal, interpersonal, and group conflicts.

9. *Conflicts with formal organizations.*[23] Problems of this type occur between an individual and another person, but the difficulty is not with the person per se, but with a position or role in an organization. The person in the role represents the organization which is perceived to be withholding desired services or otherwise acting against the best interests of the client. Adolescents, for example, do not experience authority in school and law enforcement agencies as particular persons, but as strangers or impersonal enemies who make demands on them. Another example is common distrust of the welfare system. The conflict occurs with a representative of the system, but the major dissatisfaction is with the policies, procedures, values, or functions of the system itself.

10. *Maladaptive group functioning.*[24] Difficulties often occur at a group level of functioning. The condition or situation that is thought to be undesirable is dysfunction in the properties of the group. Interpersonal relationships may be unsatisfying to the members or dysfunctional to the welfare of particular individuals and the group as a whole. There may be lack of mutual affection and acceptance among members. The members may be unable to enjoy each other. The group may need to isolate, scapegoat, demean, or glorify one or more members. There may be discrepancies among individuals' orientations to love, authority, and group identity or conflicting loyalties between members of the group and between the family and other significant persons in the environment.

The composition of a group may be faulty, for example, when a foster child is placed in a family inappropriate to his and the family's needs or when a group is so large that individual needs are unknown or ignored.

The roles in the group may contribute to inadequate group functioning. There may be a missing role, as when one parent separates from the family or an elder child leaves home, requiring a redistribution of the tasks performed by the missing member. Some members may perform their roles inadequately, resulting in disequilibrium and conflict. Members may disagree about what to expect of a person in a particular role, or they may not be clear about roles and responsibilities. There may be lack of sufficient differentiation, constancy, and flexibility in the social organization of the group.

Patterns of verbal and nonverbal communication among the members are often faulty so that individuals lose touch with each other. There may be lack of opportunities for some or most members to express their concerns, opinions, and desires and to learn how these tie in with concerns, opinions, and desires of others. There may be inappropriate balance between the demands for self-disclosure and privacy. There may be inadequate mechanisms for making decisions and solving problems that affect all members of the group. Patterns and means of communication are closely tied to the achievement of individual and group goals. There may be little mutual understanding of goals. If goals are known, there may be lack of support of individual goals or lack of means to achieve group goals.

All these factors are interrelated and interdependent, since a group is a system of interdependent parts. As a result of the interaction among many facets of the group, there may be lack of cohesiveness. The members are not attracted to each other and to the welfare of the group, resulting in apathy and lack of group identity and loyalty. Such groups do not share common goals, values, and norms and are unable to meet the needs of the members.

These categories do not meet requirements for a valid research classification, for there is overlapping among them and they may not be exhaustive of all types of problems. Neither are they established once and forever. They are to be used flexibly and varied as they are further tested in practice.

Medical Diagnoses

The use of medical diagnoses by social workers is a source of some confusion. It is generally agreed that if physical disease is suspected, a physician makes the diagnosis. Even so, the social worker needs to be alert to symptoms that suggest an illness, to the symptoms of drug use and their effects on people, and to the psychosocial aspects of illness and handicap. Changes in personality that seem to occur suddenly may be responses to organic disorders. When a medical problem is suspected, it is necessary to rule out the presence of organic conditions, through referral to, or consultation with, physicians.

Concerning diagnoses of mental illness, the social worker needs to understand the meaning of the term and its possible implications for a particular social work service. Many social workers become quite skilled in recognizing the major characteristics of mental dysfunctions, as classified by the American Psychiatric Association. But social workers do not claim to cure the illness; rather, they "treat people who have such conditions."[25] Within each category of mental illness, there is a wide variety of capacities and difficulties in relationships with people. It is the social worker's responsibility to identify the problems in psychosocial relations and to make the psychosocial assessment.

The Use of Classifications

Typologies are for use. The utility of such schemes rests in part upon how adequately the scheme covers the range of situations with which it deals and, in part, upon how competent the practitioners are in applying the scheme to their practice. Following several principles can assure the proper use of typologies of problems.[26]

1. The problem should be based on facts, not inferences, and defined in operational terms. Rather than referring to a weak ego, for example, one would set forth the difficulty in particular ego functions; instead of labeling a person as a rejecting mother, one would describe the behavior that is interpreted as rejection.

2. Classifications are nothing more than tools that alert the practitioner to major combinations of relevant factors, and they are useful in communicating the central tendency of the condition with colleagues.

3. The particular classification that is used affects what is perceived and how the perceptions are organized for action. In formulating a problem, knowledge beyond the classification needs to be used in order to arrive at a useful assessment. If a classification of mental illness has been made, for example, knowledge of psychosocial relationships, normal developmental phases, capacities, and environmental influences need also to be taken into consideration. The social worker is interested not in a particular symptom, but in clusters of feeling, thinking, and behaving that seem to fit together. The evaluation is of one or more patterns of behavior or set of environmental obstacles, not of a person or family.

4. Classification is a means for ascertaining what characteristics a person or family has in common with other individuals or groups within a population category; but assessment emphasizes also what is unique, that is, how an individual or group differs from others of its type. This is the well-known principle of individualization.

5. The problem is viewed not as within a person only, but as characteristic of his interaction in a particular situation. What may be regarded as dysfunctional behavior in one situation may not be so regarded in a different one. When a person is ill, for example, the expectations are different than when he is well. A problem may be specific to certain situations only, as when a child is aggressive at school but not at home or when an employee is conforming on the job but not in his personal relationships. The worker, therefore, is concerned with variations of effectiveness of functioning in different social systems—whether ineffective functioning in one system is influencing ability to adapt elsewhere and whether successful functioning in one system can be used as a bridge to more effective functioning elsewhere.

6. The social worker who undertakes service with a client who has a particular type of problem does not permit the label to obscure the value of using a variety of procedures and interventions in a variety of systems, as appropriate to meet the client's needs.

7. The search for understanding is reciprocal between a practitioner and a client. In line with our values, clients have a right and responsibility to participate actively in the process. While the social worker is trying to understand the client-situation configuration, the client or clients are trying to understand themselves or their situation. They are also trying to understand the practitioner's attitudes and ways of work. They are conveying messages about their purposes, aspirations, concerns, and expectations. They not only react to the worker's communications, but they actively contribute information and evaluate the worker's tentative ideas about their functioning. Such feedback serves either as a correction or a reaffirmation of the worker's analysis of the situation at a given time.

Content of Assessment

The content of assessment is derived from the purpose of social work, selected knowledge from the biological, psychological, and social sciences, and the nature of the major needs or problems in psychosocial functioning. Information that is clearly relevant to the particular situation is elicited about the individual, family, or formed group in its environment. Assessment takes into consideration the major characteristics of the individual, family, or group and the environment. In relation to a particular client system, the practitioner seeks to understand the needs or problems in terms of their meaning to the persons concerned. Problems and goals are closely interrelated: a goal is often one of alleviating some problem that interferes with satisfaction in an aspect of living or of enhancing existing capacities and opportunities. A goal is a hoped-for outcome or desire to have something be better.

Human systems are goal-directed; goals are powerful motivating factors. A person's positive motivations and aspirations are at least as important as are his problems; determining the goals that an applicant desires, therefore, should be paramount. The practitioner starts with an applicant's interest in having something be better. The applicant may be clear about what he hopes for, or he may have only vague feelings of discontent with himself or with something in his situation, or both. He may be articulate or need help to express himself. But the determination of at least some temporary goal, a hoped-for outcome, guides both worker and client in their further deliberations. The goals are evidenced by the person's verbal statements about them, but also by the nature of his participation in the individual or group session, his reactions to the worker's part in the process; the topics he initiates, elaborates on, or avoids; his posture and tone of voice, and so forth. If he is a participant in a family or group situation, his responses to other members' statements about goals provide cues for the practitioner. In families and groups, concern is with individual goals as these interact with those of other members.

In assessment of goal-directedness, the practitioner asks questions about the extent to which the individuals and the group recognize their goals, the clarity of the goals to each person involved; the extent of support, conflict, and agreement about the goals; the capacity and motivation to do what is necessary to achieve the goals; and the availability of resources for implementing the goals.

In addition to problems and goals, the functioning of the system is assessed, utilizing the major constructs that were described in the preceding chapter: boundary, integration of biological, psychological, and social aspects of behavior, progressive differentiation, social structure of status and roles, steady state, patterns of communication, and the interaction between systems and their environments.

CASE ILLUSTRATION

The family consists of Mrs. Alice Sanders, Roger, Susan, and George, Jr.
Principal client: Roger, age 17, 11th grade, public high school.
Mother: Mrs. Alice Sanders, age 47, reference librarian, Irish Catholic, divorced for one year. Prior to the divorce, she worked only fifteen hours per week. She has custody of the three children. She has maintained ties with a sister and brother, each of whom has several children.
Susan: age 15, 9th grade, public high school.
George, Jr. (Georgie): age 12, 7th grade, public junior high school.
Father: George Sanders, age 48, policeman, Dutch-English Protes-

tant, remarried four months ago. His new wife, age 50, had been a widow and has two grown children. She does not work. Mr. Sanders provides child support for the three children by court order, which the mother considers to be inadequate. Mr. Sanders instigated the divorce proceedings; his major reason was opposition to the time the family was spending on church affairs and his wife's insistence that she accept an offer for a very good position that would make use of her degree in library science. He felt that her place was in the home. He has visiting privileges, but has seen very little of the children since his remarriage.

Presenting problem. Roger was brought to the emergency room of a large urban hospital by his mother, sister, and brother following a severe digestive upset, dizziness, and loss of consciousness. The diagnosis was diabetes. The family is fully insured for health care. In an initial conference with the family, it was learned that the attack occurred at a buffet supper at the family's church at which Roger was reported by his mother to have gorged himself. The mother was very upset. She expressed a mixture of deep concern about Roger's health and great anger. For several months, she has known that something was wrong with Roger; she had tried to get him to the doctor, but he refused to keep the appointments she made for him. He had always been overweight until recently, when he suddenly began to lose weight rapidly, craved sweets, needed to urinate frequently, and became irritable at home. He had been a good student until this semester when his grades dropped precipitously. Earlier medical treatments have been for colds and influenza. A heart murmur was discovered when he was ten years old. Although no organic damage to the heart was found, his mother forbade his participation in sports and strenuous games. His mother had hoped to get him interested in a young people's group at church, because Roger seemed to be a loner. Susan was very solicitous about her brother, and offered to tell the school vice-principal why Roger would be absent. She said that a friend of hers has diabetes and was told she inherited it from her mother. She asked if that meant she and Georgie would get it, too. Her mother became irritated and said it certainly did not come from her side of the family: it is their father who is responsible. Georgie said nonchalantly that he was not worried—he does not eat all the time like Roger does. When it was suggested that the entire family attend the next informational meeting about diabetes to learn about the disease and what they could do to help Roger control his illness, each first said he could not come for various reasons, but when the nurse emphasized its importance, they agreed to attend the meeting.

During a brief interview with Roger two days later, he indicated that a lot of fuss was being made about nothing and that he was ready to go home. When reminded that this could not happen until the necessary amount of insulin and the best diet were determined, he said he didn't see why he had to stay in the hospital. It was "no big deal." He did agree that that the social worker could return to talk with him after lunch.

Needs and problems. The preliminary information suggests that there may be multiple problems that are influencing Roger's psychosocial development, the future of his health, and the functioning of the family. The social worker will test out further the meaning of the illness to Roger and other members of the family, and their emotional reactions to it. There are clues that the family possesses insufficient knowledge about the illness and its psychosocial implications. The worker will seek to learn about the effect of separation from their father on Roger and his siblings; changes occasioned by the mother's full-time employment; the meaning of the mother's labeling of Roger as a loner; the effect of the marital conflict on the present family functioning, and the present functioning of the family as a system. His use of a framework for assessment will contribute to his understanding of the psychological and social factors that influence the course of the disease and its impact on the patient and his family. In accordance with professional values, he will secure only that information that the family members are willing to present. The social worker will note the capacities and strengths that have become evident. These include the mother's high educational level and apparent success in a professional job; Roger's good achievement in school, indicating academic potential; and the other children's apparent success in school. He will note that the mother did show deep concern for Roger, in spite of the anger and frustration, and that Susan seemed to care enough for Roger to report his illness to the school.

Family members were able to cope with the crisis sufficiently to reduce their upset and accept a recommendation to attend an informational meeting.

Boundaries. Roger is an adolescent boy and a subsystem of his primary family system. He is part of mother-son and sibling subsystems. He is also a very part-time member of his father's new family system. He is a member of a Catholic church and a student in a large urban high school. He is now also a patient in a hospital. The worker will want to learn more about the interdependence between Roger and these varied systems; for example, the extent to which he feels identified with his primary family and his father's family and the influence of both systems on his efforts to cope with the consequences of having diabetes. The initial information suggests that Roger may not now be open to information about the nature of the illness and its consequences for his daily living. Although mother and siblings have agreed to attend an informational meeting, it still is not known how open they will be to the changes that Roger's illness will make in their relationships. The father and his new wife will need to be considered, as will the mutual influence of Roger and the other systems of which he is a part. Further understanding of the interdependent systems will aid the social worker in deciding who should be included in the client system and what systems might be influenced in behalf of the primary client, aided by his evaluation of which persons in the system show the greatest motivation and capacity to cope with change. He will assess whether or not the family boundary is still firm, or if the family is moving toward disintegration due to changes in family composition and roles.

Integration of biological, psychological, and social factors. The social worker will use his knowledge about the multiple causative factors, the necessary treatment, and the developmental course of diabetes. He will consider the impact of this knowledge on Roger and significant others in his social network. The fact that Mrs. Sanders seems to need to protect Roger because of a heart murmur may be contributing to difficulties in his mastering psychosocial tasks of adolescence. The worker will be alert to clues concerning the adequacy of Roger's ego functioning in terms of its defensive and adaptive functions, and as it relates to Roger's status as a patient. He will consider whether Roger's initial tendency to deny the severity of the illness is a rigid defense or a flexible effort to protect himself until he has some time to familiarize himself with his new health status. He will note what other defenses are used as protective devices. He will attempt to ascertain Roger's motivation to control the illness or to resist the daily insulin injections, urine testing, dietary restrictions, and exercise which are necessary components of the medical regimen. He will note the attitudes about, and efforts made by, Roger to adapt to the regimen. He will be concerned with the influence of the illness on Roger's self-esteem, sense of identity, and relationships with peers. Similarly, the worker will explore selectively for patterns in the ego functioning of other members of the family as these may hinder or facilitate Roger's adaptation. For example, he will test out the early clues that Mrs. Sanders has a tendency toward overprotection, a need to control, and to blame others for Roger's situation. He will try to get clues as to the meaning of Roger's refusal to keep medical appointments—for example, rebellion against his mother's attempts to control, a defense against great anxiety about the symptoms; a rationalization for failure to achieve in school; or other secondary gains that the symptoms might make possible for him.

The nature and quality of Roger's relationships with members of his family and significant others will be important determinants of whether or not he adapts effectively to the illness. In the statement of presenting problems, there are hints that there are both positive and negative aspects of Roger's relationships with members of his family. Roger's feelings about separation from his father are unknown. Divorce, however, is always stressful for children, and the early remarriage of one parent often exacerbates the problems. Roger's rebellion against early medical care and the deterioration of his school performance may be related to the marital conflict and seeming abandonment by the father. It should also be noted that Roger may be deficient in friendships with peers, which are so important in providing support and motivation. The worker reviews what he knows about midadolescence as a phase in biopsychosocial development, and the normal stresses that accompany maturation and the need to master new tasks. In Roger's case, illness and family conflict may contribute to difficulties in coping with the stress. But

Roger may also be competent in other ways and have many areas in which the ego is functioning effectively. Roger's phase of development is related to the phase of family development which has been affected by the maturation of each child, the change in family composition, and the full-time employment of the mother.

Structure: status and roles. In order to understand a person in his social networks, the social worker will want to analyze the individual's role sets and the ways in which reciprocal roles are functional or dysfunctional to the individual and the system involved. In Roger's case, there is already some evidence that his role as pupil no longer gives him satisfaction, and that is of concern to his mother. He apparently lacks adequate roles as a friend with peers. He has just been assigned a new role as patient with a serious chronic illness. At the time in the life cycle when there tends to be some rebellion against authority, Roger is faced with meeting new and rather rigid responsibilities for carrying out the medical regimen. The demands of the illness influence the roles of other members of the family who will find ways to support Roger in his new responsibilities, take over his responsibilities to the extent possible, or sabotage his efforts to follow medical recommendations.

Steady state. The social worker will seek to evaluate the state of the system in terms of the sources of stress that tax the adaptive capacities of the clients and the ways in which the persons involved cope with the stress. Any serious illness is stressful for the patient, his relatives, and other significant persons. Because of Roger's illness, the family cannot return to its prior state. The pattern of roles and emotional relationships is bound to change as Roger and his relatives adapt to changes occasioned by the chronic illness which requires changes in daily living. It has already been noted that members of the family were very upset when Roger suffered a serious digestive upset and lost consciousness. By the time they left the hospital, however, the steady state was at least partially restored. The worker knows that this family has recently undergone the stress that accompanies divorce, the threat of educational failure of the oldest child, and possibly also the mother's new employment. It is necessary to explore further the family's situation to determine the severity of the stresses on each member and their ability to cope with them. The extent to which the mother's relatives and friends of the family are able to provide support to the family needs to be ascertained.

Communication. Since the patterns and content of communication are often keys to the satisfactions and effectiveness of an individual's interaction with other people, the social worker will assess the ability of the individuals in the system to listen, to hear, and to understand each other. He will consider the extent to which communication is blocked by anxiety, emotional reactions, lack of acceptance and affection, or language patterns. In Roger's case, he will want to know more about how the family members communicate with each other, both in terms of the manifest content and the emotional messages that are exchanged. He will be particularly alert to how they engage in interchanges concerning attitudes toward Roger in his new status and the responsibilities for the medical regimen.

Environment. The social worker seeks to understand and evaluate the environment in terms of the opportunities, gratifications, obstacles, or frustrations it provides for the achievement of individual and family goals. The family is usually the most important environment for a child. Other groups and associations support, complement, or conflict with the family's values, goals, and opportunities. Concerning Roger, an analysis of the previous areas of content should provide an evaluation of the effect of the primary family, mother's extended family, and father's family on Roger's primary health and psychosocial development. The other systems which influence the situation are school, church, mother's employment, and networks of acquaintances and friends. The family has adequate health insurance, but there may be other financial constraints or lack of social resources that interfere with the optimal functioning of the family. The worker will want to evaluate further the extent to which Roger and his family are isolated from, or included in, extrafamilial social relationships, groups, and associations. The health care system itself is a crucial environment in determining the quality and continuity of care and the opportunities available for maximizing health. It determines the particular services that can be offered to the patient and family. Its connection with other health and social resources determines largely the extent to which other services may be mobilized in behalf of the family, as these become evident.

These guidelines for psychosocial assessment need to be used in accordance with the values of the profession that are translated into the principles of maximizing the participation of the clients in exploring and understanding themselves and their situations, clients' rights to privacy and equality of opportunity, and individualization. They need to be used flexibly, depending upon the client's readiness and conditions: the functions, organization, and pattern of services that are relevant to the type of agency or other setting to which the client applies or is referred. The practitioner recognizes that the whole is more than the sum of the parts. In a sense, as he examines each of the areas in the framework, he is distorting the reality of the situation for "these processes occur simultaneously and are in continuous interaction with each other, each affecting and being affected by the other."[27] It is in reflective thinking about the significance of the data obtained that the essence of the client system-situation gestalt is brought to light.

Analysis of Adequacy of Functioning

Within any given culture, there are norms or expectations that are used to judge the extent to which a person or group is functioning adequately. Assessment of a person's position on a continuum, ranging from very effective to very ineffective functioning, cues the worker into both problems and capacities. Although norms are necessary, rapid changes in the conditions of life and life style pose problems for both workers and clients in assessing the adequacy of functioning. Such assessment is made, not against absolute norms, but in relation to adaptation which is primarily "a reciprocal relationship between the organism and its environment."[28] Changes in either the person or the environment can bring about a state of adaptation in which there is a fit between the person and his environment that is favorable to the person's survival. There are certain average expectable situations or average atypical situations with which a person deals. The term "average expectable" signifies that which is within the range of expectations for the fit between person and environment.[29] According to this idea, expectations are differentiated according to such important influences on psychosocial functioning as sex, community, school grade or occupation, status of health, race, ethnicity, religion, and social class. The social worker seeks to learn the client's perceptions of, and attitudes toward, the norm of the different subsystems of his environment. It is to be noted that there is always some range of acceptable behaviors that are functional in the client's social context.

Assessment of behavior needs to take into account such judgmen₁, as whether the behavior is age- and sex-appropriate, how long it ha persisted, whether it is a reaction to change in circumstances such as death of a loved one, illness, or arrival of a new baby; whether it is socially acceptable behavior in the client's sociocultural group; the extent of disturbance in terms of whether the behavior interferes with only one or several areas of functioning; the type, severity, and frequency of symptoms; and whether there are changes in behavior of a kind that are not expected in terms of normal maturation and development. Although the worker does not focus on symptoms per se, he does need to know their significance. Rutter gives an example that nail biting tends to be an indication of stress, but is not associated with psychiatric disorders. In contrast, "disturbed peer relationships are more commonly associated with psychiatric disorders and, as such, warrant more serious attention."[30] It is important to be clear about the amount of suffering the symptom causes the client; the extent to which it prevents him from achieving his goals; the ways in which it interferes with normal progression in development; and the effect of the behavior on others.

Although there are many variations within normal adaptations, Cox has concluded that in psychologically mature adults, certain "themes or trends are most nearly universal and timeless: firm anchorage in reality, warmth and caring for other persons from an increasingly giving posture, productivity in work suited to ability, responsibility to the small and large social group, secure sense of self, development of a value system, and resilience under stress."[31] But such factors as illness, unemployment, and discrimination may make these criteria unrealistic for otherwise well and striving adults.

Making judgments about the adequacy of a person in relation to norms cannot be avoided, but it poses problems. One challenge is in ascertaining the influence of socioeconomic status and ethnicity on psychosocial functioning. Although there are certain characteristics, for example, that differentiate one group from another, efforts to define these characteristics, often combined with personal and institutional racism, may lead to negative stereotyping. Persons in positions of power, including social workers, come to expect stereotyped behavior and plan and act accordingly.[32] This difficulty points to the need for sound and current knowledge about social class, race, and ethnicity.

Another challenge to judgments about adequacy of functioning stems from a tendency to hold absolute criteria. Writing about the family, Goldberg notes that consciously or not, practitioners carry some ideal about what normal family life is or should be; there is an unrealistic model concerning what is good, adequate, or ideal family living.[33] In reality, there are few objective and universal criteria. Terms such as authoritarian husband, overprotective mother, and rejecting parent are used in varied ways, without precision, and without regard to the expectations for parental behavior in particular cultures. Extended families do exist and are functional in many cultures, including Asian, Mexican, and American Indian cultures. Goldberg provides evidence that, at least in London, the modern family is not isolated, as is so often stated. Three-generation families exist. The nuclear family is often embedded in a close network of family and neighborly relations.[34] Such research dispels certain myths about the family. It is to be remembered, however, that many families are indeed isolated from sources of support. Another myth is the one that the more separate and distinct are the roles for men and women, the better it is for them and their children. In opposition to this traditional myth is acceptance of more joint and interchangeable roles for men and women. Pollak indicates that there are great variations in patterns of family structure that are within a normal range. He refers, for example, to the fact that concentration of authority in one member of a family is probably not an expression of pathology. More often it is an expression of the history, religion, and ethology of a population group. It may be pathological, however, if it occurs when it should not be expected to happen, according to the culture of the group to which the person belongs.[35] Yet, individuals and families may need to deviate from the norms of their cultures if they are to exemplify the values of human dignity and justice for both sexes.

Goldberg suggests that, in spite of difficulties, there is a way of determining the effectiveness of family functioning. In the family which is adapting fairly successfully there is "a tolerable fit between what members of a family seek from each other and receive in return, and also perhaps a fit between their values and ways of living and those of the social group or network to which they belong."[36] It is to such interactional patterns among members of groups and with their reference groups then that assessment should be addressed.

The social worker takes into account the fact that all phases of human development overlap; each person has his own rate of maturation and development within what are average expectations; there are many variations within a normal pattern of functioning; and the norms themselves are in a process of change. The standards that a person sets for himself in relation to those that others set for him influence his success or failure in the major tasks in each phase of the life cycle. A person's feeling about his assigned roles, the way he interprets them, and his responses to the expectations of others give clues to the fit between the person and his environment. A person may adapt well to one situation and poorly to another. The worker, therefore, is concerned with variations of effectiveness of functioning in different social systems—whether ineffective functioning in one system is affecting ability to adapt elsewhere, and if successful functioning in one system can be used as a bridge to more effective functioning elsewhere.

In eliciting data from the client system, the worker's own values influence greatly the information he seeks and the inferences he draws from the data. He is guided by the values and ethical principles of the profession, as elaborated in the preceding chapter. His own personal values may, however, make it difficult to implement professional values. Often, he may not even be consciously aware of their effect on his practice.

Awareness of one's own values is essential, for they determine choices and actions, including goals, perceptions of capacities and problems, and the means to be used in the helping process. The practitioner needs "to realize that he sees others through the screen of his own personality and his own life experiences."[37] Some individual and family values are changing rapidly, offering many more options for choice. These relate, for example, to sexual behavior, forms of family structure and composition, marital separation, joint custody of children of divorce, self-gratification, and individuation. With a variety of fairly acceptable life styles, a practitioner may unwittingly impose his own preferences on clients' views of themselves and their situations.[38]

Following the psychosocial study, however brief, in which pertinent facts and feelings have been obtained, the actual assessment consists of the analysis of the individual-group-environment gestalt. The purpose is to identify the most critical factors that are operating in it, and to define their interrelationships. It is the worker's professional opinion about the facts and their meaning. It is his understanding of the configuration of the facts in order to determine how the person, family, or group can be helped. Somers and Perlman have referred to this process as one of problem-solving by the worker, done through a process of reflective thinking.[39] It is a logical process, although it incorporates intuitive insights.[40] Realistic appraisal provides the basis for action that should be guided by facts, not myths. What is to be understood is the nature of the need or trouble, the factors that contribute to it, the participants' motivations and capacities, and an assessment of what can be changed, supported, or strengthened in the person-group-situation configuration. To be properly understood, an individual or group is assessed in relation to the particular category of clients who have similar characteristics. It is to be reemphasized that classification pertains to certain aspects of the functioning of an individual or group, not to the person or group as a whole. Assessment is not completed when a problem or condition has been classified. There remains the need to construct some explanation of how it has come to be the way it is. A worker draws inferences from what he learns about the person-situation configuration and relates these judgments to the service that can be given. The behavioral science theory that he uses determines largely the inferences he will make.

Explanations, according to Lewis, are most useful when they account for all of the known facts and suggest others not previously identified.[41] The explanations that are arrived at through logical thinking are not for all occasions, but applicable to a particular case only. Lewis illustrates the point by noting that not everyone who has been subjected to social injustice has developed the same responses. The assessment must explain how a particular individual or family was actually victimized and what its responses to this event did or did not bring about. Not everyone who has experienced the death of a parent or spouse responds to this event in the same way. The assessment should explain the connection between a particular death and the functioning of a particular person or family. Strengths as well as difficulties are located as the worker seeks for alternative explanations. Such an approach tends to deemphasize stereotyping of client systems, through establishing the unique as well as the common responses to factors that contribute to a particular condition. In searching for explanations, it is usually necessary to give some attention to the nature of past experiences that have precipitated or contributed to the current condition. There may have been a gradual building up of inner and outer stresses; or there may be truly traumatic experiences from the past that contribute to the current difficulty.

Accurate assessment requires the ability to consider alternative explanations of behavior. Solomon gives the example of a child who is assessed as being discriminated against in a new school or, alternatively, as a child who is having difficulty adapting to a new school in which she feels isolated and lonely. Assessment requires determining which alternative is most probable by means of careful exploration of one's own feelings and exploration with the client.[42] Roger's school failure, for instance, may be a reaction to the build-up of stresses in the family, including the loss of a meaningful relationship with his father; it may be a reaction to the previously undiagnosed physical condition; it may be a reaction to changes in some aspect of the school itself; or it may be due to some combination of these alternative explanations.

Social workers intend to understand the present, but they intend also to influence the future. They are interested in preventing a harmful event or further damage from occurring as well as in promoting desired events. The worker has tremendous authority in assessment;

but so, too, do the clients, for they are full participants in all aspects of the process. The assessment is tentative, to be modified in the crucible of client system-worker interaction.

Sources of Information

The psychosocial study of the individual-group-situation configuration is accomplished through a variety of means.

Epidemiology, according to Meyer, is as essential for a social worker as for a doctor.[43] Knowledge about the characteristics of caseloads and the common needs of people living in an agency's catchment area is important in setting priorities for service. Preventive, developmental, and community action services are based on knowledge of the extent of the problem or condition and the demographic characteristics of persons affected by the condition. Even in treating one individual, neglect of epidemiological data can distort the reality of the lives of people. If, for example, a social worker assumes that a seven-year-old girl who is failing in school, both academically and socially, is an isolated instance of deviance, she is treated individually and labeled as a deviant. If, however, a survey is taken of the school population of seven-year-olds, the social worker may discover that the condition is widespread, especially among children from minority ethnic groups or those living in poor neighborhoods. Such a survey was made in one large city, resulting in the implementation of social work services under the joint auspices of the public schools and a voluntary agency.[44]

Although the worker still has a responsibility to help the initial client, the incidence of the difficulty also suggests broader programs of reaching out to offer services to all those who share a common condition or of participating in community action toward solutions to the problem. Awareness of the common need of families for information about diabetes and its consequences, for example, resulted in the provision of informational meetings for patients and their relatives in the hospital in which Roger was a patient.

The direct service worker has a responsibility beyond that to his clients. Agencies should be concerned with translating private troubles into public issues.[45] When a worker has encountered a number of similar needs or difficulties among those whom he serves, it becomes a public issue. He has a responsibility to address himself to the policy issue, at least by reporting the situation to relevant persons and groups in the community who can work on it. Through this process, social problems of significance to many people are identified and a start is made in the assessment of their nature, extent, and severity.

WORKER-CLIENT RELATIONSHIP

The relationship between a worker and the individual or group is a crucial source of information for use in assessment. A practitioner can learn much about an individual or a group through examining his own spontaneous reactions. The idea is that emotional reactions are provoked by clients. A worker may identify strongly with a person, desire to become intimate with him, or have feelings of pity, hopelessness, anger, or rejection. The worker considers not only what it is within him that stirs up these reactions, but also what there is in the relationship between worker and client that results in such behavior. It is often true that a person or group elicits similar reactions from other people also; a pattern of interpersonal behavior that is destructive to the client may be involved. The other side of the reactions of the worker, of course, is the client's reaction to the worker. Some of the reactions are realistic perceptions of the other people, but some of them are in the nature of transference or countertransference reactions. It is a two-way process: both worker and client behave in ways that affect the other: a process of mutual influence is occurring.

INDIVIDUAL INTERVIEWS

The most frequent source of data for use in assessment is the personal interview with a prospective client in which facts about himself and his situation are elicited and in which there is exploration of his view of his needs and situation. Individual interviews are thought to be especially useful in understanding and clarifying the particular goals that a client hopes to achieve and his reactions to the available services and the conditions under which they are given. They offer an opportunity to explore feelings and information which, at this time, might not be shared within the family or other group until there is enough trust and support by a worker for doing so. They are useful in screening, referring, and preparing individuals for experiences in groups. It must be remembered also that many persons are not living in a family, so they need to be interviewed individually at the outset.

JOINT AND FAMILY SESSIONS

Increasingly, joint and family sessions are used as the major procedure or as supplementary to interviews with individuals. Joint sessions usually consist of two clients, such as husband and wife or parent and child. There are special values in the use of joint and family interviews for purposes of assessment. In a nationwide survey of agencies affiliated with the Family Service Association of America, there was more use of joint than of family interviews, but the values for both types were similar.[46] With the exception of one local association that was opposed to all multiple-client approaches to diagnosis and treatment, all respondents were enthusiastic about the many diagnostic values of joint interviews with couples who were seeking help for marital problems. Although fewer social workers used interviews with family units, those who did concurred that there were unique values in both modalities. The values stemmed from the opportunity provided for simultaneous observation and evaluation of both partners or the entire family. The most frequently mentioned value was improved understanding of each individual and of the interactional patterns among them. Family sessions revealed interaction in ways similar to joint interviews, but there was a sense of increased subtlety of understanding and greater illumination of marital relationships and family functioning.

Five major contributions of joint and family interviews to the assessment of marital problems were found:

1. They reveal often hidden strengths and positive mutual bonds within the marriage and the family that may become essential therapeutic aids.

2. They illuminate the way in which family members interact with pathological destructiveness, restrictiveness, and mutual pain.

3. They provide greater clarity about the life situation of the couple or family, especially when home visits are used.

4. They make possible greater speed and accuracy in assessment.

5. They provide improved opportunities for the worker to observe the impact of treatment on the couple and the members of the family.[47]

From a review of the literature and this empirical study, Couch concluded that there is emerging a fairly consistent approach to assessment. There is a decided trend toward emphasis on the current situation, although historical data are not being neglected. Another trend is to assign to intake the same worker who will have ongoing responsibility for the case, so that assessment and treatment are interwoven.

Finally, the diagnostic microscope has been fitted with a wide-angle lens, with the result that the picture under scrutiny looks different. No longer does the individual loom largest, with marriage, family, workaday world and the wider society seen as background for him. Instead, he is now viewed at one and the same time as a unit and as a functional part of various groups, each of which is in turn part of a larger cluster—the marital combination, the family group, the work group, and similar face-to-face associations. Beyond these, the wider society and the great universe itself form, as it were, concentric circles infinitely expanding outward, with no hard and impenetrable lines dividing the individual unit from the marital or family constellation or from other family groupings and the encompassing wider circles.[48]

Similar values accrue from meetings of clients in small groups for purposes of assessment: for example, with adoptive parents, children referred to child guidance centers, and patients or their relatives.[49] Such group procedures have been found to have values similar to those of family sessions, but with additional values in providing insight into the nature and quality of relationships with peers. In children's groups, the relationship with an adult practitioner gives clues concerning strengths and difficulties in relationships with other adults, both parents and others with whom the child has an association. Such groups augment the limited information provided by parents, teachers, nurses, and doctors. In one family service center, it was found that groups provided an accurate and vivid vision of the child's level of functioning.[50]

The Assessment Summary

Each source of information provides some similar data, but also different perspectives on the needs of individuals and families. The extent and nature of the initial process of assessment depend upon the purpose and function of the agency or other auspice, the presenting needs or problems, and the purpose of the service. The social worker can become overwhelmed by the amount of data that it is possible to secure unless he has some clear ideas about patterns and interconnections. The following questions serve to remind him that he ought to consider certain matters that make a difference in the choice of a mode of service for the client and choice of a plan for intervening with the client system and its environment.

1. What types of problems are of concern to the client and the worker?

2. How and when did the need become evident or the problem develop and what are the precipitating factors?

3. What are the core intrapsychic, interpersonal, group, and community factors that have put stress on the client and interfered with his adequate or optimal functioning?

4. What goals and aspirations, recognized by the client, might serve as a beginning focus for help?

5. To what extent is each client motivated to accept and use the help of the worker or other resources? What are indications of positive motivation and what are the nature of resistances to the use of service?

6. What are the strengths in the individual, the group, and the network of social systems that can be supported and developed further in behalf of the clients?

In collecting data to answer these questions, it is reiterated that information should not be sought that will not be put to use in offering and rendering service.

The initial assessment leads to a plan for service. In order to develop a plan, however, the worker requires a conceptual framework about the alternative procedures and techniques that are available to him and the rationale for their use. The process in which these patterns of behavior are imbedded is social treatment. It is a complex constellation of means by which the practitioner contributes to the clients' efforts to reach goals that are related to the enhancement of psychosocial relations.

CHAPTER FOUR

Social Treatment

Social treatment is a process in which a social worker uses selective means to help clients to achieve their goals related to the enhancement of their psychosocial relations. Their goals are achieved through the acquisition of new perceptions, attitudes, and behaviors or through situational changes. A system perspective emphasizes that there are mutual and reciprocal influences among the parts: change in one part of the system affects other parts; any change upsets the steady state to some extent; a system needs inputs of new information in order to avoid entropy and to move toward a new steady state; a system corrects its operations through a process of feedback; the system and its environment influence each other; and similar goals can be achieved from different initial conditions. The social worker has available to him a repertoire of clusters of techniques. He selects a particular technique, according to his cumulative understanding of the person-group-environment system.

Numerous attempts have been made to develop categories or clusters of techniques or other forms of help in casework and group work. These sets of techniques and attitudes are often also referred to as procedures, tasks, skills, or interventive acts. In spite of somewhat different perspectives, there is considerable agreement about a number of major clusters of intervention. These clusters are: relationship, support, structuring, exploration, clarification, confrontation, education-advice, and facilitation of interaction. These procedures are based on theoretical propositions about the dynamic processes through which change is brought about. They are generic clusters of techniques and attitudes in the sense that they are applicable to work with different levels of systems and to both direct and indirect service activities.

Relationship

In individual treatment, emphasis is on the nature and quality of the relationships between the social worker and the clients. In work with families and other groups, there is an equally important emphasis on the relationships among the members. In all models of practice, except perhaps behavior modification and task-centered practice, relationship is accorded great importance as a dynamic for growth and change. Basic to all aspects of practice is the planned development of a relationship, defined in terms of the client's needs and capacities. The relationship itself has potent and dynamic power for influencing feelings and behavior. It is not only a context for treatment, it is also a dynamic element of treatment. According to Perlman, "relationship is a catalyst, an enabling dynamism in the support, nurture, and freeing of people's energies and motivations toward problem-solving and the use of help . . . . It is 'a human being's feeling or sense of emotional bonding with another.' "[1]

Although there are varied definitions of relationship in social work, its essence is a sense of being connected psychologically with one or more persons. The dynamics of relationship in treatment are related to the basic needs for love and social connectedness. Perlman has said that love is an emotionally charged investment of the self outside the self in a caring and empathic way. Social connectedness refers to the feeling that one is recognized and included in a social system—a sense of being meaningfully connected with another or others.

A helpful relationship requires a set of values, attitudes, and interpersonal skills that reflect the concern for others and knowledge about social relationships. In order to develop and sustain a relationship that has the qualities that help clients to feel loved and connected socially with another or others, the worker indicates that he is concerned for the client's well-being, that he respects him, accepts him, and desires for him to be happier in some way. In the relationship, the worker becomes a reliable environment—reliable in the consistency of attitudes and reliable in time and place.[2] The values of social work are thus implemented.

Social workers have long referred to the ideal relationship as being characterized by qualities of warmth, acceptance, and understanding.

Many other helping professionals with different theoretical orientations also agree about the importance of these qualities. The three ingredients of the client-worker relationship that cut across divergent theories of psychotherapy, counseling, and social work are accurate empathy, nonpossessive warmth or acceptance, and genuineness.[3]

Accurate empathy or empathic understanding is the capacity to project oneself into the feelings and experiences of another so that one understands what the other feels and experiences, but without losing oneself in the process. Empathy is, in Rogers's words, "to sense the client's private world as if it were your own, but without ever losing the 'as if' quality."[4] It involves cognitive and affective abilities. It requires the capacity both to feel emotion and yet to remain separate enough from it to be able to maintain perspective and accurate perception of oneself in relation to others.

In exhibiting empathy, the worker attends to both verbal and nonverbal cues from clients. He attends to his own somatic feelings which are sensed as shared with the client. He questions within himself whether his responses might be distorted. He displays the four behaviors that have been identified as required for empathy. They are: (1) accurately perceiving the client in his situation; (2) allowing a client to express his feelings fully; (3) holding distortions of perception in abeyance; and (4) separating his own feelings from those shared with a client. Accurate reception of messages from clients is complemented by accurate feedback to clients. These behaviors result in the communication of messages that convey understanding of the person in his situation.

Nonpossessive warmth is a term used to indicate the practitioner's acceptance of, or love for, the client. In Rogers's view, nonpossessive warmth means caring for a client, but not in a possessive way or to satisfy the practitioner's own needs. It means caring for the client as a unique person, with a right to have his own feelings and thoughts.[5] This quality is akin to what social workers have referred to as acceptance.[6] Acceptance involves a nonblaming attitude and warmly positive affect. It does not mean that the practitioner does not make judgments about his clients but that, although he evaluates, he does not condemn. He knows that all behavior is meaningful and serves some function, even when the behavior seems destructive to the self or others. He accepts the person, even though he cannot condone some of his behavior. Acceptance, according to Perlman, means taking the person as he is. It implies liking a person and lending oneself to him in order to meet his needs with a sense of respect for his right to retain his own identity.[7]

Genuineness or authenticity is the third ingredient of a helping relationship. An effective practitioner does not present a facade. To be genuine does not mean that the practitioner discloses his own feelings and problems to the client, but rather that he does not deceive the client about himself or situations. Genuineness requires considerable self-awareness so that the worker's verbal messages become integrated with his feelings and he is able to control his negative or defensive responses so they will not be harmful to people.

Scales have been developed for measuring each of these components of the worker's relationship with individuals and groups. Evidence from research in counseling and psychotherapy suggests that these three qualities make a difference in the outcome of service.[8] The outcomes seem to hold true for a variety of counselors and therapists regardless of their theoretical orientation, for a variety of clients, and for both work with individuals and work with groups. Although the worker must feel empathy, acceptance, and genuineness for the client, the client plays a part in eliciting these qualities. It would seem, then, that the presence of these qualities is a product of the interaction between the client and the practitioner.

Within social work, too, there is evidence that these qualities are primary factors in both continuance of treatment and positive outcome. Ripple and associates found that a relationship in which the social worker has warmly positive feelings toward the client increased motivation and was an important factor in whether or not a client continued in treatment.[9] Sainsbury, reporting on a study of families with multiple problems, found that clients preferred workers who were informal, patient, and caring, and who displayed warmth, empathy, and ethical integrity toward all members of the family.[10] From a nationwide study, Beck and Jones concluded:

This factor [relationship] was found to be twice as powerful as a predictor of outcomes than any other client or service characteristic covered by the study and more powerful than all client characteristics combined. An unsatisfactory relationship was found to be highly associated with client-initiated disengagement and with negative explanations by the client of his reason for terminating.[11]

Several theoretical explanations seem to account for the value of these qualities in practice. One explanation is that they are potent positive reinforcers that elicit a high degree of positive feelings from clients.[12] Positive feelings increase the client's self-esteem, decrease anxiety, and increase the level of acceptance communicated to others, thereby reciprocally increasing the positive appeal and reinforcement received from others. Feeling accepted, understood, and cared about tends to enhance self-esteem and feelings of being valued by other people. In an atmosphere in which a person feels he is valued, he is free to explore his feelings and ideas, set forth realistic aspirations for himself, and develop motivation toward achievement of his goals.

Another explanation is that the relationship itself is a source of gain because the client has a sustained relationship with others without getting hurt: the relationship provides a safe environment.[13] A person's intimate feelings and concerns can be discovered and evaluated only if there is mutual trust between worker and client. When the worker is genuine, accepting, and empathetic, then the client tends to feel free to communicate his feelings, concerns, and ideas. When the client perceives that the worker is attempting to understand, rather than to judge, it is not necessary for him to cling to dysfunctional defensive maneuvers.

With some clients the relationship is in itself a corrective emotional experience. It does not repeat the condemnations, rejections, or authoritarian controls that have characterized one or more significant relationships in the past. Clients often expect that practitioners will respond to them as they feel others have done. Through consistent attitudes on the part of the worker, the client is able to change his feelings and behavior that have a destructive influence on him.

Relationships develop through verbal and nonverbal communication in which both realistic and unrealistic forces operate. An emotional bond between two or more persons operates at both conscious and unconscious levels. According to psychoanalytic theory, a client may displace feelings or attitudes that he experienced earlier toward a member of his family or other very significant person in his life. The client interprets the current relationship in terms of earlier ones. He expects that the worker will respond to him as he perceives that his parent or other significant person would have done. The worker, however, does not respond in the anticipated ways. He expresses empathy, acceptance, and authenticity; and he responds to the client in his role as a social worker, not a parent. Through experiencing this different relationship, and sometimes also through developing understanding of the transference reactions, the client enhances his ability to relate to others on a realistic basis.

Identification is another important concept relevant to the use of relationship. It refers to a person's adoption of some real or imagined characteristics of another person. It is a desire to be like another person and to model oneself after the other one, largely on an unconscious basis. Clients often identify with social workers with whom they have essentially positive relationships. As a client perceives the worker to be empathic and helpful, he may tend to assume attitudes, behavior, and aspects of appearance similar to those of the worker. In some instances this is conscious modeling, but usually the client is unaware that he has incorporated values or patterns of feeling, thinking, and doing into his personality.

In groups there are special intricacies in the use of relationships. To be able to accept, empathize with, and express genuineness with multiple persons strains the capacities of the social worker. The members' own difficulties and capacities in relationships influence the worker's use of himself with each and with all. Rivalries for the worker's acceptance and attention, the flow of positive and negative feelings among the members, and contagion of trust and acceptance or of distrust and suspicion occur. To reach out warmly to one member with whom one feels empathy cannot be at the expense of others. Members respond to differential attitudes of the worker and to each other, with both realistic and unrealistic responses. Transference reactions and identifications develop among members as well as with the worker.

Whether individual or group, the nature of the relationship is not determined solely by the practitioner, for he is an interacting component of the system. His special role within the system, however, gives him primary responsibility for the development of an effective working relationship with his clients. Empathy, acceptance, and genuineness are necessary, but not sufficient, ingredients of successful treatment. Within a generally positive relationship the worker makes differential use of other techniques that help clients to achieve their goals.

Support

To support a person means to sustain or keep steady, to give courage, to express faith and confidence, and to give realistic approval to an individual or group. Supportive techniques sustain the motivation and capacity of people while they are using a social service. Clients have varied degrees of positive and negative motivation to enter into and use treatment. Particularly at the beginning, there is some natural anxiety, doubt, and uncertainty; but later on there are also times when some aspects of the situation become threatening. At these times, motivation is sustained by reducing the threats. Support from the practitioner—and in a group, from other members as well—tends to keep anxiety at manageable levels. As anxiety lessens, the client feels comfortable enough to remain in the situation and develops confidence that he will not be hurt in it. In accepting help, he recognizes that some changes will be expected of him. These anticipated changes may be threatening. In individual treatment, the client may fear the loss of self-control, invasion of privacy, inability to meet expectations, loss of self-esteem, or the demands of the intimate relationship. In families and other groups the client may also fear a loss of status, possible recriminations by other members, loss of individuality, rejection by others, and fear of exposure of self to others. In order to minimize these threats, the ego needs to be supported in its efforts to cope with new and difficult situations. What is supported are the client's capacities, constructive defenses, and efforts to work toward goal achievement.[14]

In system terms, the steady state needs to be maintained in reasonable balance so that the upset is not beyond the person's coping capacities. A moderate level of tension may motivate a person to attain a goal, but when tension becomes extreme, it is disruptive and even incapacitating. Support is an important motivator, not only because it reduces anxiety and enhances self-esteem, but also because it is a prerequisite to change through other means. Its importance is suggested by research that found that the revelation of important information about oneself in situations of support was beneficial to participants, but that self-disclosure before the group was able to respond supportively was not helpful.[15]

The social work relationship is itself a means of support through which clients are sustained in their efforts to use the clinical experience for their benefit. Feeling accepted, receiving empathic responses, and being helped by someone who is genuine is a rare experience for many clients. People often bloom when they are the beneficiaries of such a relationship. In groups, there is the additional potential of mutual support among the members. The worker sets the tone for mutual support through expressing the expectation that members will become able to do this themselves. To a large extent, however, the members become supportive of each other as they become aware of their common purposes, interests, and needs and as they work out their positive and negative feelings toward each other. They become supportive of each other as they feel trust and security in the worker, as they come to identify with him, and to integrate some of his patterns of support into their own personalities.

Support is demonstrated through a variety of specific techniques, implemented according to the worker's understanding of the individual's or group's feelings and readiness at a given time. Providing opportunities for appropriate ventilation of feelings and concerns is one major form of support and instillation of hope is another.

VENTILATION

People need support in their efforts to express their genuine feelings and concerns. A client tends to feel supported when he is accepted by the worker and has his full attention and, in groups, when he has the acceptance and attention of other members.[16] When he feels supported, a client finds courage to express feelings and thoughts that would be suppressed in usual situations, to expose some of his vulnerabilities, and to dare risk trying new things. As feelings of love, satisfaction, and happiness are expressed, these feelings are reinforced if the responses to them are supportive. Feelings of anger, hostility, hopelessness, and fear also are often expressed, usually leading to a reduction of anxiety. If a client can recognize the universality of his feelings, as well as their unique meaning to him, his anxiety tends to lessen. Feelings often lose some of their intensity and hold on a person once they are expressed to, and accepted by, other persons. But more important, once expressed, feelings are open to examination and clarification. Clarity about feelings can lead to changes in behavior. By being able to identify and describe a feeling, for example, a child may learn to substitute verbal symbols for harmful actions. Ability to associate emotions with words supports the ego's capacity to cope with them.

Ventilation, however, is not necessarily helpful. It is the nature of the worker's response to the content that determines its value to the client. In a group, the members' responses are also influential. The worker does not try to alleviate all anxiety, because some tension is used for productive work on problem-solving. Some guilt is essential to the development of sound ego controls. Likewise, a certain degree of anxiety about a future experience can spur efforts to prepare oneself adequately for the event.

One task for the social worker is to decide how much expression of emotion and experiences should be encouraged and when further expression should be discouraged. The test is in the client's responses to his own expressions: these responses may be a reduction of anxiety or an increase of it. Some persons do not get relief from ventilation but become more self-centered, angry, anxious, or aggravated and unable to recognize, understand, and cope with feelings. In family and other groups, the continuous and often repetitive outpouring of feelings by one member can stir up a variety of negative feelings toward that member on the part of others. The worker needs to be aware of his own feelings toward both the ventilator and the recipients of these feelings; he needs also to be aware of the feelings and reactions of all those involved in the experience. Expressions of anger and hostility are often difficult for others to accept, but they cannot be used constructively or modified unless they are brought out into the open for all to experience. They cannot be dealt with adequately if the practitioner or members of a group retaliate against the negative expression of feelings or actions. Support is not given through cutting off feelings or discounting the impact of them on self and others. On the basis of knowledge of the interaction between the client's feelings and behavior and his own and others' feelings and behavior, the practitioner plans what his particular next message will be.

INSTILLATION OF HOPE

Support is given through demonstrating interest in a client's efforts and progress, encouraging his efforts, offering realistic assurance, and expressing hope that things will be better. Some realistic hope is necessary to enter into a relationship, remain in it, and make optimal use of the opportunities it provides. The social worker recognizes and builds on the strengths of the individual and group; he positively reinforces the progress that has been made. Realistic reassurance instills hope that things can be better, thereby enhancing motivation for trying to change oneself and one's situation. In order to be reassured by comments made by the worker or by another member, the client must feel some trust and confidence in that person. The worker may reassure a client about the normality and acceptability of his feelings, behavior, or situation. Such reassurance is based on realistic knowledge about, and appraisal of, the client in his situation; otherwise, the worker is being deceitful or not genuine. Such attitudes are sensed by the client. When realistic reassurance cannot be given, it is apt to be more supportive to acknowledge the difficulties and to suggest what can be done within a difficult situation. Denial of reality is not supportive. In using reassurance as support, "relief comes not from self-understanding but because the worker in whom the client has placed confidence has said in effect that it is not necessary to be so worried. The dynamic is not one of reasoning but of faith dependent upon the client's confidence in the worker's knowledge and good will."[17] Expressing confidence in a person's capacities and recognizing his achievements, or at least his efforts, is often preliminary to the development of self-confidence. It is a powerful incentive to continue to try new solutions or to continue on a successful path.

In using reassurance and encouragement, the social worker needs to be realistic in his appraisal of the client, including the client's own perceptions of his abilities. Expectations for a client's behavior are implied in the giving of encouragement and reassurance. The question is how to set reasonable expectations without arousing the client's fear that he may disappoint the worker. Demonstrating that the worker will continue to accept the client regardless of his performance is essential. Self-confidence is built not only by incorporating into oneself the worker's verbal expressions of faith, but by having opportunities to be successful. In some helping situations, mastery of tasks attuned to the client's abilities becomes a major means of help. Structuring experiences so that clients may succeed in them is a means of providing support. The development of social competence has been typical of work with children, but it is just as important in work with adults who have very poor ego functioning or who have been deprived of earlier opportunities for mastery.[18]

Support may be given through verbalization, nonverbal demonstration of the worker's interest, the provision of experiences, or referral. The social worker's activities need to be based on sound judgment about the individual's needs and, if the unit of service is a group, the group climate at a given time. Even when a practitioner's intent is sound and his acts appropriate, they may not be perceived as supportive by the persons to whom they are directed. The support may not be accepted because the person distorts reality, or because he is unable to accept evidence of concern and acceptance from another person or group. To the extent that a worker is sensitive to the feelings and needs of the client and, in a group, to their relations with each other, his use of supportive techniques is apt to be effective. Certainly, the social worker's efforts to sustain the motivation and enhance the capacity of the clients toward achievement of their purposes is an important ingredient in serving people well.

Use of Structure

Clients are influenced to move toward the achievement of their goals through a process of structuring the situation. The intent of the social worker is to create a special environment conducive to the achievement of goals that have been mutually determined by worker and client system. The techniques in this category comprise activities by the worker concerning "the structure and direction of the interactions with the client."[19] For work with families and small groups, it is necessary to add "and interactions among the members." The objective of structuring is to create an optimal milieu for work. It primarily lays the groundwork for techniques more directly concerned with influencing attitudes and behavior.

The policies, procedures, and ways of work of an agency provide a framework within which the worker operates. Prior to each session with an individual or a group, the worker prepares for it in order to enhance the value and use of the session. He reviews pertinent records or other data in order to clarify the direction of his efforts. He follows up on a client who might have missed an appointment or been absent from a group meeting; he makes decisions about whether new persons should come to the session, such as a member of the family, a new member for a group, or a resource person. He arranges his office or another room for the session.

Space carries psychological connotations for those who use it. It provides a boundary and anchor for a given set of actions.[20] The particular physical environment has great influence on the behavior and transactions among all participants in the endeavor. Attractive surroundings facilitate the development of relationships. A constant location tends to enhance the consciousness of the relationship, whether worker to individual, worker to group, or member to member. It connotes a sense of being together for a particular purpose. The arrangement of furniture enhances or hinders intimacy and the rate of participation of those who are present. It sets certain expectations for participation and indicates the status of participants. A formal arrangement in which a worker sits behind a desk in a large chair and a client sits opposite him in a small chair may convey a message to a client that he is to maintain distance from the worker. Chairs in rows or along walls cause people to look straight ahead and tend to inhibit conversation, except with those on each side of them. On the other hand, chairs arranged around small tables or in an open circle tend to draw people closer together.

Nationality and other subcultural differences, as well as personality factors, lead some people to prefer greater or lesser distance from others, and the worker needs to be sensitive to these differences. People who desire closeness with particular others usually choose locations close to others, while those who prefer distance tend to sit farthest from others. Those who intend to participate less will probably seat themselves farthest from the central action. Flexibility in arrangement of furniture provides some choice for clients.

In order to work together effectively, the worker and clients need to be clear about the policies and procedures concerning purposes of service, use of time, duration and frequency of sessions, fees, principles of confidentiality, and the major focus and content of treatment. Such agreements provide a boundary within which the worker and clients are free to operate. Such policies and procedures should be used flexibly and changed in accordance with client needs and capacities. Achieving clarity about the structure of the service reduces ambiguity and confusion, thereby releasing energies for working toward the agreed-upon goals.

Realistic limits are important forms of structuring. In limit setting, which is directed at the control of behavior, the worker's activities are intended to help the individual or group to adapt to the realistic demands of the environment. Such limits are more acceptable than is the use of personal authority. A person needs to learn to meet these demands and to be protected from the destructive tendencies of self and others. Some people need to learn to overcome too rigid conformity to policies and rules in order to develop spontaneity in relationships and to use their capacities in more creatively adaptive ways. They need permission to try out different modes of behavior. The social worker needs to balance the use of permissiveness and of limits, based on differential assessment of the client in his situation. Structural controls are not an end in themselves but serve as a means to the goal of self-control and self-direction.

Exploration

Exploration is one of the dominant sets of techniques used in social work practice. It is a means for examining a situation by bringing facts, opinions, and feelings into the open so that sufficient understanding of the person-group-situation configuration is obtained to work toward goal achievement. It is used to elicit necessary information; to bring out details about experiences and relationships as the client perceives them; and to examine the feelings connected to the relationships and experiences. Through exploratory techniques, the worker draws out descriptive material, possible explanations, and emotions connected with the facts and explanations. It is an important step in the problem-solving process. Along with support and structuring, exploration lays the groundwork for techniques more directly intended to influence the individual's or group's psychosocial functioning.

Reid and Shyne have divided exploration into two types: exploration about the client's situation and his relation to it; and explorations about the client's own behavior.[21] The first category includes inquiries about external circumstances, characteristics of other people, and interactions with others. The second category concerns the client's understanding of himself—his feeling states, personality characteristics, and patterns of functioning. This formulation follows Hollis's earlier distinction between reflective discussion of the client's person-situation gestalt in the present or recent past and reflective discussion of the psychological patterns, dynamics, and development of the client's behavior.[22] In this latter form, exploration is used to encourage the client's search for understanding of himself and his situation. In most exploratory work, there is an almost simultaneous effort to obtain information to increase the worker's understanding of the client and to direct discussion or activity into productive channels for understanding self and others. It is assumed that, as people disclose more about themselves and their situations to others, they not only reveal themselves to the others, but also to themselves, which sets in motion a process of clarification.[23] Through exploration, the worker helps the clients to recognize and identify the various aspects of a particular situation and then extend or elaborate on this understanding.

The expression of feelings has been given much attention in the literature. Earlier, it was noted that ventilation of emotions often relieves anxiety and is a form of support. Exploration, however, goes beyond ventilation. Yalom, in writing about curative factors in groups, has said: "It appears that the strong expression of affect is one indispensable part of the therapeutic process, but it is a part of the process and, in itself, not productive of change." He suggests that it is the "affective sharing of one's inner world and then the acceptance by others" that seem of paramount importance.[24] It is not merely releasing feelings, but exploring them with the worker and often also with others that is important.

Although self-disclosure of facts about oneself and one's situation and the feelings about these facts is of value, expression may often need to be contained. The client may get much gratification from talking about himself, without being able to understand himself or his situation better, and without being able to progress toward any change. He may get caught up in his own sense of hopelessness or helplessness or in a repetitive recital of content. In such instances the worker needs to break through to seek elaboration of the material and to refocus the communication to secure new facts, feelings, and alternatives. In group situations, the members' responses to the nature and amount of self-disclosure by others need to be taken into consideration. The practitioner needs to note what an expression by one person triggers off in others and be prepared to deal with the consequences.

The social worker uses many different specific techniques within the category of exploration. One major set of techniques is purposeful inquiry, through which the social worker gives focus and direction to the client's efforts to ascertain, expand, and clarify information. He asks questions and makes comments to guide the client in providing essential information. He may ask direct questions to secure specific information about the client's characteristics, experiences, situations, or the meaning of these to him. He may ask more general leading questions that request elaboration of a question or comment made by a client. He may, for example, request that a client explain what happened, what the trouble seems to be, or what might be done about it. He may inquire about how a particular situation came to be. Such questions are often referred to as probing for information in order to develop the details of a situation. Such probing may be necessary to encourage the flow of verbal communication, to amplify details, to clarify ambiguities, and to ascertain how a given situation developed. The challenge to the worker is to explore in ways that do not feel like cross-examination, as often happens when one question after another is asked. Questions should be asked sparingly and in forms that do not elicit yes or no answers, but that invite elaboration of a subject.

Usually comments are more effective than questions in leading to a client's reflection on pertinent matters. A brief summary of what has been said before, a reflecting back to the client of a feeling or opinion, or a suggestion about what it might be helpful to talk about next are comments that aid the client toward fuller exploration. Some comments are in the form of sharing an observation with clients. The worker's direct observations of the client's behavior and of his own reactions to the behavior may provide important clues to the client's feelings and situation. He may comment about what he has observed or make inferences about what is taking place. The client's reaction to the observation then provides additional information for the worker and the client. In groups, the request from the worker may be that members share with each other their reactions to what they have observed about a member, each other, or the ongoing process among them.

Purposeful silence and sensitive listening are powerful aids to self-revelation and examination of self and situation. Purposeful silence often indicates that a worker is listening and following what is being said. Such a stance tends to induce the talker to continue in the same vein. In other instances, purposeful silence indicates that a client is expected to mobilize his thoughts and then express them. A worker's personal need to fill in a short period of silence with words often interferes with a client's efforts to get ready to share pertinent information.

Exploration is one of the most commonly recognized cluster of techniques and one of the most frequently used in both work with individuals and work with groups. In social treatment, it furnishes a necessary foundation for moving beyond eliciting and elaborating information to using the information for helpful purposes.

Clarification

Clarification is widely used in social work practice. To clarify simply means to make understandable. Clarification encompasses a variety of techniques which are intended to promote a client's understanding of himself in relation to significant other persons and to his situation. Several different terms have been used to convey the basic idea of clarifying something.

The best known work is that of Hollis, who has formulated six major procedures of treatment. Three of the categories deal with reflective discussion between the worker and the client. They are based on a theory that changes in a client's psychosocial functioning will be set in motion by enhanced perception and understanding, which is produced by reflective consideration of certain aspects of the client's personality and his situation. In these reflective categories the worker seeks for clarification of: (1) the client's person-situation gestalt in the present or recent past; (2) the psychological patterns and dynamics of the client's behavior; and (3) aspects of the client's past that are thought to be relevant to his present behavior.[25] In these reflective categories, the worker promotes understanding of these aspects of the client's life, largely through various forms of clarification, following adequate exploration.

Other writers have presented various techniques of clarification under different headings. Leonard Brown refers to introspection; Northen, to acts that enhance clients' perceptions of reality; and Reid and Shyne, to formulations of hypotheses concerning the client's milieu, behavior, or the interrelation between behavior and environment.[26] Most recent theorists have eliminated Hollis's distinction between the client in his current situation, the dynamics of his behavior, and developmental origins. It seems more appropriate, according to Reid and Epstein, not to separate internal and external factors, because social work's special emphasis is on interactions between them.[27]

Studies have indicated that it is difficult to separate interventions concerned only with self-awareness from those with a psychosocial focus. When researchers dealt with clients' awareness of self as a distinct area, the results have shown quite consistently that a very small proportion of techniques falls within that category.[28] Such findings confirm the proposition that social work practice is directed to the psychosocial—the interaction among person-group-environmental systems—rather than only to the intrapersonal world of the client.

Clarity of both the content and patterns of communication is basic to effective functioning. Unless a person understands the intent of messages sent to him, he cannot respond in ways that meet the expectations of others. Likewise, unless a person can convey his intents to others in ways that they can be perceived with accuracy, he cannot achieve his goals. Many difficulties in interpersonal relationships derive from inability to make clear one's desires, knowledge, feelings, and ideas. Difficulties derive also from lack of clarity about what others are saying or doing. Inadequate ability to participate actively in the communicative network of a system limits a person's opportunity to share with others and to receive validation of his feelings and thoughts from others. Inadequate communication among the participants limits severely the inputs of information into the system and hence advances entropy. Without feedback from others, there is lack of knowledge about the extent of congruence between one's own perceptions of self and situation and the perceptions of other people. Feedback facilitates change because it turns the experience of individual or group back to itself, permitting correction or extension of perceptions of self or others. If clarifying statements are understood and accepted by the client, the knowledge therein becomes a part of the client's self-awareness.

Effective psychosocial functioning requires some scheme for organizing and interpreting events. If this scheme is distorted, the person has difficulties in relating to others. Difficulties in relationship occur when false inferences are made or when there is inability to distinguish fantasy from reality. Change is brought about through more accurate perceptions of self, other persons, and institutions. Through recognizing difficulties in perception, and then acquiring more accurate and integrated perceptions, change is likely to occur.

Serious discrepancies between internal perceptions and external reality are dysfunctional. By reducing the discrepancy, a person's ego functioning is enhanced. Gradually, a person can achieve a modified cognitive system for ordering his world.

People have a tremendous store of images that are residuals of experiences with which they were associated earlier. Negative symbols associated with earlier life experiences of a hurtful nature tend to remain. These residuals need to be divested of their anxiety-producing potential.[29] Feelings tend to distort perceptions and divert energy that might otherwise be available for the achievement of desired ends. They also reinforce cognition. In a study of clients' reports on their experiences with therapists of different theoretical orientations, there was considerable consensus that the most helpful procedure, in addition to the relationship, was the recognition and clarification of feelings which clients had been approaching hazily and hesitantly.[30] Another and more recent study also found that the qualities of relationship were necessary ingredients in successful outcome, but only when combined with work toward improved cognitive understanding.[31]

Behavior, attitudes, and values are organized and supported by self-image. A person's self-image may be different from the ways others see him; his definition of the situation may be different from that of others; his image of others may be out of line with their image of themselves and, in a group, of each other. One or all of these may be present. A person, in order to change, needs to disconfirm some assumptions he has made about himself in relation to others or situations. When information does not support these ideas, there may be readiness for change. If a system is stable, the steady state may be disrupted through lack of confirmation or through disconfirmation of that idea about self or others; through induction of guilt or anxiety; or by the removal of barriers through creating a milieu of psychological safety.[32] Some upset in the system motivates a person to change, but too much tension may lead to disintegration or entropy.

Perceptions of self in relation to others may be changed through bringing to consciousness and then understanding material that was previously suppressed. Through recognizing the connection between past experiences and current responses, a person may come to recognize that the present is not the past, but that some past experiences are messing up the present. A person may modify his defenses when he sees their irrationality or harmfulness: he becomes more clear about them and their effect on his functioning. Although many adaptive patterns can be modified with little or no clarification of the relation of past to present, some destructive patterns of behavior may be modified only if a person examines and reevaluates significant past experiences and their consequences for his current functioning and future living. Growth in ego capacity is encouraged by facing and coping with the reality of one's feelings, thoughts, and behavior. In working toward adaptive change it is thought that some understanding of one's behavior is an essential prerequisite to change in that behavior. Insight is a quality of experience that may result from different experiences. It is a surprise response that occurs when a person is prepared to recognize the truth of an observation. It involves a new perception of the relationship between knowledge, emotion, and experience. It has been described as "Ah-ha" learning that occurs when a person integrates an idea that has relevance to his past or present feelings or behavior.[33] It may occur with a sense of great suddenness. It involves connections between affective and cognitive aspects of perception and behavior.

A major theoretical assumption that underlies clarifying techniques is that feeling about and perceiving oneself differently and feeling about and perceiving others differently can do much to alter behavior, attitudes, and relationships. It is a way of testing reality. Clarification is a procedure for bringing what needs to be known to awareness. It is assumed that a person may be able to alter his behavior or undertake new activities if he has a clear idea about what he wants to do if he wants to do it. Current experience can be used as a corrective in modifying attitudes and behavior, if a person is helped to examine and reevaluate the nature of significant experiences, situations, and people, and the consequences of his ways of functioning. If a formulation is understood, evaluated, and accepted by the client, it becomes a part of his consciousness of himself in relation to his situation. Awareness-enhancing techniques often help clients to work through obstacles to solving a problem or achieving a task. If clients understand the nature and perhaps also the origin of these obstacles, they are often able to overcome them. When they are not able to do so, then the practitioner can use other techniques, such as, for example, action-oriented experiences that do not depend upon verbal skills.

The major forms of messages offered by workers are those which intend to influence the client, some aspect of his situation, or the network of communication. Robert Brown calls this basic technique ascription, a specialized form of feedback that attributes a motive or characteristic to someone.[34] Such statements are used for a variety of purposes. They may be used to clarify the process of communication and point out patterns of emotions or reaction. Brown's review of the literature on social work with individuals, families, and small groups indicated that ascription was used frequently in all modalities of practice. There are a variety of specific techniques that are used to help clients to understand themselves and their situations better.

One set of ascriptive techniques is used to clarify the situation and the person's part in it. The worker may rephrase a client's statement so that the client can see his problem and situation more clearly or in a new way. This reflecting or paraphrasing is a way of mirroring behavior as it is observed by the worker. Two levels of communication are operating: the words being used and the feelings behind the words. Sometimes a person is not sure what he has said because there were so many confused thoughts and feelings connected with the words. When the worker or a member of a group can express what he heard, the client can decide whether this is what he really said or meant to say. In a group, it permits members who did not clearly hear another person to respond with a request for clarification. It may then be possible for those in the group to pursue a subject in more depth. Such an act may also enlist other members to participate, since the worker's reflection of client activity is like an invitation to react further to what is being said.

Another technique is to offer a statement that connects two events which are obscure to the client. Such connective comments aid the client to understand logical connections between aspects of his own behavior or emotions or between his behavior and that of others. Another technique is to make a statement that identifies the common ground between people. Such statements may call attention to the common needs, problems, or interests of two parties who may be in conflict. They may call attention to common feelings that underlie apparent differences. Still another technique is to identify patterns of behavior that are occurring. A worker may share his perception of repetitious forms of behavior in order to enhance the client's understanding of patterned responses or episodes of behavior and attitudes. Other frequently used types of ascription are disclosure of one's own feelings or reactions when it is thought that such sharing by the worker will contribute something important to the client system; or a specific identification of emotions by naming and describing them, thereby helping clients to conceptualize what is happening to them.

The second major set of ascriptions consists of interpretations about the meaning of behavior. An interpretation is a statement that explains the meaning of an experience to the client, an underlying motivation for his behavior, or a seeking-out of the reasons for a particular difficulty in psychosocial functioning. The focus of interpretations is on bringing into conscious awareness such feelings and experiences as are not readily acknowledged or verbalized and to aid the client to integrate these new understandings into his personality. Interpretations are generally not offered until other forms of clarification have been used to understand the situation and the person's relationship to it. Interpretive statements are usually made in tentative forms of suggesting that something may account for something else; commenting that there are explanations for an event and requesting the client to think of alternative ones; or putting an explanation in the form of a question that asks the client to consider its applicability to his situation. In a sense, any interpretation is a statement of a tentative hypothesis or a hypothetical question that is based on the worker's knowledge of people in their environments.

Interpretations are used selectively to enable a client to tie some aspects of his past experiences to his present situation. Reviewing some past situations with a client is a tool for helping him to learn from experience. The experience of reviewing patterns of experience and behavior may make it possible for a client to take a different turn, based on evaluation, to effective functioning. Hutten has said that "allowing clients to talk with feeling about past traumas when they are re-evoked by present experiences is one of the opportunities we do have to intervene 'preventively' in relation to the future."[35] She notes that the discovery of continuities of experience can reopen a person's potential for further development. Coping capacities can be released when past painful experiences can be integrated into the personality "instead of having to be cut off or kept at bay by heavy psychic expenditure."[36]

A number of principles govern the use of techniques aimed at clarification.

1. Clarifying techniques should be based on sound assessment. They are helpful to persons only if they are accurate, based on observation of the client and knowledge of human development and behavior in a network of interacting systems.

2. In working with two or more people, assessment must be made of the group system as well as of individuals. The worker needs to consider the phase of family or group development and the readiness of particular individuals to understand the what or why of their behavior, the emotional ties among the members, and the cohesiveness of the group.

3. In interpreting his perception of the meaning of feelings, behavior, or events, the worker usually offers his comments as impressions, suggestions, and opinions, not as facts. He encourages the individual or the group to test out the value of his comments and to respond to them.

4. The worker avoids generalizations that deal with the total person. Rather, he partializes the comments or questions to a particular feeling, behavioral pattern, or situation.

5. Usually the briefer and more concise the comments are, the better. It is important to present only one fact or thought at a time. Ascriptions are most helpful when they are expressed clearly, simply, and directly.

6. The worker needs to follow through with considerable exploration of the reactions of an individual or members of a group to the clarifying message. Furthermore, whatever understanding has developed needs to be repeated in different forms over a period of time if it is to result in more adaptive behavior.

7. According to most writers, interpretation is done at the conscious or preconscious levels of the personality. Usually, the focus is

on the present. Recall of the past is facilitated and past events interpreted when such recall helps the person and other participants to understand the present.

8. There are exceptions, of course, but probes for connections and interpretations of meanings of behavior are apt to be more effective with verbally accessible people with fairly good ego integration. Interpretation is a rational process—it appeals to the intellect even though people do respond with feelings as well as thought processes. Offering interpretations that explain the underlying meaning of behavior may threaten the ego's defenses; children and adults with weak egos need considerable support rather than attack. Anxiety that does not overwhelm the ego is useful so long as it is within a range that can be dealt with constructively.

9. As with any other activity, the worker's aim is to help individuals or groups to do as much as possible for themselves. Hence, questions that help people to explain feelings, behavior, and situations are usually more effective than interpretations given by the worker in that the persons are helped to find the meanings themselves. But when meaning eludes people and is considered by the worker to be important to progress, interpretations are useful and sometimes essential.

10. A special characteristic of the use of interpretation in a group is that, to be useful, it need not be directed specifically to a person. During a period when a problematic situation develops, various members may present experiences, feelings, and make relevant comments. To the extent that the underlying theme of the content is relevant to a particular person's concerns, he may derive understanding of himself and his experiences. Often when feelings or explanations are universalized, they touch closely on some member's particular concerns. This dynamic is what Konopka refers to as anonymity of insight.[37]

11. When working with more than one person, the worker needs to pay attention to the group process—the continuity of content, communicative abilities and patterns, emotional ties, and roles of workers and members. Clarifications may be directed to an individual, but only in the interest of the group. Individual reflection and introspection are pursued when they can be connected to the needs of others.

The worker finds the thread of connections between one individual's need and the needs of others. There is a tendency for social workers to direct ascriptions to individuals rather than to the group system when the unit of service is the family or peer group. If more ascriptions were directed to the group, it is likely that a greater sense of relatedness and cohesiveness would develop.

All of the clarifying techniques contribute to change in attitudes, emotions, relationships, and behavior. Lippitt, Watson, and Westley have noted that change is brought about by

> a succession of insightful reorganizations. During the learning period, the system accumulates a number of new facts or ideas which are stored away, as it were, for further consideration and are not allowed to exert an immediate influence on ways of thinking or acting. But sooner or later the system undergoes a period of insight and reorganization. The new ideas or skills or feelings—whatever has been accumulated—are integrated with the old. A new gestalt is created which carries the system beyond its previous state of awareness and being. The formation of this new gestalt is what forces the system to move; the formation of the new gestalt is what we mean by change.[38]

Confrontation

Confrontation is a form of statement that faces a person with the reality of a feeling, behavior, or situation. Its dictionary meaning is to face boldly, to bring a person face to face with something. Its purpose is to interrupt or reverse a course of thought or action.[39] It is a form of limiting behavior which faces a person with the fact that there is a contradiction between his own statements and those of other sources, that his behavior is irrational, or that it is destructive to self or others. Unlike interpretation, it is not concerned with the meaning of the behavior, but with stopping it.

Confrontations usually challenge a client's defenses, such as denial, rationalization, or displacement or they challenge unacceptable behavior. They upset the steady state, creating temporary discomfort or anxiety, thus unfreezing the system and making possible a readiness to change in order to reduce the discomfort. A confrontation disconfirms the acceptability of what is happening. It provides information that contradicts distortions or blindness to facts, directly and openly. It provides a force that challenges obstacles to the achievement of goals.[40] Confrontations are direct statements, but they need not be harsh; there can be firm challenge "with an arm around the shoulder."[41] There is a vast difference between confrontation that is accusatory, such as, "Stop lying to me," and one that deals with denial by such a statement as, "I know it's hard for you to tell me, but I already know that you are in serious trouble with the police."

There is some empirical evidence for the view that, when it is accompanied by a high degree of empathy, confrontation is an effective therapeutic technique; when employed by practitioners with little empathy, it is not.[42] Citing various studies, Nadel concluded that a challenging comment by a worker may be effective with certain clients who need more than a reduction of restraints to express their unconscious negativism. A challenge is a form of confrontation: it calls into question and takes exception to what is being said or done.[43] Confrontation may be of an individual's verbal or nonverbal behavior or of the interactional patterns among people.

In groups, it is not the worker alone who confronts. The members confront each other, often bluntly and cruelly, sometimes in appropriate ways and at other times in ways that are unduly devastating to one or more members. The worker must evaluate the impact of such statements on particular individuals and the group, following up in whatever ways seem necessary.

Education and Advice

Change, on at least one level, is associated with a system's knowing what is desirable and effective with respect to rational self-interests. Lack of knowledge contributes to ineffective functioning. Assimilation of information from the social environment is central to the process of change in a system. Positive change may be influenced by an educational process which offers the tools and resources that are useful to a client. One of the major tasks of the social worker, according to Schwartz, is to contribute data—ideas, facts, and value concepts—which are not available to the client and which may prove useful to him in attempting to cope with that part of the social reality which is involved in the problems with which he is working.[44] In one sense, all interventions by practitioners are intended to help an individual or a group to learn new ways of feeling, thinking, and doing, or to strengthen capacities. But there are times when people need new information or reinforcement of knowledge in order to make sound decisions about themselves and other persons who are significant to them. They often need specific details about community resources and their use. They often need to understand general principles of human growth and development or the implications of an illness or physical handicap for themselves or their families. They may need to learn some basic skills that can help them to enter into new relationships more effectively, as, for example, appropriate approaches to a prospective employer, teacher, household helper, or stepparent. They need information about laws that affect them concerning such events as abortion, marriage, adoption, divorce, discrimination in housing or jobs, and consumer protection. The purpose of education is to provide new knowledge and skills required for coping with a particular problem or situation.

McBroom notes that parents of infants and young children often need specific help in understanding their children.[45] Messages regarding parenthood are often confusing and lead to insecurity. Results of parent education, she points out, have been disappointing in that minimal changes in behavior result from formal classes and informational brochures. But social work groups are often effective when education is an important part of help. A group experience makes available peer support and reinforcement to increase confidence and competence to foster the child's developmental tasks. Likewise, group learning of new roles, as parents or as patients who need to accommodate to major physical impairments, can help individuals to find appropriate modes of expression and action.

In many practice situations, the social worker directs some efforts to helping clients learn to communicate more effectively with other people. With small children, the worker may teach them the elements of verbal communication. The worker may need to provide indirect modes for practicing communication through such experiences as role playing, family sculpting, art therapy, or use of microphones, puppets, word games, charades. He moves them, however, into direct verbalization when they are ready to benefit from it.

The rationale for the provision of knowledge is that people are rational and will adopt changes, given rational justification which is congruent with their own self-interest. Having accurate information is central to this proposition concerning change. Knowledge is one road to ego mastery; it is a source of power. Sharing information, rather than withholding it, provides the best safeguard against client dependency. Knowledge is provided or new skills taught when the data are clearly relevant to the client's situation and the client does not have ready access to the information. The information that is shared needs to be accurate, requiring breadth and depth of knowledge: the worker needs to be clear about the facts as they relate specifically to a particular client's needs.

Giving suggestions and advice is a special form of education. Based on his knowledge of the client in his situation the worker offers suggestions or advice to serve two functions: to give the client specific recommendations that, if carried out, may further the attainment of his goals; and to provide the client with an important source of emotional and cognitive stimulation.[46] He shares his opinions, based on knowledge, with the client. He also explains the reason for the recommendation, which is a form of information-giving. He offers advice cautiously, so as not to hamper the client's efforts to arrive at his own decisions. He offers such advice as tentative ideas for consideration by the client rather than as commands. Although workers are often hesitant to give advice for fear of encouraging dependency, they probably do so more often than they acknowledge. Clients do resent advice at times and often do not use it, but this is generally true when advice was not sought or when it was inappropriate to the client's needs.

Clients often want and need suggestions and advice from workers. In one study, it was found that clients were more likely to be satisfied with a service if the worker gave appropriate advice. The clients perceived lack of advice as lack of interest in resolving their problems.[47] In a study of groups, it was found that clients valued direct advice or suggestions given by the practitioner or other members of the group about how to deal with some life problem or important relationship.

Those who made large gains in treatment marked this item as important significantly more often than did those who made few gains.[48] In another study of clients' reactions to casework, it was reported that lack of advice-giving was the most frequent complaint about the service. If the worker was marked relatively high in the use of advice, clients were less likely to be dissatisfied than if the worker made little use of this technique.[49] In another study, it was indicated that clients tended to reject advice when it was perceived as an order to do something, but it was accepted when perceived as a suggestion for their consideration. This finding suggests that it is the way advice is given that makes a difference in its usefulness to clients.[50] In still another study, on the use of advice by eight social workers in a parent counseling program, it was concluded that working-class parents received more advice than did those of middle-class status; all of the social workers made some use of giving advice; parents' reactions to advice tended to be more negative than positive. Parents also said, however, that they liked the workers to give advice and none wanted less advice than they had received. This paradox may be resolved, according to Davis, by realizing that advice may serve an important therapeutic function other than guiding client actions. It may stimulate the client to think of alternative ways for dealing with problems.[51]

Advice is generally accepted by, and useful to, a client if it is what he really needs, if it is presented in a way that the client can readily connect to his current situation, if it is ego-syntonic, if it is presented in a manner which conveys genuine interest in the client's welfare, and if the client's own decision-making processes are engaged in responding to the advice.

Education is used not only with clients, but also with significant people in behalf of clients. A worker may, for example, give information to a teacher about a child's family situation or to a prospective employer about the kind of jobs that can be performed by a client with a particular handicap. He may give advice in the form of a recommendation that a child in residential treatment be moved to a different cottage more appropriate to his current needs. It is to be remembered that it is ethical to intervene with others about clients only if it is done with their informed consent, except under the most unusual circumstances.

Adequate psychosocial functioning is dependent upon accurate perception of self in relation to environment, which is achieved both through education and clarification. It is dependent, therefore, upon the adequacy of knowledge about the nature of the problem, the conditions in which it is imbedded, the people who are affected by it, and what can be done about it. In addition to the resolution of a particular problem, social workers often help clients learn a process useful for coping with other problems: how problem-solving skills can be applied to other situations. From the earliest efforts to develop theory for groups, John Dewey's presentation of individual and group problem-solving has been incorporated into practice.[52] Somewhat later these ideas were elaborated on as applicable to work with individuals.[53]

Decision-making is an integral part of the problem-solving process. Basically, problem-solving consists of the recognition of a felt difficulty, location and definition of the problem, procurement of alternative proposals for solution, consideration of the possible consequences of each proposal, and acceptance of a proposed solution—that is, making a decision about what is to be done about the difficulty or problem.[54] Decision involves tentative answers to such questions as, who is to implement the decision, what is to be done, when is it to be done, where and under what conditions, and why particular actions are to be taken. The decision may be affected within the person's attitudes and emotions or thinking. It may be related to actions concerning other people or the use of resources. In a group, the decision may concern an individual or it may relate to a corporate agreement or action. A decision may be a minor one or one of major concern to those affected by it. Through questions, comments, and active teaching, the social worker contributes to the client's understanding of how to cope with problems. The worker uses the other sets of techniques in the problem-solving process, but he often needs to teach the steps to be taken, provide information concerning alternative solutions and the consequences of choice. He may teach, through demonstration, ways of doing things that implement decisions. For example, a decision to budget income may need to be followed by learning about and practicing budgeting. A decision to have a conference with a school principal may need to be rehearsed prior to the actual experience.

As Siporin has said,

Making sound decisions and implementing them are fundamental aspects of all adaptive thinking and action. They are fundamental to problem-solving, and are involved in the task of assessment, planning, intervention, and corrective action in normal life and in the helping processes. We make both routine and non-routine, fateful decisions all of our lives, in secure situations or uncertain ones. . . . Choices are best made when people are informed and can actively and willingly participate in their making.[55]

Facilitation of Group Process

From a content analysis of major books and dissertations on social work practice up to 1972, Fatout concluded that work with families and other groups utilizes all of the procedures or sets of techniques described in the literature on work with individuals.[56] There are also, however, techniques that are specific to the group system, whether family or peer group. There are generic techniques, but there are additional ones that are used when the client system consists of two or more persons. The common element underlying these techniques is that of using the group interaction in order to maximize the value of the group for its members. Hartford has also noted that, in working with a group, the worker's focus is less concentrated on each individual and more on connecting members to each other so they can be of greater value to each other. The worker helps a viable group to develop and facilitates the interacting process at a given time.[57]

The social worker guides the group process so as to maximize its value as the primary instrument of treatment. In order to achieve this intent, the worker needs to understand process as a series of psychosocial interactions between and among all the participants, including the worker. Group discussion is not a series of conversations between the social worker and each member serially; rather, it engages as fully as possible each member in a group-centered interaction process, usually reflective in nature. Although the worker does communicate with specific individuals, he observes the effect of their actions on the group. As Coyle has said:

It seems to me that the primary skill is the ability to establish a relationship with a group as a group. This involves the capacity to feel at ease, in fact, to enjoy the social interplay among members and to be able to perceive both individual behavior and its collective manifestations . . . as well as to become a part of the relationships and to affect them.[58]

Focus on the group does not negate the importance of the individual. When the focus is upon interpersonal interaction, neither the individual nor the group is submerged: both are viewed as equally important. Neither can be fully understood without the other.

The social worker follows several lines of communication simultaneously: the needs and contributions of individuals related to the group; the interplay between emotion and cognition; the interplay between manifest and latent content; and the patterns of communication among the members. These thought processes get translated into the differential use of the other techniques and a decision as to whether to address an individual or the group as a whole. The techniques available to the worker are numerous; some of the worker's acts are the same as those that have been described earlier, but they are used in a different context and with a different intent.

The worker makes efforts to involve each member as fully as possible in the group. He does this through such means as inviting participation in general or of particular individuals, recognizing the contributions of each member, and demonstrating that an individual's needs and interests can be met through the group, at least partially. This is done by exploratory questions that bring out the extent to which problems, interests, and ideas are shared; or by comments that acknowledge a particular contribution to another member or the group as a whole.

Facilitating the process of the group toward goal achievement involves dealing with similarities and differences among the members. Through exploration, the worker brings out the common and diverse attitudes, feelings, and ideas about the members and their situations. He avoids engaging a person in a dialogue with himself for an extended period of time, with others as an audience. When this happens, other members tend to become passive and bored, and the group becomes ineffective as a means of help. He may need to limit the inveterate talker so that he does not monopolize the discussion. He can do this through nonverbal means, such as nodding at members who seem ready to break into the monologue; he can break into the discussion to acknowledge what the monopolizer has said and suggest that it is time for others to participate. He does not respond verbally to every contribution made by a member, for then he would monopolize the time and detract from the give-and-take among members. Rather, he requests that others respond to the contributions that have been made; he tends to address his own questions and comments to the group as a whole rather than to a particular member. This does not mean that the worker is passive. He supplements what the members are able to do. He may need to focus and refocus the discussion. He may need to suggest that the group look at one part of the issue or problem at a time and then move to consider the relationships among parts. He may share his perceptions of what is going on in the group as a means for stimulating evaluation and new directions. The principle is simply "trust the group process," but intervene purposefully when the group needs direction.

In order to maximize the effectiveness of the group, the worker seeks for the common ground that underlies individual differences, with the intent to promote mutual aid, identification among members, and group cohesiveness. There are usually common threads that underlie various problems, situations, or points of view. This does not mean that the worker does not also recognize true differences in degree or in kind. He recognizes the acceptability of the differences and points to the fact that understanding differences among people can be a means for broadening capacities in social relationships. The social worker identifies connections between one member's relationship needs and those of one or more others, with the intent of developing or enhancing relationships among members.

The practitioner recognizes the underlying agreements and explores disagreements among members in order to help the members to clarify their own positions, to understand that their position is not the only one, and when appropriate, to move toward resolution of conflicts that are created by differences. Some differences are due to lack of accurate facts or misrepresentation of facts; some are due to differences in values that concern what is desirable or worthwhile. What needs to be dealt with is the meaning of these differences in relation to a particular situation, not at an abstract level of generalization. In order to find the sources of conflict, the worker listens, and he watches the facial and body expressions of the members to understand the approvals and disapprovals, questions, or concerns. He may respond to help the group accept the right of members to hold unpopular opinions, and to accept and appreciate differences.

In facilitating interaction, the social worker may summarize his assessment of what has been going on or accomplished, with the intent of emphasizing the group process and progress or obstacles to progress. By listening objectively and registering the progress or obstacles, the worker can be an accurate reflector of the state of the discussion. This serves as feedback to the group so that it can then continue or change its course of action. When there is evidence that there are problems in the group process—such as inability to resolve a conflict, loss of morale, contagion of negative behavior, or poor attendance—the worker may share these observations with the members and engage them in a process of assessing the problem and then go on to making decisions about how the problem might be solved or at least minimized.

The worker is concerned with group process because the primary means of help when using a group are the support and stimulation that members give each other, supplemented by the worker's direct contributions to the work of the client system. Changes in attitudes and behavior occur when members are actively involved in the group; when they are able both to give and to take from others. They benefit from perceiving both their likenesses to, and differences from, others. Thus, the focus is on the development of meaningful group interaction without losing sight of individuals. Sharing of individual thought is necessary so that each member can become aware of what others are feeling and thinking and use this knowledge for appraisal of his own feelings, thoughts, and actions. Individual satisfactions are essential to the development of cohesive groups which have great influence on their members. The worker therefore needs to make sure that the group becomes a mutual aid and mutual need-meeting system.

In order to be a competent practitioner, a social worker needs a theory of practice that encompasses its purpose, functions, values, explanatory theory about individual-group-environment interaction, and processes and principles of assessment and treatment. The theory needs also to include a framework for understanding and intervening in each of the major phases of process: planning services to meet particular needs; initiating and developing a worker-client relationship and working agreement; intensively working toward the achievement of goals; and terminating the service. None is more important to successful outcome than the initial planning, which is the subject of the next chapter.

CHAPTER FIVE

Planning Individualized Services

Planning for a specific service to a client system is one of the most important processes in social work. According to Siporin, planning is "a deliberate rational process that involves the choice of actions that are calculated to achieve specific objectives at some future time."[1] It is a decision-making process through which is determined the means for achieving objectives. Plans for service should be a result of bringing together the client's and worker's assessment and knowledge as to how change can best be accomplished. The social worker, often in collaboration with others, makes certain choices concerning the nature of the services and resources to be made available to particular clients. Although planning, like assessment, is an ongoing process, certain decisions need to be made prior to and during the initial meeting with an individual or family.

Planning is necessary because social workers seek to provide individualized services to meet needs. Meyer has suggested that the primary focus of social work is individualizing, which is a process of differentiating particular people from the mass.[2] It involves paying attention to both the uniqueness of individuals and families and the characteristics they share in common. Within common human needs and situations there are particularized needs to be taken into account. Thus, a plan must be made for each individual, family, or group to be served. The plan is based on knowledge of agency policies and procedures and assessment of clients in their networks of interacting social systems.

Kurland has noted that planning has been a neglected process in social work and that "the price for lack of thoughtful and thorough planning is high."[3] Frequently, it is paid in clients who drop out, sporadic and irregular attendance, and lack of successful outcomes. It is paid also in workers' lack of confidence to take on new types of clients and new responsibilities. Main's research on social work with groups has implications for all of social work practice. One of her major conclusions is that the degree of development of individual diagnostic assessments, treatment goals, and plans for individuals was positively associated with the degree of appropriateness of the worker's use of self with individuals and with the group.[4] Treatment planning is a basis for purposeful service, and seems to be associated with the nature of the worker's engagement with the members. So the price of thoughtful and thorough planning is high in aiding the worker to use himself effectively with clients.

Preliminary planning includes decisions concerning: (1) the social context of service; (2) the needs, problems, and goals of clients that will serve as an initial focus of content; (3) the unit of service which is most appropriate to meeting the needs of an individual applicant or a collectivity of potential clients; (4) the structure of service including the composition of the worker-client system, the duration of service, and the number and type of personnel to be used; and (5) the means of entering into the service system. In relation to each of these components of planning, there are alternatives to be selected, based on the professional judgment of the practitioner, the potential clients' preference and capacities, and the organization's policies, procedures, and resources.

The Social Context

The social context for service is usually a social agency or a department of social work in a school, hospital, clinic, prison, residential institution, business, or industry. The organization is a complex network of people in interlocking social systems, such as boards of directors, advisory committees, administrators, clerical and paraprofessional personnel, and practitioners from one or more professions. Within the organization, certain groups are given authority to define the parameters of services to be given and the conditions under which they are to be given. Except in private practice, a social agency or other organization sanctions certain practices and forbids others. It has policies concerning preventive, developmental, or rehabilitative functions; eligibility requirements including fees for service; the types of clients to which service will be offered; the resources available to client and practitioner; and even the theoretical base to be used by practitioners.

Although practice must be related to organizational policies and functions, as Glasser and Garvin state, "the profession of social work must not be co-opted by organizational needs and interests."[5] Pincus and Minahan take a similar stance in insisting that the "worker must be careful not to substitute agency conceptions, policies, and practices for independent professional judgment."[6] Practitioners have both the right and responsibility to do everything in their power to influence the organizations that employ them in order to meet client needs as effectively as possible. An increasing number of practitioners are engaged in private practice. When this is so, the worker alone, or as a part of a group of practitioners, sets the policies and conditions which govern the provision of services. These workers are, however, constrained by licensing laws that define the nature of the services they may provide. They often also must relate their services to the requirements of other organizations which they may use as resources for their clients.

Recent studies indicate that virtually every neighborhood has a complex array of social structures and networks, both formal and informal. These aspects of the environment influence the quality of everyday life and can be mobilized in behalf of clients.[7] A multitude of specialized public and voluntary organizations penetrates every community, often working at cross purposes and without knowledge of each other's activities. There are also numerous self-help and mutual support groups that contribute to the welfare of their members and the community. The social worker needs to understand the community as a basis for planning in behalf of his clients.

In addition to direct services to individuals, families, and groups, the practitioner often needs to work with other people in the community. In order to be effective, he needs to have depth of understanding of the community—its institutions, resources, and networks of relationships. He establishes relationships with people who are not clients, but who can influence the progress of the client in important ways or provide necessary resources for the client. He often needs to refer clients to resources or confer with representatives of other agencies and organizations to find a solution to a particular problem; for example, a child with a severe physical handicap who requires special attention at school, physical therapy, and a group experience, in addition to individual counseling. He may need to coordinate multiple services that are required by a family, such as financial assistance, medical care, and individual and family social services. He often participates on an interdisciplinary team within a hospital, clinic, or school that has responsibility for securing needed resources and coordinating them in ways that assure their accessibility to clients and continuity of care and service; a plan for service needs to include the work that will be done with significant other persons in the environment.

Needs and Goals

Within the broad purpose of assisting people with their psychosocial functioning, the particular developmental needs and problems are varied. In the planning process, the worker considers which needs or problems of the client are appropriate within the profession's purpose and the organization's functions, policies, and facilities. He considers also which problems are amenable to intervention through direct service practice, as differentiated from those which are beyond the social worker's authority as, for example, providing financial assistance or securing a new law. In such instances, the role of the social worker is one of referral agent or resource consultant. Within these parameters, the social worker and client together identify those needs or problems that will serve as an initial focus for their work. The initial goals stem from agreement between social worker and client about what the hoped-for outcome will be, that is, what the person or group desires to achieve. Clarity of goals is essential. Goals provide the basic guide for both the worker and client in their participation in the process. They provide a framework for further assessment, for the selection of interventive procedures, and for evaluation of outcome.

The worker's preliminary planning is based on understanding the potentials for service to a wide variety of clients with a view to flexible and imaginative use of agency purposes and policies or to securing an exception to them. There is danger in overemphasis on agency purpose because some clients have needs that do not fit neatly into a current definition of purpose. One example would be the traditional statement that a family service agency aims to strengthen family life, yet couples may and often do decide to separate or divorce. Desirably, the purpose of the agency would be sufficiently flexible to make possible helping the couple to make good adaptations to the separation. If an agency has a variety of alternatives, it is more likely that service will be given according to the needs of clients. Within a general policy about purpose and services of the organization, the goals that are agreed to between worker and clients direct the activities of clients and worker. A worker will be able to serve more clients well if he uses knowledge about the psychosocial development and functioning of people and the variety of needs, desires, and goals that are congruent with agency purpose. Being able to find some thread of connection between a client's goals and agency purpose is a crucial problem-solving skill of the social worker.

One point of view asserts that goals must be limited to what clients initially say they want to achieve; another view is that the social worker uses knowledge about the client-situation gestalt to participate actively with the client in a shared goal-setting process. The latter is the perspective taken here: goals emerge from the process of assessment. The term goal is used interchangeably with objective, aim, or purpose, all of which words signify an intent to do or achieve something. In thinking about how the client can best be helped, the worker considers what tentative goals seem pertinent, considering the means for bringing about changes that result in achievement of goals.[8]

In deciding upon goals, the major focus is on the ultimate objectives to be achieved. The ultimate goal is related to the need or problem of which the client is aware. The worker and client may have different perceptions of goals. The client, for example, may state that the trouble is with her husband and that she wants him to change. As the worker evaluates what he sees and hears, he may conclude that the trouble is with the marital relationship; it is the interaction between the spouses that needs to be improved. The choice of the goal is influenced by what the client says he wants, but also by what the worker thinks is appropriate and possible. Through sharing these views, the worker and client come to some consensus about the desired outcome.

In addition to goals concerning outcomes, there are intermediate or instrumental goals through which it is anticipated that the desired outcome may be achieved. These goals are steps in the process, as, for example, when a person needs to recognize his anger or to identify a particular interpersonal conflict as one means toward overcoming depression. Or it is hoped that a father and husband with a hospitalized wife will accept a temporary housekeeping service so as to reduce unbearable stress on the family's steady state. These intermediate objectives are not ends in themselves, but goals that must be achieved on the way to the agreed-upon objectives.

Similarities and Differences in Client Systems

Planning effective services requires that the practitioner understand the characteristics of individual, family, and group systems because these qualities make a difference in the nature of the experience for both workers and clients. Each of these systems has some similarities and differences, as compared with others.[9] The basic values of social work apply, but they are implemented in different ways. Privacy and confidentiality are preserved to the greatest extent in a relationship of one client with one worker. The one-to-one relationship is controlled by the worker in relation to confidentiality, which may result in more freedom of self-disclosure. In families and other groups, respect for privacy and maintenance of confidentiality depend upon the extent to which a norm of confidentiality can be developed within the group, because there are multiple sources for transmitting information about what happens in treatment.

INDIVIDUALIZATION

Dependency on a worker is most characteristic of the one-to-one relationship, even though the worker strives to help the client to participate actively and to make his own decisions. Less dependency occurs in family or group sessions because the process itself places demands on each member to share with others. Interdependency is directly valued and demonstrated through action. In a group, the individual is required to negotiate situations, fulfill expectations, and share feelings. As Davies has written, "Seeing and feeling oneself differently and seeing and feeling significant others differently can in itself do much to alter attitudes, behavior, and relationships in important ways."[10]

The generic principle of individualization is applied differently with respect to different units of service. In the one-to-one relationship, the focus tends to be on the unique and specific characteristics and actions of a person and his situation. The client has the undivided attention of the worker. In family groups, on the other hand, individualization of each member occurs, but within the interacting processes of the group. Although the goals of each member are considered, so are the goals of each other member. But the primary goals concern the family itself—changes in the family's structure and communication systems.[11] Likewise, in formed groups the needs of each individual are important, but they fall within concern for the needs of each and all. In some groups, there may be a collective goal as well as shared individual goals. In families and other groups, each member has, in one sense, the right to equal attention from the worker, but in another sense, attention is given differentially to individuals who need the worker's help most at a particular time.

GOALS

In working with an individual, the desired change is usually in attitudes, feelings, and behavior of that particular person and in some aspect of his environment. Although he is helped to work on his relationships with other people, these others are not directly present. The expectation is that the gains made in treatment will be transferred to other situations. In families, the desired change is usually in the family system itself, in addition to changes in constituent members and subsystems. In addition to goals for individuals, it is desired that change occur within the system—its values, relationships, communication patterns, power structure, and decision-making processes. The most frequent goals are improvement in communication; clarification and improvement of role functioning; development of capacity to tackle and achieve certain common tasks and responsibilities; enhancement of positive aspects of relationships such as capacity for empathy, enjoyment of each other, and mutual support; and making decisions that are satisfactory to those who are affected by them.[12] It is expected that gains will be reflected within the family system itself and in its interaction with other systems.

In formed groups, the hoped-for outcomes are positive changes in the attitudes, feelings, relationships, and social behavior of each individual, as related to the goals specifically agreed upon with each member that are harmonious with the general purpose of the group. Individual changes occur through direct interaction with others who share certain common characteristics and needs. As in individual work, the expectation is that the gains will come to be reflected outside the group in the daily life of each individual. In both families and formed groups, there must be some common purpose for working with multiple persons simultaneously to serve as a unifying factor.

RELATIONSHIP DEMANDS

In the one-to-one relationship, there is only one interactional bond between the practitioner and the client. There is no relief from the demands and satisfactions of the relationship, except through absence or termination. Both the client and the worker have the power to break the relationship. The client is involved with only one other person who is in a position of authority. By virtue of his position in an organization or the sanction given him through licensing and his professional knowledge and skills, he has primary influence over what is done and the means to be used. This is true even though the worker seeks the client's active participation. The exclusiveness of the relationship, unless it is brief and task-oriented, tends to foster demands for intimacy in disclosing thoughts, feelings, and experiences to a relatively benign and trusting person. The client expects that his communications will be evaluated and responded to by the other person. Clients invest themselves in the relationship in various ways and with different degrees of intimacy. The relationship develops around fairly realistic expectations and perceptions of each partner. In some situations, the client will become deeply invested in his relationship with the worker and quite dependent upon him for emotional gratification. Strong identifications and positive transference reactions may develop, usually combined with some elements of negative transference. Ambivalence is ubiquitous and to be expected.

In the family, each member has a history of relationships with each other member. The members live with the assumption that destruction of the group is a threat to their emotional survival.[13] The nature and quality of these relationships is based partly on realistic experiences with each other, but also partly on distortions of perceptions of each other's intents, behaviors, and status in the family. When the family system is the unit of service, the members enter into a new arena in which the expectations are that they will share with each other and with a practitioner in different ways than have been characteristic of them. The worker is an outsider who enters into an established system of relationships, evaluates the system's functioning, and attempts to support or change certain elements of the system. The worker's primary tie is to the process between and among the members, but he must also consider each subsystem and each individual in their relationships with other individuals and subgroups. The relationships between husband and wife, parent and children, and siblings are of utmost complexity. Family relationships are almost always intense, for each member is dependent upon others and the group for meeting basic needs. For this reason, members may feel there is a great risk in entering into family treatment. There are apt to be fears of rejection or retaliation from the very persons upon whom one is dependent for emotional and sometimes also for physical survival. The social worker's influence is greatly modified by the patterns of authority that have been established in the family. Some of this authority is legally defined, concerning the power of parents in relation to children. The social worker should take care not to usurp parental authority, but should respect it and work toward changing it, if it is inimical to the family as a whole. The family will continue as a unit when the worker's particular relationship with it has terminated.

In formed groups, the situation is initially quite different. The practitioner's responsibility is to initiate and develop a system of relationships among people who often have had no prior acquaintance with each other. He needs to develop his relationship with each member and with the group as a whole, which consists of the intricate network of changing relationships among the members. As in work with individuals, the worker and the members come together for a limited period of time. The worker influences relationships in order that the group can become the principal means of help, yet also eventually become no longer necessary as a source of psychological and social support for the members.

The intensity and intimacy of relationships vary with the purpose of the group and the needs of the members. Relationships may become very intense; nevertheless, they are diluted by the larger number of interactional bonds and the limited time that members spend together. Strong identifications may develop between one or more members and the worker, or between two or more members. As cohesiveness develops, there is often strong identification with the group as a whole. Transference reactions often develop between certain members and the worker, often predominantly positive, but tinged with negative aspects. There is the added complexity of transference reactions among the members themselves. The patterns of reactions, based on a combination of realistic and distorted perceptions of others, create a very complex network of positive and negative ties. The practitioner's influence is reduced by his presence in a group in which members influence each other. This shared authority requires that the worker understand and then either support or challenge the processes among members rather than assume direct control, except when members are unable to control themselves. The group, with its competing demands, shifting alliances, and complex emotional network, does not allow for the protection of an individual to the extent this may occur in the one-to-one relationship. But the group does afford more psychological space for each individual, permitting him to move into relationships of greater and lesser intensity, according to his own readiness and interpersonal needs.

EXPECTATIONS AND SOURCES OF HELP

The nature of the worker-to-individual or individual-to-group relationship is a source of help. Lieberman said that in our culture, help is expected to be given by a particular person—whether bartender, lawyer, physician, or clergyman—in a context that is private, intimate, and exclusive.[14] If referred to a group of people who are seeking help, a person is in an ambiguous situation in which there is little tradition to guide him, for such groups are different from the educational, work, or recreational groups with which he has had prior experience. In a one-to-one relationship, the individual is exposed to a stable person who is the major definer of reality. The practitioner, who has professional knowledge and skills that the client does not have, is the major source of input of new information through which the client learns new attitudes, new ways of coping and behaving.

Lieberman pointed out that this generalization about expectations for help does not take into account the fact that help is often first sought within families or from persons in the extended family network; and that in some cultures decisions about one member are made by the group. Help in a group, therefore, is more representative of real-life situations. In groups, an individual is exposed to an array of other persons who are both giving and receiving help. The power of the group is the "authenticating force of one's peers. . . . The experience of consensual validation by peers is a much more powerful, stimulating, and important experience than is the fact of acceptance by one other human being."[15] In groups, stimulation and support come from multiple sources. There are many people from whom to learn, with whom to identify, and with whom to interact. In research on the experiences of social workers with groups, Tennant found that two thirds of the workers noted the value of motivational and support powers from peers. They thought that clients come to understand and accept their needs and problems by hearing others ask and answer questions about their strengths and difficulties. Clients are motivated to engage in solving their problems by being with others who also have problems and who are using help in working on them.[16]

FOCUS OF ACTIVITIES OF THE WORKER

In the one-to-one relationship, the worker's activities consist of observing, listening, assessing, deciding, initiating, and responding directly to the client's verbal and nonverbal communications. The focus is on the uniqueness of the particular client's needs and problems. The key factor that distinguishes service to families or couples from work with individuals and most other groups is the direct intervention of the practitioner in an operating social system that exists as such outside the treatment situation and consists of members who share each other's lives and who are important to each other. The practitioner enters the system to help the members understand its structure and processes and make desired changes or maintain its adaptability in the face of threat. In formed groups, the worker's activities are to help the members develop a new system that has potential for meeting their needs for a limited time and for the maintenance and eventual termination of the system. The source of help is the multiplicity of feelings, viewpoints, and resources that provide stimulation and support for efforts to change.

Flexible Use of Units of Service

Within the approach to practice described herein, a flexible and individualized consideration of multiple alternatives for meeting the needs of clients is valued. This approach is not congruent with organizational policies and practices that limit service to casework as a one-worker-to-one-client endeavor or to a worker-group or worker-community endeavor only. Nor is it congruent with policies and practices that require that services be given through only one type of activity, for example, verbal communication, play therapy, behavior modification, or transactional analysis. The essential principle is that the social worker and the client agree upon the particular modality or combination of these and on the focus of service, based on understanding a wide range of alternatives.

Other writers have expressed a similar philosophy of service.[17] In a survey of 146 social workers in family service agencies, Couch found that a large majority of workers and agencies favored a flexible use of individual, couple, family, and group modalities in the treatment of marital problems.[18] In a survey of seventy-six publications that described direct treatment of children, Hinchman found that individual treatment is viewed as one part of a more comprehensive plan. He found that individualized, flexible, multiple approaches to treatment were highly preferred, with considerable regard for social interaction between children, their families, and significant other persons and resources.[19] In another review of social work literature, Flanzer traced the development of the relationships between casework, family work, and group work, and identified a form of service in which the primary characteristic is planned integration of two or more modalities for the same client.[20] In a recent book, Ormont and Strean claim that combining individual and group treatment is exceedingly effective.[21] Kaplan has presented information that by making casework, group work, and coordinated services of a professional team available to aged patients in long-term care facilities, the aspirations of the staff were enhanced and the personal and social functioning of the patients was improved.[22]

Not all prospective clients need service through multiple modalities. The challenge to the practitioner is to aid the client to decide which one, or which combination, shows promise of being most productive in relation to the goals of service. To meet this challenge, social workers need knowledge of the common and specific characteristics of types of systems and the needs and characteristics of each individual. They need to be able to select a target system, that is, any persons the worker attempts to influence in order to accomplish the goals.[23] Work with people who are not themselves clients in behalf of clients is very important. Thus, other systems may need to become the target of intervention; for example, in addition to helping a school child with social difficulties that hinder learning, a parent or teacher may need to be involved.

CRITERIA FOR SELECTION OF UNITS OF SERVICE

Clear criteria for the use of individual, couple, family, group, or community services do not exist. Professional judgment is required.

Statements about indications and contraindications concerning the use of different modalities are often contradictory. Any decision needs to be based on an assessment of the persons who are involved in the situation, the goals of the service, and the values and risks involved in varied modalities of practice. Understanding the special characteristics of different forms of treatment is essential to planning a service for an individual or a family.

The individual client-social worker dyad, with its unique characteristics of privacy, one-to-one communication, potential for intimacy, and exclusiveness seems to be the treatment of choice under certain conditions. Individual help is chosen when a client needs to have some psychological distance from a living group, such as a family or dormitory, in order to be able to perceive it more realistically and to evaluate his place in the system. It may often be the preferred approach for exploring and resolving problems not suitable for discussion in the presence of family members or peers, whose needs might redirect the focus and divert the content from the task at hand. It is usually preferred when a person has a salient need for rapid restoration in a crisis situation and either does not live in a family or the family cannot be engaged in the helping endeavor. It is probably preferred when the situation requires a person to make a crucial, specific, personal decision that has long-term consequences for him and others, and when he needs to do the problem-solving work free from undue influence exerted by peers or family. Examples are decisions about whether or not to have an abortion, relinquish custody of a child, drop out of school, file for divorce. In such situations, individuals need to clarify their feelings and thoughts as to what they really want to do, make a decision, and consider and face the consequences of the decision for themselves and significant others.

When a marital couple has separated, individual treatment is best, according to findings from a large study based on the counselors' ratings. Once separation has occurred, partners need the one-to-one relationship to sort out, cope with, and integrate the trauma and anxieties stemming from separation.[24] The individual modality is undoubtedly superior for some recently separated couples, but not for all. Brown claims that groups are especially well-suited where divorce counseling is needed. The presence of others in similar situations provides perspective. A person is able to give and receive support, guidance, and challenge to confront and resolve feelings about the former spouse, sex roles, and expectations. Individual sessions, however, may be used for special problems, such as financial settlements or custody issues.[25]

Some people refuse to participate in family or group treatment; the only alternative then is individual help. This is true also if a person is imbued with the idea that his problem is so unique and difficult that he can only be helped by an expert and that the presence of other clients would dilute the change effort.[26] Some persons are too fearful of groups or they are governed by a value that forbids discussion of personal feelings and problems with others. It may be that these are the people who most need a corrective group experience. Nevertheless, individual help is required, at least until the initial resistance to family and group forms of help can be modified.

Controversy exists concerning the desirability and effectiveness of working with children in direct treatment. In a review of the social work literature on direct treatment of children, Hinchman found that most writers thought that a child should be treated, as should one or both parents; and others thought that a child was best served through treatment of the family as a unit. Those writers who favored direct service to children thought that although the family is crucial in child development, the child has his own reactions to, and ideas about, what troubles him and what is happening in the environment.[27] He is, as Austin said, "a person in his own right and is not simply a reflection of his parents."[28] Children have the capacity to grow and change, to help themselves, and to share some responsibility for their behavior. Direct treatment of children is given either through the one-to-one relationship or through experience in a group. Other writers argued that children grow and change through positive changes in their environments, particularly in their parents' attitudes and behavior or through placement in a more benign environment, such as a foster home or residential center.

Work with families and their subsystems, such as a marital couple, is particularly useful when the difficulty is in the functioning of the system itself. Examples are ineffective patterns of communication, lack of satisfying relationships among the members, lack of clarity about role expectations, conflict among the members concerning goals and decisions, and inadequate ways of coping with problems in daily living. Perlman notes that joint and family interviews may be uniquely suited to the clarification of role requirements, role allocations, and role performance within the family, since the participants can simultaneously become aware of their own perceptions related to those of others and may mutually experiment with revised role definitions.[29] They may not be suitable when hostility and rejection are extreme, without compensating warmth and support.

There seems to be considerable agreement that working with couples together, either in joint interviews or in groups of couples, is most appropriate when marital conflict is a major problem. In a large study by the Family Service Association of America, for example, couples treated together showed significantly greater change than did those treated through individual interviews, as rated by both counselors and clients. Treatment of couples in groups was also found to be more effective than individual interviews.[30] Gurman came to similar conclusions. He surveyed seventy-three journals and concluded that conjoint treatment of couples generally produces the best results, although in certain circumstances each of the other forms may have particular advantages. The rationale for this choice is that marital maladjustment is an entity having its own dynamics and ecology apart from individual maladjustments; therefore, one treats the marital pair. Groups of couples with marital problems were almost as beneficial as conjoint treatment and were superior to that form among people who divorced. The group modality also seems to produce the highest social as well as marital adjustments.[31] In another study, by Macon, joint treatment and group treatment of marital problems were found to be equally effective.[32]

It was noted earlier that individual work may be preferred when one or more members are separating from the family; conversely, work with the family is indicated when the family has "emotionally, some sense of being or wishing to be a family."[33] In some instances, the goal is to form a new family or cement a fragmented family. When a crisis is brought about by a precipitating event that affects group composition or roles, the family is usually the preferred mode of treatment. Examples of such situations are the death of a member, illness, a role transition, crisis, or unemployment.

Formed groups are found to be especially useful in certain situations. They are most useful when the main problem concerns relationships with others. The special values of peer groups, according to Benne, are that as a person interacts with others, he develops awareness and acceptance of self in its uniqueness, strengths, and limitations; he experiences interdependence with others so that help can be both given and received; and he comes to a positive appraisal of differences and conflicts among members as potentially constructive.[34] Green and associates report, for example, that:

> We see numerous Mexican-American women, anywhere between 18 and 45 years of age, who are torn by overwhelming conflict to meet their own needs and establish independent lives, yet cannot leave home because of the immense burden of guilt they would suffer for rejecting their families. In terms of therapy, these women often benefit most from a group experience. They need the support of peers in order to handle the resulting guilt, and the group itself serves as a vehicle for the family transference that must be dealt with.[35]

The peer relationship component of groups may make them particularly valuable for adolescents and adults who are threatened by authority figures. The sense of belonging to the group can reduce suspiciousness toward persons in positions of authority. When a number of individuals or couples are available who have a common need or problem, the formed group is an effective modality. Many people need to learn what impression they make on other people and to practice new interpersonal behaviors in a social situation which is removed from their daily routines and relationships and in which feedback comes from other members, in addition to that from the practitioner. The perspective provided by multiple views of problems, people, and situations provides a context for reality testing, and makes the group particularly desirable when clients have distortions in perception of themselves and others. Socially isolated people may overcome a sense of alienation from others in a setting that fosters acknowledging needs and problems and sharing common feelings about selves and others in a climate of mutual acceptance and support.

When intense relationships with other significant persons are fraught with frustration, dissatisfaction, or conflict, help is often best given outside the social system in which the conflict occurs. Groups are the modality in which a person can learn new attitudes and patterns of relationships, once removed from the original source of the difficulty. Examples are instances of sibling rivalry, adolescent and parent conflicts, or a stormy relationship with a teacher or employer. Even when there is a problem in family functioning, which usually indicates service to the family unit, a member may benefit from a group service, as when a person may not be able to bear his anxiety about family sessions or cannot trust the worker to protect him from retaliation by other members. In a group experience, the relationships with the worker and other members can begin at whatever level of participation the person is ready for until, through observation of what happens to others, he learns that the worker is interested in all and that there is enough caring, acceptance, and empathy to go around. This experience may make it possible for him then to benefit from help within his family.

McBroom, from intensive study of socialization, has concluded that the group is the most natural and effective modality for intervention when people need assistance in the process of socialization. "There is a direct connection between interaction and motivation. Therefore, primary groups are the optimal setting for socialization: they promote maximal feedback and the chance for alternatives and experiment without disaster."[36] Social competence, the general purpose of socialization, is developed through relationships with other people.

> The very terms of socialization theory suggest that group work is usually the method of choice: the social interaction aspects of personal change are enriched and accelerated in the group as a socializing environment. The goal of social competence assumes functioning in a group rather than in isolated activities. Indeed, socialization as the organizing principle of the individual's social development embraces all those processes which enable him to participate in groups. It is only through social interaction that the self rises and takes on meaning.[37]

McBroom sees the major targets for socialization efforts to be populations at risk such as new parents; parents whose children have atypical needs; deprived and displaced adults; persons facing major change or loss in family and work roles, body image, or body function; and those experiencing radically altered social expectations and opportunities.

Practical matters need to be recognized and taken into account in making decisions about the type of service to be offered or provided. Obviously, one of these considerations is client choice. People have different attitudes toward, and different experiences in, individual, family, or group modalities, which influence their motivation to use a particular type of service. The important point, however, is that the choice should be an informed one, so that the client can understand some of the benefits, risks, and consequences of a particular decision. Another consideration is the obvious one that, if a person is not currently a part of a family constellation, the choice is limited to an individual or formed group modality. The size of an agency and its caseload, or the caseload of a private practitioner, influences the extent to which formed groups can be utilized. There must, of course, be a sufficient number of applicants or clients with a common need to make possible the formation of a group.

There is a tendency to regard group modalities as less time-consuming than work with each individual separately. Whether or not this is true depends upon the purpose of the group, its structure, and the characteristics and needs of the members. More time is involved in the initial planning process in selecting and recruiting appropriate members for the group and in keeping records of both individual and group progress. More often than not, interviews with some individuals are necessary to help them to use the group effectively. The sessions tend to be longer than is customary in working with an individual.

The Structure of Service

An important part of planning concerns decisions about the structure of service. Important elements of structure are: composition of the client system, size of the client system, number of practitioners, duration of service, and length and frequency of sessions.

COMPOSITION OF THE CLIENT SYSTEM

The particular constellation of persons who interact with each other is an important determinant of whether or not the participants will be satisfied with the experience and the hoped-for outcomes will be achieved. In a worker-individual situation, the decisions about composition are relatively simple: they involve the assignment of a particular client to a practitioner. Often this is done in as simple a way as assigning a client to whatever worker has the time to undertake the service to him. But if there is more than one alternative available, attention should be given to the compatibility between worker and client. In some instances, the sex, race, ethnicity, social class, or age of the worker relative to the client could be factors to be considered. Wide differences in these characteristics tend to create social distance between client and worker.

Kadushin has summarized the literature on the influence of race on worker-client interaction. He suggests that the difficulties in cross-racial contacts may account in part for the higher attrition rates of black clients who apply for a social work service. There are contradictory findings about the effect of race on the use of service, partly because variables of race, social class, nationality, religion, and sex overlap and intertwine. There is evidence that some clients may prefer workers of the same ethnicity as their own, and others may not. There are difficulties as well as advantages in matching worker and client. The effects of matching are not uniformly positive: "Too great a similarity between interview participants risks the danger of overidentification and loss of objectivity; too great a dissimilarity makes for greater difficulty in understanding and empathizing."[38] Solomon asserts that social workers can learn to work across ethnic lines and describes the essential skills of a nonracist social worker. These essential skills are: (1) an ability to perceive alternative explanations for any behavior; (2) ability to observe verbal and nonverbal cues that will help in discovering which explanation is most probable for a particular client; (3) ability to feel warmth, concern, and empathy for people regardless of their ethnicity; and (4) ability to confront the client when he misinterprets or distorts the true feelings of the practitioner, thus heightening self-awareness and competence in relationships.[39] The conclusion seems to be that the attitudes and competence of the practitioner are more significant factors than are race and other personal characteristics in determining outcome.

Families and other autonomous groups, such as a street gang, already exist. The social worker enters the group for a limited period of time and with a special role. Some members of these groups may refuse to participate in the social work endeavor, thus modifying the composition of the system with which work is done. In some families, the composition of the group changes with the addition of a foster or adopted child or with the loss of a member. When a person is to have a long-term placement in a family or an institutional facility, the selection of the caretakers is crucial. The fit between a person and his environment has great influence on his psychosocial functioning and also on the welfare of the other people involved. One current controversy concerns placement of a person across ethnic and religious lines. It seems clear that when differences are too marked, the newcomer may feel that his new living arrangement is so foreign and ego-alien that he does not belong. In addition to adapting to ethnic and racial differences, other differences, such as state of health and social class are to be considered. These differences create the need for mutual adaptation by all concerned. There is the anticipated stress that accompanies the need to develop new relationships and often also to relocate in a new community. Sensitivity to such factors is essential in making an appropriate placement, whether it be a foster home for a child, a halfway house for a discharged mental patient, or a long-term care facility for an elderly adult. There is evidence that transcultural placements can be effective—that it is the combination of many interdependent factors, rather than one alone, that leads to a successful placement.[40]

Groups for clients are often formed by a social worker alone or as a member of a team.[41] Several major procedures are used:

1. There is selective intake and placement according to some specific criteria relevant to the purpose of the group. Examples would be therapy or counseling groups.

2. Membership is by choice of an individual; that is, there is self-selection of those who choose to join a group. Members are attracted to a group by its purpose or task: they perceive that it will meet a

personal need. Examples would be some parent-education groups, consciousness-raising groups for women, or groups for single parents.

3. Members are in a group because they share some common situation with others. Group composition is determined by inclusion of all persons who share a particular status or experience. Examples are living groups in institutions, patients facing discharge from mental hospitals, or ambulatory patients on a pediatrics ward. Individuals may or may not have a choice as to whether or not they become members of such groups. Regardless of the type of group, the practitioner and agency exert some control over its membership.

It is in relation to formed groups in which the social worker makes the decision concerning whether to suggest membership to an applicant or client that there is most concern about group composition. "The very fact of group mixture in itself," according to Redl, "may sometimes play a great part in what happens in a group, even when the best conditions and the most skillful professional leadership are taken for granted."[42] If persons are placed in unsuitable groups, they may become a serious disturbance to the group, be harmed by the experience, or drop out of the group. If the composition of a group is faulty, it is less likely to become a viable and cohesive social system.

Knowledge of the factors that influence the participation of people is used by the worker to determine which ones seem most crucial to the purpose and the anticipated focus of the group. There is no such thing as a perfectly composed group, but it is important that the worker know with what he is dealing in this respect. Two basic questions to be raised are: Will an individual benefit from the group? Will he be able to participate in such a way that his presence will not interfere seriously with the realization of the purpose of the group for others? This is true for families as well as for formed groups.

Although there are many opinions about criteria for group composition, there has been little systematic study of who fits together in groups. Perhaps the most generally accepted principle is what Redl calls "the law of optimum distance": groups should be homogeneous in enough ways to insure their stability and heterogeneous in enough ways to insure their vitality.[43] This principle is based on the premise that the major dynamics in a group are mutual support and mutual stimulation among the members. Some balance is necessary so that no single member represents an extreme difference from other members, for this usually makes integration into the group unlikely. Clients who represent extremes on any one factor of significance in human relationships are usually not placed together.

McBroom has given two examples of the fit or lack of fit between a person and a group.

1. A young man suffering from a progressive and deforming illness was included in a therapy group. All other members were older women in far advanced stages of the illness. For obvious reasons, it was not possible for these patients to become a positive reference group for him and he assessed the experience concurrently and in retrospect as a negative episode in his illness and treatment career.
2. A group organized for patients with a progressive and fatal illness included members of both sexes, divergent ages and disease stages, and a spouse, parent, or adult child of each. This group, unlike the other, was diverse but not unbalanced. It offered sufficient complementarity to permit the interaction to become supportive to all members.[44]

Different results obtain from different combinations of people. It is really inappropriate to refer to groups as either homogeneous or heterogeneous; rather there will be certain common characteristics that make for a sense of commonality and certain differences that provide different inputs into the system.

The most important consideration in group composition is its purpose. The specific goals and needs of prospective members should be those that can be met through the purpose of the group. Whatever the purpose, it is essential that there be some common need or problematic situation to provide some focus for the content of group life. Goals of individuals need to be complementary and in harmony with the general purpose of the group.

Similarity in descriptive attributes can enhance the functioning of a group. People hesitate to join groups in which they feel very different from the other members. Similarity makes for compatibility and facilitates communication. Members of groups who share the experience of being in a similar stage of psychosocial development tend to face common life tasks to master and certain common interests to pursue. Within the several stages in the life cycle, differences in age influence group participation, but are more important in childhood than in adulthood. Sex-linked values and norms of behavior in our culture are important to the development of identity and successful role performance, even though these are changing rapidly. There are also values and norms for heterosexual relationships. Grouping by age and sex is often useful in that these similarities provide support for learning social roles. Yet, at other times and with different purposes, people need to learn new patterns of relationships directly with members of the other sex or with people of different ages.

There is a tendency for small groups in our society to be based on similarity in cultural values and practices associated with social class, race, religion, and nationality. Differences in such characteristics tend to separate people from one another in work, play, education, place of residence, and life style. These factors may be relevant to the purpose of the group; for example, when groups are formed to work toward improved interracial relationships, or to help members of a minority group to accept their own cultural background as a basis for integrating this facet into their basic sense of identity. These factors may not seem relevant to the purpose of the group but, since cultural differences influence attitudes, patterns of behavior, and interests, they cannot be ignored. They must be recognized. Plans must be made for utilizing differences as positive dynamics toward growth and change rather than as impediments to such movement. In some instances when there are language differences, there is a need for bilingual and bicultural workers.

There has been a tendency to place people with similar medical diagnoses in the same group. Such a common diagnosis tends toward the development of empathy among the members and protection from social ostracism. But, in relation to certain handicaps this may be a questionable practice. Handicapped people should have a chance to interact with other people. In one major program, physically handicapped children and normal children have been purposefully placed in the same group.[45] Delinquent youngsters have participated in groups with normal ones. In one research project, it was concluded that children labeled as delinquents could interact with a normal population with at least minimal success and minimal adverse effects on the normal members.[46] In another project, it was found that educable mentally retarded clients could be placed successfully in groups with those of average intelligence.[47]

The social worker is concerned not only with the nature of the capacities and problems of people, but with modes of coping with problems. How individuals express themselves, deal with tension and conflict, and defend themselves from threat and hurt influence the nature and content of group interaction. Diversity of ways of coping with problems facilitates the exchange of feelings and ideas among members, providing there is a potential for a strong bond in relation to the purpose and focus of the group. An individual's tendency to withdraw from relationships or to reach out aggressively to other people is especially important. Usually, extremely shy persons are not placed with extremely aggressive ones because of what is referred to as shock effect. Members who are too far from the behavioral level of others in the group may find themselves in intolerable inner conflict, stirred up by the faulty placement. An individual's ability to communicate through the use of verbal symbols is another important factor. If a group is to use predominantly verbal means of communication, the ability to express oneself verbally is essential. A nonverbal person often finds his problem intensified in a group of very active, talkative members. In groups of relatively nonverbal members, however, there is need, for some who can stimulate conversation at a level others can achieve.

When members live together and their problems are those of communication, relationships, and cooperative living, it is usually desirable to work with the unit as a whole. Examples would be a cottage group in a residential setting, a small group foster home, or a family. It is necessary to add the caution that sometimes people need to get away from their family or residence in order to look at it more objectively, and to consider and practice new patterns of behavior which later can be tested out in the group itself.

Closely related to purpose of group and characteristics of individuals are the agency policies and conditions that influence the particular persons to be included in a social work endeavor. Administrative considerations play an important part in determining who the practitioner will be and who can become a client. Policies determine such important matters as fees for service, the physical facilities available, the schedule of hours that an agency is open, the geographical areas from which clients come, and money available for expenses connected with using a service. Size of agency is itself an influence: the number of clients affect the criteria that can be taken into account in forming new groups. Such practical considerations often make possible the use of only a limited number of other criteria in determining the composition of a group. If the variety of factors is considered in planning for a new group, however, whether or not they can be implemented, the practitioner begins his work with knowledge of the influence of composition on the development of the group.

The importance of group composition as a crucial element in planning for social work with groups is underscored by a study by Boer and Lantz. In comparing a group in which composition was planned with another group in which it was not planned, the authors concluded: "The groundwork of membership selection that occurs before the group has as much importance in determining member commitment, attendance, and therapeutic results as does the ongoing group process."[48]

SIZE OF THE CLIENT SYSTEM

The dyad of worker-client is, of course, the smallest system. The smaller the group, the more it demands that each party become fully involved in it, the greater are both the potential and the demand for intimacy of relationships, the least anonymous are the actions and reactions of participants, the higher are the rates of participation of all parties, and the greater is the influence on each member. In the dyad, however, it is to be remembered that the balance of power is with the worker. In working with a couple, usually a marital or parent-child pair, there is actually a triangle, a three-person group. There is a tendency to develop a majority subsystem of two and a minority of one: the third person has the balance of power. At the beginning of treatment, the social worker is the outsider who has the balance of power. He disturbs the steady state. He is seen as either threatening the pair relationship or as serving to cement it. The smaller the group, the stronger are the pressures on each individual; so also the access of a member to the worker and of the worker to each member is easier. The smaller the group, the greater is its flexibility in modifying goals to meet the changing needs of individuals. With some groups, particularly those of children and adolescents, if a group is larger than eight to ten members, the worker cannot readily be available to each individual. In some instances, there may be more than one worker. It must be noted that too small a group may disintegrate with absences or withdrawal of members.

As the size of a group increases, each member has a larger number of relational ties to maintain. Formality in leadership tends to emerge and so do clearly defined subgroups. As groups enlarge, there is a tendency for more communication to be directed to the worker than to other members. Messages tend to be directed to the group rather than to particular individuals. Beyond a membership of eight to ten there is greater anonymity and also greater difficulty in achieving consensus in decision-making. A larger group tends to have greater tolerance for direction from a leader, and the more active members tend to dominate the interaction.

NUMBER OF PRACTITIONERS

Another issue in planning is the decision to have either one practitioner or co-workers who share responsibility for giving service. Traditionally, the usual pattern has been one worker, regardless of the size of the client system, but some social workers espouse the use of more than one worker.

One value of co-workers is that this procedure may improve the accuracy of the assessment and the objectivity of workers. One practitioner may observe something that another misses. A worker's perception of the group may become more realistic when tested against that of a colleague. The worker who is less active at a given time can note reactions of less verbal participants as well as those engaged in the immediate give and take.[49]

A second major value is the enrichment of treatment. A division of labor between workers makes it possible for one to focus on major themes of a group nature while the other can respond more frequently to individual concerns. It makes it possible for one worker to confront while the other provides necessary support or for one to reinforce the support given by the other. It provides more opportunities for learning new ways of communicating and problem-solving since the client can perceive how the workers communicate with each other and handle their differences. Workers thereby serve as models for clients. If the co-workers are of different sexes, an advantage is that they model sex roles for members and serve as objects of identification for members of the same sex. They also can model appropriate heterosexual relations. Yet, in a world in which sex roles are changing rapidly, the workers' own views of appropriate sex roles may be in conflict with those of one or more clients. There are different perceptions concerning definition of appropriate sex roles. The co-worker relationship is sometimes thought to symbolize the two-parent family which provides the potential for using the service as a corrective emotional experience.

The use of co-workers seems to be desirable in some groups where there is a realistic need for more than one worker, depending upon the size of the group, the nature of the content, and the needs and problems of the members. One example would be an activity group that is composed of children who are deficient in ability to verbalize feelings and ideas and who require a great amount of individual attention within the group. Another example would be a large multiple-family group, composed of several families who are also having family therapy. By participating in the multiple-family group, the practitioners are able to further the plan for integrating two forms of help.[50]

The most frequent use of more than one practitioner is as a vehicle for training practitioners, as distinguished from providing particular benefits to clients. A less able and less experienced worker can learn from observing another worker and from the feedback he receives from his colleague.

The rationale for the use of only one practitioner with a couple, family, or other group concerns the effect of additional workers on the group process. With the addition of a second worker, there is much greater complexity of relationships and communication with which each participant must cope. There is a subgroup of workers and another one of members. Each member must relate to the practitioner subsystem as well as to each of the workers in it. The balance of power shifts from the members toward the workers. With two or more workers participating, opportunities for members to participate are lessened. Each member of the group must develop and cope with a relationship with at least two professionals, which dilutes the intensity of the worker-individual relationship and the worker-group relationship. Each member must fathom the differences in expectations that each worker has for him and for the group. Members come to realize the fact that two practitioners are seldom truly equal in status, skill, and experience. They usually identify one of them as the primary leader and the other as his assistant. Being an assistant is not the same as fully sharing the authority and responsibility that are implied in the co-leader relationship.

Difficulties in working together are likely to be detrimental to the progress of the group. Frequent difficulties are those of rivalry for the love and attention of the members; struggles for power to influence particular individuals or the group's structure or content; pressures on each worker to prove his ability and to do at least his fair share of the work; and a tendency to divert primary attention from the group to the relationship between colleagues.

The practical matter of cost in time and money is a factor to be considered in making decisions concerning the number of workers assigned to a client system. The use of two workers is more than twice as expensive as is one worker only. Time is spent not only in individual and group sessions. If co-leadership efforts are to be successful, the practitioners need to review together each session, to work through their difficulties in roles and relationships, and to engage in ongoing planning together.

In one study of fifty therapists in conjoint family therapy, it was found that experienced therapists gradually reached a point of diminishing returns in satisfaction with co-therapy. They came to prefer to work as the sole therapist because they considered this to be a more effective way to serve clients.[51] In a survey of psychologists, psychiatrists, and social workers, it was also found that the more experienced practitioners no longer preferred the co-worker role.[52] A review of literature on outcome research on marital therapy indicated that no support was found for the view that co-therapy is more effective than treatment by a sole practitioner.[53] More research is obviously necessary to shed light on this subject. It seems most appropriate to use co-workers with large groups as in multiple-family therapy, with groups of couples, or in network therapy involving members of the client's extended family or neighborhood.

DURATION OF SERVICE

In work both with individuals and with groups, a major tendency has been to perceive service as ongoing without planned termination, with some notable exceptions. Perhaps this was due at least partially to the fact that most early social work was directed to the poor or disabled who had multiple problems, often including the need for continuous financial assistance or socialization into the American system. Although there has always been some emphasis on brief or short-term service, it has accelerated greatly in recent years. In reality, except in public welfare and group service agencies, most service has been short-term, but not necessarily planned as such. Most services developed for preventive purposes are short-term. Crisis intervention, travelers' aid, task-centered practice, and behavior modification are forms of practice which make planned use of limited time, both in work with individuals and with groups.

Several studies have found that short-term treatment in social work is at least as effective as continued service.[54] The advantages of short-term treatment are numerous. There are fewer unplanned terminations. A time limit discourages the often potentially destructive development of undue client dependency. It enhances a sense of hopefulness that positive changes will occur. Some people, particularly men, are more willing to participate in a time-limited service than in a long, continued one. Planned short-term treatment is thought to be most effective when the goals are improving communication, restoring equilibrium, or changing attitudes and behavior in particular defined situations, and when the focus of the service is on experiences in the present.

Some individuals and families need continued service beyond the six to twelve weeks usually considered maximum for short-term service. The issue is not whether brief or continued service can be effective, but rather under what circumstances brief service is preferable and under what circumstances extended service is preferable. There have been several demonstration projects of longer term services that have led to successful outcomes. These projects have included work with very troubled and disadvantaged young children, disturbed acting-out adolescents, regressed schizophrenic patients, and multiple-problem families.[55] Certainly some people can benefit optimally from brief service; others need a longer period of time.

•

LENGTH AND FREQUENCY OF SESSIONS

There has developed a convention of one-hour, weekly sessions as predominant in social work with individuals and slightly longer sessions for groups. Such a plan is suitable for certain client systems. Some clients need to be seen more frequently, however, or for longer sessions. One example would be an emergency in which a child has run away from a foster home. In such an instance, the worker needs to spend considerable time with the child and the foster family during a period of a few days. On the other hand, young children or severely disturbed, psychotic patients can tolerate only very short sessions, especially during the early phase of treatment. A convention also exists that practitioners work daytime hours on weekdays, an unfortunate situation. Many clients can come only during late afternoon and evening hours, and people do have emergencies on weekends. There is increasing recognition that working hours need to be adapted to the situations of clients if services are to meet their needs effectively.

Means of Entry Into the Service System

The extent to which a potential client is motivated to use a service influences the plan for service. The means by which an applicant takes the first step to contact an agency or a practitioner has great influence on his use of the service. Some potential clients seek help voluntarily; others are involuntary clients. The voluntary client's decision to apply for service is often the result of a number of interrelated decisions. He has already recognized that he wants something which he thinks an agency or a private practitioner might be able to offer. The desire may be for a resource such as financial aid, adoption, foster care, or medical treatment; family planning or family life education; counseling or therapy for some personal or social problem. In Kadushin's words:

> The prospective client who contacts the agency to schedule an interview has then made a decision which is the end result of a number of prior decisions, namely that she has a problem with which she wants the help of some professional person and has further identified the social agency as the source of such help.[56]

Many applicants make such decisions and are considered to be voluntary applicants. They may be self-referred or have been referred by another person. They may have learned about the service in varied ways. They may have learned about it through a representative of another organization, such as a teacher, employer, or judge. They may have learned about the service through the agency's publicity, as when a counseling service in a university publicizes its services to all students or when a youth-serving agency announces that it is starting a vocational exploration service for high school students and dropouts.

There has been increasing interest over the years in reaching out to prospective clients who do not seek service. In these instances, there is an active search for persons whom the worker or agency perceives to be in need of help. Reaching-out approaches are used in schools when the initial concern is usually expressed by a teacher or administrator who then tells a social worker about the pupil's needs. The child or his parents may or may not respond positively, but an agency of the community has decided that help should be offered. Cases in probation, work with delinquent gangs, and protective services in child welfare are other examples of this approach. These may become services that people want once they know about the positive intent of them, or people may be required to accept them or suffer some undesirable consequence.

Several authors make the point that a basic distinction appears between the roles of voluntary and involuntary clients. The voluntary role is assumed by the person because he hopes for some benefit from the service for himself or his family. Initial positive motivation, however, may vary from a strong desire to some reluctance to enter into an agreement with a social worker. The involuntary role is ascribed to the person because of some other status he occupies, such as being a parolee or because of some acts he is judged to have committed, such as child abuse. Initial motivation is a transient factor. People who come with high expectations of having a need met may lose this motivation during the course of the initial sessions if the worker is not attuned to their needs, their feelings about requesting service, and their psychosocial situation. People who come with active resistance can develop motivation to use a service effectively.[57] Webb and Riley conducted research that indicates that voluntary initiation of a service is not required for successful involvement of the client.[58] Results of such demonstrations as the St. Paul family-centered program for multiproblem families, work with delinquent gangs, and services to hard-to-reach adolescents indicate that many initially unwilling clients can be reached and can make good use of social work help. Other authors state that people can be changed even when initially they do not want to try, that motivation can be created.[59]

Even voluntary clients have ambivalent feelings about applying for a service. They almost always have some anxiety about a new experience: they have no way of knowing how they will be received and what will happen to them; they are hesitant about their own abilities to meet the practitioner's expectations. There is a sense of stigma attached to certain types of problems, such as a man's inability to provide for his family; certain illnesses such as epilepsy and cancer; and such behavior as child neglect and spouse abuse. The still prevalent ethic in America that people should be independent and pull themselves up by their bootstraps makes it difficult to admit a need for help.

The voluntary or involuntary aspect of service will have direct bearing on the process in the initial phase of service. It influences the length of time needed to achieve mutually acceptable goals and an effective working relationship between worker and client system.

In addition to the voluntary or involuntary initial motivation for service, other matters greatly influence the use of social work services. Ready accessibility of needed services is essential. Being kept on waiting lists reduces motivation to use a service. One study found that applicants who had waited the shortest period of time accepted the service when appointments were offered. In another study, it was found that one half of the applicants who had to wait nine weeks or more dropped out. Several other studies have confirmed the relationship between premature dropouts and length of waiting between sessions. Applicants who have longer waiting periods are less apt to keep their appointments. Agencies and practitioners, therefore, need to devise means for offering prompt help to those who need it.[60]

Case Illustrations

A LIFE EXPERIENCE GROUP

Social context. A new social worker in a senior citizens' center that served a lower middle-class Irish and Italian community had the task of determining what social work services were most appropriate to the needs of participants. The center offered a nutritious lunch to anyone over age sixty-two and had a variety of recreational and social activities. Coffee was served at the center in the morning in order to encourage socialization among the participants. Many of the participants had needs which required them to use other community resources, such as financial aid programs, alternative housing arrangements, and health facilities. The staff noticed that many clients did not make use of these services.

Need. From observations of the informal interactions among clients and from conferences with other staff, it became evident that additional services were needed by some clients. As the social worker interviewed participants, they shared their experiences in daily living and some of their concerns and problems. She became aware of concerns that were common to many of the clients: being a widow or widower, illness, fears of old age, family conflicts, and loneliness.

Selection of modality. Based on this information, it was noted that numerous problems were common to clients. The worker decided to offer a group experience to those who could benefit from what she called a Life Experience Group. She chose this title because she had learned that many members disliked staff who always focused on their problems or reacted negatively to suggestions that they might need therapy.

Means of entry. The worker posted a sign-up sheet, limited to twenty-five persons, to indicate interest in becoming a member of a Life Experience Group. She then met with each individual who had signed up, eliciting information about their current needs and situations and engaging them in thinking about what they might want from such a group. She gave information about what they might expect the group to be like, its general focus and expectations for members. She explored their readiness to share some of their own interests and personal concerns with others. A few people immediately responded that they couldn't do that. Others had concerns about such issues as housing and economic security, for which they needed immediate personal help. They were referred to particular staff members who could be most helpful to them at this time.

Structure. The worker had observed that most people left the center soon after lunch. She discovered that most of them used the afternoon for shopping, cleaning, and cooking and did not wish to remain at the center in the afternoon. She also recognized that the time of the group meeting should not conflict with popular center activities, such as a film or card party. She therefore decided to offer the group in the morning for one hour once a week.

Based on the pregroup interviews, twelve persons—eight women and four men—were selected for the group. They ranged in age from sixty-four to seventy-two. All had expressed difficulty in dealing with changes in their lives, such as death of a spouse or friend, aging, or conflict in family relationships. All indicated a desire and willingness to talk about these concerns and the problems they were facing. For all, participation in such a group would be a new experience. It was agreed that members would try the group for ten weeks, at which time they would evaluate progress and reassess whether continuation was indicated.

Purpose. The purpose of the group was discussed with the members, related to their own expressions of needs and what they wanted to be better in their lives. All agreed that the purpose of the group would be to gain in understanding themselves and their situations and to increase their ability to deal more effectively with the problems they were facing. Within this general purpose, individual goals for each member would be clarified.

AN INDIVIDUAL SERVICE

In the senior citizens' center, the social worker's exploration of the psychosocial needs of the members resulted in the provision of individual counseling for some of the members. One of these women was Mrs. O'Neill, age sixty-seven, who became a member of the center the day the social worker interviewed her. She was brought to the center by a friend and neighbor.

Means of entry into the service system. When the social worker approached Mrs. O'Neill with a desire to learn how the center might be helpful to her, she burst into tears and mumbled that nothing could help her. She was very upset, but gradually shared her concerns with the worker. Her husband had died two months ago and her life was not worth living without him. She was offered an immediate private interview, which she eagerly accepted.

Need. In exploration of her situation, the worker identified Mrs. O'Neill's need for support in the mourning process, help to make plans concerning her living arrangements, and help to resolve interpersonal conflict with her daughter. Mrs. O. has adequate income and wants to try to live independently, but her daughter is putting pressure on her to sell her home and move into a retirement home.

Goals. Based on a preliminary assessment of the client's immediate needs and her motivation to use help, the worker and client agreed to work together to relieve some of Mrs. O.'s anxiety about her future without a husband and to make a decision concerning her living arrangements. It was hoped, also, that Mrs. O. could find some way to relieve the tension with her daughter.

Selection of individual modality. Because Mrs. O'Neill was very upset and had been unable to participate in activities at the center, the worker offered her personal interviews, which were eagerly accepted. The worker also recognized that improvement in the relationship with her daughter would probably indicate joint interviews, but decided that Mrs. O. was not ready to use this modality. Mrs. O. also needs to develop new relationships, and, in addition to individual interviews, the worker will try to involve Mrs. O. in center activities and relate her to other clients with whom she can find some common bond.

Structure. Because Mrs. O. seems to be in a state of crisis, it was decided that the worker will meet with her twice a week for approximately an hour after lunch. The worker suggested that five or six weeks should be sufficient to achieve the goals, but that this arrangement would be evaluated before the end of that time. Mrs. O. was unable to consider the duration of the service because she felt she just did not see much hope for anything better in her life. She did accept the idea of meeting with the worker twice a week, but added that she would like to be able to call the worker between times if she is too upset. The worker agreed to this request.

Summary

Preservice planning has been presented as a problem-solving process in which a social worker uses knowledge to make decisions about a plan of service to be negotiated with a particular person or category of people. The required knowledge concerns the social context, the client system's needs, capacities, problems, and resources; the purposes that social work has accepted as within its professional domain and a specification of goals to guide the social worker's activities; the characteristics and values of the major modalities of practice; the structural components of client systems; and the means whereby clients get connected to a service. Through preservice planning the social worker strives to influence the conditions that are most likely to foster the effective use of a service which has been designed to meet the needs of particular people. Through effective planning, the social work experience becomes a significant environment for all those who participate in it.

CHAPTER SIX

The Initial Phase

Initial interviews have been presented as part of a process of planning individualized services to people. In such situations, a prospective client enters into a service system through some form of intake, which literally means to take in applications or requests for service. It is a process in which a request is made by or in behalf of a person, family, or group and a decision is made about the disposition of the application. The essential tasks in intake are to clarify the nature of the request; orient the applicant to the available services; determine the applicant's eligibility for and motivation to use a service; decide which particular service will be most suitable to the applicant's needs; and clarify the next steps in the process. The basic focus is on exploration of client need in relation to available resources. The intent is to facilitate the processing of an inquiry in the best interests of the applicant.

The Initial Interview

The social worker needs to prepare himself for the initial interview with an individual or group. He reviews whatever material is available, such as reports of telephoned requests for appointments, face sheets, or application forms completed by the applicant in advance of the interview. He uses his knowledge about biopsychosocial functioning of individuals as he thinks about the characteristics of the applicant and their potential influence on the initial encounter. He thereby uses available data for what Kadushin calls "anticipatory empathy," an effort by the worker to consider imaginatively the person in his situation.[1] Schwartz has a similar idea which he calls "tuning in," an effort by the worker to get in touch with feelings and concerns which a client may have about coming for help.[2] Within his general understanding of persons who have certain characteristics, he reminds himself that each individual and each family within a category is unique. The worker considers his own feelings concerning his preliminary expectations about the person, as reflected through whatever information is available to him. Kadushin says that

> Adequate preparation increases the interviewer's confidence, diminishes anxiety, and ensures a more positive start to the interaction. Since many routine problems to be encountered in the interview are thought out and resolved in advance, the interviewer's mind is freed to deal more adequately with unanticipated problems during the interview.[3]

The worker, however, needs to be alert to differences in expectations, so that he can really begin where the client is at the time. In some instances, the interviewer does not have facts about the applicant: he has only general knowledge about agency services and policies and the types of people for whom the services are designed.

The worker prepares for the interview by arranging the physical setting in order to reduce the applicant's anxiety and enhance participation in the process. He arranges the furniture in ways that optimize the potential for ease of communication and makes available materials, such as ash trays for adults and toys for children, that may reduce initial anxiety. Such seemingly minor details make a difference in the way the interview proceeds and in the applicant's satisfaction with it. Most intake interviews take place in the agency, except in reaching-out approaches when home visits are frequently made or when a worker makes a contact with a natural group, such as a gang.

Before a practitioner can offer service to an applicant, preliminary answers to a number of basic questions are sought. It is neither necessary nor possible to have complete information about a person in order to make a preliminary judgment about the suitability of a particular service for him. The worker begins with seeking whatever facts are clearly relevant to the decision to accept a person for service. He then continues to add to his knowledge as he judges what additional information will be helpful to him and to the applicant in making decisions concerning acceptance or rejection of a request for help. There needs to be a mutually acceptable definition of the need or problem and the type of service that is offered.

Exploration of the needs of applicants, in relation to available service, centers on the following questions:

1. What is the major request? What is the need the applicant is seeking to meet or the problem as he perceives it? Is the request one which the agency or worker can accept, at least tentatively?

2. How did the person, family, or other group happen to come to this particular agency at this particular time? What precipitated the decision to apply or to accede to the demands of a referral group?

3. What is the applicant's purpose or goals in terms of hoped-for outcomes? What does he hope will be different or better? Is there an immediate or short-range goal that can serve as a basis for further exploration?

4. What are the applicant's expectations concerning the nature and focus of the service? How do these mesh with the worker's expectations and the agency's resources?

5. What can be offered by this agency or this practitioner at this time? Does the applicant meet eligibility requirements or can these be waived? Is there need for further exploration in additional interviews? What alternatives or combinations of services are available—individual, family, group, or environmental interventions? Which modality seems most suitable to the client's needs at this time? If an appropriate service cannot be offered, can an alternative plan for referral elsewhere be developed?

6. What are the next steps in the process to assure that the applicant gets the necessary service? Will the same worker continue with the client.? If not, who will meet with him next time? When? Where? How can he get connected most easily to the next step?

PROCEDURES AND PRINCIPLES

The form and length of the intake process vary depending upon the agency's purpose, functions, and policies and the need for which a service was designed. The simplest form of intake occurs when participation is voluntary and when the service is designed to serve whoever responds to publicity about a program. Such services are usually preventive or developmental ones. Examples are parent or family life education, crisis intervention centers, or groups for prospective adoptive parents. When people respond to such recruitment, there is usually a registration process in which essential identifying information is secured that is necessary for determining eligibility and agency accountability. Brief interviews usually take place to provide information about the service so that the applicant's expectations are within the intent of the program, to screen out persons who might not be suitable, to orient applicants to the nature of the service which is being offered, and perhaps to inform them of alternative services that might be appropriate. Essentially, in this type of intake, the process is largely one of self-selection and registration of clientele who meet the eligibility requirements. Even though the initial interview is brief and informal, the intake worker is sensitive to the applicant's desires and motivation and is the crucial bridge to a meaningful service.

In some organizations, application and intake procedures are formal and continue through a period of study, diagnosis, and planning for treatment prior to the assignment of a client to a regular worker. Sometimes a group experience may be a part of the preliminary process, used for purposes of assessment and planning.[4] A conference with an entire family, often in its home, may take place in instances in which faulty functioning of the family as a group is thought to be central to the problem of an individual or of the family system. The most prolonged intake procedures usually occur in health clinics. A social worker may be assigned to interview the applicant to determine his eligibility and to make a psychosocial study of his problems and situation. Often the applicant is seen also by other members of the diagnostic and treatment team, such as psychologists, psychiatrists, physicians, and physical therapists. It is in the meeting of the professional team, then, that a decision is made about whether or not the case will be accepted and, if so, the type of treatment to be offered. The needs of applicants are assessed in relation to the constellation of individual and group services which comprise the functions of the organization. Whatever the procedures, the applicant should be assigned to a service immediately rather than placed on a waiting list.

A number of principles have been proposed to guide the intake worker.[5] They are to be used flexibly, with due regard for the client's initial presentation of self.

1. The social worker expresses clearly, simply, and explicitly his understanding of the purpose of the interview. Such statements enable the client to respond appropriately and allay initial confusion and anxiety. He solicits reactions to his statements and gives additional information as it is needed by the applicant.

2. The worker is sensitive to the applicant's situation. He elicits facts and feelings, according to the applicant's readiness, without requiring undue exposure of self. He views the client as the primary source of information. Data are collected only if they have a bearing on the request or need.

3. The worker treats the person, family, or group as an applicant until there is acceptance of a client role and an initial agreement on the nature of service to be given. Except when client status is compulsory, he has no right to interfere in the life of another person until that person has given permission.

4. The worker establishes a time-limited relationship which is characterized by interest in each person present, acceptance, positive regard, and an attitude of hope and encouragement.

5. The worker acknowledges the applicant's ambivalence about accepting a service and about becoming a client. He recognizes and accepts the feelings, and clarifies the general purpose and nature of the proposed service; and he engages the applicant in a problem-solving process directed toward making a tentative decision about the use of a service.

6. The worker maximizes the applicant's motivation by working to achieve an optimal balance of hope and discomfort. Realistic hope of a favorable outcome is encouraged; problems are defined as capable of resolution with effort; and realistic expectations are identified.

7. The worker takes responsibility for helping the applicant to meet eligibility requirements, or to modify the conditions, when possible, and when such changes are in the best interests of the applicant.

8. The worker, in interviewing more than one client simulta-

neously, elicits participation by all in each aspect of the initial problem-solving. He individualizes each person while he searches for the common threads and common goals.

9. The worker, if the applicant decides to continue, engages him in a problem-solving process concerning a tentative choice of at least a short-term goal to be worked toward in the next session.

The data for the worker's initial assessment of client need began with the first information he received about the applicant and his situation. During the initial interview, he has explored the facts with the client, using them in order to understand the individual, couple, family, or other collectivity in relation to one or more alternative services. He has reached a preliminary assessment which leads to a decision about an applicant's eligibility for service according to the requirements of a particular agency or private practitioner's priorities. The assessment leads to a joint decision about whether or not an applicant wishes to continue, at least for another time. If the decision is to continue, the worker who does the intake may continue with the case or the applicant may be assigned to another social worker for individual, family, or group help, or for some combination of these modalities. Knowledge about the particular value and characteristics of each modality, as described in the chapter on planning, guides the worker in assisting the client to make a decision about the type of service he will accept.

The social worker's relationship with a prospective client may begin at the point of the person's application for service or referral to a service. It more often begins once the decision has been made to try out an agreed-upon service. Whatever has been learned about the client system-environment in the intake process needs to be conveyed to the worker who now has responsibility for the case. If a person is to receive service through a formed group, the worker usually has one or more interviews with the individual in order to establish an initial relationship. Such interviews provide an opportunity to explore the person's reactions to placement in a group, to clarify expectations, and determine what benefits the group might offer. The new member, likewise, has an opportunity to become acquainted with the worker. Such interviews tend to diminish the anxiety and confusion which are characteristic of first sessions of groups in which all participants are strangers to each other. Since people are often referred to groups because social relationships are difficult for them, they need help to try out the group situation. Through one or more preliminary interviews, a relationship may be initiated between the worker and the member which can serve as a bridge for member-to-member relationships within the group.

The fact that a tentative decision was made at intake for a client to continue does not mean that the work of the early phase of service is completed. Usually it takes time for the worker, who has been assigned the case to develop a working relationship with the client system, to clarify the purposes and ways of working together, and to prepare the individual or group for actively working toward the achievement of desired goals. The principles that were enunciated for the initial interview guide the practitioner during the remainder of the initial phase. Planning, assessing, and treating are interrelated processes. They incorporate professional values and knowledge about clients in their interacting social relationships.

Development of Relationship

RELATIONSHIP AND EMPATHY

An important task in the early phase of service is to achieve the quality of relationship that will make it possible for the client to have confidence in the worker's genuine concern for his welfare. In work with groups, an additional task is to develop relationships among the members. Clients cannot have confidence in a worker until they have tested the worker's concern for them. Trust does not develop all at once. It develops as clients have experiences that successfully test the worker's interest in them, through observing the worker's responses to their verbal and nonverbal behaviors. Achievement of trust is relatively easy or hard, depending upon the extent to which clients previously have achieved a basic sense of trust. If a person has not worked through fairly satisfactorily the basic issue of trust versus mistrust, he repeats feelings of being unloved or rejected; he is often suspicious of other people; and he lacks confidence in himself and others. Each new relationship offers some occasion for mistrust until the unknown becomes familiar. With an appropriate amount of support, acceptance, and empathy from the worker, clients who have a healthy sense of trust will move rather quickly into an appropriate relationship with the worker. The less their ability to trust, the more difficult this will be. As clients develop trust, they gradually become ready to take more risks in participation in the helping process.

Understanding the ambivalence of clients and the flow of emotion between worker and clients and among members of groups is essential as a base for using these often conflicting desires and feelings for the benefit of the clients. One of the greatest concerns of a new client is with his relationship to the worker and, if in a group, to the other members. One concern has to do with acceptance by others. The client may wonder: Will the worker like me, be interested in me, and accept me? Will I like the worker? If I am in a group, will the other members accept me and will I accept them? Will I be ignored or rejected? Who is the worker's favorite client? The fear of not being loved often runs deep and pervades much of the initial behavior of clients in new situations. Closely related to the issue of love is that of intimacy. The client may ask himself: How much will I need to disclose my thoughts and feelings? How close will we get to each other? Will my privacy be violated so that I am forced to reveal my most innermost self to another? The third major concern of most clients is the issue of power and control. The client may wonder: Who will control what goes on? How much freedom will I have? How much can I determine what will happen? How dependent will I have to become to get what I yearn for? How will the information I provide be used? The clients ask these questions in many ways, but seldom in the form presented here and often through nonverbal means. The worker needs to be sensitive to their feelings and reactions and to be able to control his own feelings and reactions toward them.

As the social worker comes to understand the way in which a client perceives his relationship with the worker and with other participants, if there are any, he has an opportunity to support these perceptions or to help the client to modify them. His acceptance of the client, ability to empathize with the client, and his authentic behavior are the major influences on the clients' attitudes. As worker and client develop mutual understanding about the goals toward which they are working and about their respective roles, their positive feelings toward each other are enhanced. In families and groups, in addition to the client roles, the ways in which members enact their roles influences the nature and value of their interpersonal relationships. The worker therefore supports the patterns of behavior that are growth-enhancing and that are satisfying to the persons concerned. He actively works to change the patterns of roles that are not complementary or that are dysfunctional for an individual or the group.

Self-awareness. Through his own attitudes and behavior, the worker tries to convey acceptance, accurate empathy, and genuineness. He faces numerous challenges to his skill in facilitating the development of relationships that will further the client's goals. In order to develop an effective working relationship, he needs to be sensitive to his own interpersonal needs. He learns to recognize that each client has a particular psychological meaning for him. He may react with fear, hostility, affection, or overprotection: some clients trigger such reactions. A clinging, dependent client, for example, may reactivate an unresolved dependency need. An elderly client may stir up feelings of inadequacy or fear of aging and death. A client who complains continuously about other people may stir up feelings of impatience.

It is hard for some workers to accept conflicts as constructive and useful in problem-solving, so they tend to deny the conflict, which only erupts later in less constructive ways. It is often difficult to deal with personal questions relating to age, race, education, or marital status because they are mistakenly perceived as threats to professional competence. Such potential difficulties require that the worker have self-understanding and an ability to recognize the meaning of these reactions for his work with clients. He can replace these nonhelpful reactions with acceptance and empathy, which helps the client and reduces the worker's discomfort and anxiety in relation to them. Such achievement is illustrated by a report from a student:

Mrs. James did not come for her second appointment. Before I telephoned her about this matter, I read my process notes from the previous interview. I was shocked to recognize how judgmental I had been: her style of life and values were so different from mine. I had unintentionally passed judgment on her in a negative way, and I think she must have felt my lack of genuine acceptance. In evaluating the case with my supervisor, I recognized certain strengths that I had overlooked because of my concerns about her life style. In the telephone conversation, I was pleased that I was able to express genuine concern for her and that she accepted another appointment. She kept that appointment and we were able to establish a good relationship.

Other special problems in relationships often emerge in work with families and other groups. Many social workers have difficulty in expressing empathy with all members of a group and with the group as a whole. They may tend to identify with children against their parents or with shy, conforming members more than with outwardly aggressive ones. They may take over parental roles rather than help the parents to learn to be more effective. They may find it easier to accept positive statements than to deal with the negative aspects of relationships among members. They may find it difficult to feel comfortable with the considerable testing of them that takes place through such means as rambling discussions, provocative questions or comments, or disruptive activities. If a group is composed of clients from more than one ethnic category, social class, or religion, workers are challenged to help the members to bridge the differences among them. As workers become more able to recognize and then control these difficulties, they become able to enhance the development of a sense of cohesiveness or group bond, which is the result of the degree to which members have achieved psychosocial closeness to each other. This bond, in turn, provides a strong motivation for members to continue in the group.

EFFECT OF CULTURE ON RELATIONSHIPS

Ethnicity and social class of client and worker influence the development of effective working relationships. Characteristics of the worker interact with those of the other participants in the process. First impressions are important. Each person, worker and client alike, often unconsciously tends to evaluate the other in terms of certain stereotypes which are based on ignorance or preconceptions about differences between them and on prior experiences with apparently similar people.

Depending upon prior experiences with people of other races or ethnic groups, a quality of mutual strangeness may pervade the initial meeting. Both parties to the relationship feel uncertain about the other's feelings and expectations, with accompanying suspicion or fear. A white worker usually feels guilty because of his membership in a racist society and because of his feelings of discomfort when he is with a client who makes him feel uncomfortable.

Stereotyping is a major deterrent to developing and sustaining effective relationships. Some practitioners are not able to respond to a client of a different race as a unique person, instead of as a symbol of a particular category of people.[6] It is imperative that cultural differences be recognized and respected and that ethnic identity be fostered. Attention to culture must not, however, be at the expense of individualization. Cooper indicates that if ethnicity is overemphasized, clients "tend to lose their individual richness and complexity: there is the danger of no longer treating people—only culture carriers."[7] A worker may emphasize ethnic factors to such an extent that individual problems and solutions become obscured. Kadushin makes a similar point that a worker needs to have awareness of his reactions to racial differences. If he exaggerates race as a factor in treatment, he may oversimplify the client's problems and attribute certain difficulties to race that may be due to other difficulties in psychosocial functioning.[8] The point is important, but lack of emphasis on culture may also oversimplify the client's problems. Cultural factors need to be viewed as they interact with psychological and environmental ones in a particular situation.

Race is a problem in social work practice; it is a problem to be worked on, particularly when the race of the client and worker differ.[9] Clients from minority groups have valid reasons for initial distrust of white practitioners because many white people are prejudiced and discriminate against nonwhite people in many subtle and overt ways. The barriers between white workers and clients of different races need to be recognized and dealt with early in a relationship. Traditionally, practitioners have tended to avoid color differences. If a worker is able to communicate his awareness of the ethnic difference in a sensitive manner, the potential for developing a helping relationship is enhanced and the client is more apt to continue with the worker than if these differences are denied or ignored. The worker begins to bring differences into the open by introducing the subject at an appropriate time and then responding sensitively to the client's feedback.[10]

A wide range of individual differences exists within each ethnosystem and there is considerable overlapping among the groups, but there still are some recognizable constellations of values that are unique to each major ethnosystem. The practitioner needs to bridge the social distance that exists between himself and his client: he must be able to move toward the client. Such movement requires that the worker "understand the values and norms of another cultural system, of one's own system, be aware of where differences lie, and accept both as legitimate."[11]

Clients who have experienced discrimination are often particularly sensitive to the social worker's attitudes in the initial contact. They value being treated with respect but they have often not been so treated. Effective work with clients requires that the worker observe those formalities that are overt indications of respect, such as proper introductions, use of titles and surnames, and shaking hands. Such formalities are important to black clients who have been denied these symbols of courtesy. They are important to people of other cultures also. An example is given by Velasquez and associates who point out that the Spanish language includes two terms for use in addressing another person, depending upon the person's status in terms of both age and social role. Addressing a person who is older or in a position of authority by his first name is not perceived as a friendly gesture, but as lack of respect: a social worker is in a position of authority and therefore should be addressed by his surname and title. It is a sign of disrespect for a Latino client to disagree with a person in a position of authority. If unaware of this cultural norm, a worker may misinterpret silence or acquiescence as resistance, which militates against the development of a relationship characterized by mutual trust.[12] Another example is provided by Aguilar. In the Mexican-American culture it is the custom to have an informal and personalized conversation before entering into a business transaction.

In making initial contacts with Mexican Americans, it is essential to begin the interview with an informal and leisurely conversation.[13] Hammond also emphasizes the importance of informality and personalized contacts in establishing relationships with native Americans.[14]

Within many Asian cultures there is a similar expectation that time will be taken for social amenities and for getting to know a person before "getting down to business." The offering and acceptance of a cup of tea is frequently an important part of setting a climate which will be comfortable for the discussion of problems.

In some Asian cultures, for example the Japanese culture, respect for authority is a basic part of behavior expectations. For persons reared in very traditional families, it may be exceedingly difficult to disagree with someone in a position of authority. The social worker in such a situation must be very careful not to press family members for agreement or a conclusion before there is sufficient comfort to express difference. In a cultural situation where the expectation is to agree with the expert, it becomes important for the worker to pose options and to foster discussion rather than assume that the first "yes" signifies agreement or support of an idea. Etiquette may dictate agreement when an "expert" makes a suggestion. The worker needs to develop a climate that is sufficiently supporting to allow for discussion and sufficiently safe to allow for expression of feelings rather than the enactment of expected role behavior.[15]

Cultural differences may intensify feelings of suspiciousness and distrust toward the worker. Problems in relationships often derive from differences in perceptions of social institutions. Social workers may view police, schools, recreation centers, public welfare departments, and health facilities as supportive and protective agencies. Some clients, however, associate such institutions with unsavory past experiences of failure, rejection, devaluation, or ethnic prejudice against them. There is ample reason for them, therefore, to distrust the social worker and the social agency until the worker can demonstrate his interest, acceptance, empathy, and ability to help. Social institutions are potential resources for clients, but their effective utilization is dependent upon the clients' perceptions of, and prior experiences with, them. If the worker understands the basis for clients' attitudes, he can then find ways to help them make use of available opportunities.

Anger of an oppressed person toward institutions may be displaced onto the worker. Even when a worker displays acceptance, empathy, and authenticity, the client may not feel that the worker cares for him. The client may distort the worker's intent and behavior. A worker is often hesitant to discuss such problems with the client. But in order to develop the understanding of self and others that is essential to social competence, a client needs to have a worker who can explore the feelings that the client has toward him and then, when indicated, confront him with the facts of distortion. When the worker is too threatened to open up the issue, "the client is denied an opportunity to learn something about himself and how he relates to others."[16] The worker's failure to explore the problem with the client interferes with the development of a helping relationship.

White workers attempt to defend themselves in many ways against the anger and distrust of some clients of other races and against their own feelings of guilt toward members of minority groups. They may deny the ethnic differences, overidentify with a client, or set lower expectations for him than they would for a white, middle-class client. On the other hand, they may feel a need to set such high standards that the client is doomed to failure. They may have fantasies that they can make up for all of the client's past deprivations. The basic solution is introspective efforts to recognize their feelings and then to focus on the client in his situation, with efforts to accept him as a unique individual and to empathize with him.

Workers of minority ethnic backgrounds may have some of the same difficulties in relating to clients of a different race. As is true when white workers connect with clients, the minority worker needs to be able to accept his own and the client's ethnicity.[17]

When worker and client share a similar ethnic background. it is often easier for the worker to accept and empathize with the client. Similarity between worker and client may provide the client with a positive model of his ethnicity. Matching worker and client in regard to ethnicity has the advantage of fostering a sense of comfort in sharing certain identifiable physical and social characteristics and of understanding the culture into which both were socialized. It is, however, easy to overemphasize the similarities within a category and to fail to take into account the many individual and family differences. It has been noted, for example, that in black client-black practitioner relationships, problems often develop due to the practitioner's tendency either to deny his common tie with the client or to overidentify with him. In spite of sharing a common racial experience, unless the worker can recognize his own countertransference reactions and learn to control them, it is unlikely that an effective working relationship will develop.[18]

There are both positive and negative implications for work across ethnic lines. It is possible to capitalize on the values that come from learning about and facing differences as well as from learning about and facing similarities. The social distance between people can be reduced. In Kadushin's words:

> If the worker's professional training enhances the ability to empathize with and understand different groups and provides the knowledge base for such understanding, the social and psychological distance between worker and client can be reduced. If the gap is sufficiently reduced, clients perceive workers as being capable of understanding them, even though they are the products of a different life experience.[19]

Ethnicity interacts with social class, complicating the potential barriers to effective worker-client relationships. Social class differences largely determine the people with whom one associates and with whom one feels comfortable. Unless a social worker is tuned in to the importance of money and other material resources in relating to people, he is apt to blame the client for certain problems in social living. Stereotypes about a culture of poverty or of the limited potentials of poor people interfere with developing truly helping relationships that build on strengths and hopes for a better future.

Questions are raised about the influence of gender on the development of relationships. There is concern by many women that counselors and therapists tend to perpetuate sex-role stereotypes, and this "may harm rather than help their patients by training them to conform to narrowly defined roles and adjust to unhealthy life situations."[20] From a review of research on psychotherapy and behavior change, it was concluded that the effect of the therapist's sex as an effect on outcome has not been confirmed.[21] Nevertheless, as with ethnic and social class differences, social workers need self-awareness and sensitivity to sex-role issues. It is probable that the attitudes and values of the practitioner, rather than sex per se, are of primary importance in the development of a worker-client-system relationship.

CONFIDENTIALITY

Even though confidentiality is a professional value, many people who come for social work service fear that the social worker will violate their rights to privacy by revealing what he knows about them to others and that such information will harm them. Certainly, a client is assured that the worker will try to hold in strict confidence what goes on in the social work situation, except under certain circumstances. When foreseeable, these exceptions need to be explained to the client. Common exceptions to confidentiality are the use of information within the agency for purposes of supervision and collaboration, presumably for the benefit of the client. In some agencies, it has become customary to use audio- or videotapes and direct observations of clients for training and research purposes. Clients have a right to refuse to participate in such experiences without penalty; and they have a right to know the details of how the information will be used, to whom it will be made available, and under what conditions. These details should be provided in written form and informed consent secured in writing. When clients are children, their parents need to sign consent forms. The careless use of such documents can harm clients, who then have every right to protest against invasions of privacy. Parents may need to be informed about certain aspects of the treatment of their children. The worker must be clear about how much assurance he can give that what he learns about clients will be held in confidence. In order to disclose information about themselves and their situations, most clients need to be assured about the confidential nature of the relationship.

A particular dilemma for social workers is that they usually are not protected by immunity to giving information, through statutes that grant privileged communication to protect clients in legal proceedings unless the client waives this privilege. Several states have some degree of privileged communication for clients of social workers, usually as part of licensing laws.[22] Even in these instances, certain information is not privileged; for example, certain medical conditions must be reported as must child abuse. A practitioner does not violate the principle of confidentiality if he is required by law to report specific information or if the client's behavior poses clear danger to himself, as in attempted suicide or danger to others, such as intent to kill or to commit other crimes. Giving information to insurance companies, turning over unpaid bills to collection agencies without informing the client, giving information relative to taxes, and providing information about a client to his employer are invasions of privacy and hence unethical behavior on the part of the social worker, unless he has the client's informed consent to divulge such information.

In work with families and other groups, there is an additional concern with the ethics of each member in the use of information he receives about other members. As members disclose their feelings, ideas, and experiences to each other, the worker cannot make promises about the members' use of knowledge about each other. But this fact does not absolve him of ethical responsibility. He makes clear to all that he hopes that members will be able to express what they feel and think without fear that he will share this information outside the group, unless he informs them about it first and, when possible, secures their informed consent. In this respect the worker serves as a model for the members; in addition, he expresses expectations that they will hold in confidence information they derive about each other.

Motivation and Resistance

Motivation is "the amount of pressure a client feels to effect change in his problem situation."[23] The pressure stems from the perceived gap between what is and what ought to be and from perceived possibilities of closing the gap. Engagement in the use of help requires recognition of some need or problem that is appropriate to the services offered; acceptance of some responsibility for a part in the situation; willingness to share feelings, thoughts, or experiences with a practitioner and often also with members of a family or formed group; and a decision to invest energy, time, and perhaps money in the effort. When a decision about these matters is made by a client, he is motivated to use the help that is offered.

It was noted in an earlier chapter that some clients initiate a request for service because they expect benefit from so doing and that some come because they have been sent by others, but do not perceive that they need the service. When clients initiate the encounter or respond positively to a reaching-out approach by a worker, they are likely to be motivated to use the service. Such clients are usually ready to learn about the service, to engage in decision-making concerning the particular service to be used, and to become involved with the worker in exploring specific needs or problems and working toward mutually derived goals. When clients reject the idea that service will be beneficial and are not ready to engage themselves in using help, the initial phase will be prolonged. The worker can anticipate that there will be considerable denial or projection of problems on others and great ambivalence about becoming involved with the worker. The worker will need actively to enable such a client to find some goal, no matter how small, that he is willing to work toward. At the same time, he will need to deal with the ambivalence and projection that block the movement into relationship. Even though the client denies the problem or the possibility of any positive change in it, he does have some dissatisfaction with himself or his situation. The feelings of discomfort can be brought out through direct statements that a person thought the client was in enough trouble to send him for help, and through exploration of his feelings and ideas about that fact, the persons who referred him, and the circumstances that led to the referral. There is usually some thread of concern that the worker can pick up, such as being able to do something different enough "to get dad off your back," or to "keep you out of jail."

An example of a client who was initially resistant to service is Billy, a sixteen-year-old black boy, who was referred to a youth-family counseling center by the local police department. Because he was involved in three auto thefts within a period of five days, the police regarded this case as one that merited our attention. The social worker, a black man, was assigned to study the offense, the child and his family, and the environmental influences affecting his behavior in order to recommend whether the family could be helped by our agency or what other plans should be made for Billy. A report from the school indicated that Billy's schoolwork is poor and that his conduct both in and out of class is unsatisfactory. Teachers report that he is sullen, defiant, and uncooperative. His choice of companions and activities is questionable. He has not, however, been in trouble with the police before this time.

Billy lives with his mother, Mrs. Grant, in a rented five-room house located in a residential neighborhood of modest homes. His mother has worked periodically in the past, but she is now unemployed and receives AFDC payments. She has been in poor health most of her life. She is a deeply religious person and insists that Billy practice his religion seriously and engage in church activities. Soon after completing high school, Mrs. G. met and became pregnant by Billy's father. Although he refused to marry her, they lived together for several years. She reported that he beat her on numerous occasions. She left him and soon after married Mr. G., whom she divorced a year later because of his heavy drinking and irresponsibility.

Billy did not keep his first appointment, so I arranged to meet him at school and we had our discussion in my car as I drove him home. He is average height for his age, slight in build, rather nice looking in appearance, but his face was clouded with a somewhat depressed look. Initially, he was extremely defensive and brusque. He seemed to be expecting a punitive, authoritarian approach and was acting accordingly. I told him who I was, the agency I represented, and explained why I was here. I remarked that, as he knew, the police and school were concerned about his behavior. I was here to get acquainted with him and his family and to talk with him and his mother about any difficulties they were having.

Billy relaxed slightly, and I asked if there were any questions he wanted to ask me. After a long silence, he said that he wanted to know what the outcome of all this would be. I said that I could understand his anxiety about what was going to happen next because of the seriousness of what he had done. I wished I could tell him, but I would have to know more about him and his situation before I could honestly tell him what my recommendation to the police would be. Billy said that was fair, but he hoped it wouldn't take too long because he was very nervous. When I asked about these feelings, he said that he did not think he could take being sent away to be locked up with "nothing but boys for six months or more." I said I thought I could understand his not wanting to be sent away from home, but was there something particular that worried him about living with other boys. He replied that he had heard many stories about what went on in forestry camps and that boys who had been in juvenile hall for a long time "might do anything." After some additional exploring, he was able to admit his fear of homosexual attacks by other boys. . . . Later, in our discussion, he said that it was always black kids who get sent away.

I said it was clear to me that he had a lot of worries about what might happen to him and that he was wondering himself about how he got himself into this mess. With his voice reflecting pent-up feelings of anger and resentment, Billy said he got so fed up with things at home that he just couldn't take it anymore— he just doesn't care anymore. I wondered if there were things he could tell me about what gave him such feelings. He replied that his mother refused to let him have a car even if he got a job to pay for it. She also denied him permission to obtain a driver's license even though he had successfully completed driver's education. He got so tired of begging and pleading that he decided he'd have a car even if he had to steal it, and now he's in a worse mess than ever. . . . As he complained about his mother, he became more and more excited. He resented the fact that everything he wanted was refused him: all decisions about him have been made by his mother and her relatives. . . . I agreed that sometimes kids think their parents will never understand them, which makes them pretty mad.

I said I had learned from him that he and his mother have difficulties in getting along together, and I would like to try to help both of them to work things out so that there would not be these bad feelings between them. Billy remarked, with some bitterness, that his mother and relatives just did not trust him, and he gave examples of what he meant by that statement. I said he seemed to think that no one can be of much help to him, perhaps including me. He did not respond to this statement. I asked if he would be willing to try to work with me to talk more about his feelings and the things that bothered him, and to meet with me and his mother to try to find ways to get along better. He said he was willing to try anything.

When we arrived at his home, I told Billy I would meet him after school next week. Billy said he could use someone to talk to because he was so discouraged that he did not know which way to turn. I walked him to the door, where we were greeted by Mrs. Grant. I told her of my plan to see Billy again next week and hoped that she would agree to meet with us to discuss the family's problems. She expressed concern about the trouble Billy was in, and agreed to be home to meet with us.

In an analysis of this interview, the social worker thought he had overcome some of Billy's initial resistance that seemed to be related to his perceptions of the worker as a punitive person, the worker's power to make a recommendation about the disposition of the case to the police, a sense of hopelessness and despair, and a great lack of trust in adults. He reached out to Billy by meeting him in familiar surroundings and driving him home in his car, thus creating an atmosphere of informality. At the same time, he presented himself and his responsibility clearly. In the communication between the worker and his client, the worker observed and responded to Billy's nonverbal behavior, gave Billy opportunities to ask questions and answered them simply and honestly, explored and understood Billy's feelings and his perceptions of the problems in an accepting way, and felt and conveyed an attitude of empathy through words and manner. He offered some hope that Billy's relationship with his mother and other adults could be improved. He selectively used techniques that are most appropriate in the initial phase in the categories of support, structuring, exploration, education, and clarification of purpose and roles. He gained considerable information that will be helpful in formulating a biopsychosocial assessment as a basis for a viable treatment plan.

Most new clients, like Billy, are not completely motivated to use a service. Even when they apply voluntarily, they begin with considerable ambivalence. They simultaneously have antithetic emotions and attitudes. It is natural for people to have mixed feelings about other people and situations; they come to new experiences both wanting and fearing them. It is anxiety-provoking to find one's way through a maze of customs and procedures that are specific to a particular kind of service. In order to gratify some of their desires, clients have to deny others. Being a client requires giving as well as receiving, and it requires some degree of involvement of self in the process. In group situations, the demand for giving as well as receiving is perhaps even greater than in the one-to-one relationship.

There are multiple reasons for resisting the help that is offered and often desired.[24] It is difficult for some clients to identify with the role of client and accept help from a professional person. Clients may be reluctant to admit that they need help from an outsider. They may regard inability to cope adequately with their difficulties or to provide necessary resources for themselves as serious weakness. If they value independence more than interdependence, they believe that they should be able to "pull themselves up by their own bootstraps." If they need financial assistance or other tangible resources, they may feel humiliated and embarrassed at having to secure these through social agencies or they may feel ashamed to request a reduction in usual fees. If they have been victimized by an unjust and racist society, they may feel hostility toward agencies that are a part of that society. Some people find it difficult to accept a role as client because they associate the present experience with similar past experiences that were unpleasant. If they have had prior experience with a social agency, and were dissatisfied with the content, process, or outcome, they may not expect that it can be better this time. These are examples of obstacles to achieving a positive identity as a client.

Resistance in the early phase may be related to fear or, at least, to uncertainty about the unknown. It is natural to feel fearful about what any new endeavor will entail and hesitant about becoming involved in it. Use of professional help is a new experience for most clients so that they lack adequate knowledge of what is expected of them and what they can expect of the worker and of other members, if they are in a group. They may fear they will not be able to meet expectations and thus fail again. They may doubt that their needs and goals are appropriate to this particular situation.

Resistance may take the form of reluctance to become involved in a relationship with a social worker and also with other clients, if the service is given through a group. Some insecurity or even psychic trauma is natural as a person meets with one or more strangers. Entering into new relationships is often particularly difficult for clients who are having difficulties in relating to other people. Anxiety about relationships varies from minimal concerns to deep paranoid terrors. Entering into a new relationship stirs up earlier conflicts about a person's acceptability to others, trust versus distrust, exposure of all of one's vulnerabilities to others, fear of being controlled, and fear of closeness and intimacy.

Children are often reluctant to discuss difficulties at home or at school because they are dependent upon their parents, guardians, and school personnel. They fear that what the worker shares with other adults will be used against them: they fear collusion between the worker and other adults. Work with a child almost always involves work with the significant adults in his life. Full confidentiality cannot be promised, but it is reassuring to the child to be told that the worker will be talking with certain adults, the reasons for doing so, and what kind of information will be shared and what will not be shared. As a worker prepares himself to work with a child alone, as part of a family, or as a member of a group, he can imaginatively reflect on what it would be like "to walk in the child's moccasins." He can reflect on the possible mood of the child when he comes to the first session: fear of being seen as bad or sick; fear of losing control of his feelings; doubt about a strange new adult who is neither a teacher, doctor, parent, relative, nor recreation leader. As he gets started with a child or a group, a simple statement introducing himself and explaining what they will be doing together tends to reduce anxiety and prepare the child for his part in the process.

As the worker senses evidences of anxiety, he can universalize the experience by telling the child that this is a place where lots of children come and that when they first come, many don't know what will happen and it feels scary to them. Exploring for, recognizing, and responding to the child's response is crucial. Inviting the child to ask questions about the worker's initial statement of orientation often leads to personal questions about the worker's status and interests. The worker usually gives the sought-for information directly and briefly rather than requesting reasons for the question or turning it back to the child. Children want to know and need to know something about the worker, if they are to admit him into their lives.

Clients often fear change itself because any change disrupts the steady state. They may fear that change will disrupt existing social relationships, roles, and abilities, causing more loss than gain in outcome. Those members of families who are content with their present roles may resist efforts that threaten to alter the existing patterns of authority, communication, or decision-making. After all, there can be no guarantee that acceptance of help will result in achievement of the client's goals or even that the efforts to change will not have a negative consequence for some aspect of the client system.

Apparent resistance to using help may be related to a pervading sense of hopelessness or despair. Some clients have problems of long standing that seem so serious to them that they have given up hope that things can be better. They believe that positive change is impossible, either because of environmental conditions, such as feeling that "you can't beat the system," or because of feelings of inadequacy to perform in the desired way. Such clients often have practical obstacles that interfere with the use of help, such as physical impairments, lack of money for child care, suitable transportation, or difficulty in arranging appointments during work hours. Workers must be able to help such clients to feel some hope that something can be better.

The amount of hope and encouragement given during and immediately following the initial interview is associated with continuation in treatment, according to Ripple.[25] She reports that discouragement by the worker is almost always associated with discontinuance. Discouragement was characterized by blandness and neutrality toward the client, no offer of hope that the situation could be improved, and no specific offer of an early second appointment. In order to want a service, a person must have some discomfort about the current situation, but also some hope that something can be done about it. From another study, Fanshel drew similar conclusions.[26] Zalba, in studying continuance in private family agencies, confirmed the finding that discontinuance is related to the optimism of the worker. A higher rate of continuance was associated with higher optimism about the outcome of the services. In cases in which there was both low optimism on the worker's part and great severity of client's problems, the discontinuance rate was highest.[27] In another study, Boatman found that appraised hopefulness had a discernible influence on workers' activities.[28] It is clear, than, that the worker needs to communicate to the client his expectations that there can be improvement in some aspect of the psychosocial situation, so as to evoke hope in the client.

Social workers, as well as clients, have some ambivalence about undertaking a new case. They have some fears and doubts that are similar to those of clients. They may feel uncertain about whether or not they can be helpful to a particular individual or group. They may be concerned about how clients will perceive and evaluate them and whether or not they will accept them. They may fear that they will encounter unmanageable resistance, especially if a client is not self-referred. They may be so engrossed in what appears to be serious pathology that they feel hopeless about the client's ability to use help. They may fear acting out behavior on the part of the clients, as in excessive aggression. They may expect that some clients will make overwhelming dependency demands on them.

Learning to handle retaliatory resistance is an important key to a beginning relationship. To some extent, resistance constitutes a rejection of the worker. In acting against what a worker has to offer, the client stirs up feelings of annoyance or frustration. If resistance is not understood and dealt with, it is natural for the client to retaliate. A client, for example, avoids the worker by failing to keep an appointment; the worker avoids discussing this with him. A client keeps changing the subject; the worker fails to request that he stay with the topic. When a worker knows a client is lying, he may retaliate by failing to challenge the client, by drawing him out to further fabrication, or by trying to trap him. There is a tendency to avoid directness because of fear of provoking hostility. If a worker understands the feelings that are aroused by the client's behavior, he can challenge it in a nonpunitive and nonaccusatory manner. Being direct is essential, but it is not to be confused with being directive.[29]

There is a tendency for social workers to regard all objections or opposition on the part of clients as negative. Hamilton has cautioned that the client may not want some aspects of the service for many very good as well as poor reasons.[30] The worker needs to evaluate the meaning of the defenses against involvement in treatment; they may indeed be reactions to inappropriate means used by the social worker or to the worker's own fears or insensitivities to the needs and abilities of individuals or groups. Clients from cultures different from the workers may be motivated to have help, but have a different view of the process. Levine notes that one major cause of group resistance occurs when the worker has directly, or through a subsystem, forced his will on the group without negotiations with members. He notes that most resistance represents a power struggle between the worker and one or more members.[31]

Violations of cultural values and role expectations often generate resistance. An example concerns a nine-year-old Korean boy whose behavior in school was intolerable.

The school had referred the boy and his mother to a child guidance clinic, but the family refused to go. The trouble at school got worse until finally the boy was suspended. The principal called the school social worker for help. The worker, in turn, consulted with an anthropologist to ascertain whether cultural factors might influence the way she tried to work with the family. Through this consultation, she got much help. She learned that the Korean father is usually dominant. The father makes the decisions concerning family members and resents outsiders who exercise control. Male children have high status in the family, and education is extremely valued.

With these and other facts to go on, the social worker contacted the father for an appointment at the office, to which he might want to bring his wife and the boy. When the family came, the worker asked the mother and child to remain in the waiting room while she talked with the father. This procedure apparently conveyed to him the worker's knowledge and acceptance of the importance of recognizing his authority as head of the family. The father appeared grieved and upset at his son's disrespectful behavior. The worker pointed out the boy's realistic intellectual capacity and outstanding abilities. She emphasized how much the boy could benefit from education, providing he could learn to behave differently in school. She suggested that the father take the child to the clinic, tying the need for the clinic to the parent's desire to be a good father, just as he would want to take the child to a doctor if he were physically ill. In response to the father's concern that the clinic would take over his responsibility for the son's behavior, the worker emphasized that the clinic would not do that, but rather would join hands with him to help his child. He would still be the head of the family, but the clinic might want to work with the mother also. When he asked about getting his son back into school, the worker said that she would recommend his reinstatement. The mother and boy were brought into the conference, and the referral was successfully accomplished.

Understanding the nature of ambivalence toward entering into a new endeavor suggests certain intermediate goals to be achieved in one or more early sessions. The worker wants to help the client to become oriented to himself and the helping situation, and he wants to tip the balance of ambivalence toward enough positive motivation for the client to return, at least for another try.

Within a dynamic flow of communication, the social worker introduces the client to himself and the helping situation. He provides what information is necessary to overcome doubts about how goals will be determined, the respective roles of worker and client, and policies and procedures that have a direct influence on the situation. He invites the client to identify his needs, concerns, and goals and to express what he thinks will be expected of him. He responds to support the client's views or to clarify the differences between the client's goals and expectations and the realities of the service offered. Accurate information is an essential ingredient in accepting help from another.

Through sensitive listening and observing, the social worker evaluates evidence of positive motivation. He looks for clues that might indicate resistance. They are myriad. There may be denial that there is a problem or insistence that one can handle it alone. There may be projection of the problem onto others. Resistance may be connected with the use of time: forgetting to come, arriving late, or giving signals that indicate a desire for early ending of the session. It may be indicated by failure to follow certain procedures, such as completion of a registration or application form. It may be related to the nature of participation: refusing to answer questions even if these were appropriately asked; avoiding relevant subjects; blaming others for their predicament; changing the subject; monopolizing the conversation in a way that shuts out the worker or other members; or using such defenses as denial, rationalization, or displacement in discussion of needs or problems. If there has been transfer of an individual or a group to a new worker, the clients are apt to show resistance to the change through comments that compare the present worker with the former one or that test the present worker's knowledge of their situations.

Accurate assessment of the presence of adequate motivation is not easy. Clients' motivations certainly influence their use of service, but the worker has to assume a part of the responsibility for enhancing or weakening motivation. Bounous, in a study of 106 women and their 8 workers in a family service agency, found that 28 percent of the clients dropped out after only one interview, without discussing their intentions with the worker or without agreement between worker and client that discontinuance was appropriate. The worker's perceptions of client motivation tended to be inaccurate. The workers had predicted that almost none of the clients would discontinue. When clients were highly motivated, the workers tended to underestimate their acceptance of counseling as a preferred means of help, the amount of responsibility they felt in relation to a problem, and the support from significant others for their getting help. They tended to overestimate the severity of problems and the clients' perceptions of the severity of the problems.[32] These findings indicate that workers need to give more attention to a client's strengths; to focus attention on the relative value the client places on getting help at a particular time in a particular agency, and on the degree to which the client is willing to assume some responsibility for changing the problem or situation.

Expectations and Working Agreement

One major focus of the initial phase is development of a partnership between the social worker and an individual, family, or group in which all parties have a common understanding of the enterprise in which they are engaged. Many recent writers refer to this task as contracting between a worker and a client system. Siporin defines a contract:

> A contract is a consensual, mutual agreement and acceptance of reciprocal obligations and responsibilities, with a promise to perform certain tasks and to deliver certain goods within some time period. Usually there is also a sanction or penalty for failure to perform expected behaviors; the penalty may be to terminate the relationship, pay back the goods, or pay damages. A contract has the effect of providing authority to take certain actions, including to do something to or for the other party of the agreement. A contract is usually written and often enforceable by law.[33]

There are some objections to the use of the term contract in social work practice. A social worker would neither desire to invoke sanctions against a client system nor would he have legal authority to do so. A client would likewise find it difficult to invoke sanctions against a worker for failure to perform expected behaviors. Many clients, particularly those with low incomes, have had negative experiences with contracts concerning rents or installment purchases. For these reasons the term contract should be used with caution, at least in communicating with clients. Whether or not the term is used, the worker and clients develop a set of flexible agreements regarding the essence of their work together.

Perlman states that the social worker and client form "a pact that is the basis of an ongoing productive partnership between client and agency."[34] The worker gives information; he affirms what the client expects and what the agency can offer; he clarifies the conditions for working together and the responsibilities of each to the endeavor. Other writers similarly emphasize that the working agreement sets forth the goals of the service, the needs or problems to be addressed, the reciprocal roles of worker and client system, the model or theoretical orientation of the practice, and the unit or system through

which service will be given.[35] Such mutual agreements are fundamental in determining the direction, structure, and nature of the service. But flexibility is necessary if working agreements are to be tools
in treatment. Flexibility makes it possible to redirect efforts, as appropriate to the needs of clients or according to changing environmental circumstances. There is a danger that if an initial contract is
formal and very explicit, it can become a "corrupt one," as when
the initially stated goals of clients are specified in the contract and
conceal more important unavowed ones.[36] Much earlier, John Dewey
warned that aims cannot be completely formed in advance:

> The aim as it first emerges is a mere tentative sketch. The act of striving to
> realize it tests its worth. If it suffices to direct activity successfully, nothing
> more is required, since its whole function is to set a mark in advance, and at
> times a mere hint may suffice. But usually—at least in complicated situations—
> acting upon it brings to light conditions which had been overlooked. This calls
> for revision of the original aim; it has to be added to or subtracted from. An
> aim must, then, be flexible; it must be capable of alteration to meet circum-
> stances.[37]

A tentative working agreement is derived from shared experience
in exploring the client's needs and situations. Its major values are
that it gives both the worker and the client a sense of involvement
and participation, and it signifies mutual commitment and responsibility. It provides a common frame of reference for the participants
so that each one is clear about what is expected of himself and others.
It provides a foundation for periodic review of progress and next
steps. Congruence among the parties to the agreement leads to effective functioning, and failure to achieve congruence promotes mal-
adaptation and hinders directed activity.[38] With the rise of incongru-
ities, individuals are working at cross purposes, and the worker's
efforts tend to be diluted and diverted. Congruence allows a worker
and client system to establish and sustain a working alliance.

PURPOSES AND GOALS

The purpose for which people engage in a joint venture is a pro-
pelling motivation and a necessary condition for successful action.

Dewey has stated clearly the meaning of the word "aim," used synonymously with goal or purpose: "An aim denotes the result of any natural process brought to consciousness and made a factor in determining present observation and choice of ways of acting."[39] He also explains:

> Since we do not anticipate results as mere intellectual onlookers, but as persons concerned in the outcome, we are partners in the process which produces the result. . . . The net conclusion is that acting with an aim is all one with acting intelligently. To foresee a terminus of an act is to have a basis upon which to observe, to select, and to order objects and our own capacities.[40]

In the early phase, the social worker attempts to clarify the purposes for which he is able to offer service. Oxley notes that to begin with a client where he is means understanding his hopes and expectations. What he hopes for is an expression of his aims or goals. When a client comes to see a worker, he has some idea, however vague and general, about the agency where he is making his request for assistance or to which he has been sent by another person. The client's initial expectations about the purpose may be based on knowledge, rumors, or attitudes that seeking service is degrading or that it is respectable. These ideas influence the statements he makes about the reasons for coming or being sent to this particular place. The client is deeply concerned with determining if he can get some particular needs met and under what conditions. It is not his responsibility initially to understand the agency's function and to gear his requests accordingly.[41] It is the worker's responsibility to clarify what help can be given in relation to what the client desires.

The worker does not determine the purpose or goals for the clients; he explores with them their reasons for seeking assistance or having been referred by someone else. To clarify goals he must seek expression of perceived needs, problems, and aspirations. If the system is a family or other group, he explores each individual's goals, but also each one's ideas about the group and its relevance to his goals. The group will have problems in functioning if there is incompatibility between the worker's goals, individuals' goals for themselves, and shared purposes of the group. There must be some common elements among the members' goals as these interrelate with the general purpose for the group.

Goals are hoped-for solutions to the problems of clients or to their need for enhancement in some area of functioning, as perceived by them and the worker. The presenting request may or may not be the one that is most crucial to a client's welfare or that can be dealt with through social work practice. Wants and needs are not necessarily synonymous. A common example is a request by a parent for correction of a child's behavior, when the need is for changes in family relationships and interaction. A request by a hospital patient for a particular service may be a device for seeking assistance with more complex problems, some of which may not be clear to the client. People have goals which they avow. They have others of which they are aware but which they do not express until they sense trust in the worker and the situation; and they have some important goals of which they are not initially aware but which become clear to them as they explore their situation. It is impossible to make an agreement about goals of which the applicants are not aware; they cannot make a choice unless they know what the alternatives are. Self-determination is much more complicated than asking a client what he wants, and using that as the aim of service. An example illustrates the need for alertness to the latent content of a client's messages about goals. A social worker recorded:

Mrs. Gandy's child, Jim, was referred to the clinic because of his serious acting-out behavior in school. While we were exploring the feelings about the referral, she said that she understood Jim, but the teacher certainly did not. She gave many abstract explanations about his problems. She wanted me to help the teacher to understand Jim because that was all that Jim needed. She said several times that she loved Jim and he loved her and that she never got mad at him because she understood him so well. As she talked about her relationship with Jim, her physical appearance and tone of voice suggested to me that she really was feeling depressed. When she interrupted her monologue, I said that I heard her saying that everything was fine between her and Jim, but I felt she looked as though she might be feeling sad or upset. I tried to convey the empathy I felt by posture and tone of voice. After a brief startled silence, Mrs. Gandy lowered her head and started to cry. I offered her a Kleenex and remained silent. She then slowly told me that she was very upset. She knew down in her heart that she really was a failure as a mother. She felt completely hopeless about it all.

Having acknowledged her feelings to herself and to me, she could move toward exploration of the factors that were contributing to the situation, including her part of it. She requested help for herself in relation to Jim, as well as help for Jim.

In analyzing this incident, the worker reported that she commented on the difference between Mrs. Gandy's verbal and nonverbal messages, after deciding that it would be appropriate to share her observations with the client. Before doing this she considered how the client, as recipient of a message, might respond to it. She recognized her own initial hesitancy to share her observation directly with the client. She felt somewhat anxious about upsetting the client's steady state by puncturing a necessary defense. She felt uncertain about her ability to deal with the response should the client become angry with her or reject the message. She examined her own feelings toward Mrs. Gandy, recognizing that she felt empathy toward her, and knowing that her own feelings could convey as much as the words.

The message was encoded and transmitted to Mrs. Gandy through words, gestures, and tone of voice. The message was received first with a startled response, but with a minimum of distortion, which is not always so. To have a message sent through appropriate words and gestures depends upon adapting one's vocabulary to that of the recipient. For a message to be received, there must be shared definitions of meaning.

Mrs. Gandy received the message that was sent and responded to it by crying and then disclosing previously unacknowledged feelings. The worker remained silent in order to give the client time to ventilate her feelings, to think about the message, and to convey her acceptance of the crying. The client was ready to hear the message and was able to decode it accurately, in spite of her strong emotional response to it. If the worker's message had been ignored or seriously distorted, the client's response would serve as feedback to the worker, who would try again to formulate and send a more helpful message.

In order to clarify problems and goals with clients, the social worker needs to communicate with acceptance and empathy, listen to the client's latent as well as manifest messages, accurately assess the client's behavior, and act in relation to this understanding. These skills in communication are applicable to all facets of the interaction process. Realistic goals depend upon shared knowledge of the situation and possible alternative outcomes.

In groups, realistic goals depend also upon understanding both the avowed and unavowed goals of each member. An individual may make statements about his goals, but he also gives the worker clues as to what he desires through what he talks about and how he responds to messages from others. In groups, most members search for common concerns and experiences as they discuss their reasons for coming, and gradually they relate their own particular goals to a common purpose.

One group had as its purpose, as formulated by the social work department in an urban high school, the preparation of pupils to make a satisfactory transition from intermediate to high school. Information about the group was given by the students' advisers, and those who were interested were randomly assigned to groups. They did, however, have the right to express a preference for having a friend in the same group. The size of the group was eight to ten members in order to permit individualization and opportunities for all members to participate actively. Group meetings were held for fifty minutes, during an activity or study period. In the group there were five girls and four boys, ages fourteen and fifteen:

As the bell rang, the pupils came straggling in. Only Tom and Curtis came together, chatting happily. Concha came in, noticed Yvonne and said, "Oh, hi, how are you today?" and sat beside Yvonne. The social worker invited them all to pull their chairs up into a circle so they wouldn't feel lost in such a big room. They all did this, except Melissa, who remained several feet from any other member. The worker then introduced herself and suggested that the members do the same. She then gave a brief introduction, reviewing the fact that they had all expressed an interest in a group in which they could help each other to get a good start in this great big high school. Most young people, she said, find it tough to move from a small intermediate school in which they were the high-status students to a big school in which they are now the youngest ones. She asked for comments about whether that is what they remembered about the group. Tom said that was what he understood, and the others all indicated their approval.

The worker said there might still be uncertainties about what they could expect to happen if they decided to stay in the group; that they would talk about the things that were of greatest concern to them, so they should try to find out what they think are some of the difficulties in being here. Betty and Sue both raised their hands to speak. The worker mentioned that they did not need to raise their hands, that she hoped they would talk informally with each other, that this was not another class but an informal discussion group. She then suggested that either Betty or Sue could talk first.

Betty said that she thought this group was a good idea, so she would start. "I don't know whether what I say is what you want," looking directly at the worker, who said that whatever she wanted to say would be just fine. "Well, it's so lonely here—I haven't run into any of my old friends from James School. I just don't know anybody." Concha said that she felt exactly that way too, that she was not in the same classes with kids she used to know, except for one person. The worker looked at Sue and said she had been one of the first to say she wanted to talk. She said that she had just wanted to say exactly what Concha had just said. Curtis said that he's lucky because he and Tom know each other well and they're lucky because they got in the same group. Tom added that they've been friends for a long time, but it still feels very strange here. The interchange stopped, so the worker commented that so far several members had mentioned loneliness and the desire for friends—perhaps they'd like to work on that. Yvonne said she'd certainly like to find out ways in which she can make friends and participate with other kids in activities. There was general consensus about this in the group, except that Melissa had not actively participated. The worker then suggested that maybe there were other things that bother them, too. Curtis responded: "Yeh, there's a lot of gang fighting on campus and the Chicanos are all beating up the rest of us." Juan, who is of Mexican background, almost screamed, "Now I've heard it all—it's the Anglos who always start it."

Curt: Oh, so you are in a gang?

Juan: Hell, no, I'm just as scared of the gangs as you are, but you don't need to put me down because of my race.

Curt: Well, you say you're not in a gang so don't take what I said personally.

Juan: Well, you did accuse me of being in a gang and you had no right to do that.

Curt: I didn't really mean that, but the kids in the gangs—

Tom: It's just that Curt and I really got it yesterday—but you're o.k., Juan.

Betty was whispering loudly to Concha and said, "Concha, you should speak up." Concha, also a Mexican American, said she guessed we were all afraid of gangs. This goes back to having friends. She wondered how we could be a part of things if we stay out of gangs. "But I have another real bad problem," and then silence. The worker asked if Concha felt she could share it with the group. Concha: "Well, have any of you been to gym yet?" All indicated they had been. Betty said, "It's just awful," and Concha said, "Do the boys have to take showers naked with others like we do?" The boys all indicated that they did. Only Joe emphasized he wasn't bothered by this—that he thought it was fun. Concha: "Well, you can have your fun—but it's so embarrassing."

The worker said she thought they would want to talk about that some more, but reminded the group that the time was almost up. She then reviewed the major concerns that had been expressed and said they were good examples of what could be worked on in this group so they could all make a good transition to the high school world. There was general nodding to these comments. She reminded the members that the plan was for the group to continue through the first half of the semester, twice a week, during sixth period. Tom asked what days. The worker said it could be Monday and Wednesday or Tuesday and Friday—did they they have a preference? Tom asked why not Monday and Thursday? The worker said if that would be better for all of them, she could make it then. There was a unanimous vote for Tom's suggestion, and Melissa spoke for the first time, saying she'd like that much better. They all left the room together, with much chatting in a friendly way.

In groups, then, the worker states simply the general purpose for the group and invites exploration of its relevance to their situations. He begins to identify common goals related to the concerns of the members. He clarifies the structure of the group, allowing group decisions when possible. Orientation to the purpose and structure of the group and initial goal-setting activities takes place within a major focus on psychosocial relations: encouraging participation, accepting feelings, permitting the exchange of difference and conflict that can be dealt with by the members, and reinforcing positive ties among the members.

When a family comes for aid, it is usually because a problem is described as that of one member—often a child or a spouse. The family often does not regard the need as some type of change in the functioning of the family system. In such instances, there is lack of congruence between worker and client system about the problems and the purposes of the service. The worker, therefore, has the task of redefining the client system as the family, recognizing that all members are involved. As Freeman says, "the struggle between the family and the therapist to define the problem is the heart of the first stage of family therapy."[42] The worker uses his influence to reorient the family to the idea of improvement in family functioning, as distinguished from individual or subgroup functioning.

Work with young children also poses special difficulties. They rarely have a conscious desire for help. The need is recognized by a parent, nursery school teacher, or doctor; sometimes even with little cooperation from the parents. The child does know, however, that he is in trouble or "bad," and he is exceedingly anxious until he knows the reasons for being brought to an agency. He can understand the purpose of the service, if it is described simply, clearly, and accurately in terms he can comprehend. After an initial period of defensiveness, he is usually relieved to know and makes good use of the service.

Several studies have been made on the use of purpose in social work practice. Failure to clarify goals is a source of problems in ongoing treatment. Based on a study in six family service agencies, Schmidt found that when workers made a purposeful effort to formulate objectives and communicated these to clients, a high proportion of clients accurately perceived and agreed with the objectives. When workers did not specify objectives, the majority of the clients did not understand how interviews were intended to benefit them. There was incongruence between the goals of the worker and the client. The goals of clients were more often related to concrete resources, while those of workers were more abstract and psychological in nature.[43] In another study, Raschella found that clients served in outpatient mental health centers were less likely to drop out prematurely when there was a high degree of congruence between worker and client in the specification of the goals of service.[44] Levinson reviewed sixty-one articles on social work with groups and found that the major goal of the practitioner was often some change in individual behavior, even though collective effort to change the clients' environment was often needed. When purposes of members and workers were in accord, the groups tended to operate optimally to achieve their purposes. When the worker ascribed the purposes for the group, these tended to be rejected by the members, leading to dissolution of the group.[45]

Conflicting ideas about the purpose of the service need to be resolved during this phase of treatment. The worker does not impose his ideas on the clients, but he does share them and he shares his reasons for making suggestions that might be different from the client's initial formulations of goals. In the end, however, the worker recognizes that until a client system and the worker have come together on the goals, the chances of successful service are slim.

ROLE EXPECTATIONS

Clarification of the expectations that clients have concerning the behavior of each in their respective roles is an important determinant of the outcome of the service. A major concern of new clients is finding an appropriate role in relation to the worker and other participants, if any. They have questions about whether or not they want to and can do what is expected of them and whether or not they made the right decision to apply for service. In order to clarify expectations, the practitioner explores with the client how his expectations fit with the client's expectations. The worker needs to orient the client to what it means to be a client in this particular situation. The client needs to respond to these messages from the worker, expressing his feelings about them and understanding of them as they relate to his situation. As messages are exchanged, the nature of the client's expected participation becomes clarified, leading to mutual understanding of each other's part in the process.

The process of clarifying expectations requires that the clients be able to enter into verbal interchanges with practitioners. Not all clients are ready and able to verbalize their feelings and attitudes. Polansky and his associates have studied what they refer to as verbal accessibility, which is the degree of the client's readiness to use words to describe his feelings and basic attitudes. Verbal accessibility is determined by a complex of elements: the client's capacity for self-observation, his motivation, his freedom to communicate verbally, and the worker-client relationship.[46] Relatively nonverbal clients can be helped, however, if the worker uses nonverbal activities through which clients may express themselves and through which their capacities for verbally expressing their feelings and attitudes may be increased.[47]

As in other areas of practice, the worker's lack of knowledge about cultural norms may limit the client's initial participation in the process of working toward mutual expectations. A client may expect, as is probable in the Japanese culture, that he should give only polite answers to questions, suppress strong feelings, be indirect in his patterns of speech, and be apologetic for the slightest lapse.[48] If the social worker does not understand the values on which such behavior is based, he is apt to interpret these behaviors as resistance rather than as efforts to behave appropriately in an ambiguous situation. If the worker is able to understand the meaning of the behavior, he can respect it, listen attentively to the client, and gradually reduce the ambiguity in the situation for the client.

Another obstacle to achieving mutual understanding of role expectations, often unrecognized by workers, is conflict concerning authority. The client needs to come to understand the nature and extent of the worker's legitimate authority, and the worker needs to come to understand the client's need to control or to submit to the worker's authority. Clients may attempt to control the process and content in many ways, as for example, by using either silence, long monologues which are difficult to interrupt, or coming late or leaving early. In families there may be the struggle of one member to control the messages sent or the behavior of others or to expect the worker to control the process of communication or the behavior of members. In formed groups, there is often a struggle for power among the members or between the worker and the group. The conflict is perhaps extreme when the group is a natural gang or a group which has appointed or elected officials. Whether it pertains to individual, family, or peer group, the usual initial pattern is for the clients to accede to the worker's authority; then challenge some aspects of it; and gradually develop an appropriate balance of control in the worker-client interaction. There is almost always some testing of the extent of the worker's ability to control or to relinquish control to the clients. This struggle is prolonged when workers are ambivalent about their responsibilities or fearful of losing control of the situation. When clients discover that they have both rights and responsibilities to participate freely within certain agreed-upon parameters, both the relationship and the motivation for change are enhanced.

Developing a working agreement between worker and client system assumes that social workers perceive accurately the clients' expectations of the worker's role. In her research, Clemenger found that one important intermediate goal is achieved by the worker during the beginning phase: the worker develops accurate assessments of the way that clients perceive his role. Such assessment is essential to the selection of appropriate means for help. She also found that accuracy of assessment was reduced when the clients were mentally ill and distorted reality, which made it difficult for workers to understand how the patients perceived them. Accurate assessment was also impaired when workers viewed the behavior of certain members to be negative; when they thought of members in stereotyped terms, such as passive-resistant, noncommunicative, or domineering. The tendency to stereotype distorts the worker's skill in assessment. Generally, however, most workers are able to communicate the components of their roles quite accurately to clients, and clients are able to perceive them accurately.[49]

CONTENT AND FOCUS

The desired and the actual content of interviews or group sessions may be a matter about which clients and workers are in agreement, or there may be misperceptions by clients of what they are expected to talk about or to do and what they prefer to do. The content provides the focus for the interchange between worker and client. The new client has many questions about what he will be expected to do or talk about.

In beginning with a client system, much of the content concerns mutual expectations. In a study of expectations in groups, Brown found that the ability of the social worker and the group to focus on the topic of mutual expectations during the first meetings enhances the satisfaction of members with the outcome.[50] Discussion of expectations leads to congruence between worker and members on their attitudes toward the group. They share similar perceptions concerning the experience. Social workers in groups in which agreement was highest initiated the discussion of expectations in the first meeting. These workers helped the members to stay with the topic and deal with their resistance to clarifying expectations. They were able to pick up from nonverbal cues that indicated that a member might be ready to react to something that had been said earlier. They were able to recognize and encourage expressions of feelings about the experience. In contrast, in groups in which agreement was low, the workers were less likely to initiate the topic and to deal with it in early sessions. In one group of parents, for example, it was never clarified whether the group would focus on personal or family problems of members or engage in social action. The major conclusion of this study was that developing mutual expectations as early as possible is significantly related to the effectiveness of group functioning and member satisfaction.

In beginning with a client system, exploration with clients about what they prefer to discuss or to do provides a natural base for understanding their primary concerns and their readiness to deal with particular issues. Rosen and Lieberman studied the relevance of content to expectations of clients. The purpose of the research was to discover "the extent to which the content of an interactive response is perceived by a participant to be relevant to, and in agreement with, his own definition and expectations of the content to be dealt with in the treatment relationship."[51] The major finding was that there is need for clear worker and client orientation to the purpose of the interview which assists the worker to keep the interview focused on relevant content. Thus, content is directly related to purpose.

In a study of two groups of adoptive parents there was consensus that the topics most preferred by members were legal procedures in adoption, knowledge about parent-child relationships, informing a child that he was adopted, and the reasons for placing a particular child with particular parents. It was found to be important for the worker to initiate and maintain appropriate focus on topics that clients deemed to be important. It was suggested that attrition is related to the extent to which clients' expectations about content are met.[52] Sufficient commonalities among members are a requisite for continuing interaction over a period of time.

EFFECTS OF WORKING AGREEMENT ON OUTCOMES

There is support from research for the principle that mutual agreement between worker and clients concerning goals, roles, and content is fundamental in determining the direction and quality of the service.

Several studies have compared clients who continue in service with those who discontinue when the worker judges continuation to be desirable. In one of the first major studies, Ripple and associates found that factors associated with a high discontinuance rate were:

the worker's irrelevant or minimal effort to clarify the problems; low perceptiveness and lack of sensitivity to the client's presentation of his problem and situation; inadequacy or absence of explanations of agency services; and an incompatible or opposed view of the problem vis-à-vis the client. When there was agreement about purpose and realistic expectations of help, there was a very high rate of continuance. The most decisive factor was clarity of expectations and mutual agreements.[53] Several other studies tend to confirm the principle that clarification and agreement about expectations are essential ingredients in continuance.[54] In a survey of research in the field of family service, Briar found that factors associated with continuation were adequacy of communication between client and worker, client's attribution of responsibility for the problem to himself rather than to others; and the appropriateness of the client's attitudes and expectations regarding the worker and treatment. His conclusion was that "the degree of congruence between the worker and client in their definitions of the client's situation has been found to be strongly associated with continuance in all studies that have examined the factor."[55]

Clarity and consensus about expectations not only prevent discontinuance, but also have a positive effect on progress in problem-solving. In a study of groups, Garvin found that when the worker accurately perceived the expectations of members, his responses tended to be more appropriate and there was significantly greater movement in problem-solving than in instances in which the worker did not perceive the members' expectations correctly.[56]

The working agreement between worker and client concerning goals, focus of content, and respective roles constitutes the plan for action. It is to be remembered that the plan is a flexible one, to be changed by mutual decision between worker and client. As the worker engages in a decision-making process with clients concerning these agreements, he is working simultaneously to engage the client in the process. He does this through attention to relationship, enhancement of motivation, and establishment of patterns of communication.

The plan for service is based on a preliminary assessment, knowledge about modalities and structures of service, and clarification of goals, roles, and content. One example follows:

Annette, a sixteen-year-old girl of Italian Catholic background, came to a free clinic because she was pregnant and did not know where to turn for help: she was in a mess and just did not know what to do. Exploration of the inquiry brought out the facts that she was not married, lived with her mother, age 37; and her father, age 42; two brothers, ages 14 and 10; and two sisters, ages 12 and 7. Her father was a carpenter and her mother a housewife. She was in the eleventh grade in a parochial school. When she thought she might be pregnant, she went to her doctor, who promised not to tell her parents but advised her to do so herself. He suggested that she go into a maternity home and give up the baby for adoption. He offered to help with these arrangements. She was very upset at the time and just did not want to do what the doctor suggested—at least she didn't think so. She said that this was the most embarrassing thing that had ever happened to her. She went to the clinic because it was near her school and she saw a poster about the clinic which said it gave confidential pregnancy counseling. She had walked around the block several times before getting up enough nerve to go in.

The boyfriend with whom she had sexual intercourse denied any responsibility for her pregnancy. He was 20 years old and a college student. She thought they really loved each other and she went too far one night: "It was an awful thing to have done and here I am pregnant and it's the only time I've had sex." When she told him she was pregnant, there was a big fight between them, after which he insisted he would never see her again, saying, "It's your baby and your problem—don't put it on me." She dared not tell her parents because she knew they would disown her forever. Furthermore, she would be expelled from school as soon as her condition became known. She did well in school and had hoped to graduate with honors and go on to college, but now "that's all over for good." She brought out these facts and ideas, with a considerable amount of gentle questioning and probing by the worker. At one point she said, "I can't believe it, but you're not lecturing me about the mess I've got myself into." Several times she burst into tears, but regained her composure when the worker accepted the tears and supported her efforts to talk about her concerns.

At the beginning of the interview, the worker had assured Annette that she had come to the right place. She assured her that whatever she told the worker would be held in confidence, unless she gave the worker permission to share information with others in her behalf. Following the exploration of the facts of the case and Annette's feelings about them, the worker reiterated that she could get pregnancy counseling at the clinic. She gave her information about the clinic and its operating procedures. In response to the worker's inquiry about what she thought she might want to happen, she burst into tears and then said, "Just what you've done—listen to me and understand—but I just don't know what I can do." The worker outlined briefly a number of ways that some clients found help: health information and care; individual counseling; group counseling for young women who have similar concerns; and working with families of clients. To the latter, Annette shuddered and gasped, "Oh, no," to which the worker assured her that this would not happen unless she came to decide it would be a good thing to do. Annette asked if the worker could give her advice as to what she should do. The worker said she could help her to think through what she wanted to do about the baby, mentioning the alternatives of abortion, raising the child herself, or adoption. Annette said, "That's exactly what I want—I just don't know what to do."

On the basis of Annette's own desires and the worker's preliminary assessment, she decided to offer individual counseling to Annette. She thought that Annette was in a state of great emotional distress, as a reaction to the pregnancy and its consequences for her family, other social relationships, and for her future plans. She was very concerned about the responses of family and friends to her situation and she was upset about her boyfriend's rejection of her. She had a great deal of anxiety, guilt, and self-blame. She seemed well-motivated to use help: even though she was very upset, she was able to communicate facts, express feelings, and identify major concerns. She demonstrated ability to enter into a relationship and to accept the worker's part in the process.

The worker explained that she would be glad to continue to talk with Annette on a regular basis, and that making a decision about the baby and her future would not be easy because there were many things to be considered. She reiterated that the final decision would need to be Annette's; mentioned some of the things they would need to talk about; and how she thought she could be helpful. Because Annette expressed a strong need to make the decision as soon as possible and the worker also thought this was very important, a plan was agreed upon for Annette to come twice a week for an hour immediately after school for the next few weeks, with the aim of making a good decision about the outcome of the pregnancy. If additional time was needed, this would be possible.

At this time, the worker did not emphasize that it probably would be necessary to involve the parents and significant others at some point. These matters will be brought up as soon as Annette is ready to consider them.

In relation to this interview, social work values are evident. Belief in the dignity and worth of the individual are reflected in the worker's acceptance of Annette, treating her with respect, assuring her about confidentiality, encouraging freedom of expression, and individualizing the process and plan of treatment, according to mutual perceptions of Annette's needs. Social justice was exemplified by informing Annette of her right to have access to resources and to make decisions, based on knowledge concerning the goals of treatment, the outcome of pregnancy, and the modality of practice. The value of interdependence was exemplified through encouraging Annette's participation in the process and recognizing the network of social systems of which Annette is a part.

The worker's actions were based on explanatory knowledge about behavior from a biopsychosocial perspective that will result in a fuller assessment of Annette's needs, problems, and capacities as these interact with supports and limitations of the social environment. In developing an initial and flexible plan of treatment, the worker used knowledge about the major concepts of planning. She made selective use of techniques of social treatment with considerable emphasis on support, use of structure, exploration, education, and some clarification. With Annette's participation, she not only elicited appropriate information and arrived at a tentative treatment plan, she also enabled Annette to feel accepted, understood, and less anxious; to understand herself and her situation better; and to engage in a problem-solving process regarding an important decision. Thus, assessment of the person-situation configuration, initial planning, and social treatment go on simultaneously.

Movement into Work Phase

The major focus of the social worker's understanding and activities in the initial phase may be summarized as:

1. Orienting the individual, family, or group to the general purpose, structure, and plan of the service and to the respective roles of client and worker
2. Initiating a social work relationship with the individual and, in families and formed groups, initiating relationships among the members. (In this endeavor, the qualities of acceptance, empathy, and genuineness are paramount.)
3. Motivating an individual or a group to want to use an appropriate service, which requires recognition of ambivalence and resistance and making efforts to enhance positive motivation
4. Developing a working agreement that is arrived at through joint decisions about: (*a*) the nature of the needs or problems to be dealt with; (*b*) one or more goals relevant to the client's needs and, in family or formed groups, some common purpose to

serve as an initial focus for the worker-client system's effort: (c) the content and means to be used in working toward the achievement of the initial goals; and (d) the responsibilities of worker and clients in their respective roles

5. Utilizing techniques within all of the major categories, with special emphasis on support, structure, exploration, education, and clarification, based on understanding of the client system and the interactional process.

Movement occurs along two parallel lines: developments in the relationships and the achievement of tasks related to the goals. The worker assesses verbal and nonverbal clues that indicate the client system is moving into a more intensive work phase. There are evidences of trust in the worker and, if a group, in each other; dissipation of much of the ambivalence about needing and using help and about the relationship with the worker; some self-disclosure of both positive and negative feelings, experiences, and ideas and some confidence that it is safe to do these things; some acknowledgment by clients that they have some responsibility for themselves and their situations and for working toward goals; some mutually acceptable norms and patterns of communication; and some degree of commitment toward continued working together for mutually agreed-upon purposes. When the worker recognizes these clues, he can move toward a focus on more intensive attention to the tasks and problems per se. The next phase has its own characteristics and therefore calls for some different emphases on the worker's part.

CHAPTER SEVEN

The Core Phase:
System Maintenance and Development

No clear demarcation between phases of process is possible, but there comes a time when the worker and individual or group recognize that they have reached an agreement to work together toward some mutually acceptable goal. Clients have come to a preliminary decision that the service has positive meaning for them in terms of satisfaction in the relationship and the desire to achieve a realistic purpose. They have demonstrated sufficient positive motivation to continue beyond the initial stage. In groups, there is sufficient acceptance among the members that they are able to work together with some capacity for mutual support and mutual stimulation. In family situations, they have accepted the worker into their family for a limited purpose and period of time. They have accepted, at least partially, a need for improvement in the structure and process within the family unit as well as perhaps in individuals and environment.

Gradually, clients tend to become more secure in the situation. As this happens, they share more of their feelings, experiences, and opinions. They are willing to risk more exposure of themselves to others. Verbal communication becomes less scattered, more focused, and more concentrated on particular issues. There is less blaming and projecting onto others as clients take more appropriate responsibility for their own behavior. In families and formed groups, members recognize more of the common threads of values, attitudes, opinions, and interests, but they also allow for individual differences and differentiation of self from others. In the one-to-one relationship, there is a stronger attachment to the social worker and the experience; in formed groups, the attachment to each other and to the group is important to most members; in families and other groups, there is recognition that by working together, both individual and group needs can be met. Cohesiveness develops.

In order to have this phase of treatment become optimally useful, clients and workers need to test and arrive at some consensus concerning a particular style of working together. This process involves the development of shared norms that define how the participants will interact: for example, the rules that govern communication, the ways in which differences and inevitable conflicts will be handled, and the degree of freedom to experiment with ways of expressing feelings and behaving. The desired norms are those that accredit freedom of expression, acceptance of difference, experimentation with new ideas and behaviors, optimal client participation, and realistic responsibility for one's part in the process. In families and other groups, there needs to be a norm that individual goals are important and pursued when these are not inimical to the goals of others and to the general purpose of the group. These norms implement professional values. The particular style of interaction that results differs with each client system, for it is a dynamic cyclical process that engages all of the participants in a search for more effective ways of feeling, thinking, and doing. The content of interaction varies with the purpose of the endeavor and with the problems, capacities, and life situations of the clients.

In helping an individual or a group to work toward optimal goals, the social worker simultaneously pays attention to the maintenance and further development of the system itself and to the achievement of new understandings or tasks that are essential to goal achievement. In earlier sessions, the worker's primary focus was devoted to the development of a socioemotional climate that would support the client or members of a group in efforts to have something be better or different for them, and also the development of a working agreement. In order to maintain and further develop the helping system, the social worker engages in continuous assessment of the structure and process of the interaction among participants. It is important to keep the action system functioning so that it can serve as a vehicle for goal attainment. Entropy is prevented. The steady state must be maintained within reasonable parameters at the same time that clients are attempting to make desired changes. Problems are apt to arise that hinder the clients' abilities to achieve their goals. The worker should be prepared to deal with them. The most frequent problems tend to be in the realm of relationships, roles, resistance, and communication.

Developing and Sustaining Relationships

The dyad of worker and client, the worker with a marital couple or family, and the worker with a formed group comprise systems of interpersonal relationships in which there is an ebb and flow of positive and negative feelings toward oneself and others. During the early part of this phase, patterns of relationships emerge, based on the complementarity of need on the part of all concerned in the areas of love and affection, control and power, and inclusion. Self-esteem and positive identity are attributes that contribute positively to the ability to develop relationships that are appropriate to a particular situation.

During this phase of practice, the predominant qualities of relationships are mutual trust, acceptance, and interdependence. The relationship with the worker is predominantly positive and based on realistic perceptions of client and worker roles. In family and group situations, there is less dependence on the worker, with mutual aid becoming a prominent characteristic. The client gradually comes to feel accepted for what he is. He comes to trust himself and the worker sufficiently to reveal more and more of himself to the worker, and, if a member of a group, to other members. This does not mean that the worker is passive: he listens intently; he demonstrates empathy, acceptance, and genuineness; and he intervenes actively when clients need his expert knowledge and skills.

Within the general atmosphere of mutual trust and acceptance, there will be some hostility and jealousy toward the worker. So, too, will there be strong feelings of dependency, identification, love, and intimacy.[1] These strong feelings are more noticeable in therapeutic than in developmental and preventive situations. The worker uses his knowledge of ego psychology and social relationships to make sense out of behavior which often seems irrational. Some hostile feelings toward the worker are very natural reactions to realistic situations in which an individual or group has every right to feel irritated as, for example, when a worker has been late for an appointment, failed to inform the client about a change of time for the session, or made a promise that he did not keep. In other instances, hostility may be in the form of resistance to avoid involvement in discussions of painful subjects. Facing things in himself that he finds difficult to tolerate may anger a member; thus, he projects the reason for his discomfort onto the worker. Feelings may be displaced or projected from other life experiences. One example follows:

> In a play group, Tommy, age 5, had an eating problem. At refreshment time Jenny was playing mother. She called to the others to come and eat. Tommy stuck his tongue out at the worker, who commented that he had bad feelings about eating. He made an angry face and said, "Go away." This behavior was typical of the struggle that Tommy and his mother were having around the problem of eating.

In such ways, hostility may be expressed against the worker who represents a parent or other significant person in the client's past. Clients often complain about persons in authority—father, boss, teacher—when it is the worker toward whom they have the feelings of hostility. Even though such hostility stems from feelings that were realistic in the past, the irrational elements are not appropriate to the person's relationship with the worker. Likewise, some clients with a need to be the "one and only" cannot bear to tolerate the fact that the worker has other clients with whom he has a close relationship. They develop fantasies about the worker's relationship with other clients and become jealous or feel rejected by the worker. Clients may feel criticized by a worker when the worker's comments were intended to be constructive. Some clients are extremely sensitive to subtle nuances that indicate less than total acceptance by the worker. Clients, however, may anticipate criticism and interpret noncritical comments or questions as criticisms.

Clients often develop strong positive feelings toward the worker that are expressed in a desire to have him to oneself, difficulty in sharing, strong overidentification, or prolonged dependency. In some instances, clients want to be nurtured by the worker, unconsciously expecting what they expected, but did not get, from their parents.

They may endow the worker with even more power than the worker has. They may withdraw from the relationship if they become overwhelmed by the intensity of their feelings. They may fear becoming totally dependent or helpless. Some clients present themselves as being very independent: with trust and reassurance, they can dare to express needs for help from others. Some clients present themselves as being helpless and, perhaps, also hopeless, incapable of doing anything on their own. Here the worker must give a great deal of support, but also work toward self-direction.

These unrealistic feelings toward the worker are often referred to as transference reactions, that is, the unconscious and inappropriate repetition of reactions and feelings from the past in a present situation. They involve a reliving of past experiences by transferring reactions from earlier to present relationships. The worker's effort is to develop and sustain the relationship on a realistic basis. He does not actively encourage these feelings and actions, but evaluates their impact on the progress of the work. He cannot ignore them. They need to be recognized and understood and dealt with as they occur.[2] At times when the client is ready, the worker may comment on the underlying feelings. He may comment that, although a client sees him this way, he is not his parent or teacher. He may comment that the client has said he reminds him of his father and perhaps the client expects him to behave that way.

In group situations, the worker needs to understand that there may be multiple transference reactions not only to him, but also among the members.[3] When an atmosphere of trust, acceptance, and mutual aid has developed in the group, feelings which have been taboo may be expressed. Group interaction often facilitates the expression of hostile feelings toward the worker as a symbol of authority. When one member dares to express hostility, other members may react with shock. When they realize that the worker does not retaliate but continues to accept the person, they become more able to express their own conflicts toward the worker. A process of contagion has occurred. Along with the worker, the members come to understand that the feelings displayed do not always have a rational basis. Irrational attitudes are easier to see in someone else, yet gradually the implications of one's own behavior become clear. A member may be stimulated by the special characteristics of other group members which remind him consciously or unconsciously of earlier relationships with parents, siblings, or significant others. Sibling rivalry is often reenacted in group situations, with certain members reminding one of being the less-favored child in the family.

As clients develop relationships with the worker, they often request personal favors. These may vary from a small child's request that the worker take him home, or give him the toy he has been playing with, to an adult's requests that he go to lunch with him, lend him money, or do other such favors. The worker's understanding of the meaning of the request determines his response. Early in this phase a client may be testing the worker to clarify their respective roles; he may be wanting reassurance that the worker really cares enough for him to give or do something special; he may be seeking means to have more time with the worker and turn the relationship into a personal one. The worker can ask the client about his reasons for requesting the favor. Such requests for time, attention, or gifts are handled within the agreed-upon norms and rules, and according to the worker's judgment about the effect that granting or refusing the request will have on the progress of treatment. In a family or other group situation, of course, the worker's relationship with other members must be taken into account.

Gradually, as clients begin to trust the worker and each other, if they are in a group, and as they develop more confidence in their own abilities, they tend to identify with the worker. Such identification is manifested in various ways. They may begin to dress like the worker or imitate some aspect of his appearance or mannerisms. They may comment that they try to think about how the worker would handle a particular situation. They may comment that they did something to please the worker. Often such enthusiasm is an unconscious incorporation of some part of the worker into themselves. Gradually, they move from identification with the worker to an enhanced sense of their own identity.[4] Such identifications occur also among members of groups. They enhance the sense of relatedness and, in addition, lead to changes in attitudes and behavior. The worker tends to foster identifications, but also to help them move to an enhanced sense of their own identities and mature object relationships.

Other special challenges to the use of relationship occur. One example concerns the management of seductive behavior. These sexual advances are not limited to the worker-client dyad, but may also take place within families and formed groups. In one study, it was found that encounters with seductive behavior were common.[5] These experiences were mildly to markedly discomforting to the workers. Some workers felt angry that their professional interest, concern, and caring had been misinterpreted. It is possible, of course, that workers themselves might unwittingly behave toward clients in seductive ways, based on their own interpersonal needs. To be able to recognize one's feelings and refocus the relationship on a professional basis is the challenge to the worker.

Since each person, including the social worker, brings to the relationship his own history of social experiences, the worker needs to become aware of his own reactions and to understand those of his clients. It is indeed difficult, if not impossible, for social workers to relate with the essential qualities of acceptance, empathy, and genuineness to all clients and also to understand the dynamics of the relationship between them. When the worker transfers to the client reactions from his own past experiences which are inappropriate to the situation, this phenomenon is referred to as countertransference. When a worker feels irritated with a client, becomes uncomfortable, or defensive, he needs to recognize that the dynamics of transference might be operating.

Another potential problem is related to a tendency by workers to empathize more readily with one member of a family or group than with another. In a relationship with one client, the worker's empathy may make it difficult for him to see that client's significant others realistically. Often, for example, a worker finds a small child very appealing and tends to blame the parents for the child's difficulty. Unconscious parental urges may be stimulated by the neediness of clients, and these attitudes may reinforce the client's needs to look for gratification that he lacked in earlier phases of development, rather than to work toward more satisfying and effective relationships in the present. In sessions with a mother and child, a worker's positive feelings for the child and the child's responses to them might arouse jealousy or fear in the mother. When the worker gets cues that such a situation is developing, he reflects on his own attitudes toward child and mother. He may then be ready to talk with both parties about his awareness that the child wants all of his attention and that the mother has feelings about this; that the worker is there for both of them. In one such situation, the worker encouraged the mother to share in the child's play. Combining doing with talking provided opportunities for the mother to learn to deal with the child. By observing the worker and child together, the mother was able to see the child's positive attributes; in turn, the child discovered pleasure in getting approval from his mother. The relationship between worker and client was enhanced, and the tie between mother and child was strengthened.[6]

Changes in composition upset the existing relationships and require adaptations by all participants in the process. There are times when a worker changes jobs or is assigned to new responsibilities. When he leaves a client and a new worker is assigned, the client needs to deal simultaneously with the feelings about the worker's leaving and with the problems in establishing relationships with the new worker. In both individual and group situations, the clients must repeat the tasks of the initial phase because the new worker is a newcomer to an ongoing process. The worker needs to review and update the working agreement with the individual, family, or group. In families, additional members are often brought into the treatment process; this upsets the steady state and changes the content of the sessions. Even though the new participants are members of the family, they have not been participants in the family counseling or therapy sessions. It takes time to assimilate them into the work with the family.

In groups, membership turnover influences orderly movement. A new member needs to become oriented to the group, develop relationships with the other members, and test their perceptions of goals and expectations: he is in the initial phase of treatment. The older members need to adapt their roles and contributions to the group to take into account the needs of the newcomer. The system may have difficulty in including the newcomer, and the newcomer may have difficulty in accepting other members or the group's norms and process. When intimate relationships have been achieved, a newcomer can feel great discomfort in trying to become part of the group. The usual anxieties about entering a new situation are aggravated by the sense of intruding into an existing system of relationships.

One example of the difficulty for an individual and a group in adapting to a new member concerns a young adult therapy group in which most members had been together for several months. No members had been added since the end of the first few sessions. The group had developed a sense of cohesiveness and had been engaged in discussions of intimate relationships. One afternoon, just as the group was beginning, a stranger arrived, saying that she had been referred to this group. The worker had not prepared the group for this event, but introduced Genevieve to each member. The members were polite to Genevieve and made efforts to orient her to the discussion. At the worker's suggestion, they returned to the discussion that had just been started earlier, but they never got to sharing deep concerns.

Genevieve attempted to give advice to the others about their problems. After the session ended, the newcomer left but the others lingered. When the worker indicated they might be upset about the new member, each one expressed much anger toward the worker for having permitted this to happen and for not having let them participate in making the decision. Jack said, with sadness, that it had taken them so long to be able to trust the worker and themselves. Sallie agreed, and said it would be hard for them to really share themselves again. The worker said she had no idea they would react this way; she just thought that a group experience would be good for Genevieve. She thought the group should be able to work it out. The members all left, without saying goodbye to the worker. In an individual conference with Genevieve, the worker found out that it had been a devastating experience for her. She felt the members' great discomfort and hostility and just couldn't seem to fit into what was going on.

It is possible for a practitioner to use such experiences for the benefit of all concerned, but he needs great sensitivity to the emotional interplay among members and the readiness of people for such experiences. Likewise, when a member leaves a group or withdraws from family sessions, the structure and process of the system are changed, necessitating new adaptations on the part of all concerned.

Assessing and Changing Roles

The social worker recognizes that the pattern of roles in any relationship is a crucial influence on the viability of the client-worker system. How an individual perceives the role of client and behaves in that role is an indicator of the usefulness of the service to him. In marital and family treatment, role conflict or lack of complementarity interferes with the system's ability to achieve its goals. The focus of treatment may, therefore, center on the patterns of roles in the marital or family relationship. These patterns of behavior may be either functional or dysfunctional to the welfare of the clients.

Other roles emerge out of the interaction among members of the family or within the worker-individual or worker-group relationship. In worker-client interaction, clients may assume such roles as controller or dominator, conformist or nonconformist, scapegoat or victim of circumstances. Clients often get stereotyped into these roles by the worker's response to them or, in groups, by the responses of other members to the person in the role.

The well-known role of scapegoat is an example.[7] It causes distress to the scapegoat and to the social worker who is confronted with such a phenomenon. In families and other groups, a steady state is often maintained at the expense of one member who becomes the object of the displaced hostilities of others. The scapegoat becomes a symbol of some disturbance in the dyad or group. Members are protected from recognizing their own tensions by displacing them onto another. The scapegoat tends to be a person from whom others do not fear retaliation. Although the primary dynamic is the group's need to place a person in such a role, the scapegoat is not a helpless victim. He unwittingly behaves in such a way as to maintain the pattern of behavior. Scapegoating is produced by the existence of tensions among people which have not been resolved satisfactorily in other ways. In families, the sources of tension may be associated with unavowed conflict in cultural value orientations. Since people have been socialized to accept particular values and patterns of relationships, some differences are present in any relationship. The conflicts may be within families or between families and extended families around patterns of expectations for performance or traditions and customs to be observed. The conflicts may be between the family and the expectations and customs of the community.

In a one-to-one relationship, when it becomes evident that a client has become a scapegoat in his family or other group, the worker is limited to helping him to understand what is going on in his relationship with others and the part he plays in provoking hostility. Some understanding may make the role more bearable and relieve the scapegoat of feelings of guilt and anger by finding an acceptable channel for the release of feelings. Since the scapegoat meets the often unconscious needs of others, the ideal situation for working with the problem is intervention in the family or group which needs to scapegoat one of its members. This is a difficult task for the worker, especially in a family because there the pattern has often been established over a long period of time. The worker finds ways to bring the tensions and conflicts into awareness and to clarify the stresses that result in the projection of hostilities onto a particular member, to clarify the pattern of relationships, and to discover alternative ways of dealing with the needs that result in the behavior. The techniques of support and exploration are used first, but confrontation is usually necessary. Gradually, the worker can move toward clarifying the meaning of behavior and trying out new behavioral patterns.

The monopolizer is another common dysfunctional role, whether it occurs in the worker-client dyad, families, or preventive or therapeutic groups.[8] The role often meets the person's emotional need to maintain control and ward off anxiety in a way that, if maintained, disrupts the relationship or prevents the goals from being achieved. The person feels compelled to talk, becoming anxious when the worker or other members take over. Often the talk is repetitive ventilation of feelings or experiences. Some ventilation is valuable. Continuous pouring out of negative feelings, experiences, thoughts, and problems without stopping to reflect on them or trying to change the dissatisfying conditions becomes nonproductive. In situations outside the social work one, such ventilation is also harmful to the development of social relationships that are mutually beneficial. Some clients who have been able to give and take in communication revert to monopolizing when they become anxious. Workers often become irritated with this pattern of behavior. In groups, other members develop resentment of the monopolizer. They tend to react through silent hostility, feelings of helplessness, fear of trying to change the situation, or blaming the worker. The pattern tends to be self-perpetuating since the more the monopolist talks, the more he senses the irritation of others and the more anxious he becomes. He is too anxious to give up the center of the stage. His tendency to monopolize is a self-protective device. For these reasons, it is important for the worker to attend to the problem as soon as possible.

In dealing with a monopolizer, the worker's task is to interrupt the pattern of behavior, first through supportive means, such as finding something that can be acknowledged as a positive effort and then stating that he would like to respond to the client's message. In a group he might interrupt long enough to comment that other members might like to respond. If these techniques do not work, then the worker needs to confront the monopolizer with a direct request that he stop talking because his prolonged talking is not being helpful to him. Later he can help the person to deal with the anxiety or need to control that underlies the pattern of behavior. In groups, he also may need to help the others to learn to interrupt and enter into the discussion or activity.

Scapegoats and monopolizers are but two of the patterns of behavior that tend to be dysfunctional. Among the other roles with which the worker needs to be concerned are the isolate, who lacks psychological bonds with his associates; the clown, who seeks acceptance by offering himself to be laughed at, usually with an undercurrent of contempt for self and others; and passive-aggressive roles. Whatever the pattern of behavior, the parts are interdependent: there is an interrelatedness between individual needs and the needs of the dyad or group in the creation and maintenance of such roles. Thus, the desirable interventions are with the systems of relationships.

Motivating and Reducing Resistance

Identification with the social worker and feelings of trust and mutual acceptance provide powerful motivation for continuation. In such an atmosphere, anxieties and fears are lessened and hopefulness is increased. Clients are not apt to remain in treatment if they believe that some positive changes in themselves or their own situation are not possible. They need to have and to perceive that they have the power to achieve some change.[9] In the last chapter, it was noted that there must be hope that relief from discomfort, pain, or dissatisfaction with the current situation can occur. There must be enough discomfort with the steady state for a person to desire some further development or change in the situation. Thus, the worker needs to work to maintain a balance between discomfort and hope as the client tries to change in some way. Usually he can recognize that progress is being made. In this phase he feels hopefulness as he or the group of which he is a part achieves some desired gain. Mastery of situations strengthens the ego and success tends to build on success. What might have been a vicious cycle of hopelessness-failure-greater hopelessness gets replaced with a cycle of hopelessness-success-hopefulness.[10]

Even within a general atmosphere in which individual and group motivation is high, there will be periods of time when apathy or discouragement sets in. Particular clients resist efforts by the worker or by other members to work on difficulties or obstacles to goal achievement.[11] When anxiety increases beyond a tolerable level the client defends himself: he resists. During this phase resistance represents an effort to hold on to the familiar and fear of trying out other ways of feeling, thinking, and doing. According to Ackerman, "it reflects the patient's need to place a fence around the most vulnerable areas of self in an attempt to immunize the self against the danger of reopening old psychic wounds."[12]

The major principle to guide the worker is that he respects the client's need to protect himself and does not arouse more anxiety than the client is able to deal with at a given time. Certain of the worker's activities may arouse anxiety. In families and groups, certain activities of other members may arouse anxiety in one or more members. In order to advance expectations and achieve certain gains, it is necessary that some anxiety be aroused; the crucial factor in treatment is whether clients have the ego capacities to cope with the disturbed feelings. Confrontation is more often used now than it was in the initial phase of treatment, but it tends to arouse anxiety and hence resistance. What is to be conveyed is not condemnation or withholding of acceptance, but a direct leveling with the client that something has to change. Such challenges make it possible for clients to visualize alternative ways of behaving or alternative decisions related to problems. Confrontation which strips defenses is harmful; the worker needs to allow time to provide support to the person in his efforts to understand the intent of the confrontive message and to work it through.

Interpretations of the meaning of behavior may also be resisted, either because the worker expresses a truth that the client is not yet ready to recognize or because the worker has really misunderstood the meaning of the situation. It is hard to face the intensity of deep feelings and it is no wonder that clients defend themselves against such understanding until they have developed enough self-esteem to accept these aspects of themselves. Secrecy leads to resistance. When a client keeps a secret from the worker he is making it impossible for the worker to help. When a worker withholds information from the client because he has promised the source that the information would be confidential, he cannot use it for the client's benefit. In therapeutic groups, resistance often occurs because there are secrets between one or more members and the worker which are not revealed or discussed in the group session.[13] Resistance similarly occurs when there are secrets among members of families and the worker or a member attempts to open up the secret area for examination. These areas of secrecy create barriers.

The specific interventions of the social worker in overcoming resistance are as varied as the reasons for the resistance in the first place. But, to be worked with, the resistance must be acknowledged and brought to the client's attention. The worker may comment that he has noticed a particular thing has happened. He brings to conscious awareness the expectations, disappointments, or anxiety that work against continuance of effort. His next move depends upon the response from the client. He may invite ventilation of the feelings of anxiety, hopelessness, or fear that create the stalemate. He may provide support in the form of realistic reassurance to reduce threat. He may universalize the problem, acknowledging that it is natural to be uncertain about the consequences of efforts toward change or that distrust is often realistic due to times when trust has not been earned. He may engage the individual or group in exploration of the situation. At times the worker will use confrontation to disrupt the steady state in order to overcome apathy, denial, or avoidance of a particular issue. He may offer facts that have not been recognized or encourage the client system to search for facts on which to base a decision about moving into a feared area.[14]

Communication

In the core phase, patterns of communication become established, and there is need to maintain those that are functional and seek to modify those that create barriers to goal achievement. The worker needs to be particularly sensitive to the client's ability to understand what he is trying to communicate and, at the same time, to test out his understanding of the messages being sent by the client. Self-evaluation by worker as well as evaluation of the adequacy of the client's communication is necessary. Among the characteristics of communication to be taken into account are: clarity of speech; change of topic; the transactions that do not get completed; who is in control and under what conditions; the appropriateness of affect; the message about relationship that is imbedded in the words; and congruence between the manifest and latent content.[15] In work with more than one client at a time, the task is more complicated in that the worker needs to understand the meaning of the messages sent by him or by one member to each individual and to the group as a whole. He needs to assess the speaking order: who speaks to whom; who is left out; who speaks for whom. For example, if mother talks to father, does the child usually interrupt? If the oldest child talks, does the father lecture? The nature and extent of each person's participation influences the individual's use of the service and also the progress of the group.

Clients often need help to learn how to communicate more effectively in a particular situation so that they are understood by others and, in turn, become able to understand others. This process lays the groundwork for other forms of change. Modeling and teaching communication skills are important parts of the worker's activity. Change in dysfunctional communication patterns may lead to change in interpersonal behavior, and enhanced capacity for effective communication may result in more positive responses from other people.

During the earlier sessions, some satisfactory patterns of communication between worker and client were developed. In families and groups, patterns among the members were adequate to develop a working agreement and satisfying enough for clients to have continued. But, as the content of the sessions shifts and as increased demands for active participation are made, new difficulties arise. In other instances it may take a long time for clients to be able to communicate verbally in effective ways. Examples are in work with very disturbed children who have been verbally inaccessible or psychotic patients who have great difficulty in making themselves understood and in understanding the messages of other people.[16]

To enter into verbal communication with other people requires many interrelated skills. It requires ability to listen to others and to make sense out of what is heard; present information in such a way that others can understand the message; relate what one is saying to the ongoing discussion; subject one's feelings and ideas to the scrutiny of others; consider the rights of others to express themselves; physically face those with whom one is interacting; and enter into the mood of the interaction. These skills are required of both worker and clients. These demands are present in the client-worker interaction and in family and group interaction.

The worker has special responsibilities for the process and content of communication. He decodes the vocabulary and grammar of the client's language, which may be unfamiliar to him. He encodes his messages in a form understandable to the client. He may fail in communication with his clients due to differences in language, stemming from social class, age, regional, or ethnic differences. He needs to understand that there are varied linguistic styles for expressing feelings and ideas. There are cultural differences in volubility, intensity, and colorfulness to be taken into account. While accepting the client's style of speech he needs also to ascertain its suitability to the varied roles the client carries. Speech that is functional at home in one's subculture may be dysfunctional at school or work. These different expectations may create conflict within the client and in his interpersonal relations. The worker may need to spend some time with the client in an effort to make his language serve his purpose rather than otherwise. He does not imitate the client's style of speech. He accepts it and he may pick up on particular words and phrases that reflect the client's mood or meaning. It is primarily his tone that carries the message of nonjudgmental acceptance. He communicates in an authentic way, but avoids the use of professional jargon.

In working with individuals or families who have dysfunctional patterns of communication, the primary goal of treatment may be to help clients to communicate more effectively. Minuchin and his colleagues have described intensive work with twelve multiproblem ghetto families, including at least two delinquent children. These families often exhibited patterns of communication that were extremely dysfunctional to each member and to the family as a whole. The therapists served as teachers of talking. The members needed help over a long period of time to clarify to whom they were speaking, to learn to listen, to repeat what they had heard, to request that others respond, to ask for clarification of messages, and to recognize and change patterns of communication.[17]

The worker helps clients to identify the roadblocks to effective communication. These were noted earlier, as when one person dominates the coversation or withdraws from active participation. One illustration is the treatment of a family consisting of Mrs. Kopper, who is in the final stages of getting a divorce; Mr. Prince, who has been living with her for several months and whom she plans to marry when the divorce becomes final; her two children—Cathie, age 4, and Tommy, age 8. Tommy was brought to a mental health center because of severe temper tantrums and refusal to talk. One part of the treatment plan was to work with the two adults in relation to Tommy's needs. The worker recorded:

> For several weeks Mr. Prince participated very little in the discussion, despite my efforts to draw him out. Mrs. Kopper speaks for both of them. His silence has appreared friendly. He often smiles or nods, which behavior was interpreted by me as agreement with Mrs. Kopper's statements. Feeling uneasy about Mr. Prince's continued silence and noting a sudden and fleeting look of distress on his face, I said I wondered if his silence might mean that he did not really agree with Mrs. Kopper's opinion that the status quo was just fine for both of them. This comment led to a flood of feelings about how awkward the present arrangement is for him, how uncertain he feels about the ambiguity of his place in the family, and how uncertain he feels about his responsibility to the children once the marriage takes place. Thus, an area of conflict was opened up at a new level of comunication. I recognized that I should have been active much earlier in bringing him into the conversation.

The focus of work with the couple then shifted, with their agreement, to recognizing the differences between each person in feelings and perceptions of the situation, helping them to listen actively to each other and check out with each other the accuracy of perceptions about the message; expressing both loving and caring feelings and hostile ones in a nondestructive manner, and then moving into decision-making concerning their futures.

Some forms of family treatment are based almost entirely on changing the communication process.[18] For many individuals, families, and small groups, however, improved communication is not the primary goal for its own sake. Rather it is sought as a tool on the way to achieving the major purpose of improved social relationships.

As the practitioner assesses and influences the way the client-worker system is developing, these efforts result also in positive changes in the clients' patterns of behavior. For "the relationship between task and socioemotional activities is complex."[19] If clients are able to develop meaningful relationships with the worker and often also with other participants, it is expected that they will carry these attitudes and abilities over to other vital relationships. If they can sustain motivation to work toward their individual or collective goals, the sense of hope and successful effort will be carried with them after they leave the social work situation. Similarly, if they have been able to modify their role behaviors and communicate more effectively within the helping system, these gains may be transferred to other social situations. Thus, as the worker is paying attention to the maintenance and development of the system, he is simultaneously intervening to help clients meet their needs and solve their problems in psychosocial functioning. In the next chapter, primary attention will be given to interventions that are intended to influence directly the clients' understanding of themselves in their situations, and to solve particular problems in social living.

CHAPTER EIGHT

The Core Phase: Achievement of Goals

In order to enable the client system to move as rapidly as possible toward the achievement of its goals, continuous assessment is necessary. Assessment is now aimed at understanding the particular goals, needs, problems, and capacities of the individuals being served. The worker finds ways to use capacities and reduce obstacles within the person and environment that prevent the attainment of goals. Although the worker has to make his own evaluation of the clients in their environments, the more important task is to involve the client in the search for appropriate understanding through exploration and reflective thinking.

The worker's major activities in the helping process vary with the particular situation. Usually, however, he intends to help clients to increase understanding of themselves in their situations, resolve identified problems, develop greater social competence, and reduce obstacles and enhance opportunities in the environment.

Understanding Self and Others

Acquisition of more accurate perceptions of self in relation to others is a frequent focus of treatment in the core phase. In order to help a client to achieve this, the practitioner utilizes his knowledge about biopsychosocial functioning. He needs awareness of his own values as these are like or different from those of the clients. The extent to which a client can improve in self-understanding is partially dependent upon the accuracy of the worker's assessment of the client's view of himself and others. The client's perceptions may be distorted by the stereotypes used by the worker to account for the client's behavior. The worker needs accurate perception of his own tendencies to view the difficulties and the strengths of a client as due to a characteristic such as being poor, rich, a fundamentalist Protestant, or belonging to a racial category. As Solomon has pointed out, there is also an opposite trap for the worker, namely, that he view a black client "as just another person," failing to recognize the influence of race on the practice experience.[1] She describes dilemmas and skills required for effective work with black clients, but they have general applicability. One basic skill of the effective practitioner is "the ability to perceive in any behavior, others' or one's own, alternative explanations for that behavior, particularly those alternatives which the self might most strongly reject as false."[2] This skill requires sensitivity to one's own stereotypes and feelings toward others. It also requires the use of knowledge from the behavioral sciences about the different and similar values and experiences of the subcultures within society, taking into account the disagreements among scholars about these ideas. Consideration of alternatives can help the worker to hold in abeyance his own biases and use these generalizations as possible explanations only, which may or may not hold for a particular individual, family, or group. Rather than thinking of a client as representative of a category of people, he assesses the extent to which he possesses the attributes of that group. This is the essence of individualization: it occurs only when one can distinguish a client system from what is general for most people in a particular category.

Striving for self-understanding is based on the theoretical assumption that if a person can understand how his values, emotions, patterns of behavior, and prior experiences have contributed to the current problems, he becomes able to distinguish which attitudes and behaviors best serve his goals. He can then decide how he can behave differently or what needs to be changed. It is assumed that the more accurate the perception of inner and outer reality, the firmer is the foundation for effective social functioning. More accurate perception of other significant persons may lead to changes in attitudes and behavior toward them.

One example is a fifteen-year-old girl in an orthopedic hospital. Gerry, in a fit of rage, tore the cast off her arm. She was in pain and crying. In a response to my statement of concern about her, she went into a loud tirade about the nurses, blaming them and saying that they all hated her—in fact, everybody hated her. She pled with me to do something about it. After she regained her composure, she said that the nurse told her she would just have to wait until an intern could come to replace the cast—that she knew better than to tear it off. She defended herself, saying she really did not know what she was doing. I said in a soft voice that she had certainly caused herself a lot of pain and trouble. She started to cry again. I said that it seemed to me it was a very painful way to express her anger. During the ensuing silence she became calmer and said, between sobs, that this was the second time she had done this. "Can't you help me?" she asked. "I'm in trouble." I said, "Yes, you really are in trouble with yourself and with other people, too." I suggested that I first see about replacing the cast and then she might want to have several talks with me. She asked, "Oh, could you?" I said that perhaps through such talks I could help her to find better ways of expressing all that anger. She asked if I'd come back soon. I said I would after the cast was replaced. This critical event led to enhanced understanding of herself in relation to others.

When people are anxious, there is a tendency to cling to the familiar and to avoid risking further upset in the steady state. Through social work help, there can be opportunities to correct errors in one's assumptions about the world by checking these assumptions against those of the worker, thus getting corrective feedback. In groups there is the further opportunity to test these assumptions against those of one's peers. The particular purpose and quality of the relationship provide a different context in this respect. In daily living, the reciprocal nature of a person's behavior in relation to others leads them to respond in ways that confirm his expectations: certain patterns of behavior become self-perpetuating and self-defeating. If a person anticipates rejection, for example, he tends to behave in ways that bring rejection. A vicious cycle develops which needs to be broken. In the social work situation, the person does not have his inaccurately perceived ideas confirmed; rather, he is supported and challenged toward different ways of perceiving himself in relation to others.

Acquiring self-understanding requires that a person disclose aspects of self that may be frightening and painful to him and which he fears will be unacceptable to the practitioner and, in groups, to other members as well. Experimentation with different ways of behaving requires wading in unknown waters. To venture into this arena requires that a relationship of trust has been developed among the participants. It requires that the worker use supportive techniques in assisting the client to enter into reflective discussion of self and situation.

Nine Spanish-speaking mothers, of low socioeconomic status living in a barrio of a large city, accepted an invitation to join a group at a community mental health center to learn about child development and how to bridge the cultural differences between them and the dominant culture. During the first meetings, the women tended to be formal and reserved in their behavior, and it took time for them to trust the worker and each other sufficiently to be able to disclose their feelings and concerns, but gradually cohesiveness developed. The members became more able to share with and support each other. When one member mentioned a marital difficulty and received acceptance from the group, others began to disclose their difficulties, too. The worker, a Spanish-speaking graduate student in social work, recorded:

> Corita said that her husband used to mistreat the children severely and found her repugnant when she was pregnant. Lupe said, "That's my situation, exactly." Juanita then spoke about her husband's infidelity. Corita interrupted to say that she had actually been hospitalized as a result of strain due to her husband's infidelities. . . . Juanita said she had domesticated her brute through ignoring the bad and giving and doing. The ladies laughed in acknowledgment, but the feelings of being devalued were very evident. I was at a loss as to how to help them, because these women have so few realistic alternatives. I suggested that here, in this room, we could at least unburden and there was much general approval. *"Todo en confianza,"* said Joty, "all in confidence." Everyone nodded, and several repeated the phrase. Much more emotion was being expressed than ever before: anger, hurt, self-blame, and worry, but also some laughter, caring, and sharing.

Very quickly, the women became able to participate in reflective discussion about themselves, their husbands and children, and the neighborhood conditions that made life difficult. One example was Corita's recognition that she tended to be overprotective of her eight-year-old daughter.

> During the next session, as the group discussed their attitudes toward their children, Corita was still concerned. I said that sometimes our concerns toward our

children reflect certain fears of our own or experiences we have had. Corita then disclosed the fact that she did feel she had to protect her daughter from harm, but maybe she goes too far. But, she just did not want to have happen to her daughter what she had gone through. She became silent, so I asked if she would want to tell us about this. After a thoughtful silence, she said that when she was her daughter's age, she had been molested by her stepfather. She felt dirty, ashamed, and used for such a long time. I saw the concern and shock in the ladies' faces. Touching Corita's arm, I said I thought I could understand how she wanted to protect her daughter. Then Lupe said, "And you feel so helpless, don't you? I still feel dirty and helpless. My guardian molested me when I was only nine and I just didn't know what to do about it. I felt trapped." She's been trying to help her daughter become more independent, rather than quiet and meek like she was. I noted that we respond differently to similar trauma and we have so much to gain from each other's views of things. There was general nodding. Juanita said that our meetings are a good thing. All agreed.

As the women brought up problems and feelings related to sex, the worker learned that they had very little accurate knowledge about human sexuality, so she provided some education about this, as the members requested it and were ready to use it. Several members had been raped; several had been and were being physically abused by their husbands as were their children; and there were other examples of maltreatment. Gradually, the women came to explore and recognize their feelings and reactions to such treatment and then to consider what alternatives they had. The first proposed solutions ranged from just taking the abuse for the sake of the children to actually giving up the marriage. Gradually, alternatives became apparent. Corita, for example, gained enough self-assertiveness to discuss the issue with her husband. She said:

"Because of our group, I have been able to stand up to my husband and tell him I do not fear him. Since then, he has not laid a harsh hand on me nor beaten the children. I wanted you all to know." Her sense of pride was evident. This comment elicited much joy and encouragement to hold her ground. Juanita had long been upset because her husband disowned their oldest daughter because she married a black man, and he forbade Juanita to see her daughter. The group really rallied around Juanita, giving her much sympathy and support, and sharing with her their ideas about how she might deal with the situation.

It took much time before Juanita decided that no one could keep her from her child and she was able to confront her husband and go on her own to visit the daughter, without dire consequences. These are but two examples of the way in which a sense of self-worth and confidence replaced earlier feelings of self-blame, worthlessness, and powerlessness.

Through reflective thinking about the person-situation configuration, clients test their capacities to modify misconceptions they have about themselves, other people, or situations. They come to more accurate perceptions of reality. Perception is a function of the ego. The way a person perceives himself, other people, or situations depends upon the external event and the interpretation of the event. The interpretation depends upon the person's values, his cultural perspective, past experiences with similar events, and the nature and strengths of his defenses. There are a number of reasons for lack of understanding. Clients may lack knowledge that is essential to understanding. They may, for example, lack knowledge about normal development and normal reactions to events: they mistake the usual for abnormality or vice versa. When normal expectations for physical, psychological, and social development through the life cycle are not understood, what is normally expectable behavior is often regarded as deviant or, on the other hand, problematic behavior is not recognized as such. Similarly, lack of knowledge about physical handicaps and illnesses and the effect of these on the psychosocial functioning of patients and their relatives is a common source of misconception. Lack of knowledge about sex is another frequent example. In such instances the provision of facts, according to the client's ability to accept and understand them, is necessary. The client can make best use of the facts if there is discussion of their meaning to the client and persons in his social network.

Commonly held prejudices are often determinant of a person's inability to perceive himself and others accurately. When one is prejudiced, perception is distorted. One perceives individuals as representatives of categories which have been devalued. Prejudice may be based on ethnicity, poverty, age, sex, or being on welfare, and both interferes with a person's opportunity for relationships with others and harms the others. There is usually great resistance to acknowledging that one is prejudiced; there is a tendency to deny this attitude and rationalize the reasons for one's attitude and behavior toward others. Recognition of the fact is the first step toward change. Factual information is essential but seldom sufficient to bring about changes in attitudes and behavior. Alternative techniques to be used are ventilating feelings, followed by examination of the basis for the feelings; raising questions about actual events that seem related to the prejudice; or providing experiences with the victims of prejudice. Understanding and empathy reduce prejudice. Empathy can be developed in clients as well as in workers through a variety of techniques: requesting that the person try to put himself in the place of the other; asking him to express how he thinks it would feel to be in that situation; being influenced by empathic comments by the worker or members of groups.

Irrational beliefs about oneself are forms of lack of self-knowledge. A low self-image or lack of positive identity leads many clients to deprecate themselves and engage in self-defeating patterns of behavior. "I am not loved"; "I can't do it"; "I'm really ugly"; "If you really knew me, you'd know how rotten I am." All these are messages that often convey irrational beliefs about oneself. Self-evaluation is a process that determines an individual's level of self-esteem, his beliefs about his ultimate worth. Along with self-evaluation goes a process of self-definition, through which one acquires a sense of identity or beliefs about who and what he is. Both sets of beliefs are developed through relationships and experiences with other people who confirm or contradict the beliefs around which responses from others interact with his own perceptions.[3] A change in self-esteem requires that a person test the assumption that if others know certain things about him, he will be rejected. Identity and self-esteem influence how a person relates to others and are influenced by the person's perceptions of the responses of others to him.

The social worker can provide conditions, through the relationship, that allow the client to test the validity of his beliefs about his worth and identity. When possible, a worker can use external realities to correct distortions in perception of self such as, for example, "John just said he loves you very much—didn't you hear him?'' Members of groups offer a broader arena for such testing than is true of one-worker-one-client relationships.

Transference reactions, earlier discussed, are a special instance of distortion of perception. Clients may react to the worker or to other members in ways that were appropriate to an important person in their earlier experience but which are not appropriate in the current situation. This phenomenon is apt to be more intense in long-term than in short-term treatment and it is apt to be more intense in individual than in treatment with couples or in groups. In multiple-person situations, however, there is the added complexity of transference reactions directed toward other members of the family or group.

Reflective thinking is the concept used by Hollis in her classification of types of procedures used by social workers. The term is used in the sense of involving mental consideration or contemplation.[4] The worker asks questions or makes comments that are intended to encourage or contribute to: (1) the client's understanding of himself in relation to his current situation or immediate past; (2) the patterns and dynamics of the client's behavior; and (3) aspects of the past that are thought to be relevant to the present situation. By far the most work is in the first category, helping the client to reflect on himself in relation to his situation in order to understand it better and hence be able to change it when desirable. The primary technique used by the worker in this endeavor is exploration, followed by clarification or interpretation.

In dealing with difficulties in accurate perception of the person-situation constellation, the worker provides essential knowledge and requests the client to consider its meaning to him and how he can use it. He draws out the client's thoughts and feelings about himself and the situation and reactions to current situations. He requests that the client think about possible explanations for the problematic situation. He may universalize feelings in order to indicate the naturalness of feelings about a particular circumstance, such as the notion that people often have angry feelings even when they love someone. He suggests that clients try to express exactly how they feel, and he may need to label the emotion and seek their response to the idea that they are feeling angry, fearful, or loving toward the persons involved in the situation. He asks them to consider the things in the environment and in his responses to these things that contribute to the reactions. Through such clarifying techniques, he helps the clients to move from manifest content to recognition of underlying patterns of feelings, relationships, and behavior.

In some instances, it is helpful for the client to reflect about dynamic and developmental factors so that he learns how his emotions and thoughts work for or against him. The worker may encourage him to search for possible reasons within himself for his feelings; he may call attention to a discrepancy between fact and feeling or he may recognize inappropriate behaviors. The worker may note that a pattern seems to be emerging in the way the client feels and thinks about different situations, making comments to help the client to discover the pattern. When the client is ready, the worker may interpret his use of defenses in a tentative manner. One worker said to a client, for example, that when things are hard for us, we tend to deny that this is so in order to protect ourselves. Sometimes when a client does not recognize difficult behavior, an interpretation from the worker may help. An example is a comment: "There seems to be some connection between your anger and the death of Jimmy that we need to try to understand." However, unless the client recognizes the behavior as ego-alien or unprofitable, he will not seek to understand or change it.

During the course of treatment, earlier experiences in the person's or family's past may be brought up by the client himself or when the worker decides it is desirable to elicit such information in order to remove an obstacle to progress. There are times when making connections between an event in the past and a present difficulty is necessary. Certainly the search for roots is almost an obsession in today's world. Much talk about the past is done to ventilate anger or to justify or defend a present position or behavior. Even so, for a person to recall an important event and his reactions to it may be crucial to change present feelings and behavior.

An example is of an adult who was adopted when he was four years old and wanted to find his biological parents. He became able to say that he feels abandoned and rejected by them and that, not even knowing who they are, makes him feel strange and abnormal. His current dilemma is that his wife of fifteen years has just taken a job which requires her to travel several days each month. His income is very adequate, and she does not need to work. He also worries that she will abandon him, in spite of every realistic evidence to the contrary. The early feelings of being abandoned seem to be resurging in the present. Thus, clarification of the present fears of abandonment as related to earlier events may be helpful.

Viewing behavior from a developmental perspective may help the client to change his definition of his own behavior or that of significant others. Looking at what precipitated a problem can help put it into perspective. The perceptions of the past events may be accurate or distorted: only if it is possible to test the reality of the events seen as traumatic can either worker or client know the fact. But the important issue is the meaning of the perceived event to the person and its influence on his current psychosocial functioning. The worker's focus is on the influence of these events on the present attitudes, relationships, and problem-solving capacities of the individuals involved.

In family and group situations, when one member recalls historical material, the worker needs to assess its impact on other individuals and on the progress of the group. He needs to decide whether the nature of the past experience and its influence on current functioning is such that it can be worked with in the multiple-client situation. If the person is a member of a group, it may become clear that his situation is so different from that of other members that he needs individual treatment in addition to the group. The worker also needs to decide whether a change in plans is required in order to deal with the matter. In some instances, for example, short-term treatment may need to be extended.

Seeking for the meaning of behavior or emotions involves bringing them into conscious awareness when they can be recalled with assistance. When the worker suggests explanations, these are related to the particular pattern of behavior, emotion, or situation—not generalized to the personality. The practitioner refrains from interpretation of unconscious processes: his focus is on conscious and suppressed material.[5] The worker generally approaches internalized conflicts as they are manifested in social adaptation, interpersonal relationships, realistic aspects of the cultural milieu, and the realities of the living experience.

Explanations that are intended to enhance understanding of the meanings of feelings or behavior are helpful only under certain conditions. The interpretations should be accurate. If they are correct, they reveal an underlying theme that can serve as a basis for further reflection and action. Inexperienced practitioners have a tendency to jump in to present interpretations based on their own need to show how smart they are. Adequate prior exploration is necessary. The worker or client who makes comments about the meaning of behavior needs to seek feedback to the message sent and to work toward evaluation of its meaning to the intended recipient. The most effective comments are made when the individual or members of a group who are the recipients are nearly ready, but unable to discover the meaning for themselves and to relate it to the broader situation. The understanding that has occurred needs to be worked over in different forms. Some redundancy provides an important safety factor in clarifying the use being made of the new understanding.

In a study of the use of ascriptions by social workers from twenty family sessions which were tape recorded, several criteria for their successful use were formulated.[6] An ascription was defined as a form of comment in which a characteristic is ascribed to a client or a group. It is a form of feedback. Ascriptions include comments aimed at clarifying behavior and situations and interpreting the meaning of behavior. It was found that workers often have difficulty in communicating the intent of their messages effectively. The comments which were most effective were those that were clearly stated and contained only one basic idea; accurate, specific, and to the point; focused on the central problem under consideration; offered in a mood of sharing a perception with a client and in words that were consonant with actions; and offered in a tone of voice that was supportive and nonthreatening. The comments tended to be effective when the worker was sensitive to the feelings and differential readiness of clients, thereby conveying acceptance and empathy. They were effective when the worker avoided taking sides in arguments and did not attack defenses; focused on relationships and interactions among people; encouraged clients to respond to the statement and allowed adequate time for the response; and offered opportunities for members to respond to each other. The comments tended to be effective when they related primarily to process as distinguished from manifest content; when there was emphasis on positive feelings and behavior as well as negatives; and when an ascription got at a theme that drew the members' ideas together.

Ascriptions were judged as not helpful to the clients when the worker's statement included numerous ideas so that the client did not get a cue as to which idea he was to respond to, or when too much information was given in a single message; such messages were vague, ambiguous, long, complex, and difficult to understand. Ascriptions were not helpful when the worker inappropriately interrupted a client, allowed one member to respond for another, did not return to the first member's concern when others had interrupted, or inappropriately changed the subject. They were not helpful when they enhanced defensiveness and withdrawal from participation. One of the judges summarized one worker's use of ascriptions with the comment, "How we can deluge the client with words." Such volubility is something to be watched. Although the research on the use of ascription was limited to meetings with families, it can be assumed that many of these findings would apply as well to work with individuals and formed groups.

These evaluative comments indicate the crucial importance of self-awareness and relationship. They point out the need for skills in communication and in accurate assessments of clients and their situations. The worker needs to decode the client's grammar, vocabulary, and style of speaking, and decipher both the manifest and the latent meaning. He needs to recall what went before, pay attention to the sequence of material, interpret the meaning to himself and be reasonably confident about his judgment, modulate the tone of voice, and have faith in the individual's and group's ability to participate appropriately in the process. In groups, the social worker needs to build on and support the members' capacities to support or question the comments and actions of each other. When the members confront each other or offer interpretations about the meaning of an individual's behavior, the worker needs to assess the motivation of that person as to its intent, the effect of the message on the member or members toward whom it was directed and on the group as a whole, and the readiness of the group to use it. Based on diagnostic considerations, he needs to support the efforts of the sender of the message, encourage the group to elaborate on the ideas, or suggest that there are better ways to think about the matter. Gradually, the members become more able to empathize with and understand each other and thereby become more helpful to each other. The work is most apt to be effective if the worker can help the members to identify common themes that relate one member's situation to those of others.

In groups a special characteristic of the use of techniques for enhancing understanding of self and others is that a contribution, in order to be useful to an individual, need not be directed specifically to him. During the time when a particular problematic situation is being explored, various members may present their experiences, express their feelings, and make relevant comments. To the extent that the underlying theme of the content is relevant to a particular person's concerns, he may derive understanding of some aspect of himself and his experiences. Often, when feelings or explanations are universalized, they touch closely on some member's particular concerns. This is what Konopka refers to as anonymity of insight.[7]

Verbal communication alone is not the royal road to understanding of self in relation to environment. Actions often clarify what people are thinking, feeling, and doing. Videotaping and replaying a session may enhance awareness of both verbal and nonverbal behaviors. Role-playing may be used to help a client become more aware of repressed feelings and patterns of relationships, with the worker taking the part of a family member or the client playing both roles himself. In families and formed groups, various members may participate in role-playing and in its analysis and evaluation.

Controversies within social work concern the value of self-knowledge as a viable goal, particularly with clients of ethnic minorities or low incomes who need practical resources and opportunities for achievement. Solomon notes, however, that self-knowledge is necessary in order to have the power to solve problems. The value of knowledge is not for its own sake but as a "means of identifying those forces operating in the problem situation which can be controlled by the client, that is, upon which he can exert some form of power."[8] Particularly with clients who have negative self-images, the worker needs to demonstrate that the search for understanding is in the interest of opening new opportunities for them to be more able to control their own life situations.

There is some evidence from research for the idea that acquiring self-knowledge is effective. In one study, clients reported that increasing their understanding of their problem was one of the two elements of greatest importance to them during a brief service. A statistically significant correlation was found between clients' reports of increased understanding and improvement in the problem at the follow-up.[9] In another study clients rated understanding of self and others as most helpful.[10] Enhanced understanding should lead to decision-making concerning maintaining patterns of behavior that are functional and satisfying and changing those aspects of self which are self-defeating and which contribute to the misery of others.

Problem-solving Capacities and Patterns

One frequent goal of service is to work toward some decision that will be satisfactory to the individual and to the social systems that are affected by the decision. Clients often have difficulty in making or evaluating decisions. Problem-solving is a process through which intrapersonal, interpersonal, and intergroup conflicts are resolved. The decision concerns an individual in his social context or a common action of a family or other group. In social work practice the worker's emphasis is on the effectiveness of the decision itself, learning a problem-solving process, and implementing and evaluating the decision. Underlying this construct are ideas of people's ability to make choices and to change themselves and the environment.

Every individual and every group has learned to cope with problems in particular ways. Positive motivation, built on some sense of hope and clarity of goals, is essential to effective problem-solving. So, too, is clarity of understanding of who are the contributors to the problem and the particular part of the client in its evolution. One aspect of evaluation is of the ego qualities necessary for problem-solving, including accurate perception and judgment. It is to be remembered that problems are not only intrapersonal, but usually involve a person's interactions with others. They are often in the nature of dysfunctional patterns of behavior within families, groups, and organizations. They are often due, at least in part, to lack of resources in the community for meeting needs. In work with some client systems, the major purpose may be the resolution of a particular problem. In other instances there is a realistic problem-solving component within a process that is more inclusive. As a person makes a particular decision and carries it out effectively, other benefits accrue, such as more satisfying relationships among the participants; the improved relationships may, in turn, facilitate the solving of other conflicts that arise.

Problem-solving may be focused on coping with or resolving a problem of an individual or it may be in the nature of a group problem. In the latter instance, the group goals must be clear and there must be a group decision-making process that is appropriate to the capacities of the members and the goal to be achieved. Internal, interpersonal, and group conflict is always present to some extent. Although conflict occurs in a worker-individual system, it is more overt in family and group systems. The system's tolerance for conflict, its ability to identify the underlying issues, and the interconnections with other systems in the environment are important components of assessing capacity for decision-making.

John Dewey's formulation of problem-solving has been incorporated widely into social work practice theory.[11] Problem-solving emphasizes a rational and logical process for coping with questions and difficulties. It recognizes also that there is a flow of thoughts, ideas, and emotions and both conscious and unconscious elements. Emotions influence cognitive processes.

> In actuality, too, problem solving in social work probably proceeds, not linearly, but by a kind of spiral process in which action does not always wait upon the completion of assessment and assessment often begins before data collection is complete.[12]

Nevertheless, Dewey's steps provide the model for reaching some decision and action.[13] The steps in the process are:

1. Recognize the difficulty. Some state of doubt, hesitation, perplexity, or difficulty is recognized by one or more persons. There is a felt need to find some solution to the difficulty. In social work practice the difficulty may be recognized by a client, a worker, or some person in the client's environment. The worker often observes patterns of behavior, conflicting messages on the part of the clients, silence in response to questions, or comments that indicate some doubt or concern that was not recognized by the client system. Such an observation needs to be shared in order to ascertain if the client system recognizes the difficulty.

2. Define and specify the problem and the goals. The process involves formulating specific questions or aspects of the problem and its component parts. The difficulty, as initially presented, may not be the problem selected for focus. In exploring the ramifications of the situation it may become evident that there is a core difficulty underlying the original one. It may be one part of a constellation of interrelated problems from which either a core problem or one part may be selected. It involves analysis of the problem to clarify who is concerned about the difficulty and what it means to those concerned about it. In this step, there is exploration of feelings about the problem. There may be some intrapsychic conflict about the difficulties and the goals; there may be contradictory or ambivalent emotions and responses within a person. If the problem is a complex one, a particular aspect might be chosen as the immediate focus of worker-client-system interaction. Decision-making is involved in defining and selecting a problem. In fact, a series of decisions is made in each step of the problem-solving process.

In families and other groups, each member may have different feelings in intensity and kind about the nature of the difficulty and the hoped-for outcomes. There may be different perceptions about the nature of the problem, stemming from differences in life experiences, personal and cultural values, and norms. It is not unusual for members of a family to be caught up in a vicious cycle of arguing and disagreeing, accusing and defending, without awareness of the issues that lead to the dysfunctional behavior. This may happen also in groups, particularly of children. Unless the sources of conflict can be defined and some goals for change identified, there cannot be opportunity for change. Before a problem can be solved, the participants in the process must arrive at a common understanding of the issue.

3. Consider alternative proposals for solution. The next step is eliciting suggestions for possible solutions. Suggestions may be offered by both the client and the worker. Facts need to be obtained in order to assess the suitability of each proposal to the achievement of the goal. The choices to be made need to be based on realistic available alternatives. The only alternatives that are available are those that are within a cognitive field of experience related to past personal experiences and social and cultural characteristics, and the social and physical environment of the participants. The potential consequences of the alternatives need to be considered, although there tend to be unanticipated consequences of the choices made.

Considerable reflective thinking on the meaning of the possible solution to the clients and significant others is essential in considering alternatives for action. Thinking through the facts about the problems, according to Perlman, "requires coming to grips with it, probing into it, facing up to the feelings which it excites or with which it is charged, and working with the mind and also the spirit and the body to achieve mastery over it."[14] Alternatives are based on different constellations of values, resources, and role sets. Thus, some understanding of self and situation is required for analysis of alternative choices; one's attitudes, emotions, values, and norms of behavior influence decisions as to which alternatives are acceptable and which are not. The possible choices are influenced by the availability of support systems in the family and community. Many blocks to problem-solving are imposed by society. There may be lack of appropriate resources or there may be rigid policies which deter any viable choices. Certain stigmatized groups are objects of discrimination and thereby lack power to achieve their goals. As alternatives are considered, some will be recognized quickly as either not feasible or not worth further consideration; one or more will be seen to have the potential for a sound decision.

4. Decide which alternative to accept. This necessitates excluding the other proposals and evaluating the probable consequences of the decision. As in all steps of the process, the result is not based only

on rational thinking; unconscious factors, values, experiences, and external factors are powerful forces in choosing. Often, there is a spontaneous recognition that a particular decision seems right. Sometimes the choice is arrived at through a cognitive process of summarizing the problem and goals, the advantages and disadvantages of each alternative, and the reasons for the particular choice. In families and groups, there may be mild disagreement or great conflict in arriving at a choice. Depending upon the way the system has learned to recognize and manage conflict in the past, a solution that is reasonably acceptable to all will develop or the conflict will be solved by means of elimination of dissenting members, subjugation of some to the power of others, compromise, or majority rule.[15] In some instances when conflict cannot be resolved, the system itself may disintegrate.

Clients often need help with rethinking the proposed choice in light of their goals, the resources available, the strength of motivation to implement the decision, and the consequences of this anticipated decision.

5. Plan a course of action for putting the decision into operation and clarify worker and client roles in implementing the decision. The plan involves clarifying the actual steps to be taken and the persons to be involved in the process.

6. Implement the decision and evaluate the results. When an individual or group acts on a decision, another series of subproblems needs to be faced. There may be a need to find an alternative way to enact the decision. Obstacles may be encountered in the abilities of the client system or in the environment. Once an effort to act on the decision has been made, the results need to be evaluated. There may be a sense of great success or achievement or the results may not bear much resemblance to what was intended.

An illustration of the use of decision-making within an ongoing social work service concerns the Cohn family, consisting of Mr. C., age 43, an engineer; Mrs. C., age 41, homemaker and part-time clerk; and Bill, age 17, only child. During the intake interview, the presenting problem was Bill's unacceptable behavior. The problem became serious about a year ago when Bill's school grades dropped precipitously. He had done well in school up to this time and had also worked after school. Both parents complained that Bill was lying to them, had lost respect for them, and was very mean to his mother. Both parents felt that Bill was destroying their relationship with each other. Mrs. C. and Bill had frequent fights about how he spent the money he earned on his part-time job. After one of these fights, Bill had left home and stayed with a friend all night. Bill, too, was concerned about the fighting and thought his parents were too strict and restrictive. A friend suggested that the family call the Community Mental Health Center for counseling, which Mrs. C. did. Mr. C's goal was for Bill to quit school and join the army, where he would get the discipline he needs. Bill's goal was to stay home and graduate from high school. Mrs. C. felt caught between husband and son. During the first two months of treatment, the goal was to achieve resolution of the conflict about Bill's immediate future and to improve the relationships and social climate of the family. The plan was for individual conferences with Bill, joint interviews with the parents, and family conferences when these seemed to be indicated. The worker recorded:

After two months, I got three telephone calls in quick succession from all three of the Cohns. Each said it was impossible for them to live together any longer and that there had been a physical fight between Bill and Mr. C. Both parents said that their doctor had advised them to file an incorrigibility petition with the Juvenile Court. They did not want to do this, but had agreed that Bill should join the army. When, in each instance, I suggested the family come in for a conference, each agreed to do this at the suggested time.

Family interview. All three of the Cohns were quiet, expectant, and waiting for me to begin. I said I understood that the purpose of the conference was to understand the immediate crisis and then to come to some decision about Bill's future. I asked the family how it would like to begin to work on the trouble. Mrs. C. began in a short burst of whining anger, "I have tried, but he [pointing to Bill] just gets at me; for no reason at all he explodes and threatens me." Her sister and her doctor have both told her that if she keeps on getting aggravated, it will kill her. She doesn't want to make Bill leave, but she doesn't see any other way out. I commented, "Things really seem bad, then." She nodded, and tears came to her eyes.

I turned and looked at Mr. C. He began hesitantly, then forcefully said that he agreed with his wife. He talked about his own frequent stomach upsets and his doctor's advice to get the boy out of the home. I looked at Bill and asked if life at home seemed this bad for him, too. He said, in quiet anger, that he is really mixed up; he seems to be the one who's done most of the trying, but when he gets just a little out of hand, they make it worse. He wants to finish school, but since they want him out, what is there to do?

I asked if they had come here to tell me they had already reached a decision—that Bill was to leave home. No one answered me directly. There was a long silence. Mr. C. seemed uncomfortable, shuffled around, and looked at his wife. She, in turn, became tearful and talked about her helplessness in view of Bill's terrible temper. Mr. C. repeated much of what Mrs. C. had said. Then Bill very quietly asked, "What else is there to do?" I asked Bill if he wanted to enter the army. He said firmly, "No—I do not—but maybe that's the only way out." I asked the parents if they wanted me to agree that Bill's going into the army was the only way out. There was another long silence.

Mrs. C. broke the silence, saying, "I don't know. I don't know anything anymore. Look—this is my only son, but when he starts fighting with his father . . ." (Silence)" I asked, "And what happens then?" She responded, "I was caught in between and almost killed. But, of course, I want Bill home. I've worked to keep him, but he'll soon be gone anyway and I've got to live with my husband." I said, "You seem to feel that your son wants to stay but your husband wants him to leave and the whole thing is up to you." She answered in desperation, "Yes, he told me that if Bill doesn't go, he will." I commented that was a tough position to be in and turned to Mr. C. He acknowledged that he had said that to his wife and even meant it at the time. "And I still think no child should be permitted to disrupt and destroy his parents." I said, "And this is what you feel Bill is doing." After a silence, he said, "Yes." Bill said, "You see it is stacked against me." Neither parent replied.

I said I wondered if the parents would respond to Bill's comments. (Silence.) Then I asked, "Do you want me to say the only possibility was for Bill to leave home?" (Silence.) Mrs. C. started to cry quietly—then she said almost inaudibly that Sam (her husband) wants Bill to go and Bill wants to stay. "I just have to choose between them . . . but which one is going to hate me?" (Silence.) I asked, "And which one do you think will hate you?" She said, "Maybe they both will . . . then I'll be left all alone." I asked how this felt to Mr. C. and to Bill. Mr. C. said, "But that's silly. Bill is my son, too. It's hard to know . . . when I'm mad I want him to go, but when I sit here and think about it, I'm not sure." Looking directly at me, he said, "Remember what we talked about before—how mad I still am that I was thrown out of my home. I was denied an education." I said, "And you can't help acting toward Bill as your parents did toward you." He said, "Yeh—and that's not fair to Bill . . . but I just can't seem to get over it." I asked Bill if he knew about his father's experience. He answered, "Yes, that's why I can't understand what my parents are doing and that's why I want to finish high school and even make plans to go to college."

Mrs. C. turned toward Bill and shouted, "Then, why don't you behave so it can happen?" Bill replied with anger, "Here we go again . . . here we go again . . ." Then, more softly, "But, I'm not saying I've done nothing wrong. I did get out of hand on Sunday. But most of the time I do try. . . . And when I go off a little bit, you make it worse and then things just build up . . . then Dad suddenly gets into the middle of it." I asked Bill, "Are you saying that the fight usually starts with your mother over some small thing? Then you try to stop, but mother keeps it up—then father interferes and the fight between you and Dad becomes explosive?" He said, "I just wish Dad would take a stand that's his own—not just follow Mom all the time." Mr. C. said, "You know, in some respects, the boy is right—that's what happens." (Silence.)

I asked the group where they wanted this discussion to go: are they here still to find out how Bill can leave in a good way or how they can all live together? This time Mr. C. answered clearly, "I want Bill home." Mrs. C. said, "So do I, but things must change." And when I asked, "Who must change?" Mr. C. said, "I guess all three of us." Mrs. C. nodded.

There was a noticeable change in the atmosphere. For the first time father and son sat back comfortably in their chairs, but mother was still very tight. She said she hoped they could work this out, but wanted to know how this could be done—there had been a terrible fight. I suggested that we talk about the fight. All began to talk at once. I said it would be helpful, not only to me, but to everyone, if we really began from the beginning and tried to hear what each was saying.

After a detailed review of the fight and each person's reactions to the incident, I summed up the major facts. Further elaboration was presented, after which I commented that the parents were angry and ashamed because the landlady had to intervene. Bill felt unjustly accused because it was Mr. C. who had struck the first blow, and both Mr. C. and Bill felt that Mrs. C. had triggered the actual fight. All three were silent, but seemed very thoughtful.

Then Mr. C. commented that he was thinking that they all wanted to stay together—but they couldn't go on the way they'd been. When I asked him to summarize the way it had been, he said he thought they ganged up on each other without even trying to figure out what was going wrong. Mrs. C. then broke in with further incidents of Bill's money demands, his schoolwork, and his girlfriends. It was Mr. C. who reminded Mrs. C. that Bill had a part-time job and was now doing much better in school. Mrs. C. said this was true, then repeated many of the things that worried her and concluded with, "If only they will take some worries away from me." When I questioned the "they," she said, "my husband." He said part of it was his fault—he had let his wife take most of the responsibility for Bill. Bill seemed to want him to be more of a father. Both mother and son became immediately supportive. He said that he loved them both and would try to do his part in helping them to get along together. Bill said he wanted to try to make it with them, and Mrs. C. said perhaps she could do some things differently, too. I asked if there was still uncertainty about wanting Bill to stay at home. Each one said he'd like to try to get along better with the others. I commented that our time was up; that they seemed to agree they wanted to try to have Bill remain at home; that they seemed to be feeling better now; but that they needed to realize there would be some setbacks until they were able to make some of the changes. I arranged for another appointment with the family. Since the problem is primarily one of unsatisfactory family relationships, the major modality of treatment should be the family unit.

Decision-making is an ongoing part of the social work process, but what is being emphasized in this section is a decision necessary to resolve a major problem of concern to an individual or group. As with the Cohns, often the decision to make a change in self or circumstances contains some risk for the client and significant others. A successful experience in decision-making should lead to enhanced ability to deal with other problems as they emerge.

There are a number of general principles for the worker's use of his relationship with clients and differential interventions in helping clients to use a problem-solving process for making decisions. These are evident in the Cohn case. The conclusions from Somers's survey of the literature on group problem-solving have been drawn upon in developing these propositions.[16]

1. Problem-solving is a major activity of the social worker as he makes ongoing assessments of the client system's readiness and capacities to work through each step of the process. It goes on in the worker's thinking before, during, and after each session with an individual, family, or group. This activity is related to the collaborative problem-solving work that occurs between the worker and the client system and to the parallel work that clients do between and during sessions.

2. The capacities of both the worker and the client system for self-observation and understanding of self in particular situations must be stretched and fully employed in the problem-solving work. Thus, understanding of self and others is an important component of problem-solving.

3. Active participation of the client, all members of groups, and the worker is essential to effective and productive problem-solving.

4. The worker's responsibility is to assist the client and members of groups to solve their own problems to the greatest degree possible. Only when people are enabled to solved their own problems do they

develop power to have some control over their lives and situations. The worker stimulates and guides the process, but does not take over what individuals and groups can do on their own.

5. The worker assists the clients to maintain a focus on reality in their problem-solving work, so that the resulting decisions are appropriate to the agreed-upon goals, their life situations, and available internal and external resources.

6. The worker intervenes directly, making differential use of techniques in order to help the clients to maintain focus; deals with the interrelationship among feelings, attitudes, relationships, and thought processes as these influence decision-making; strengthens coping efforts; supports and fortifies the clients' egos; and recognizes and works through intrapersonal, interpersonal, and group conflicts that impede effective problem-solving.

Enhancing Competence

Changes in perception of self and others and ability to make decisions do not necessarily lead to effective functioning; there must also be change in responses to other people. The client needs to do something more effectively. Achievement of competence in the performance of tasks related to problems in social relationships is often a goal of practice. The worker needs to assess the extent to which persons have mastered the tasks associated with each phase of psychosocial development relative to their age, sex, ethnicity, and environment. In helping clients to achieve competence in the performance of particular tasks or roles, the social worker primarily uses an educational process. Goldstein differentiates the educational role of the social worker from that of the schoolteacher. In social work, "the learning process is primarily directed toward the acquisition of knowledge that will aid in the completion of certain tasks or in the resolution of problems related to social living."[17] In order to adapt more effectively, people need the necessary knowledge and skills.

Decision precedes action. Once a decision has been made the client needs to implement it, but he may not know how to do this effectively. A decision to seek to adopt a child, for example, requires accomplishing a series of tasks culminating in the legal adoption. A decision by a teen-ager to enter college requires that he know how to make application and submit necessary papers. Other clients may need instruction and guidance in relation to their roles as parent, spouse, sibling, or employee. Some may need to know how to get out of debt through budgeting and managing their money. In some instances, the worker will refer a client to a specialized resource for help, as with vocational tests or informal and formal classes. In other instances, he actively assists the client in securing the necessary information or skills.

Demonstration, role-playing, and rehearsal are common tools used to prepare clients for dealing with difficult situations. Planning with the client to try something out, then report back, evaluate the effort, and plan next steps, helps to build confidence to try new ways of dealing with stressful situations. Participating actively and responsibly in the effort to change one's behavior is a step in building competence and confidence. The worker maintains a relationship, encourages the client to try out new patterns of behavior, and offers support for experimentation with new behavior that may prove rewarding. In groups, mutual support from members is an additional dynamic.

Task-centered practice, as formulated by Reid and associates and Studt, may be appropriately used with some clients individually, as part of families, or in groups.[18] The focus is on task performance, that is, a sequence of actions that people must follow in order to improve their functioning in a particular social situation. Within the literature, there are differences of opinion about whose goal determines how the task is to be defined and how and whether various tasks are related to each other. In Studt's formulation, working on a task is preceded by an analysis of the client's social context, giving consideration to relationships among persons as these support or interfere with desired functioning, and by the articulation of tasks for both client and worker within a perspective of the client-situation-system and with an agreed-upon goal. Studt describes a situation in which there is a common task for a population of institutionalized clients, namely, preparing themselves to live acceptably as members of an open community. Such a formulation utilizes interventions with individuals, groups, and communities as well as the provision of concrete services.

The theoretical assumption underlying work toward enhanced knowledge and skills is that the ego is strengthened as a person develops effective means of communication and has reasonably clear perceptions of himself and his situation. It is also strengthened as people have confidence in their abilities to perform roles in ways that are personally satisfying and that meet reasonable expectations of others. Mastery of tasks leads to self-esteem. The ability to think needs to be tested in the crucible of experience. It is especially important to have opportunities to master tasks in areas in which a person has previously found himself lacking.[19] Thus, in social work, help in developing competence is related to the problems of the clients. It is thought that "social competence leads to increased ego strength which, in turn, enhances capacity to cope with conflict and anxiety. Increased coping capacity may then lead to increased competence."[20]

The growth in the use of education as a major component of service has been tremendous in recent years. Educational activities are used for both preventive and therapeutic functions. There are a large number of educational groups for parents or for relatives of patients, usually short-term in structure. One recent example illustrates the use of short-term groups for parents of children who had identified problems in school. Two types of groups were organized: activity and discussion.[21] For some parents, activity groups were judged to be most suitable. These tended to be people who were less verbal and more cautious about verbalizing feelings or foreign-born parents who were still struggling to learn the English language. Many mothers who joined the activity groups were suffering from feelings of apathy and isolation. In a safe and supportive environment, communication flows between verbal and nonverbal modes of expression and moves from superficial to meaningful levels. Erikson's concept of mastery as the key task in latency was found just as relevant to adults who had been underachievers and who were suffering from low self-esteem. In addition to activities, common concerns about parenting and school were discussed, decisions were made, and solutions to mutual problems were sought.

Another project was a family-life education camp established for the treatment of child abuse. The program had as its goals: (1) to teach parents new and constructive parenting skills; (2) to develop skills in interpersonal relationships; and (3) to eliminate child abuse practices. The emphasis in all aspects of the program was on four major concepts: self-esteem, self-gratification, mutual sharing, and empowerment. Through the development of skills, self-esteem was enhanced, and parents learned ways to gratify themselves without becoming emotionally dependent on their children for satisfying their psychological needs. Through mutual sharing in groups, parents could apply these skills to finding and using friendly support systems in the community. By learning to take responsibility for their part in the abusive events and in the group activities and discussions, they developed power to control their own lives. The use of didactic and experiential techniques accompanied the use of verbal discussion. The writer concluded that most effective in the "treatment of an abusive parent was a massive dose of hope, self-esteem and education."[22]

In child welfare, there is professional concern about fostering the strengths of natural parents in order that children may be maintained in their own homes. Working with parents to make this possible requires development of their skills and education. Talking it out in treatment is frequently secondary to activities engaged in with parents—accompanying them to appointments, teaching them household management and menu planning, and helping them to understand children's needs. Whittaker confirms the need to aid natural and foster parents to develop better child-rearing practices. When a child is first placed in a residential facility, he argues, "the basic purpose of child helping should be to teach skills for living."[23] Competence needs to be developed in basic social skills such as how to make a friend, how to let someone know you like him, how to join a game, defend oneself with peers without resorting to fighting, or negotiate with an adult. Mastery of such skills enhances self-image and increases the likelihood that more and more difficult challenges will be attempted. Such skills can be carried over from the residence to daily living in the community.

The need for short-term educational help in abortion counseling is a current focus in social work practice. Many girls and women who decide to have an abortion need to be prepared for surgery and to have psychological support in relation to the usual anxieties of fear of pain, body damage, helplessness, and even death. For many patients there is guilt about the decision to abort and the usual anxieties take on special meaning when medical care is associated with sexuality and reproduction. Preparation includes accurate information, responses to particular questions and concerns, education, and anticipatory guidance to strengthen the individual's ability to deal with a temporary disorganizing experience. Such preparation may be done with patients, individually or in small groups. Often there is need to follow up with sex education geared to developmental needs and family planning.[24]

In a two-year nationwide study of 920 adolescents, ages twelve to eighteen, Konopka reported that sex education was incredibly poor.[25] One girl, for example, said, "When I found out I was pregnant I didn't even know what pregnant meant and I went to the nurse and she told me, 'that means you're going to have a little baby.' I said, 'What?' And then I told my parents and knew I had really been bad." Many girls did not even know about menstruation. Many had had their first sex experiences in their own homes with fathers, brothers, relatives, or mothers' boyfriends. They had enormous fear of being used sexually. The sample of girls was drawn from both urban and rural settings in twelve states and from all racial, religious, ethnic, and socioeconomic backgrounds. In a similar study of sixth-grade girls, Buckley also found tremendous ignorance about sex.[26] Unless sex information is accurate, related to the developmental phase of the person, and discussed in terms of particular situations, it is often not integrated into the personality.

In his research on family therapy with families living in urban slums, Minuchin and associates discovered the value of the use of tasks within a treatment session to help members deal with conflict among two or more members. The practitioner actively guides members in learning how to observe the process that is going on among other members and instructs family members in role playing in order to learn new and unfamiliar ways of dealing with conflict. These action-oriented techniques are accompanied by identification of intrapersonal and interpersonal obstacles that emerge as new efforts to solve conflicts are attempted. The intent of such role playing is "to induce a vivid awareness of hidden patterns and underlying motivations while at the same time providing an opportunity to express new ways of attacking a problem.''[27]

These are a few illustrations of the use of educational techniques, used in conjunction with other procedures, to help people gain the competence and confidence that enhance psychosocial functioning.

Influencing the Environment

A living system requires constant transaction with its environment in order to maintain differentiation and impede entropy. Inadequate opportunities for interchange tend to isolate individuals and families from the larger social structure and to cut them off from inputs of an economic, educational, and social nature.[28] Food, clothing, shelter, and transportation are essential to physical survival; so, too, are social relationships that nurture and support developmental processes. Social relationships can become more satisfactory and adaptive patterns can change positively in response to favorable experiences. A harsh physical environment, too limited a cultural milieu, and inadequate social and educational opportunities create obstacles for a person. Gross social pathology, denial of civil rights, unhealthy and unfair employment practices, and ethnic segregation or other forms of group isolation affect the personality and its coping capacities. When the difficulty is between a person and a depriving environment, efforts must be made to change the particular part of the social system so that it can support, rather than impede, the person's efforts toward more effective functioning. Reducing environmental stress enables a person or a family to regain a satisfactory steady state, and the provision of more adequate opportunities contributes to his psychosocial development.

Modifying environmental obstacles requires that the social worker move into one or more systems in the client's social network. Such work is "a goal-directed process, undertaken after (1) a diagnostic evaluation of the social environment and (2) an assessment of the individual's specific capacities, needs, and desires have been formulated."[29] It requires the differential use of knowledge and skills in practice. It requires, however, the specification of goals and procedures that are appropriate for influencing people who are not in roles of client or patient. They are rather potential supporters and helpers.

From the early days of social work to the present time, it has been emphasized that the social worker does not "treat the individual alone or his environment alone, but the process of adaptation which is dynamic interaction between the two."[30] In promoting a radical approach to social work, Rein notes that both individual and social change need to be included. He says that "a radical casework approach would mean not merely obtaining for clients social services to which they are entitled or helping them adjust to the environment, but also trying to deal with the relevant people and institutions in the client's environment that are contributing to their difficulties."[31] The environment is seen as a series of concentric circles of interacting systems of influence.

Services in Behalf of Clients

SOCIAL SUPPORTS

Clients need support from significant people in order to work toward their goals. The support of the participants in the practice situation is important, but it is seldom sufficient. The social worker needs to take into account the extent to which the environment provides support for a client. In one study of adolescent probationers, reconviction rates were significantly related to lack of support at home, work, or school, and to crime contamination. Those with the greatest difficulties in the environment were least likely to show satisfactory achievement.[32] In an earlier study in a family service agency in which adults had interpersonal conflicts, continuance in treatment was strongly associated with support of the clients' efforts by other people. If other people were indifferent or opposed to the clients' efforts, clients were less likely to continue.[33] Thus, a frequent task for the social worker is to seek support from significant others in enhancing the motivation of clients in the use of service.

Work with family units is often the service of choice. But when a client is receiving individual or peer group help, work with his relatives is often an important component of the worker's role. The worker may initiate conferences with one or more members of the family, aimed toward securing their support of the service planned with the client. When a child is the principal client, the minimal involvement of the parents or guardian is that of granting informed consent for the child to be served for a particular purpose. The focus should be on strengthening the relationship of the client with his family.

In addition to the family, the worker needs to assess the supportive potential of educational, work, recreational, or other groups to which a client belongs. There may not be an organized group but a network of social relationships that can be mobilized in behalf of the client. According to Caplan, "kinship and friendship are the most important types of primary social relationships which can be used as support systems."[34] A support system is one in which significant others help the individual to mobilize his personal resources; provide the material means and skills that are essential to improve the situation; and provide emotional support for efforts to cope with the problems. Networks are composed of people and relationships and are systems of mutual aid.

Self-help groups, which have become ubiquitous in our society, are alternatives to natural networks for the provision of support and mutual aid to people with common needs or problems.[35] An important means, then, for supporting clients is to connect them with appropriate social networks or self-help groups as a supplement to professional service. This involves a process of referral.

RESOURCE CONSULTATION

The social worker may refer clients to supportive networks or to other health and social agencies for help with needs that cannot be met within his agency. Referrals to employment agencies, work-training programs, health and medical care, or religious organizations should be part of treatment if clients are to be helped to function at more nearly their full capacity. Some writers refer to this service as a brokerage role in which the worker serves as a link between a client and a resource. Solomon has broadened the concept of the role to that of resource consultant. Resource consultant is the preferred term rather than broker, advocate, or mediator because a consultant directs his attention to the client's capacity to use his personal resources and skills in his efforts to achieve his own goals. The provision of resources in the form of financial assistance, housing, and health care is crucial, but the trick is to provide them in such a way that they do not reinforce dependency and powerlessness. "The resource consultant role is defined here much more broadly than that of resource dispenser or resource provider; it involves linking clients to resources in a manner that enhances their self-esteem as well as their problem-solving capacities."[36] The client's participation in the process is extensive: the consultant offers his knowledge and expertise to the client.

The effective use of a resource requires that the client have a great deal of knowledge and skill. Essentially, the consultant shares his knowledge, provides encouragement, and gives advice that is essential to the client's decision to use a resource. Effective consultation requires that the worker has assessed the client's needs for particular resources, and that he has accurate information about available resources and the conditions for their use. The worker then needs to call the client's attention to, and give appropriate information about, the alternative resources that might be available to him in solving a problem or providing opportunities to enrich his life or the lives of members of his family. He needs to clarify his reason for suggesting a resource and to work with whatever ambivalence the client may have about it. He needs to engage the client in the problem-solving process toward making a decision to use a resource and selecting the most appropriate one. The client, and often his family, should be prepared as fully as possible to know how to proceed in making application to the agency or organization and meeting its eligibility requirements and intake procedures. He should be prepared to make optimal use of the resource. The worker may also need to consult with the responsible person in the receiving agency, with the full knowledge and consent of the client, in order to assist that person to aid the client in becoming eligible for and using the service. A worker can thus pave the way for the client, without taking away from the client's use of his own skills in getting a desired resource.[37]

In the use of resources, the major emphasis is not to refer a client away from the agency, although this may be necessary if the client's needs cannot be met therein. It is rather to provide additional resources, often not within the province of social work practice itself, which will enrich the lives of clients and provide additional opportunities for them. The nature of the resources may be as varied as a special library, tutoring, a music class, recreational activity, employment service, provision of a Big Sister or Big Brother, or a leadership training group. In working with families, for example, a child can often benefit from a camp or day care experience so that, in a supportive and nurturing environment, he can take advantage of opportunities for making friends, developing competence in activities that facilitate normal development processes, and find relief from an unbearable burden at home or in the neighborhood. Other types of groups, such as Scouts, Camp Fire Girls, and those under the auspices of community centers and Ys, are designed to enhance social development through the provision of interpersonal and social experiences. Likewise, referrals of adults to informal classes for learning new activities that might become hobbies, such as cooking, sewing, photography, or camping, can be sources for the development of self-esteem, social relationships, and new interests in life.

Many clients have inadequate financial and health resources, or do not know how to apply for and make use of those that are available. In such instances, there may be a serious problem in the client's eligibility for service or in matching client needs to available resources. The worker may then need to serve as mobilizer of resources. Many individuals and families need active help from a worker in finding appropriate resources, getting connected to the appropriate people who can meet a need, and following through on the use of the resource. When resources are not available to clients, the worker may need to serve as an advocate.[38]

Advocacy. In serving as an advocate, the worker is spokesman for the client. He presents the client's case to some official, argues its merits, and engages in bargaining concerning the outcome. When a particular obstacle to the use of a resource comes to the fore, the worker and client together determine whether it is within the power of the client to take steps to alter the unbearable situation, with the support, encouragement, and guidance of the worker. If the decision is that advocacy is necessary, the worker proceeds to take action. As an advocate he is not neutral; he is a partisan representative of the client. Even so, he allows the client to participate as fully as possible. Depending upon the nature of the cause, he recognizes that it might be more effective to secure legal aid for the client rather than undertaking advocacy himself.

Becoming an advocate for a client is often desirable, but requires that the worker be clear about the ethical judgments and skills that are necessary.[39] It is possible that in arguing a case for his client, other aggrieved persons who have equally strong claims may be deprived of their entitlements because they do not have advocates. If he argues, for example, that the director of a residential treatment center should make an exception to policy so that his client might be admitted, this decision might be at the expense of other children who have equal need for the placement. So long as there are scarce resources or resources of poor quality, some potential users will be denied the opportunity. In order to make an appropriate decision concerning advocacy, the worker needs to be aware of his own biases, including a tendency to want to do for other people rather than work with them. He needs to have made an accurate assessment of his client's needs and capacities, the effect of the desired action on his ability to function effectively, and alternative means to solve the problem. He needs knowledge of the legal rights of people and organizational policies by which scarce resources are distributed and eligibility determined. He needs the technical skills of persuasion and manipulation that are somewhat different from the techniques used in other aspects of his work.

Placement. Provision of new environments through placement of clients away from their own homes is another use of resources. This is a highly skilled service which usually involves the worker in making fateful decisions about the environment of a client and the welfare of all parties to the process. Even if placement is not the treatment of choice, the worker bears the awesome responsibility to help the client to adapt to the new environment and to minimize the risks and maximize the potential benefits of the placement. The environment has great influence on a person's sense of self-esteem and identity and the opportunities available to him for satisfying social relationships and psychosocial development. Placement involves the physical and emotional separation of a person from one natural life situation, often a family, and his adjustment to a new environment. In a sense the client is moving out of one group and into another one. It is always an anxiety-producing experience for all concerned.

The social worker may be a resource consultant, helping voluntary clients to find a suitable retirement home, temporary foster home, residential school, or camp. In other instances, however, the worker has considerable power to select the home or facility and to monitor the process. He often has the power to accept or reject adoptive applicants or foster homes and to select the children to be placed in a particular home or facility. The placement may be compulsory by court order. Working with the person being placed and both the old and new family or group involves a direct counseling service, of which helping the person to use the resource and helping others to make it effective are integral parts. Placement requires working with many different people in the community; finding suitable foster homes, adoptive homes, or institutional placements; working with organizations in the new neighborhood relative to the client's needs such as, for example, schools or health resources; interrelating the various systems involved so that they work in the interests of the primary client—the natural parents, child, and foster parents. The worker should also be giving services to children and parents in their own homes and neighborhood, so as to avoid the need for placements to the extent possible.

COLLABORATION

Social workers influence the environments of clients by conferring with significant others—those persons in the ecosystem who have or can have special meaning for the client. Such people appear to have a part in creating or exacerbating the problem or they have some power to modify the problem or to assist the client to cope with it. The purpose of the conference may be to influence the other person to change his attitudes and behavior toward the client, to secure change in the client's situation, or to enhance the worker's own effectiveness.

The worker may meet with representatives of other organizations which serve the same client to plan for dividing responsibilities among them and finding ways to coordinate their services for the client's benefit. The worker may meet with teachers, principals, parents or foster parents, judges, or employment agents. He may provide them with information about the client and make suggestions that bring about a positive change in the relationship between the client and the other person. He may successfully suggest a new environment for the client, such as reassignment to a less-pressured job or a special class. He may report on the client's enhanced motivation or progress, thereby setting in motion a chain reaction in the client's favor. His ethics require that he engage in these activities only with the knowledge of the client and, except under special circumstances, with his informed consent. If the worker engages in such efforts in a spirit of mutual benefit, he will discover that the significant others make valuable contributions to his own knowledge and skills.

In order to serve his clients most effectively, the worker often needs to work collaboratively with members of other professions, such as education, medicine, psychiatry, and law.[40] Each participant needs to understand the values and goals of the other disciplines. Each needs to respect the specific contributions of the others and be willing to share some tasks. In any collaborative effort, there needs to be a mutuality rooted in respect for the contributions of each member of the team. It is imperative that the worker understand the goals, functions, and structure of each discipline and the problems with which it deals. He needs to be clear about his own contribution to the team's effort. He must be able to recognize his own and others' feelings of differential status, competitiveness, and turf, and be able to participate effectively in the management of interdisciplinary conflicts for the benefit of clients. Indeed, there is a considerable amount of overlapping among disciplines. The worker recognizes that clients are deeply influenced by the social climate, the most crucial aspect of which is the nature of relationships among the staff.

Beyond Client to Community

There is little controversy concerning the profession's responsibility to prevent, abolish, or remedy social ills that have a deleterious effect on the functioning of people. The issue concerns the selection of social problems about which social workers can be held accountable for having the necessary knowledge and skills for influencing change, as contrasted with the broad problems that must be attacked by the economic-political system and citizens joining together in broad collective action. A special concern is clarification of the responsibilities that a social worker has for social action when he is employed primarily to provide direct services to, and in behalf of, people who need them.

One conceptualization of the role of the direct service worker in influencing the community limits his responsibilities to certain activities. He documents needs and social ills as these are revealed in his practice.[41] He contributes his findings through agency channels to those persons who formulate social policies, draft legislation, and engage in community organization and social action. As members of staffs and committees, he may participate in reviewing policies as they affect clients and in making decisions about policies and procedures. He may represent the agencies in organizations that are working toward improved services or legislative changes. Thus, he engages in collective efforts to create resources and formulate policies that will bring better services to both clients and the general public.

Other schemes would extend the responsibilities of the practitioner beyond service to, and in behalf of, his clients. One useful formulation is that developed by Middleman and Goldberg.[42] These authors believe that a practitioner has concern for a particular individual or family which has problems, but he has concern also for a general category of people who share problems similar to those of the client. In deciding with whom to work, the choice may be to work with (1) the client in his own behalf; (2) others in behalf of the client; (3) the client in his own behalf and others who have similar problems; and (4) others in behalf of a category of people who have a particular problem or condition.

The first category comprises educational, developmental, or thera-

peutic services to the individual, family, or group that is the benefi-
ciary of the services offered. The second category comprises the
range of activities in work with significant others in behalf of the
client system. In the third and fourth categories, the worker extends
his service to others who may not be his clients, but who have unmet
needs. In his engagement with a client system or with others in behalf
of the client, the worker becomes aware that other people have a
need similar to that of the client. In such instances, he may develop
a system of help that benefits both the original client and others who
accept the service. Many educational and therapeutic groups are organized when a worker recognizes that others share similar problems
or needs and that a group experience will be beneficial to the original
client and other clients or applicants as well. The preferred service
may not be a group, but some other form of service delivery.

Organizations for single parents are examples of this approach to
practice. A mother with concerns about herself and her child is
helped to locate others in a similar situation. Recognition of the need
for self-help and mutual support in facing and coping with the many
difficulties that accompany such a status leads to the idea of a self-
help group for the original client, but also for other parents who desire such a service. Solomon has noted the importance of providing
opportunities for the client to become a service provider.[43] Being
able to give as well as take builds on the strengths and skills of the
client, enhancing self-esteem and competence. Such opportunities occur when a client is helped to participate in meeting his own needs,
but then reaches out to help others with similar needs.

Some self-help or mutual aid organizations have moved beyond
concern about the particular difficulties of the members to taking social action. One example is a community service that emerged from
work with a parent of a physically handicapped child. Recognition of
the need for mutual support in facing and coping with the many difficulties that accompany such a parental role led to the idea of a self-
help group for the original client, but also to the organization of
groups for other parents who desire such a service. The members
engaged in social action to get appropriate educational programs for
all such handicapped children and to lobby for legislation that would
open up opportunities for all physically handicapped people.

Another well-known example is the report of the development of a program of multiple services.[44] The case began with a complaint from a client about the condition of her tenement apartment. She came to the agency in desperation because she was unable to run her household without utilities and had exhausted her financial resources. In this case, the worker decided that action was necessary to change the system. The tenants, including the original client, were involved in fact-finding and decision-making. Numerous techniques were used to help the tenants to ventilate their feelings of anxiety, hopelessness, and anger; sort out the varied perceptions of the situation; and move on to decision-making. Direct services were provided to the original client and to other individuals and families at the same time that efforts were made to intervene with public agencies in behalf of the tenants. This service began in behalf of one client, which led to serving a group of clients suffering from similar circumstances, but then went further to work with nonclients in behalf of a larger population being injured by bad housing conditions. This was a team effort in which social workers in direct service collaborated with city planners and community organizers.

When clients join together with others for the purpose of achieving some change in the environment or to resolve a conflict between two or more systems that affect them, considerable educational and problem-solving help from the worker is often indicated. They often need considerable encouragement to continue with the project. They may need to learn to communicate in new ways with persons in positions of power and to select and use leaders appropriately. Such community activity involves the workers in using one-person interviews with clients or with community representatives, guiding the process in task-centered groups, and supporting and educating people as representatives in intergroup or interorganizational relations. Although the major focus is on the task to be achieved, the participants often achieve personal gains also. To learn how to engage in group problem-solving and to make individual and collective contributions to a solution to a common problem is a source of power for subsequent efforts to bring about community change.

In order to function well enough to participate toward the achievement of an external task, the needs of the members for help with personal and interpersonal problems must not be so great that they cannot maintain focus on the external goal. The group must have access to strategic people who can offer support and use their power to aid in goal attainment. It must be thoroughly informed about the nature and extent of the problem and able to defend its proposed solution.

The social worker's roles in the community, beyond efforts in behalf of clients, are largely determined by the organization that employs him. He has particular assignments for which he is held accountable, but he also has some opportunity to set his own priorities. He may or may not be free to organize new services for people who are not clients of the agency. He can, however, use his professional knowledge and skills to influence policies and procedures within the agency and in the community toward the goal of improved and extended services to people.

Social workers constantly need to remind themselves that an individual, family, or group does not exist in a vacuum; it is a part of a network of interlocking and interdependent social systems. The means for achieving improved psychosocial relationships are through the appropriate use of individual interviews, group interaction, and environmental interventions. The procedures of social treatment apply equally to work with client systems and to work with significant others in their behalf. The content of the work is determined by the particular set of intermediate goals that, if achieved, will result in effective service and satisfied people.

CHAPTER NINE

Termination and Transition

Termination is a dynamic and vital process in social work.[1] It is more than a symbol of the end of treatment: it is an integral part of the process. If properly understood and managed, it becomes an important force in integrating changes in feeling, thinking, and doing. These changes, though, are of little value to the clients until they can apply the benefits gained in everyday relationships and achievements. Social work treatment is always time-limited. "The goal of treatment," said Gordon Hamilton, "is always to help the person return as soon as possible to natural channels of activity with strengthened relationships."[2] Treatment beyond the point that the person's natural growth can be resumed may interfere with the natural potential for growth and lead to continuing dependency.[3] What happens to a client when it comes time to terminate may make a critical difference as to the nature and extent of gains that will endure. If a person is helped to face the meaning of the social work experience and to leave it with a sense of achievement, he may well be prepared to use what he has learned in his roles and relationships in the community. He may be more able to cope with the other separations that will confront him throughout his life.[4]

Ending an experience needs to be done in such a way that professional values are implemented. Ideally, an individual has entered into a relationship in which he has been helped to achieve his goals, felt that he has been treated with acceptance and respect, and encouraged to participate actively in the process and to make his own decisions, with due regard for the welfare of self and others. A somewhat intimate and interdependent relationship has been achieved with the practitioner. In families and groups, in addition to each individual's relationship with the worker, the members have found mutual acceptance and respect and have participated actively in a process of mutual aid and interdependency. Now, the breaking up of the client-worker system needs to be done in such a way as to implement the values of the profession.

The decision to terminate and the process of ending make use of the knowledge essential to the biopsychosocial system approach to practice. A worker-client system has been formed and sustained for the purpose of achieving particular goals. Now, the knowledge about biopsychosocial functioning in environments is used to help the worker-client system to break up in a way that benefits the clients. Particularly useful are perspectives on the life cycle that incorporate the concepts of loss and separation related to the significance of social relationships to people in each phase of development, and that explain the ways that the ego defends itself against, copes with, and masters the experience.[5] When faced with loss or separation, the steady state is upset. There are certain expectable emotional and behavioral reactions to the threat of loss. The feelings of loss are also accompanied by satisfactions with the social work experience and a resulting sense of positive achievement and competence to face the challenges of social living without the assistance of a social worker. The nature and intensity of the reactions to termination depend upon many circumstances, such as length of service, reasons for termination, past experiences of clients with loss and separation, and the extent of meaningful relationships and supports in the environment.

If termination is to be a meaningful and growth-producing experience, the social worker has a number of important instrumental goals to achieve during the final phase of service. These are to help the clients to:

1. Evaluate the progress they have made, acknowledge the realistic gains, and accept the fact that the experience is ending

2. Set priorities for work on pressing problems or tasks that are still unfinished and that seem crucial to the clients' progress

3. Work toward stabilizing and strengthening the gains that have been made

4. Resolve the ambivalence about leaving the relationship with the worker and, in the case of formed groups, with the other members

5. Work out the conflict between acknowledgment of progress and giving up a meaningful relationship and experience

6. Use the social work experience as a frame of reference for continued efforts toward achievement, through tying this experience more directly to their subsequent life tasks and relationships

7. Make transitions toward new experiences, such as follow-up sessions or referrals, as indicated.[6]

Reasons for Termination

Termination occurs for a number of reasons, some of them planned as an integral part of treatment, and some of them unplanned or unanticipated. Ideally, termination occurs when a person, family, or group no longer needs the professional service. Clients are terminated when a defined purpose has been achieved. When planned termination occurs, a social worker and client have made a judgment that sufficient progress has been made to enable the person or family to continue to consolidate the gains without the help of the worker and sometimes also without the help of a group. All people have problems in social living, but usually they can cope with the problems with the support and help of families, friends, and other significant people in the community. It is unrealistic and generally unhelpful to continue service until a total "cure" has occurred or until clients have achieved their full potential. The challenge is to predict that sufficient progress has been made so that the client or family can maintain the gains and possibly also continue to progress without social work help. The process of termination itself is an important part of treatment.

During the planning process, the worker and individual, family, or group had agreed upon an anticipated length of service, usually with flexibility to shorten or extend the time as needed. Sometimes the nature of the service determines the approximate number of sessions, planned and understood from the beginning. This is typical of crisis intervention, parent or family life education programs, task-centered practice, and services to patients who are to be hospitalized for a fairly predictable length of time.

In a study made of thirty-three clients and their eleven social workers in family service agencies, it was observed that termination was planned in approximately two-thirds of the cases. In the majority of these cases, the social worker and client concurred in the decision to terminate; clients were actively involved in discussing the ending; and plans were made to end gradually.[7] The workers purposefully tried to use the termination phase for therapeutic purposes. The main reasons given for ending were that the goals had been achieved, clients were ready to function independently, or additional sessions would result in limited productivity. These were middle-class clients who were generally satisfied with the social worker and the outcome of service.

In the one third of the cases in which termination was not planned, the situation and outcome were quite different. These clients who withdrew tended to be of lower socioeconomic status whose decision to use the service had not been fully voluntary. They either felt they had achieved what they wanted or, more often, were dissatisfied with the service: there were problems in worker-client interaction; lack of agreement concerning goals and expectations; or lack of open communication between worker and client. Thus, there were earlier cues that should have alerted the worker to problems of motivation and communication.

Termination may occur due to certain factors in the client and his use of service. There are times when little progress has been made. Recognition of this state should result in reevaluation of the plan for service and the development of one more suitable to the client's goals, needs, and capacities. If neither worker nor client can work out a shift in focus that is acceptable to both of them as a basis for further work together, termination occurs. There are times when entropy takes over: a group disintegrates before the goals have been achieved, due to loss of members or unresolvable problems in the group's structure or process. There are times when a client needs to withdraw from treatment because he is unable to meet the minimum expectations for his behavior. Bolen, writing about termination in a residential treatment center, has indicated that early termination of an individual is sometimes necessary. Even though institutions are geared to allow for a wide range of problematic behavior during the course of treatment, there are limits to what behavior can be tolerated.[8] Extremely aggressive or assaultive behavior, for example, usually falls outside the acceptable boundaries. The possibility of danger to self or other clients may require the transfer of such a person to another setting which is considered to be better equipped to handle the behavior.

Other factors often contribute to unplanned termination. Changes in individual or family situations often result in premature termination: for example, a move to a new community, a change in work or school schedules, a long illness, the removal of a child from treatment by the parent, lack of continued eligibility for service, or other situations over which the worker and the agency have no control. Another set of reasons includes those over which the client system has no control, occasioned by changes initiated by the worker or other person in the agency. Workers may be transferred from one assignment to another by administrators, financial exigencies may force the ending of services before the clients are ready to terminate, or the worker may leave the agency for a variety of reasons. Occasionally the worker's own needs may motivate him to terminate a case when the client is not ready. Fox and associates note that workers may precipitate termination: "When the child does not get well fast enough, when the transference becomes negativistic, or when a family's goals differ from the worker's goals, the result may be felt as a narcissistic wound and lead to discontinuance of treatment."[9] The solution to such problems lies in enhancing the worker's self-awareness and abilities in assessment and evaluation. These situations are, in a sense, failures of workers—not clients.

Whatever the reasons for termination, the worker has a responsibility to help the client to use the ending phase for his benefit.

Reactions to Termination

The ending of a meaningful experience stirs up a variety of feelings and reactions. Just as clients had feelings of anticipation and dread at intake, so do they have strong feelings about ending. Schiff says:

Of all the phases of the psycho-therapeutic process, the one which can produce the greatest amount of difficulty and create substantial problems for patient and therapist alike is the phase of termination. It is at this time when the impact of the meaning in affective terms of the course of therapy and the nature of the therapist-patient relationship is experienced most keenly, not only by the patient but also by the therapist.[10]

It is, however, the reawakening of old losses in the present that makes this phase useful for modifying conflicted emotions, stabilizing gains, and motivating further progress in whatever time remains.

Doubt, hesitation, and unresolved tugs between positive and negative feelings are characteristic of the termination phase. Most terminations contain elements of both happiness and sadness. Clients may recognize the progress they have made or feel badly because they have not achieved their vision of the ideal outcome. They may want to move on to other relationships and experiences without being dependent upon the worker or a group; yet they may also want to continue the gratifications received through the relationship with the worker. In groups, gratification also comes from a sense of belonging to a system that has provided mutual support and stimulation for positive changes in self and situation. Clients may feel good about the prospects of termination one day and then feel despair another day. The mixture of positive and negative feelings is described in work with young children:

If the therapeutic relationship has had any real meaning for a child, he will naturally have ambivalent feelings in ending it. It is sad to say goodbye to someone who has been loved for a while and to whom one feels grateful, but it is a satisfaction to become independent of help and to be freed from the obligation to keep appointments that sometimes interfere with other interests and activities. Moreover, the child has been brought to the clinic because the parent was dissatisfied with him. If, at the ending, the parent is better satisfied, this adds to the child's happiness in the termination of treatment, which becomes proof that the parent is no longer dissatisfied with him. So, the desirable aspects of ending may well outweigh the regrets.[11]

Although each person will have his own particular feelings and reactions concerning termination, certain themes have been identified which give clues for understanding what is happening and what to do about it. Writers of both work with individuals and work with groups liken the termination process to the initial phase in terms of the number of diversity of reactions by clients. A typical statement is: "Anxiety over coming together that was experienced in earlier stages, now is felt in relation to moving apart and breaking the bonds that have been formed."[12] Considerable agreement is found among the writers that the termination stage has several subphases of emotional reactions to the final event. Whether in individual or group services, the most basic reactions seem to be denial, anger, mourning or grief, and separation resolution.

When confronted with the reality of termination, clients frequently deny that termination is imminent or that the experience has been of value to them. Denial serves as a defense against facing the impending separation and the feelings of loss and anxiety associated with it. Clients may deny that they were told that the relationship would not last indefinitely. They may protest that they are not ready to leave or even that problems are worse than ever. Sometimes denial is more subtle. Some evidences of denial may be long atypical silences when termination is mentioned; numerous references to loss scattered throughout the interview or group discussion; or changing the subject when the worker tries to explore the meaning of separation to the individual or members of a group. A variation of the usual denial maneuvers may be exaggerated independence, which is not an accurate reflection of the person's level of functioning. A person may act stoical and need to appear strong when confronted with the loss. These reactions, too, are defenses against acceptance of the anticipated loss. In groups, the denial may be expressed through superficially greater cohesiveness than before: the group strengthens its bonds against the threat of the worker or agency.

Angry reactions often overlap with denial. Clients may react with anger to what they perceive as abandonment, rejection, or punishment. There may be what Schiff calls the "unspoken rebuke" aimed at the worker for leaving the client.[13] Anger may be expressed in such phrases as: "So, you're kicking me out"; "I guess you never did care"; "It doesn't matter—I never did get help here anyhow"; or a simple, "So what?" One example is a worker's interview with a fifteen-year-old girl who had been talking about how much better things were going for her in school now. There was much recognition by both Susie and her worker that her behavior at school had improved and that her relationships at home seemed better also.

> Toward the end of the interview, the worker said she wanted to bring up something with Susie for her to think about so they can discuss it more fully next week. Susie asked, "What is it?" The worker said, "I think we should talk about your not coming here any more after summer vacation begins." In a startled voice, Susie asked, "B-b-but why?" The worker said that they had talked about how much better things were for her now. She thought Susie was almost ready to get along without social work help now. Susie said, "Ohh—I still need you—things really aren't good at all." Then and after a long silence, "So—you're just like everyone else after all." To worker's query about in what ways, the response was, "Letting me think you really care about me when you really don't." Then she cried.

This incident illustrates the sudden disruption of a trusting relationship with a client who had previously been deprived of positive relationships with her parents and other adults.

A major theme in the termination phase is that of loss and separation, both in terms of feelings among the participants in the social work service and also in terms of opportunities to work on old conflicts about loss and separation. As Bywaters says, "closure is an opportunity to choose, face, and accept separation and to experience the survival of loss and evidence of new strength and mastery."[14] The desire for dependency is reactivated and there is a need to retest relationships, as was done in earlier phases. To the extent that a worker or members of a group become loved and valued by a client, the client will feel a deep sense of loss and will need to mourn the loss. Thus, as Bowlby indicates, "separation anxiety is the inescapable corollary of attachment behavior."[15] When clients face the reality of their feelings about the loss that is inherent in termination, they react with expressions of sadness and engage in reflective thinking about the situation.

Regression to earlier patterns of behavior is one frequent reaction to the reality of separation; negative symptoms that had been alleviated may reoccur. Through the reemergence of symptoms, clients attempt to prove that they still need the service as much as ever.

Dependency on the worker may increase. In groups, eruption of previously settled conflicts may occur. The conflict between the acknowledgment of improvement and the fear of the loss of the worker's love and attention can end in an explosion of problematic behavior. A child who has stayed in school and improved in his relationships with teachers and peers may suddenly become a truant or get into a serious fight with another pupil. A father who had long since given up abusive behavior toward his wife may strike out at her again in a fit of anger. A young adult may sass his employer and endanger his job. Green reports that:

> I have known children with a six- and seven-year history of enuresis who dried up during several months of treatment, but who often had bad lapses during the ending phase. When assured that no one was trying to get rid of them, many of these youngsters could talk about how many more visits they would like to have. Some would say impulsively that they would come forever, or a thousand times. Yet, in a surprising short time, they could whittle that down to two or three visits and be free of enuresis in the same short time.[16]

Another example is of an inexperienced worker and a nine-year-old boy who was brought to a child guidance clinic because he was stealing frequently. His symptoms had been gone for several months, and he was ready to terminate. On their last day together, the worker took him to his favorite place for ice cream. There, for the first time in the worker's presence, he stole something. The worker was unprepared for this behavior and had no understanding of it. She felt upset, angry, and helpless. The little boy knew it, but neither one of them knew what was going on.[17] In such instances, the flare-up is an indication of trouble over terminating a relationship which has been important to a client. It serves as a means whereby the client can test the worker again, as he did in the initial phase. He needs to ascertain whether the worker really does care about him and what happens to him.

Early detachment from the experience is another pattern of behavior that occurs when clients are anxious about the termination. Clients often respond to the fact of termination through flight—coming late or missing sessions. Such clients seem impelled to break off the relationship themselves, as if to say, "I'll leave you before you leave me.'' When a child in a residential treatment center or in foster care is ready to return to his family, which he has longed for, he may run away so as not to face separation from the social worker and the foster parents. He may do this to provoke people into rejecting him so that he can prove that they really did not care about him. Usually he returns within a few days, but feels great anxiety about how he will be received. If he is received back with understanding and empathy, he is able to move on to effective coping with terminations. People who have been hurt badly through earlier relationships are particularly sensitive to evidences of being rejected. They are easily triggered into withdrawal if they have a glimmer that they might be hurt again.

These feelings and reactions are not typical of all clients, but they have been observed frequently. The nature and intensity of the feelings will vary with the personal characteristics and experiences of the clients. Usually the greater the difficulties that clients have had in prior experiences with separation and relationships, the stronger will be their feelings about ending, providing the social work experience has been a truly meaningful one for them. Since social workers serve many people with disturbed human relationships, there is likely to be trouble during the termination phase.[18]

When groups have had a particularly satisfying experience in working together, the members may resist completion of the work if the relationships among them have been more satisfying than the achievement of the group's purpose. Members may delay completing the work in order to prolong the relationships. Some groups desire to continue on a friendship basis after the original purpose has been achieved.[19] Such a decision by a group usually means that it has changed its purpose to that of a social group that continues without the assistance of a social worker. Although the members remain together, they still need to face the changes and deal with the separation from the worker and often also from the agency. Many self-help and support groups have started with some members who participated in a therapeutic or educational group and then desired to maintain relationships with people with whom they shared a particular need.

In the group of Spanish-speaking mothers that was presented in the last chapter, the plan was for the group to meet for about fifteen weeks. By the tenth week, the women were reporting changes in themselves and their families. The worker, a second-year graduate student, reported:

Once the reserves were down and trust had come, the leap to relating comfortably in and out of the group sessions seemed very sudden. Several members reported that they had enrolled in English classes, driver education, or conferred successfully with school personnel concerning the needs of their children. There was car-pooling, giving of rides, sharing of telephone numbers. As the members began to feel some power over their own lives, the group tackled serious problems of members: financial difficulties, marital conflict, child and wife abuse, problems in relationships with children and school officials, and cultural conflicts.

During the last month, I directed the content of the group toward unfinished areas of concern. At the beginning of one meeting, I reminded the members that we had only three meetings left. When Juanita reported an important achievement, and then said, "I did not have the trust to try before," Corita said, "I think we have all learned to trust and assert ourselves." Then Elena said to me, "But it is so sad, for soon you will leave us." I answered, "With sadness, for I have come to care for each of you and you will soon be ready for our ending." Elena had spoken the heretofore unspoken words.

During the next session, I asked what specific issues that we had left unfinished would they like to discuss today. Elena said, "We have a thousand things—a thousand things." I responded, "You are really concerned because this group is ending." She said, "I can't talk about it now." But this elicited a spate of comments from others about their feelings; anger at me for leaving them and fears of making it on their own predominated. Mixed in with these expressions were examples of positive changes in themselves and their situations.

On the last day, the ladies came into the room carrying trays, pots, and utensils, and it became apparent to me that they had gotten together on their own and planned a meal. I expressed surprise and delight, and they responded with great pleasure. When the members took their usual chairs, Corita said they ought to talk before brunch. When no one else responded, I said that it would be helpful if they could discuss their feelings about the group—the positive and negative parts and whatever progress they thought they had made. Each one compared herself as she thought she was in the first meeting with today. Corita, for example, said, "When I came I felt like this," placing her hand about a foot from the floor. "Now I feel free and proud. I am no longer afraid; he has learned about the children because I've taught him what you said, *maestra* . . ." Juanita's eyes filled with tears as she told us she had found peace of mind, faith in herself, and capacity to live her own life so that her children would not suffer. She said she had applied for a community aide job, finally having enough belief in herself to do this. . . . Lupe shyly spoke of having gained so much in learning about the individuality of each child and how she has gained friends here . . .

After each member had spoken, I reviewed the progress that I thought had been made in the group, with emphasis on how they had slowly become cohesive, given each other hope, shared very painful experiences, and found they were not alone or unique, and thus could give strength to each other. . . . I said that I, too, had learned from working with them. . . . When I paused, Maria said, "There's one more thing." She proudly came forward with a plaque in Spanish which says:

> Mary,
> Thank you for helping us to be
> better spouses and mothers
> woman to woman.

I was overwhelmed and had difficulty expressing my thanks and appreciation. Lupe took some pictures of the group: then we feasted, socialized, and said good-by. The members had planned to continue as an informal group, and they invited me to come to their meetings any time.

The social worker concluded her record with the statement that some colleagues have questioned whether Spanish-speaking people living in the barrio will respond to group treatment. Her answer was:

That they can make effective use of a group experience is what really excites me! . . . Finally, these ladies made me aware of the natural perceptiveness and sensitivity which have made them able to bear the indignities that life has presented them. It was a humbling experience for me to see them bloom in self-awareness and self-esteem.

For many clients the termination phase is characterized predominantly by positive feelings toward the relationship and a sense of goal achievement. They come to work on a problem which is brought to a satisfactory resolution. An example is a couple who wanted to work through a marital conflict and did so successfully. The couple felt great warmth toward the social worker and expressed appreciation for her services. Their own improved relationship with each other was a great gain for them, so that the loss of the worker was not perceived as a devastating one. Another example is of work with a chronic elderly patient and his family to develop a discharge plan satisfactory to all concerned. There were serious conflicts among family members about the most desirable plan; for there was a need for members to face changes in family roles and circumstances and to consider the effect of these changes on each member. A suitable plan was implemented which was satisfactory to all parties. Termination was a natural conclusion to the problem-solving process, but there was still a need to review the work together, acknowledge its completion, and say good-by to the worker in appropriate ways.

The literature places heavy emphasis on the painful feelings and problematic behavior that tend to accompany work toward termination. It is to be remembered that there is also the positive side of the ambivalence, and in many situations this side predominates. There is, perhaps, always some sense of loss in leaving an experience that has been helpful in important ways or to which a person has contributed much of himself and his skills. It has been suggested that in groups, "the resistance to endings seems to be marked by a general reluctance to tear down a social structure built with such difficulties, and to give up intimacies so hard to achieve."[20] There is, also, however, anticipation of the ending, as is true of certain other experiences in life such as graduation or leaving the parental home. Some clients have highly positive reactions to termination, such as, "I really think I'm ready"; "You've been wonderful"; or "I never thought a group could be this great." Feeling competent to cope more effectively with life's challenges and having confidence in one's ability to do so are richly rewarding and are accompanied by feelings of satisfaction and hope. These feelings and reactions are often the outcome of working through the positive and negative feelings and making constructive moves toward new experiences and relationships.

The process of termination involves the feelings and reactions of the social worker as well as the client. Facing termination stirs up feelings about both the client's and the worker's role in the process. If an individual or group has made considerable progress, it is natural that the worker will feel pleased about the gains and about his contributions to the progress. The worker may, however, be apprehensive as to whether the client will be able to make it on his own. It is natural, too, that he will feel some sense of loss, for it is not easy to separate from persons whom one has helped within a meaningful relationship. The client is apt to test the worker's confidence in his ability to stand alone, and thus the worker must come to grips with learning that he is important to his client and that he needs to sanction and encourage the client's independence. The extent to which the worker and client are able to cope with the separation process is a major determining factor in the client's ability to use ending an experience for further growth.[21]

If a practitioner has worked hard with a client and little progress has been made, his self-confidence may be threatened and he may become irritated with, and disappointed in, the client. These feelings can lead to premature termination. Similar reactions can occur when a client, in myriad ways, stirs up feelings of hostility, irritation, or anxiety in the worker. The worker often defends himself by labeling the client as hopeless or lacking capacity for further gains. Working with such clients is difficult for both client and worker. If the worker cannot modify his own feelings toward such a client, he may need to transfer the client to another resource.

Variations in Reactions

THE STRUCTURE OF SERVICE

It was noted earlier that feelings and reactions toward termination vary from person to person, depending upon the intensity of the worker-client relationship and the client's prior experience with separation and relationships. There are other factors as well that influence the termination process. One is the purpose of the service. Therapeutic services are apt to be more intense and more permeated with problems in relationships than are preventive services which aim to facilitate the positive psychosocial functioning of people who do not usually have serious problems; hence, they are more able to anticipate and work through termination without intense emotion or negative reactions. In task-oriented interviews or groups, the fact that the participants are there to work toward some defined tasks means that somewhat less emphasis is placed on the socioemotional dynamics of the experience. This does not mean that there is not a sense of loss of relationships at ending such an endeavor. It does not mean that feelings of satisfaction or dissatisfaction are not stirred up, including the possibility of anger at the worker or the group that more was not accomplished.

The duration of the service influences the content of the ending process to some extent. Generally, short-term services of up to four months are offered to clients where problems are less severe and less chronic than the problems of clients who are offered long-term treatment. This means that the impact of termination will usually be less upsetting to these clients than to those in longer term treatment. But short-term services are not less meaningful to the clients. Although there has not been time to develop and test the durability of relationships, the greater specificity of the goals and the problems may enhance the development of a strong bond between worker and client system. The limited duration may itself be a factor in motivating very intensive work on mutually understood problems which makes clients aware of the meaning of the service to them.

In crisis intervention, which is by definition a brief service, the resolution of the crisis or at least a return to a previous steady state provides a natural time for termination which has been built in from the beginning. Little attention has been given to the ending phase of crisis intervention. Rapoport, however, emphasizes that "in brief treatment, termination needs to be dealt with explicitly."[22] Since the length of treatment is discussed in the initial interview, the ending process is anticipated from the beginning. Because of the partialized and specifically defined goal and the assumption that the state of crisis is a time-limited phenomenon, the minimum goal is achieved within a period of several weeks. It must be remembered, however, that clients in an acute state of crisis do not always grasp the idea of brief service. A client is bound to have feelings toward a worker who has been helpful to him in restoring his equilibrium, reducing his unbearable anxiety, and enhancing his understanding of the crisis situation and its meaning to him and others in the situation. One of the powerful dynamics in crisis intervention is the experience that there are people available—a worker or a group—who reach out to help at a time when one's own coping capacities are inadequate. Thus, the relationships between worker and client, or member and member, are very meaningful. Since many crises involve loss of some kind, it is essential that clients learn better ways to handle the loss of the worker or the group. Working through the termination phase can thus contribute to better facing and coping with future losses.

It has been suggested that in open-ended groups in which membership changes frequently, intensity of relationships and strong cohesion tend not to develop. If this be true, then it would be expected that termination would be less imbued with strong emotions than in other situations.[23] The important point is that the social worker have the sensitivity and the knowledge to make an accurate judgment about the meaning of himself and often also of other members to a client and that he use this understanding in the termination process, whether the service has been brief or long.

MODALITY OF PRACTICE

There are differences in termination, depending on whether the client is an individual, a family, or a group. In the dyadic relationship of worker to client, the primary emotions are related to separation from the worker and the particular service. In work with families, the family continues as a unit: it is the worker who terminates his relationship with the family. Each member of the family will have his own particular feelings and reactions to the termination, ranging from relief, to acceptance, to intense feelings of anxiety and loss. The worker has meant something different to each of them, but there is also a core family reaction to termination. In working with these reactions, the family's capacities for group problem-solving can be strengthened and their improved relations can be supported. In terminating with families, the primary issue seems to be the family's sense that it can now "make it on its own," and continue to use what was learned in treatment when it recognizes problems in the future.

In formed groups, members may terminate at different times. In open-ended groups there is a more or less regular entering and leaving of members. Even in closed groups, some members may be ready to leave before the others. In either instance, a member leaves a group that is going to continue without him. When this occurs the person who is leaving will have mixed feelings about it, but so too will the other members. The one who is leaving may display any of the feelings and reactions previously described. Those who remain may feel a deep sense of loss of a valued member; or they may feel guilty or angry because they are not yet ready to leave. The fact that one member is ready for termination may provide hope and enhanced motivation for the others. In other instances, it points up the slower progress of the others, who may react with a sense of discouragement or failure. Feelings of rivalry and competition may be aroused, supplanting the sense of cooperation and mutual aid that previously prevailed. Those who remain may feel apprehensive about new members who fill the vacancy left by the departing member. They also may react to the fact that, with the loss of a member, the system's steady state is disrupted. The remaining members have to readapt to a changed situation. When a new person enters the group, both the group and the newcomer worry about whether they will be acceptable to each other. If the members are not helped to resolve the varied feelings, they tend to project onto the new arrival the anger which is left over from the experience of loss, taking out on him the feelings they had not worked through earlier. With skillful help from the worker, every new termination provides an opportunity for the client to prepare for the time of his own termination; thus, there are both hazards and opportunities as the remaining members face their feelings and come to understand their reactions to frequent terminations.

In closed groups, in addition to the separation of a client from a worker, there is the separation of the members from one another. There is also the dissolution of a social system that has meaning to the members. In some instances, the major anxiety is related to the threatened loss of the group, not just the worker. More of the total personality is probably invested in counseling and therapeutic groups than in task-centered groups, but there is a sense of loss in ending the latter type of group if members have worked well together or an important goal has been achieved.[24] As one member of a prerelease group in a mental hospital expressed it to his worker, "I came to say good-by to you again. It's hard to do this and hard to leave after such a long time here." Then, following the worker's comment, "Yes, I know," the patient continued, "But leaving our group is hardest of all." After another supportive comment by the worker, "But it's easier knowing others are facing the same things, trying to make a go of life outside." In such instances, it would be important for the worker to help the client to say these things in the group, too. The group which is being dissolved is a meaningful reference group and a vehicle for social gratification for its members, which fact creates additional anxieties and resistances to termination. But the dissolution of a group is also an overt symbol that the progress that has been made is sufficient for the members to manage without the group. People internalize meaningful experiences, so, in this sense, the group becomes a part of them, influencing their values and norms of behavior in other situations.

Interventions of Workers

In the termination phase the social worker has many tasks to perform. With the client's participation, he evaluates the client's use of the service and assesses his readiness to end. He informs the client system that termination should be discussed. He then helps each person to resolve ambivalent feelings, set priorities for the use of the remaining time, deal with the application of learnings to social living, and plan for desirable follow-up services.

Termination, as a phase in the social work process, is related to the agreed-upon goals, the nature of the client's needs, what has gone before in the helping process, and the client's hopes and plans for the future. The complexity of the process is illustrated by the following illustration of practice.

Mrs. Swift is a thirty-eight-year-old, well-educated, white professional woman, who was married to a man who is a multiple drug abuser and actively committed to a drug culture life style. At time of intake, Mrs. Swift had a multitude of problems in psychosocial functioning: severe anxiety and other emotional reactions to stressful situations, great dissatisfaction with her own ability to develop and maintain satisfying social relationships, and marital and other interpersonal conflicts. She identified herself as "crazy" and a deviant; felt inadequate to give up what she called "a hippie life style" and alcohol, and to take responsibility for her own decisions and behavior. She used denial and projection to defend herself against facing and coping with self-defeating attitudes and behavior. She was overweight, due to compulsive consumption of sweets.

The client's own goals for treatment were to give up her self-destructive behavior, gain a sense of self-worth and adequacy, and make important decisions about her marriage and other social relationships. Prior to her application to the family service agency, she had joined Alcoholics Anonymous and Overeaters Anonymous, groups which provided considerable support for her motivation to control her eating and drinking. She recognized, however, that she also needed counseling. It was clear to the worker that despite the overwhelming problems, the client had many positive personal qualities, ego strengths, and motivation to change her attitudes and behavior.

The agreed-upon plan for service was a flexible one, with recognition that relatively long-term treatment might be indicated, and that a combination of individual and group modalities would be tried. The worker recognized that the client would need a great deal of support, but would also need to develop some understanding of herself in relation to other people. This understanding would be used in making decisions about her marriage and other options in her life and in developing satisfying relationships with people who share her new values and desired life style. In the first three months, personal interviews were used; then these were combined with experience in a small therapy group led by the worker. Following the termination of group therapy, individual sessions were continued in order to help the client assess her progress, make further gains, and prepare for termination.

The social worker recorded:

> Mrs. Swift has been in treatment for about two years. During treatment, she developed a strong positive relationship with me, characterized by great dependency needs. Gradually, she came to feel that I accepted her fully and empathized with her: a sense of mutual trust and positive regard has developed between us.
>
> As we worked together, the client was able to recognize that she had made much progress. She has remained sober throughout the course of treatment and continues to be active in Alcoholics Anonymous and Overeaters Anonymous.

She rather rapidly lost forty pounds and has maintained her ideal weight for the past year. She has separated from her husband and has filed for divorce, extricating herself from what was a destructive marriage and a life style with which she no longer identifies. She has worked out conflicts in relationships with members of her family and developed a supportive network. Her phobic anxiety reactions have almost disappeared, and she has come to understand their purpose and to be able to assert herself more affirmatively. She has maintained herself in her own apartment. During the past weeks, discussion has more often focused on her growing ability to try out new positive experiences. For the first time recently, she telephoned me—not for the usual reassurance, but to report a very positive experience. The time to terminate treatment is approaching.

Due to the intensity of the therapeutic relationship and the central themes of dependence and abandonment in the client's life, terminating will be difficult. But it will also be a real opportunity for her to solidify further the gains that have been made and experience a positive ending of a significant relationship as well as a new beginning in living without my support and help. There will be much pain for her in facing and working through the termination phase.

I began on termination by reminding Mrs. Swift of the progress she has been reporting and suggested that counseling need not continue much longer. I suggested that it might be a good idea if she began to come every other week instead of once a week. She had many reactions to this statement. She talked about knowing that she was getting ready to end, but expressed great uncertainty about her ability to get along without me. She resisted the change in frequency of sessions. She would for example, call me to request additional appointments. She begged for reassurance that she would not be forced to quit before she was ready. She anticipated the pain of separation, but she also rejoiced in her new-found confidence. I remained available and supportive and assured her that she could set the final date.

After the client expressed feelings of comfort with the new schedule of appointments, I again brought up termination. This decision followed a review of the client's progress and changes made, which she herself initiated. I restated her belief that she was ready to work on terminating, to which she agreed. I asked her if she could set a date, explaining the significance of ending well and the reason for setting a date ahead of time.

She set a date, two months away. Together we marked the remaining five sessions on a calendar. The client again expressed the fear of leaving and recounted previous endings that had not been good. She expressed anxiety about being on her own and feared that, without me, she would go back to her old self-destructive habits. We needed to spend time working on these fears. She came to recognize that the gains she has made are real and that her new-found abilities to express and understand her feelings and to know how to go about working on problems would make a return to drinking and other unsatisfying behavior unnecessary. Besides, she now has new friends who can give her support, and she can also give much to them.

I shared my own feelings of sadness at ending and my very positive feelings about the client and the work we have done together. She responded, "We're really a great team." Although this case has not terminated yet, we are well into the process, a process that is planned, structured, and purposeful. This process not only encapsulates an exciting opportunity to review and solidify the gains made during the course of work, it also provides for the client a positive, growth-enhancing separation from a valued person, along with the recognition and maintenance of an integrated self. It is a separation with love.

EVALUATION OF PROGRESS

Evaluation of the client's progress and readiness is essential. The appraisal of the quality of the service and the person's use of it is an ongoing process.[25] Evaluation involves a capacity to make sound judgments in relation to the agreed-upon goals. The ultimate test of the effectiveness of social work practice is the extent to which the persons who were served have made positive changes toward the goals that were set with them. The progress or retrogression of a client is appropriately made in relation to his particular characteristics, background, problems, and needs rather than in relation to fixed or uniform standards. This view is in accordance with the values of social work: it is in opposition to many evaluative research studies in the human service professions which have used the same tests or measurements to evaluate the success or failure of service, regardless of differences in client conditions, type of service provided, and agreed-upon goals.

In some instances, notably work with families or other groups that will continue to exist when the social work service is terminated, the concern is with changes in the structure and interacting processes of the group, as well as changes in the individuals who are part of the group. If goals for each individual and the family have been developed, evaluated, and modified periodically, they naturally become the criteria against which progress is evaluated.

Evaluation of the progress of clients is made more precise and easier for the worker if some plan is developed for tracing changes in the client's psychosocial functioning, including changes in the environment as these relate to goal achievement. Minimally, summary reports should be made at the close of intake, toward the end of the initial phase, and when termination is being considered. The first re-port would include pertinent data about (1) the individual-environ-ment configuration; characteristics, problems, capacities, motiva-tions, and opportunities; and (2) goals as identified by the client, the worker, and significant others. Based on a description and appraisal of the person's beginning in the practice situation, goals are often reassessed, revised, and mutually agreed upon among all participants in the process. As changes in the client and his situation occur, these can be noted from week to week, or periodically. These changes are usually in attitudes toward self and others, the quality and range of relationships, overt behaviors, and opportunities and obstacles in the network of systems of which the person is a part. When the client system is a family or other group, the movement of each individual is evaluated in relation to the trend of changes in the group and the impact of environmental influences on it.

According to Chin, "it is important to emphasize that evaluation studies of goal achievement or outcome are of limited importance unless the evaluation study also tries to pinpoint the components which 'cause' the degree of attainment or hindrance of goals."[26] Thus, both the process, including the worker's interventions and progress, and changes in the client's external relationships and con-ditions should be studied.

Agreement between the client's and the worker's judgments about the changes that have been made, based on a careful review of the available information, generally constitutes the basis for appraising the success or failure of the treatment. Reports of clients are consid-ered important indicators of change; so, too, are expert judgments of workers. But clients and workers do not always agree about the out-come of service. There may be marked discrepancies between work-ers and their clients about satisfaction with the outcome. In a study of twenty-five cases, Maluccio found that two thirds of the workers and clients agreed that the clients had benefitted from the service. Most clients were satisfied with the outcome: they had achieved their particular goals. Although the workers concurred with the clients' positive evaluations of the outcome, they tended to be dissatisfied with the extent and kind of changes made or they doubted the clients' capacities to deal with future problems. Maluccio suggests that, as treatment proceeds, workers tend to increase their expectations, becoming dissatisfied with the clients' achievements.[27] Workers seemed to emphasize weaknesses and negative qualities in their clients, in spite of the fact that social work knowledge of biopsychosocial functioning emphasizes human capacities and competencies.

Clearly, there is need for more accurate assessment of the results of service. Several research designs have been developed which may enhance the reliability of judgments and which take into account individualized goals for clients. These include single-subject designs and goal-attainment scaling procedures.[28] There is need also for formal evaluative research on both program and outcomes of service which, however, requires resources beyond those of the direct service practitioner.

Whenever termination is being considered, a review and an evaluation of what has or has not been accomplished, and the determinants thereof, are imperative. So, too, is a set of realistic goals for the time that remains before the final termination.

In addition to evaluation of client progress, the readiness of clients for termination needs to be considered. Numerous clues may indicate that clients may be ready to think about termination. Clients may begin to reminisce about how things were when they first came; they may comment on progress they have made. They may give evidence of enhanced self-esteem or confidence by changes in appearance or in statements about these changes. They may indicate that they are doing at home or elsewhere what they previously worked on in the sessions. They may miss a session, even though they have been regular attenders.

One example is of a family who was absent one day. When they came the next week, the worker asked about the absence. The father said they had decided to play hooky. They went to the beach, had a picnic, and played all day. There was an impish quality about their report, indicating they felt a sense of accomplishment in not coming to the session and in being able to have fun together. The worker commented on this and all of the family members agreed that was how they felt. This incident led to discussion of the gains they had made in therapy and their readiness to terminate.[29] In other instances, clients may mention that they have friends or relatives who ought to be coming to the agency, indicating that they are aware that they have been helped. Many, of course, inquire directly as to how long the worker thinks they should continue to come or say that they think they don't need to continue much longer.

RESOLUTION OF AMBIVALENCE

A major task of the social worker during this phase is to encourage the ventilation of ambivalent feelings about the termination. This process clears the air so that clients can evaluate the experience realistically. If ambivalent feelings are worked through, the client's energies are released for further work on problems or tasks. Clients can learn how to handle loss and separation through the experience they have in terminating a social work service. Fox and associates note: "The manner in which the therapeutic relationship is brought to a close will heavily influence the degree to which gains are maintained; failure to work through the attitudes and feelings related to the ending of therapy will result in a weakening or undoing of the therapeutic work."[30] One example is of work with a client individually and in a group.

Cathie, age 17, had had a series of losses in her life. The immediate crisis was a boyfriend's decision not to marry her and to break off the relationship. Cathie was pregnant. She was placed in a group of adolescents whose purpose was to assist the members to resolve an immediate crisis, using the support and contributions of other members as well as of the worker. The goals for Cathie were to have emotional support to express and clarify feelings and to reduce anxiety; to understand the situation and her part in it; and to clarify what decisions she needs to make. In individual service, the focus was to make a decision about whether to bring the pregnancy to term or to have an abortion. When the latter decision was made, the worker helped Cathie to cope with her feelings about the baby, the desertion of her boyfriend, and fears of doctors and surgery. Medical time limits put great pressure on Cathie and the worker. A great deal of help was given through the group, but individual sessions were required around the specific decision to abort and plans for implementing that decision.

When the worker reminded Cathie that termination from both individual and group help was imminent, Cathie reacted with massive denial. The denial was not broken until the end of her last session in the group when the worker asked Cathie to say good-by to the group. She reacted first with shock and then with great emotional expression of sadness and grief, mixed with considerable anger at the worker for sending her away. Because there was not time for her to work through these feelings in the group, the worker scheduled an additional interview to enable Cathie to face the experience of loss and to help her move on to carry out the plans she had made for her immediate future.

When one member is leaving a group, the worker understands that this change influences each of the remaining members and the functioning of the group. The steady state is upset. If members do not bring it up, a collective sense of denial may be operating. The worker needs to introduce the subject and explore its meaning to the members. A universalizing comment is often effective, for example, such as that people usually feel sad when someone is leaving, followed by asking them to discuss this topic. Usually, members are relieved when the issue is brought out into the open. Such discussion is invaluable to the terminating member who perceives the meaning that his leaving has for him and for others. People with long histories of damaged self-esteem find it extremely difficult to imagine that they have really helped others. The painful disruption of relationships during termination is eased for such a person when he understands not only that he is ready to leave, but also that he will be missed.

REVIEW OF PROCESS AND PROGRESS

Along with ventilation of feelings and at least partial resolution of ambivalence, the worker engages the client in a review of his progress in relation to agreed-upon goals and relevant to his particular situation. He may ask the client to discuss symptoms or particular behaviors that were of concern to him, and to present his ideas about changes made in attitudes, achievements, and relationships, including his relationship with the worker and/or other members. He may share with the client his own assessment of the client's problems and progress. In families and other groups he may share his direct observations of changes in the members' ability to communicate with each other, identify problems and make appropriate decisions, or change patterns of interpersonal behavior. He seeks for each member's perception of changes in the group's way of functioning.

A common theme during the last sessions is review of the experience and an evaluation of the extent to which clients feel they have benefited from, or been disappointed in, their progress. It is important that a client be helped to recognize and accept his part in the progress. Then he can understand that he can use some of these same understandings and skills in his roles outside the social work experience.

In families and other groups, the worker needs to accept the fact that there will be differences in progress made and that the criteria for judging progress are different for each person. This is so because, in addition to family or group goals, there are different goals for each member. It is also so because of differences in age, sex, developmental phase, severity of problems, and so forth. The worker needs to explain such differences to the group. He needs to accredit the real, even though different, progress made by each. He needs to give special help to members who feel disappointed and, if realistic, give encouragement that progress can still be made. In focusing on an individual, he needs to be sensitive to what is going on with other members.

As individuals or groups evaluate their experiences, the worker needs to be secure enough to listen to, and respond nondefensively to, criticisms of his part in the process. Such criticisms may or may not be valid, but they provide feedback for him to use in evaluating his own performance, which can contribute to his understanding of the use of himself in practice. The worker needs also to be comfortable in accepting genuine praise. One social worker in a hospital described her work with a family and its physician following the death of the oldest daughter after undergoing minor surgery. The physician, who had been close to the family and who had reassured the members that there would be no danger in the surgery, was devastated by the death, as was the family. At the end of the very long session with the worker, the physician reached out to the worker, hugged her, and said, "I really love you—you've done so much for me." The family members gave similar expressions of appreciation. The practitioner, feeling confident that she had, indeed, been helpful, and being able to both give and receive positive feelings, was able to accept this praise and derive pleasure from it.

An important part of the worker's activity is to recognize and acknowledge the progress that has been made and to explore with the client the specific work he has done to bring about the changes. Another activity is to express one's own enjoyment and satisfaction in the client's increasing strength to manage his affairs better. This requires that the worker be in touch with his own feelings about his relationship with the client so that his own resistances to termination do not make it difficult to convey these positive feelings.

PROBLEM RESOLUTION

As clients review what has happened to them, it is often discovered that some serious concerns were touched on from time to time but not dealt with adequately. Now, under the need to use the remaining time profitably, means for coping with this unfinished business may be found. Clients also often need to improve their problem-solving competence and to gain skills necessary for meeting the expectations that significant others will have for them in the near future. The worker may engage clients in discussion or action-oriented experiences to help them stabilize the gains they have made. These activities tend to be oriented to the network of systems of which the clients are a part. Further discussion of new ways of decision-making and action and of ways to apply the acquired understandings and skills helps clients to distinguish between effective and less effective ways of meeting their needs. There tends to be talk or action about ways in which the gains can be applied to varied social situations. There often is a desire to repeat earlier experiences, either those that were gratifying or those in which failure was experienced in some way. Through such recapitulation, the clients confirm their judgments that they are now more able to deal with problematic situations. Resources in the community are often discussed or used in order to foster the transition from social work help.

The worker supports clients' efforts to develop or strengthen new relationships and to find new roles in the community through which they can test and use their recently acquired knowledge and skills. He accredits their developing interests and is pleased when these take precedence over the sessions with him. Hamilton said that:

The painful aspects of terminating a helpful relationship are diminished by the clients' own growing sense of strength, by a comforting feeling of improvement because of the channelizing of his activities into ego building and enlarged social activities and interests with the realization of the worker's continuing good will and the fact that he can return to the agency if necessary.[31]

And Siporin has said that "the interventive system should be terminated in ways that link the client to the natural helping system of the community and that enable the client to continue to have access to its resources.[32]

Transition and Termination

During the termination stage there is often work to be done with others in behalf of the client system. Parents may have some anxiety about whether their child will be able to maintain the gains made and whether they can be effective in helping the child in his development. They need to be consulted and helped to consider the meaning of the social work service to them so that they can help the child to continue to progress. In residential settings or hospitals, other staff need to be notified about, or participate in, the actual decision about termination, depending upon the circumstances.

The worker needs to present and clarify the nature of any continuing relationship he may have with individuals, their families, or with a group. He makes plans with the client to be available if problems are encountered, to follow up with interviews for the purpose of evaluating the outcome of service, or for reunions with a family or group. He makes clear, when possible, that he will be available to clients if they feel it necessary to return. It is becoming usual for workers to offer some form of follow-up to clients who may simply want to review the use they have made of the service. This issue should be addressed flexibly in terms of individuals' and families' desires to use such follow-up services.

Clients who have been hospitalized or placed in foster homes, residential treatment centers, or correctional facilities often need some continuous service to help them in their adaptation to family and community life. The ideal situation is for the same worker to continue, but usually a different one is assigned for aftercare responsibilities. In such instances, the new worker needs to work with the client about the meaning of the change of workers to him. Whether the client returns to his own family or to another type of residence, he has an adjustment to make in adapting to and performing his social roles. Both client, family members, and other caretakers need to be prepared for the ambivalence and difficulties in readjustment.

At other times, a client may be referred to another service for a different kind of help. His case is transferred or reassigned to another agency or to another worker within the same agency. Transfer is indicated under several circumstances. The client may need and want further help, but the present worker is unable to continue; the client needs and wants a particular type of service that is not available in the present agency; the client and worker have reached an impasse in their work together; or a group is so seriously malstructured or malfunctioning that the defects cannot be remedied by the worker.[33] Although ambivalent, the client is willing to be transferred to another worker or agency. The decision to transfer is a mutual one between client and worker.

Clients who are transferred are often reluctant to begin with a new worker and sometimes also a new agency. It feels to them like starting all over again. It is really not so, however, because a client is different from what he was when he began with his present worker. The worker needs to clarify this point and to explain that it should be easier for him to move to another helping situation because he has learned a great deal in the present one.

Termination itself occurs at the end of the last session. When the time for ending comes, the worker helps the clients to say good-by in meaningful ways. He assures the clients that his interest in them does not stop because the service is terminating. Hope is held out that the new strengths and learnings from the social work experience will provide a foundation for each person's continued coping in his own way with everyday problems of living. He suggests that they should be able to continue to use the knowledge and skills throughout their lives. There is often a summary of the experience and a ritual to formalize the breaking of ties. The ritual may be as simple as shaking hands, saying good-by, and wishing each other well. When a social worker feels that his service to an individual, family, or group has been successful, he himself will have grown; for, in a sense, he benefits as much from his clients as they do from him. They teach him how to be a better practitioner. What he learns from working with a particular client system should make it possible for him to give even better service to the next individual or group that he encounters.

CHAPTER TEN

Summary

Clinical social work has gradually become a preferred term for that part of the profession which deals with direct services to people. Its purpose, according to a recent definition, is "the maintenance and enhancement of the psychosocial functioning of individuals, families, and small groups by maximizing the availability of needed intrapersonal, interpersonal, and societal resources."[1] It encompasses a wide scope of developmental, preventive, and therapeutic services. It is identified by an emphasis on psychosocial assessment of persons-in-situations and, based on this assessment, the use of appropriate procedures and techniques. The focus on biopsychosocial configurations represents the "sine qua non of clinical social work as contrasted with clinical practice in other disciplines."[2] As distinguished from clinical practice in other professions, the primary concern is the social context within which individual or family problems occur and are altered.

Within the definition of clinical social work, there is room for alternative theoretical perspectives and models of practice. The perspective of this book is that there is an integrated method of practice that can be applied differentially to varied situations, client systems, human needs, and settings. An integrated model of practice fosters identification with the profession of social work rather than with any one of its fragments. It affirms that there is a strong common core of philosophy, purpose, knowledge, and technology that defines the profession for its practitioners and for the public. It is in harmony with current knowledge about the complexity of human motivation and behavior. Services to individuals can be separated from those to families, small groups, and communities only for purposes of analysis. Regardless of the unit of service, the practitioner needs an holistic understanding of people as they interact within their families, other social systems, and their broader networks of social relationships. Based on an appropriate biopsychosocial assessment of the individual or family in its social situation, the social worker should be able to use any of the modalities of practice in a purposeful and planned way. The flexible use of individual, group, and environmental contexts and means of help contributes to the success of the particular individualized treatment. A fundamental principle is that the needs of the client should determine whether individual, family, group, or community modalities of help should be used singly, serially, or in combination.

Essentials of Competence in Social Work Practice

The essence of practice is doing, that is, performing roles with integrity, knowledge, and skill. In Gordon Hearn's words:

> To act with professional integrity is to act consistently within a framework of values, a framework that is shared generally by members of the profession; to act with knowledge is to act with an awareness of the rationale for and probable consequences of our actions; and to act with skill is to exercise such control that our actions more closely approximate our intentions.[3]

It is competence that counts: values, purposes, and knowledge need to be translated into effective performance. The provision of high-quality services to people is a complex endeavor. The competent practitioner has a mastery of knowledge which he can draw upon in the moment-to-moment communication with his clients. He acts in accordance with professional values and the purposes of social work. He exercises sound judgment in the use of techniques within the processes of planning, assessing, directly intervening, and intervening through the environment. He facilitates the achievement of tasks that are typical of each phase of the helping process. He keeps current with the theory and research on practice so that, to the extent possible, his actions are based on principles that are derived from research.

VALUES

Translated into ethical principles, values guide actions. The philosophical perspective of this theoretical approach to clinical social work is humanistic, scientific, and democratic. It is concerned with the whole person-environment configuration; it desires that people have opportunities to realize their potentials and to be treated as having inherent worth and dignity; and it is committed to social justice for all people. It prefers objectivity and factual evidence over personal biases. It embodies the idea of democracy as a philosophy that governs relationships among people, based on reciprocal rights and mutual responsibilities and directed toward the mutual welfare of the individual, group, and society.

A competent practitioner needs to have great sensitivity to his own personal and cultural values as these are similar to, or different from, those of his clients, those espoused by the organization in which he works, and those expressed by dominant segments of the community. He is aware of the ethical principles of his profession and evaluates his own behavior in relation to them. He recognizes conflicts in values and uses a problem-solving process in making decisions about acting in relation to the conflicts. He follows ethical principles concerning such matters as informed consent, confidentiality, privacy, self-direction, maximum participation, choice of treatment procedures, and discriminatory policies and practices.

PURPOSE AND PROBLEMS

A competent practitioner is clear about the mission of his profession and gives help within the profession's purposes. Social work has always had concern for individuals in their interpersonal relationships and in encounters with their environment. The purpose of clinical social work is to help people to function more effectively in their psychosocial relations. The social worker helps the client to identify the problems that are amenable to social work intervention and to clarify mutually acceptable goals. Changes are often desired in individuals' attitudes, perceptions, and behavior toward themselves and others. Changes are often desired also in the environment in order to provide the necessary resources and a nurturing social milieu. Most frequently, the sought-for changes are in the interrelationships of person-group-situation. The general purpose is translated into more specific goals for each client. The function of the practitioner may be to promote opportunities for the enhancement of potential, to prevent problems in psychosocial relations, or to remedy existing problems that interfere with the achievement of goals.

The needs that social workers seek to meet and the problems they attempt to prevent or remedy are consistent with the purpose. They are in the realm of psychosocial relations and environmental conditions that are barriers to the achievement of goals sought by clients. They include lack of economic and social resources, lack of knowledge or experience, emotional reactions to stress, psychosocial factors related to illness and disability, dissatisfactions in social relationships, interpersonal conflict, culture conflict, conflict with formal organizations, and maladaptive group functioning.

FOUNDATION OF KNOWLEDGE

A competent practitioner's activities are based on a body of knowledge that is consistent with values and purpose. No single source of theory is adequate to explain the complex intrapsychic, interpersonal, and societal processes that influence the adequacy of a person's or a group's functioning at a given time. In order to help people with their social needs and problems, it is necessary to have a broad perspective that incorporates knowledge about the interrelationships among biological, psychological, and sociocultural influences on individual and group functioning.

An ecological systems perspective offers a framework of concepts that aids the practitioner in understanding the relationships between people and their environments. The model of the open organismic system helps the practitioner to understand the organization, interdependence, and integration of the parts and the effects of inner and outer stresses and strains that threaten adaptive capacities. Human systems are perceived as complex, goal-directed, and adaptive units in constant interaction with other social systems.

Psychoanalytic ego psychology supplements the broad eco-systems perspective by providing explanations about the interrelation of biological, psychological, and sociocultural influences on human development over the span of life. It describes and explains the interrelated functions of the ego and the relationships between past and present, conscious and unconscious, and internal and external forces that determine human behavior at a given time. The biological sciences and medicine provide knowledge about normal growth and maturation, positive health, and physical and mental illnesses and disabilities, knowledge which is essential for assessing the impact of these factors on psychosocial functioning. Other bodies of knowledge that are relevant to social work practice are social psychology, sociology, and anthropology. They offer explanations about socioeconomic, cultural, and ethnic determinants of individual and collective behavior and about the structure and dynamic operations of families, other groups, and the networks of formal and informal relationships in a given community.

A competent practitioner makes use of knowledge in all of the major interrelated processes of practice—assessment, planning, social treatment, and evaluation, Knowledge is for use.

ASSESSMENT

A competent practitioner can assess accurately the client system-situation configuration. He makes assessments in order to understand and appraise an individual, family, or other small group, in its social situation. A preliminary assessment is an essential prerequisite for planning what should be done to enable a system to improve its functioning or to effect changes in its environment, or both.

The biopsychosocial perspective guides the practitioner's focus in exploring the situation with the client system. To achieve an accurate appraisal of the meaning of the facts that have been secured, the worker makes appropriate use of sources of information, classifications of psychosocial needs and problems, and criteria for judging the adequacy of biopsychosocial functioning in particular environments. He is able to organize the data and assess their significance for the functioning of both the individuals and the social systems with which they interact. In planning developmental and preventive services, the worker needs to be skilled in the use of epidemiological approaches to assessing the needs and conditions of populations that may benefit from the proposed service.

The preliminary assessment is a tentative one, to be elaborated and modified as the worker and clients interact in regard to one or more mutually agreed-upon goals. The content and processes need to be in harmony with the values of the profession as they are translated into such principles as maximizing the participation of clients in exploring and understanding themselves and their situations; assuring the clients' rights to privacy; and adapting both the content and process to the needs of the particular individual, family, or group. Respect for the client requires that information will not be sought unless it will be put to use in rendering the service.

PLANNING INDIVIDUALIZED SERVICES

A competent practitioner engages in effective planning, a process by which decisions are made about the nature of the services and resources to be made available to particular individuals, families, or groups. Although it is an ongoing process, certain decisions need to be made prior to or during the initial sessions. These decisions concern the social context of service; the general needs, problems, and goals of clients that will serve as an initial focus of content; the unit of attention or type of client system which is most appropriate to the particular situation, and the structure of the service. If a group service is being planned, the practitioner attends to the criteria for group composition, the size and structure of the group, and his primary role in the group. The practitioner needs to understand the concepts and principles that guide his decisions. In an important sense, planning is a problem-solving process in which a social worker uses his professional knowledge to make decisions about a plan of service to be negotiated with particular clients. The preliminary plan is a flexible one, to be changed as the clients' needs and goals become clear.

SOCIAL TREATMENT

A competent practitioner is one who uses himself in ways that truly are adapted to particular clients' needs, requiring large doses of sensitivity, self-awareness, flexibility, and creativity. No words can convey adequately the complex process of social treatment—that complex constellation of attitudes and feelings, thought processes, and techniques that is the worker's contribution to the client's efforts to achieve his goals. The goals are achieved through the acquisition of new or enhanced attitudes, perceptions, and behaviors and through changes in environmental conditions.

A competent practitioner has mastered clusters of techniques that he uses within a therapeutic relationship and supportive milieu. He is able to develop and sustain relationships with his clients and with other significant persons in their behalf. He has enough self-esteem and interpersonal competence to reach out and engage people in interacting with him and with other people. He can bridge social distance through his attitudes of acceptance, empathy, and genuineness and through knowledge of the common ground that underlies age, sex, socioeconomic, and ethnic differences. In addition to relationship building, these clusters of techniques are support, structuring, exploration, clarification, education-advice, and facilitation of interaction. Verbal communication is an important medium for help, but so too are action-oriented experiences. Appropriate use of particular media and techniques is dependent upon understanding the theory on which they are based, the values they have for achieving particular outcomes, and the phase in the helping process. Although the techniques are generic, they require differential application. Basically, it is not the techniques per se that effect changes, but rather the judicious way the worker uses them, based on self-awareness and self-discipline and on cumulative understanding of the person-family or group-environment system.

Social treatment begins with the first contact between a client and a worker and has its own particular focus in each phase of the helping process.

The initial phase. The competent practitioner understands that the major tasks to be achieved in the initial phase are initiating relationships, developing a working agreement, and establishing patterns of effective communication. In order for these events to happen, he assesses the influence of the social context, usually a social agency or organization, on the client system and on his roles in helping. He explores the clients' perceptions of their needs and problems and the goals they hope to attain. He contributes his own knowledge and opinions to the clients in an effort to achieve congruence between worker and client goals. Through exploration and education, he clarifies the structure of service and the conditions under which help can be given and engages the clients in a decision-making process concerning mutually acceptable expectations. He creates a milieu that fosters client participation, self-direction, and support for clients' efforts. Based on his preliminary assessment, he makes tentative plans for the roles he will perform in working with the client system directly and in working with the environment.

The core phase. When the social worker and the individual or group recognize they have reached an acceptable working agreement or contract, the clients are ready to move into the core phase of work toward defined goals. In helping clients to achieve their goals, the worker simultaneously pays attention to the maintenance and further development of the worker-client system and to the problems and tasks that are essential to progress. Since the action system is a vehicle for goal attainment, the steady state must be maintained within reasonable parameters at the same time that clients are attempting to make desired changes. The worker is prepared to deal with the problems in the functioning of the system that hinder the clients' abilities to achieve their goals.

As the practitioner assesses and influences the way the client-worker system is developing, these efforts result also in positive changes in clients' patterns of behavior. As the worker pays attention to the system itself, he simultaneously helps clients to meet their needs and cope with their problems. He engages the clients in a process of reflective thinking and makes contributions to the clients' understanding of their current situations, the patterns and dynamics of their behavior, and aspects of past experiences that are relevant to the present. He assists clients to make, implement, and evaluate individual or group decisions that will be satisfactory to them and to other people who will be affected by the decision. He uses activities that develop social competence so that changes in understanding of self and others and decision-making are translated into more effective social behavior. He enables clients to reduce or eliminate obstacles in the environment, or he acts in behalf of clients to change environmental conditions. Improved psychosocial relations are achieved through appropriate use of individual interviews, group interaction, and environmental interventions.

Termination and transition. Termination is a dynamic and vital process in social work. If properly understood and managed, it becomes an important force in integrating changes in feeling, thinking, and doing. A worker-client system was formed and sustained for the purpose of achieving particular goals. In the final phase, knowledge about psychosocial functioning is used to help the system to terminate, and in a way that benefits the clients. In order for this to happen, a competent practitioner helps clients to acknowledge the positive and negative feelings and resolve their ambivalence about leaving the relationship with the worker and, in the case of formed groups, with the other members. He helps clients to evaluate the progress they have made, acknowledge the realistic losses and gains, and accept the fact that the experience is ending. He helps clients to set priorities for work on unfinished problems or tasks that seem central to their progress so that the gains made may be stabilized or even strengthened. He helps clients to apply the social work experience directly to their life tasks and relationships so that they can make transitions toward new experiences.

Conclusion

In this book, a theoretical approach to integrated practice of clinical social work has been presented. The generic values, knowledge, principles, and skills have been emphasized. However, an effort has been made also to demonstrate the ways in which generic concepts are applied to varied client systems, problems, and social situations. The theory is incomplete, requiring further elaboration and tests of its effectiveness in varied situations. General theories of practice are essential, but they are not sufficient. Within the general theory, it is necessary to provide more detailed explications and illustrations of the theory as it is applied in individual, family, and group modalities and in fields of practice. More specific models may well be developed for work with children, adults, and elderly people and for services to particular racial and ethnic populations. It is hoped that many educators and practitioners will engage in study, research, and writing related to this approach to practice. Adequate theory should contribute to effective practice.

NOTES

1. Perspectives on Social Work Practice

1. Mary E. Richmond, *What Is Social Case Work?*

2. American Association of Social Workers, *Social Case Work: Generic and Specific*, p. 11.

3. Margaretta Williamson, *The Social Worker in Group Work*, p. 9.

4. Claudia Wanamaker, "The Integration of Group Work and Case Work," in *Proceedings, National Conference of Social Work, 1947*, pp. 300–310, Roy Sorenson, "Case Work and Group Work Integration," *ibid.*, pp. 311–22.

5. William Schwartz, "Group Work and the Social Scene," in Alfred J. Kahn, ed., *Issues in American Social Work*, pp. 122–23.

6. Gertrude Wilson, *Group Work and Case Work*, p. 6.

7. *Ibid.*, p. 3.

8. Bertha C. Reynolds, *Learning and Teaching in the Practice of Social Work*, p. 5.

9. Marion E. Hathway, "Twenty-five Years of Professional Education for Social Work—and a Look Ahead," *The Compass* (June, 1946), 27 (5):13–18.

10. Arlien Johnson, "Development of Basic Methods of Social Work Practice and Education," *Social Work Journal* (July, 1955), 36 (3):111.

11. Harriet M. Bartlett, "Toward Clarification and Improvement of Social Work Practice," *Social Work* (April, 1958), 3 (2):3–9.

12. Werner W. Boehm, "The Nature of Social Work," *Social Work* (April, 1958), 3 (2):10–18.

13. Harriet M. Bartlett, *Analyzing Social Work Practice by Fields.*

14. National Association of Social Workers, *The Psychiatric Social Worker as Leader of a Group;* Guido Pinamonti, "Caseworkers' Use of Groups in Direct Practice."

15. An early major effort was the work of Walter A. Friedlander, ed., *Concepts and Methods of Social Work.* More recent formulations have been those of Beulah Roberts Compton and Burt Galaway, Carel Germain and Alex Gitterman, Howard Goldstein, Allen Pincus and Anne Minahan, Judith Nelsen, Max Siporin, Ruth E. Smalley, Francis J. Turner, and James K. Whittaker. See Bibliography.

16. Council on Social Work Education, *Statistics on Social Work Education in the United States.*

17. Max Siporin, *Introduction to Social Work Practice*, p. vii.

18. Ann Hartman, "The Generic Stance and the Family Agency," *Social Casework* (April, 1974), 55 (4):199–208.

19. Carol H. Meyer, *Social Work Practice* (1970).

20. Alice Overton, "The Issue of Integration of Casework and Group Work," *Social Work Education Reporter* (June, 1968), 16 (2):25–27.

21. Carel B. Germain and Alex Gitterman, *The Life Model of Social Work Practice*, p. 2.

22. Carol H. Meyer, *Social Work Practice* (1976), p. 28.

23. A review of ten essays on social work with groups concluded that, with the exception of the one by Tropp, there is a strong movement away from specialization, based on whether an individual or a group is the unit of service. See Robert W. Roberts and Helen Northen, eds., *Theories of Social Work with Groups*, p. 390.

24. Helen Harris Perlman, "Social Work Method," *Social Work* (October, 1965), 10 (4):166–78.

25. William Schwartz, "The Social Worker in the Group," in *The Social Welfare Forum, 1961*, p. 149.

26. Ron Baker, "Toward Generic Social Work Practice," *British Journal of Social Work* (Summer, 1975), 5 (2):195.

27. Rosalie Bakalinsky, "Teaching Generic Practice."

28. Emanuel Tropp, "A Developmental Theory," in Roberts and Northen, eds., *Theories of Social Work with Groups*, pp. 198–237.

29. Hartman, "The Generic Stance and the Family Agency," p. 206.

30. Harold L. Wilensky and Charles N. Lebeaux, *Industrial Society and Social Welfare*.

31. Eveline M. Burns, "Tomorrow's Social Needs and Social Work Education," *Journal of Education for Social Work* (Winter, 1966), 2 (1):10–20.

32. Neil Gilbert and Harry Specht, "The Incomplete Profession," *Social Work* (November, 1974), 19 (6):672. See also Edward Schwartz, "Macro Social Work," *Social Service Review* (June, 1977), 51 (2):207–27; Sheila B. Kamerman et al, "Knowledge for Practice," in Alfred J. Kahn, ed., *Shaping the New Social Work*, pp. 97–146.

33. See, for example, Beulah Roberts Compton and Burt Galaway, *Social Work Processes;* Howard Goldstein, *Social Work Practice;* Max Siporin, *Introduction to Social Work Practice;* Allen Pincus and Anne Minahan, *Social Work Practice*.

34. Jerome Cohen, "Nature of Clinical Social Work," in Patricia L. Ewalt, ed., *Toward a Definition of Clinical Social Work*, p. 31.

35. Cora Kasius, ed., *A Comparison of Diagnostic and Functional Casework*.

36. Bernece K. Simon, "Social Casework Theory," in Robert W. Roberts and Robert H. Nee, eds., *Theories of Social Casework*, pp. 355–95; Helen Northen and Robert W. Roberts, "The Status of Theory," in Roberts and Northen, eds. *Theories of Social Work with Groups*, pp. 368–94; Francis J. Turner, ed., *Social Work Treatment*, Part III.

37. Grace L. Coyle, "Some Basic Assumptions about Social Group Work," in

Marjorie Murphy, ed., *The Social Group Work Method in Social Work Education*, p. 89.

38. Eileen Younghusband, "Social Work Education in the World Today," in William G. Dixon, ed., *Social Welfare and the Preservation of Human Values*, p. 7.

39. Mary E. Richmond, "The Social Case Worker's Task," in Proceedings, National Conference of Social Work, 1917, pp. 112–15.

40. Gordon Hamilton, *Theory and Practice of Social Case Work*, p. 12.

41. Bertha C. Reynolds, *Social Work and Social Living*, p. viii.

42. Herbert S. Strean, ed., *Social Casework*, p. 17.

43. Herbert S. Strean, *Crucial Issues in Psychotherapy*, p. 1.

44. Frances Lomas Feldman and Frances H. Scherz, *Family Social Welfare*, pp. 311–12.

45. Clara A. Kaiser, "Current Frontiers in Social Group Work," in *Proceedings, National Conference of Social Work, 1947*, p. 422.

46. Margaret E. Hartford, "The Search for a Definition, Historical Review," in Margaret E. Hartford, ed., *Working Papers*, p. 70.

47. For discussion of residual and institutional perspectives, see Alfred J. Kahn, "The Function of Social Work in the Modern World," in Alfred J. Kahn, ed., *Issues in American Social Work*, pp. 3–38; Wilensky and Lebeaux, *Industrial Society and Social Welfare*, pp. 138–48.

48. See Claire F. Ryder, "The Five Faces of Prevention," in Council on Social Work Education, *Public Health Concepts in Social Work Education*, pp. 107–15; Gerald Caplan, *Principles of Preventive Psychiatry*.

49. Howard J. Parad, "Preventive Casework: Problems and Implications," in *The Social Welfare Forum, 1961*, pp. 178–93.

50. Norris E. Class, "Child Care Licensing as a Preventive Welfare Service," *Children* (September–October, 1968), 15 (5):188–92. For other references see Carol H. Meyer, "The Relationship of Licensing to Child Welfare Concepts and Principles," *Social Service Review* (September, 1968), 42 (3):344–54; Martin Wolins, "Licensing and Recent Developments in Foster Care," *Child Welfare* (December, 1968), 47 (10):570–82.

51. Henry S. Maas, "Children's Environments and Child Welfare," *Child Welfare* (March, 1971) 50 (3):132–42; Elizabeth Herzog et al., *Families for Black Children*.

52. Carol H. Meyer, *Social Work Practice* (1976), p. 18.

51. Alfred J. Kahn, "Therapy, Prevention and Developmental Provision," in Council on Social Work Education, *Public Health Concepts in Social Work Education*, pp. 132–48.

54. Milton Wittman, "Preventive Social Work," *Social Work* (January, 1961), 6 (1):27.

55. See Naomi Golan, *Treatment in Crisis Situations;* Lydia Rapoport, "Crisis Intervention as a Mode of Brief Treatment," in Roberts and Nee, eds., *Theories of Social Casework*, pp. 267–311; Howard J. Parad, Lola G. Selby, and James Quin-

lan, "Crisis Intervention with Families and Groups," in Roberts and Northen, eds., *Theories of Social Work with Groups,* pp. 304–30.

56. Kurt Spitzer and Betty Welsh, "A Problem-focused Model of Practice," *Social Casework* (June, 1969), 50 (6):323–29.

57. Report of the Joint Commission on Mental Health of Children, *Crisis in Child Mental Health.*

2. VALUES AND KNOWLEDGE

1. Jane Addams, Twenty Years at Hull House, p. 123.

2. Mary E. Richmond, *Social Diagnosis,* p. 357.

3. Carel B. Germain, "Teaching an Ecological Perspective for Social Work Practice," in Council on Social Work Education, *Teaching for Competence in the Delivery of Direct Services,* p. 32.

4. Among the authors writing about approaches similar to this one are: Carol H. Meyer, *Social Work Practice* (1976); Carel B. Germain and Alex Gitterman, *The Life Model of Social Work Practice;* Richard H. Taber, "A Systems Approach to the Delivery of Mental Health Services in Black Ghettos," *American Journal of Orthopsychiatry* (July 1970), 40 (3):702–9; Florence Hollis, *Casework;* and Helen Northen, "Psychosocial Practice in Small Groups," in Robert W. Roberts and Helen Northen, eds., *Theories of Social Work with Groups,* pp. 116–52.

5. Milton Rokeach, *The Nature of Human Values,* p. 4.

6. Eileen Younghusband, *Social Work and Social Change,* p. 106.

7. For further discussion of this issue see Harry Kitano and Stanley Sue, "The Model Minorities," *Journal of Social Issues* (1973), 29 (2):1–9; Florence R. Kluckhohn, "Family Diagnosis," *Social Casework* (February, 1958), 39 (2):66–69; Helen Mendes, "Some Religious Values Held by Blacks, Chicanos, and Japanese Americans"; George Nakama, "Japanese Americans' Expectations of Counseling."

8. For a discussion of American society as a network of ethnic systems, see Barbara Bryant Solomon, *Black Empowerment.*

9. Kenneth L. M. Pray, *Social Work in a Revolutionary Age,* p. 278.

10. Charles S. Levy, *Social Work Ethics,* p. 14.

11. These major principles are derived primarily from *ibid.* and from National Association of Social Workers, *Code of Ethics,* 1980.

12. Levy, *Social Work Ethics,* p. 142.

13. Robert Chin, "The Utility of Systems Models and Developmental Models for Practitioners," in Warren G. Bennis, Kenneth D. Benne, and Robert Chin, eds., *The Planning of Change,* pp. 201–14.

14. Carel B. Germain, *Social Work Practice,* pp. 7–8.

15. For discussions of applicability of systems theory to social work practice, see Edgar H. Auerswald, "Interdisciplinary versus Ecological Approach," *Family Process* (September, 1968), 9 (3):202–15; Beulah Roberts Compton and Burt Galaway, *Social Work Processes,* pp. 97–110; David S. Freeman, "Social Work with Families"; Ann Hartman, "To Think about the Unthinkable," *Social Casework* (October, 1970), 51 (8):467–74; Gordon Hearn, *Theory Building in Social Work;* Gordon

Hearn, ed., *The General Systems Approach;* Sister Mary Paul Janchill, "Systems Concepts in Casework Theory and Practice," *Social Casework* (February, 1969), 50 (2):74–82; Gerald K. Rubin, "General Systems Theory," *Smith College Studies in Social Work* (June, 1973), 43 (3):206–19; Irma L. Stein, *Systems Theory, Science, and Social Work.*

16. Walter Buckley, *Sociology and Modern Systems Theory,* p. 41.

17. Gordon W. Allport, "The Open System in Personality Theory," in Walter Buckley, ed., *Modern Systems Research and the Behavioral Scientist,* p. 344.

18. Ludwig von Bertalanffy, "General Systems Theory and Psychiatry," in Silvano Arieti, ed., *American Handbook of Psychiatry,* p. 1100.

19. Carel B. Germain, "General Systems Theory and Ego Psychology," *Social Service Review* (December, 1978) 52 (4):538.

20. The implications of biological and health factors for psychosocial functioning are presented by Jeanette Regensburg, *Toward Education for Health Professions* and Francis J. Turner, *Psychosocial Therapy.*

21. Basic references on Freudian psychoanalytic theory often used by social workers are: Charles Brenner, *An Elementary Textbook of Psychoanalysis;* Anna Freud, *The Ego and the Mechanisms of Defense;* Sigmund Freud, *An Outline of Psychoanalysis;* Saul Scheidlinger, *Psychoanalysis and Group Behavior.*

22. Major references on ego psychology are: Erik H. Erikson, *Childhood and Society;* Erik H. Erikson, "Identity and the Life Cycle," in *Psychological Issues* (1959), pp. 18–164; Erik H. Erikson, *Identity, Youth, and Crisis;* Heinz Hartmann, *Ego Psychology and the Problem of Adaptation;* Gertrude Blanck and Rubin Blanck, *Ego Psychology;* Jane Loevinger, *Ego Development;* Robert W. White, "Ego and Reality in Psychoanalytic Theory," in *Psychological Issues* (1963), entire issue.

23. Werner W. Boehm, *The Social Casework Method in Social Work Education,* pp. 102–3.

24. Heinz Hartmann, *Ego Psychology and the Problem of Adaptation,* p. 24.

25. *Ibid.,* p. 35.

26. William C. Schutz, *Interpersonal Underworld.*

27. Anne O. Freed, "Social Casework," *Social Casework* (April, 1977), 58 (4):217.

28. Erikson, *Childhood and Society.*

29. For discussion of various ways of delineating stages of human development, see Loevinger, *Ego Development.*

30. For more detail on developmental stages of families, see Frances Lomas Feldman and Frances H. Scherz, *Family Social Welfare,* pp. 63–156; Evelyn M. Duvall, *Family Development,* pp. 106–56; Sanford N. Sherman, "Family Therapy," in Francis J. Turner, ed., *Social Work Treatment,* pp. 457–94.

31. For references on role theory, see Bruce Biddle and Edwin J. Thomas, eds., *Role Theory,* and Theodore Sarbin and Vernon Allen, "Role Theory," in Gardner Lindzey and Elliott Aronson, eds., *Handbook of Social Psychology,* pp. 488–567; and as it is used in social work practice with adults, see Helen Harris Perlman, *Persona.*

32. For discussion of these dynamics in small groups, see Helen Northen, *Social Work with Groups*, pp. 26–31; Sanford N. Sherman, "Family Therapy," pp. 470–72.

33. Walter Buckley, *Sociology and Modern Systems Theory*, p. 79.

34. Irma L. Stein, "The Systems Model and Social Systems Theory," in Herbert S. Strean, ed., *Social Casework*, p. 134.

35. For applications of communication theory to social work practice, see William Brown, "Communication Theory and Social Casework," in Strean, ed., *Social Casework*, pp. 246–66; L. Jeannette Davis, "Human Communication Concepts and Constructs"; Judith Nelsen, *Communication Theory and Social Work Practice;* Virginia M. Satir, *Conjoint Family Therapy;* Norman A. Polansky, *Ego Psychology and Communication.*

36. Kenneth K. Sereno and C. David Mortensen, *Foundations of Communication Theory*, p. 8.

37. For a good discussion of input, processing, output, and feedback, see Donald E. Lathrope, "The General Systems Approach in Social Work Practice," in Hearn, ed., *The General Systems Approach*, pp. 45–61.

38. Norbert Wiener, *The Human Use of Human Beings*, p. 33.

39. Nelsen, *Communication Theory and Social Work Practice*, p. 2.

40. Herman D. Stein, "The Concept of Environment in Social Work Practice," in Howard J. Parad and Roger R. Miller, eds., *Ego-oriented Casework*, p. 70.

41. Jerome Cohen, "Social Work and the Culture of Poverty," *Social Work* (January, 1964), 9 (1):5; for a similar view, see Solomon, *Black Empowerment.*

42. Robert K. Merton, *Social Theory and Social Structure*, pp. 233–34.

43. Marta Sotomayor, "Mexican-American Interaction with Social Systems," *Social Casework* (May, 1971), 52 (5):316–22.

44. Herbert H. Locklear, "American Indian Myths," *Social Work* (May, 1972), 17 (3):72–80.

45. Colin Greer, "Remembering Class: an Interpretation," in Colin Greer, ed., *Divided Society*, pp. 3–35.

46. Florence Lieberman, "Clients' Expectations, Preferences, and Experiences of Initial Interviews in Voluntary Social Agencies," p. 152.

47. For further information about personal and institutional racism, see *Social Work Papers* (1974), 12; entire issue.

48. June H. Brown, "Social Services and Third World Communities," *Social Work Papers* (1974), 12:27.

49. Mendes, "Some Religious Values."

50. Carel B. Germain, "Social Context of Clinical Social Work," in Patricia L. Ewalt, ed., *Toward a Definition of Clinical Social Work*, pp. 54–65.

51. Charlotte Towle, "Social Casework in Modern Society," *Social Service Review* (June, 1946), 20 (2):65–79.

3. ASSESSMENT IN SOCIAL WORK

1. In an analysis of the five theories of social casework, it was found that all five authors used the term assessment in similar ways. See Robert W. Roberts and Robert H. Nee, eds., *Theories of Social Casework*.

2. Gordon Hamilton, *Theory and Practice of Social Case Work*, p. 214.

3. Bertha C. Reynolds, *Social Work and Social Living*, p. 109.

4. *Ibid.*, pp. 130–31.

5. Bernece K. Simon, *Relationship between Theory and Practice in Social Casework*, p. 25.

6. Carel B. Germain, "Social Study," *Social Casework* (July, 1968), 49 (7):405.

7. Harriet M. Bartlett, *The Common Base of Social Work Practice*, pp. 141–42.

8. These findings are based on a survey of social workers in the Los Angeles area reported by Lola G. Selby to the Social Work Research Section, Los Angeles Area chapter, National Association of Social Workers, 1958.

9. Lois P. Case and Neverlyn B. Lingerfelt, "Name-Calling," *Social Service Review* (March, 1974), 48 (1):75–86.

10. Hans Toch, "The Care and Feeding of Typologies and Labels," *Federal Probation* (September, 1970), 34 (3):15–19.

11. Gordon W. Allport, *The Nature of Prejudice*, p. 19.

12. Nicholas Hobbs, *The Futures of Children*.

13. In their classifications of problems, the following authors include a similar category: Lilian Ripple, Ernestina Alexander, and Bernice W. Polemis, *Motivation, Capacity, and Opportunity*, pp. 22–34; Helen Harris Perlman, *Persona*, pp. 193–227; William J. Reid and Laura Epstein, *Task-centered Casework*, pp. 41–49.

14. This category is similar to that of Reid and Epstein, *Task-centered Casework*, who label it reactive emotional distress.

15. The primary architect of psychosocial phases in human development is Erik H. Erikson, *Childhood and Society*. Utilizing Erikson's phases, Meyer has charted the age-specific life tasks, typical problems, and needed services in each stage of the life cycle. See Carol H. Meyer, *Social Work Practice* (1976), pp. 73–74.

16. The literature on crisis intervention contains discussions of developmental and situational stress. For an excellent bibliography, see Naomi Golan, *Treatment in Crisis Situations*.

17. This category has been used by Edward J. Mullen, "Casework Treatment Procedures as a Function of Client-diagnostic Variables."

18. James K. Whittaker, "Causes of Childhood Disorders: New Findings," *Social Work* (March, 1976), 21 (2):91–96.

19. For a major study of filial deprivation, see Shirley Jenkins and Elaine Norman, *Filial Deprivation and Foster Care*.

20. In *Task-centered Casework*, Reid and Epstein have a category labeled dissatisfactions in social relationships.

21. This is one of Reid and Epstein's *Task-centered Casework* categories. Mullen,

"Casework Treatment Procedures," divides this category into marital relations, parent-child relations, other family relations, and social relations outside the family.

22. For good discussions of this subject, see Jack Rothman, "Analyzing Issues in Race and Ethnic Relations," in Jack Rothman, ed., *Issues in Race and Ethnic Relations*, pp. 24–37; Barbara Bryant Solomon, *Black Empowerment;* Herbert H. Locklear, "American Indian Myths," *Social Work* (May, 1972), 17 (3):72–80; Stanley L. M. Fong, "Assimilation and Changing Social Roles of Chinese Americans," *Journal of Social Issues* (1973), 29 (2):115–27.

23. This is one of Reid and Epstein's categories in *Task-centered Casework*.

24. For classifications of problems in groups, see: Charles D. Garvin and Paul H. Glasser, "The Bases of Social Treatment," in *Social Work Practice, 1970,* pp. 149–77; Leland Bradford, Dorothy Stock, and Murray Horowitz, "How to Diagnose Group Problems," in Leland Bradford, ed., *Group Development,* pp. 37–50; Allen Pincus and Anne Minahan, *Social Work Practice,* pp. 230–38.

25. Helen Harris Perlman, "The Problem-solving Model in Social Casework," in Roberts and Nee, eds., *Theories of Social Casework,* p. 167.

26. These principles are based largely on two papers: Olive M. Stone, "Diagnostic and Treatment Typologies for Social Work," and Lola G. Selby, "Discussion: Implications for the Social Work Practitioners," unpublished papers, Social Work Research Section, Los Angeles Area chapter, National Association of Social Workers, 1958.

27. Mary Louise Somers, "Group Process within the Family Unit," in National Association of Social Workers, *The Family Is the Patient,* p. 31.

28. Heinz Hartmann, *Ego Psychology and the Problem of Adaptation,* p. 24.

29. For application of this idea to social work, see Florence Hollis, *Casework,* pp. 260–68.

30. Michael Rutter, *Helping Troubled Children,* p. 41. For another good discussion of assessment of children's problems see Florence Lieberman, *Social Work with Children.*

31. Rachel Cox, "The Concept of Psychological Maturity," in Silvano Arieti, ed., *American Handbook of Psychiatry,* p. 233.

32. Cervando Martinez, "Community Mental Health and the Chicano Movement," *American Journal of Orthopsychiatry* (July, 1973), 43 (4):595–610.

33. E. Goldberg, "The Normal Family," in Eileen Younghusband, ed., *Social Work with Families,* pp. 11–27.

34. The studies to which Goldberg refers are those of Michael Young and Peter Wilmott, *Family and Kinship Ties in East London;* Lulie A. Shaw, "Impressions of Life in a London Suburb," *Sociological Review* (December, 1954), 2 (2):179–94; and Elizabeth Bott, *Family and Social Networks.*

35. Otto Pollak, "Social Determinants of Family Behavior," *Social Work* (July, 1963), 8 (3):95–101.

36. Goldberg, "The Normal Family," p. 26.

37. Gisela Konopka, *Social Group Work,* p. 94.

38. Morton R. Startz and Helen F. Cohen, "The Impact of Social Change on the Practitioner," *Social Casework* (September, 1980), 61 (7):400–406.

39. Mary Louise Somers, "Problem-solving in Small Groups," in Robert W. Roberts and Helen Northen, eds., *Theories of Social Work with Groups*, p. 365, and Helen Harris Perlman, "Social Casework," in Roberts and Nee, eds., *Theories of Social Casework*, p. 164.

40. Harold Lewis, "Reasoning in Practice," *Smith College Studies in Social Work* (November, 1975), 46 (1):1–11.

41. *Ibid.*, pp. 9–10.

42. Solomon, *Black Empowerment*, p. 301.

43. Carol H. Meyer, *Social Work Practice* (1976), p. 97.

44. For an example, see Edith Tufts, *Group Work with Young School Girls.*

45. William Schwartz, "Private Troubles and Public Issues," in *The Social Welfare Forum, 1969*, pp. 24–43; Ruth R. Middleman and Gale Goldberg, *Social Service Delivery*, pp. 25–53.

46. Elsbeth Herzstein Couch, *Joint and Family Interviews in the Treatment of Marital Problems.*

47. *Ibid.*, p. 52.

48. *Ibid.*, p. 54.

49. Sallie R. Churchill, "Social Group Work," *American Journal of Orthopsychiatry* (April, 1965), 35 (3):581–88; Martin Sundel, Norma Radin, and Sallie R. Churchill, "Diagnosis in Group Work," in Paul H. Glasser, Rosemary Sarri, and Robert Vinter, *Individual Change through Small Groups*, pp. 105–25.

50. B. L. King, "Diagnostic Activity Group for Latency Age Children," in Community Service Society of New York, *Dynamic Approaches to Serving Families*, pp. 55–67.

4. SOCIAL TREATMENT

1. Helen Harris Perlman, *Relationship*, pp. 2, 22.

2. Clare Winnicott, "Casework Technique in the Child Care Services," in Eileen Younghusband, ed., *New Developments in Casework*, pp. 135–54; for similar ideas, see Florence Hollis, *Casework*, pp. 236–37.

3. For good discussion of these ideas by social workers, see Beulah Roberts Compton and Burt Galaway, *Social Work Processes*, pp. 155–57; Joel Fischer, *Effective Casework Practice*, pp. 189–218; Thomas Keefe, "Empathy," *Social Work* (January, 1976), 21 (1):10–15; Perlman, *Relationship*, pp. 57–59; Ruby B. Pernell, "Identifying and Teaching the Skill Components of Social Group Work," in Council on Social Work Education, *Educational Developments in Social Group Work*, pp. 20–22; Saul Scheidlinger, "The Concept of Empathy in Group Psychotherapy," *International Journal of Group Psychotherapy* (October, 1966), 16 (4):413–24; and Lawrence Shulman, *The Skills of Helping Individuals and Groups*, pp. 53–57.

4. Carl R. Rogers, "The Necessary and Sufficient Conditions for Therapeutic Personality Change," *Journal of Consulting Psychology* (1957), 21 (1):96.

5. *Ibid.*

6. Alfred Kadushin, *The Social Work Interview,* pp. 49–53.

7. Perlman, *Relationship,* pp. 55–57.

8. Rogers, "The Necessary and Sufficient Conditions for Therapeutic Personality Change," pp. 95–103.

9. Lilian Ripple, Ernestina Alexander, and Bernice W. Polemis, *Motivation, Capacity, and Opportunity,* pp. 76–77.

10. Eric Sainsbury, *Social Work with Families.*

11. Dorothy Fahs Beck and Mary Ann Jones, *Progress on Family Problems,* p. 8.

12. Charles B. Truax and Robert R. Carkhuff, *Toward Effective Counseling and Psychotherapy,* p. 161.

13. Nicholas Hobbs, "Sources of Gain in Psychotherapy," *American Psychologist* (October, 1962), 17 (10):741–47.

14. Lola G. Selby, "Supportive Treatment," *Social Service Review* (December, 1956), 30 (4):400–414; Louise A. Frey, "Support and the Group," *Social Work* (October, 1962), 7 (4):35–42; Lola G. Selby, "Support Revisited," *Social Service Review* (December, 1979), 53 (4):573–85.

15. Morton A. Lieberman, Irvin D. Yalom, and Matthew B. Miles, *Encounter Groups,* p. 359.

16. For a full presentation of ventilation in work with individuals, see Hollis, *Casework,* pp. 103–6; Leonard N. Brown, "Social Workers' Verbal Acts and the Development of Mutual Expectations with Beginning Client Groups."

17. Hollis, *Casework,* p. 93.

18. For good references on this subject see Grace Ganter, Margaret Yeakel, and Norman A. Polansky, *Retrieval from Limbo;* Dorthea Lane, "Psychiatric Patients Learn a New Way of Life," in National Association of Social Workers, *New Perspectives on Services to Groups,* pp. 114–23.

19. William J. Reid and Laura Epstein, *Task-centered Casework,* p. 151.

20. For further information see Edward T. Hall, *The Hidden Dimension;* Margaret E. Hartford, *Groups in Social Work,* pp. 173–84; and Brett A. Seabury, "Arrangement of Physical Space in Social Work Settings," *Social Work* (October, 1971), 16 (4):43–49.

21. William J. Reid and Ann W. Shyne, *Brief and Extended Casework,* p. 70.

22. Hollis, *Casework,* pp. 79–81.

23. Helen Harris Perlman, *Social Casework,* p. 141.

24. Irvin D. Yalom, *The Theory and Practice of Group Psychotherapy,* p. 72.

25. Florence Hollis, "The Psychosocial Approach to the Practice of Casework," in Robert W. Roberts and Robert H. Nee, eds., *Theories of Social Casework,* p. 66.

26. Brown, "Social Workers' Verbal Acts"; Helen Northen, *Social Work with Groups,* pp. 69–76; Reid and Shyne, *Brief and Extended Casework.*

27. Reid and Epstein, *Task-centered Casework,* p. 160.

28. These findings are summarized in Hollis, *Casework,* p. 179.

29. Hobbs, "Sources of Gain in Psychotherapy," pp. 741–47.

30. R. W. Heine, "A Comparison of Patients' Reports on Psychotherapeutic Experience with Psychoanalytic, Nondirective, and Adlerian Therapists."

31. Lieberman, Yalom, and Miles, *Encounter Groups*.

32. Warren G. Bennis, "Personal Change through Interpersonal Relations," in Warren G. Bennis et al., eds., *Interpersonal Dynamics*, pp. 357–94.

33. Arthur Blum, "The 'Aha' Response as a Therapeutic Goal," in Henry W. Maier, ed., *Group Work as Part of Residential Treatment*, pp. 47–56; see also Hollis, *Casework*, pp. 59–62, 193–97.

34. Robert A. Brown, "The Technique of Ascription," p. 73; for an article based on the dissertation, see Robert A. Brown, "Feedback in Family Interviewing," *Social Work* (September, 1973), 18 (5):52–59.

35. Joan M. Hutten, "Short-Term Contracts IV. Techniques," *Social Work Today* (August, 1976), 6 (20):617.

36. *Ibid.*

37. Gisela Konopka, *Social Group Work*, p. 128.

38. Ronald Lippitt, Jeanne Watson, and Bruce Westley, *The Dynamics of Planned Change*, p. 267.

39. Marian F. Fatout, "A Comparative Analysis of Practice Concepts Described in Selected Social Work Literature," p. 133 and discussion on pp. 133–38.

40. For discussions of the use of confrontation see Perlman, *Social Casework*, p. 80; Allen Pincus and Anne Minahan, *Social Work Practice*, pp. 187–89; William Schwartz, "The Social Worker in the Group," in *The Social Welfare Forum, 1961*, p. 148.

41. Alice Overton and Katherine Tinker, *Casework Notebook*, p. 68.

42. David Hallowitz et al., "The Assertive Counseling Component of Therapy," *Social Casework* (November, 1967), 48 (9):546.

43. Robert M. Nadel, "Interviewing Style and Foster Parents' Verbal Accessibility," *Child Welfare* (April, 1967), 46 (4):211.

44. Schwartz, "The Social Worker in the Group," pp. 157–58.

45. Elizabeth McBroom, "Socialization through Small Groups," in Robert W. Roberts and Helen Northen, eds., *Theories of Social Work with Groups*, p. 276.

46. Reid and Epstein, *Task-centered Practice*, p. 172.

47. John E. Mayer and Noel Timms, *The Client Speaks*.

48. Lieberman, Yalom, and Miles, *Encounter Groups*, pp. 371–73.

49. William J. Reid and Barbara L. Shapiro, "Client Reactions to Advice," *Social Service Review* (June, 1969), 43 (2):165–73.

50. Sainsbury, *Social Work with Families*.

51. Inger P. Davis, "Advice-giving in Parent Counseling," *Social Casework* (June, 1975), 56 (6):343–47.

52. For understanding the historical development of problem-solving in social work with groups, see Mary Louise Somers, "Problem-solving in Small Groups," in Roberts and Northen, eds., *Theories of Social Work with Groups*, pp. 331–67.

53. Perlman, *Social Casework*.

54. John Dewey, *How We Think*.

55. Max Siporin, *Introduction to Social Work Practice,* pp. 170–71.

56. Fatout, "A Comparative Analysis of Practice Concepts."

57. For fuller discussion of these activities, see Paul H. Glasser, Rosemary Sarri, and Robert Vinter, eds., *Individual Change through Small Groups;* Hartford, *Groups in Social Work;* Northen, *Social Work with Groups;* Gertrude Wilson and Gladys Ryland, *Social Group Work Practice.*

58. Grace L. Coyle, "Some Basic Assumptions about Social Group Work," in Marjorie Murphy, ed., *The Social Group Work Method in Social Work Education,* p. 100.

5. PLANNING INDIVIDUALIZED SERVICES

1. Max Siporin, *Introduction to Social Work Practice,* p. 39.

2. Carol H. Meyer, *Social Work Practice* (1976), p. 167.

3. Roselle Kurland, "Planning: the Neglected Component of Group Development," *Social Work with Groups* (Summer, 1978) 1 (2):173.

4. Marjorie White Main, "Selected Aspects of the Beginning Phase of Social Group Work," p. 114.

5. Paul H. Glasser and Charles D. Garvin, "An Organizational Model," in Robert W. Roberts and Helen Northen, eds., *Theories of Social Work with Groups,* p. 87.

6. Allen Pincus and Anne Minahan, *Social Work Practice,* p. 115.

7. Alice H. Collins and Diane L. Pancoast, *Natural Helping Networks.*

8. For a similar view of goal-setting, see Florence Hollis, *Casework,* pp. 283–88.

9. For presentations of similarities and differences in client systems, see Mary E. Burns and Paul H. Glasser, "Similarities and Differences in Casework and Group Work Practice," *Social Service Review* (December, 1963), 37 (4):416–28; and Derek Tilbury, "The Selection of Method in Social Work," *Social Work Today* (April, 1971) 2 (2):9–12.

10. Bernard Davies, *The Use of Groups in Social Work Practice,* p. 38.

11. Group for the Advancement of Psychiatry, *The Field of Family Therapy* (March, 1970), 7 (78):531–644.

12. *Ibid.*

13. Shirley Luthman with Martin Kirschenbaum, *The Dynamic Family,* p. 13.

14. Morton A. Lieberman, "The Implications of Total Group Phenomena Analysis for Patients and Therapists," *International Journal of Group Psychotherapy* (January, 1967), 17 (1):71–81.

15. *Ibid.,* p. 79.

16. Violet Tennant, "The Caseworker's Experience in Working with Groups."

17. Scott Briar and Henry Miller, *Problems and Issues in Social Casework;* Howard Goldstein, *Social Work Practice;* Pincus and Minahan, *Social Work Practice;* Meyer, *Social Work Practice* (1976); and Siporin, *Introduction to Social Work Practice.*

18. Elsbeth Herzstein Couch, *Joint and Family Interviews in the Treatment of Marital Problems.*

19. Madison Hinchman, "Social Work Practice with Children and Youth," p. 158.

20. Jerry Flanzer, "Conintegration."

21. Louis R. Ormont and Herbert S. Strean, *The Practice of Conjoint Therapy.*

22. Jerome Kaplan, "The Social Worker in the Long-Term Facility," *Hospital Progress* (May, 1970), 51 (5):116–32.

23. Pincus and Minahan, *Social Work Practice,* p. 58.

24. Dorothy Fahs Beck, "Research Findings on the Outcomes of Marital Counseling," in David H. Olson, ed., *Treating Relationships,* p. 440.

25. Emily M. Brown, "Divorce Counseling," in *ibid.,* pp. 399–429.

26. Pincus and Minahan, *Social Work Practice,* p. 201.

27. Hinchman, "Social Work Practice with Children and Youth," p. 146.

28. Lucille N. Austin, "Some Psychoanalytic Principles Underlying Casework with Children," in Eleanor Clifton and Florence Hollis, eds., *Child Therapy,* p. 3.

29. Helen Harris Perlman, "Identity Problems, Role, and Casework Treatment," *Social Service Review* (September, 1963) 37 (3):307–18.

30. Beck, "Research Findings on the Outcomes of Marital Counseling," p. 440, and Couch, *Joint and Family Interviews,* p. 227.

31. Alan S. Gurman, "The Effects and Effectiveness of Marital Therapy," *Family Process* (June, 1973), 12 (2):145–70.

32. Lilian Macon, "A Comparative Study of Two Approaches to the Treatment of Marital Dysfunction."

33. Frances H. Scherz, "Family Therapy," in Robert W. Roberts and Robert H. Nee, eds., *Theories of Social Casework,* pp. 219–64.

34. Kenneth D. Benne, "The Uses of Fraternity," in Warren G. Bennis et al., eds., *Interpersonal Dynamics,* pp. 301–3.

35. Joseph M. Green, Frank Trenhim, and Nelba Chavez, "Therapeutic Intervention with Mexican-American Children," *Psychiatric Annals* (May, 1976), 6 (5):72.

36. Elizabeth McBroom, "Socialization through Small Groups," in Robert W. Roberts and Helen Northen, eds., *Theories of Social Work with Groups,* p. 280.

37. *Ibid.,* p. 299.

38. Alfred Kadushin, *The Social Work Interview,* pp. 256–57.

39. Barbara Bryant Solomon, *Black Empowerment.*

40. John G. Milner, "Ethnic and Cultural Considerations in Child Placement."

41. Major references on group composition are: Margaret E. Hartford, *Groups in Social Work,* pp. 95–138; Helen Northen, *Social Work with Groups,* pp. 93–100; Harvey Bertcher and Frank Maple, *Creating Groups.*

42. Fritz Redl, "The Art of Group Composition," in Suzanne Schulze, ed., *Creative Group Living in a Children's Institution,* pp. 76–96.

43. *Ibid.*

44. McBroom, "Socialization through Small Groups," p. 287.

45. Ralph Kolodny, *Peer-oriented Group Work for the Physically Handicapped Child.*

46. Ronald A. Feldman et al, "Treating Delinquents in Traditional Agencies," *Social Work* (September, 1972), 17 (5):71–78.

47. Edward N. Peters, Muriel W. Pumphrey, and Norman Flax, "Comparison of Retarded and Nonretarded Children on the Dimensions of Behavior in Recreation Groups," *American Journal of Mental Deficiency* (July, 1974), 79 (1):87–89; David Preininger, "Reactions of Normal Children to Retardates in Integrated Groups," *Social Work* (April, 1968), 13 (2):75–78.

48. Annette K. Boer and James E. Lantz, "Adolescent Group Therapy Membership Selection," *Clinical Social Work Journal* (Fall, 1974), 2 (3):175–78.

49. For further information, see Couch, *Joint and Family Interviews;* Otto Pollak, "Disturbed Families and Conjoint Family Counseling," *Child Welfare* (March, 1967), 46 (3):143–49; and Donald R. Bardill and Joseph J. Bevilacqua, "Family Interviewing by Two Caseworkers," *Social Casework* (May, 1964) 45 (5):278–82.

50. For further information on the values of co-therapy for treatment, in addition to the authors in the preceding footnote, see Ernest N. Gullerud and Virginia Lee Harlan, "Four-Way Joint Interviewing in Marital Counseling," *Social Casework* (December, 1962), 43 (10):532–37; Elsa Leichter and Gerda Schulman, "The Family Interview as an Integrative Device in Group Therapy with Families," *International Journal of Group Psychotherapy* (July, 1963), 13 (3):335–45; and Baruch Levine, *Group Psychotherapy,* pp. 296–305.

51. David G. Rice, William F. Fey and Joseph J. Kepecs, "Therapist Experience and Style as Factors in Co-therapy," *Family Process* (March, 1972), 11 (1):1–12.

52. Group for the Advancement of Psychiatry, *The Field of Family Therapy.*

53. Gurman, "The Effects and Effectiveness of Marital Therapy."

54. Dorothy Fahs Beck and Mary Ann Jones, *Progress on Family Problems;* Elizabeth Kerns, "Planned Short-term Treatment," *Social Casework* (June, 1970), 51 (6):340–46; Leonard S. Kogan, J. McVicker Hunt, and Phyllis F. Bartelme, *A Follow-up Study of the Results of Social Casework;* Norman Epstein, "Brief Group Therapy in a Child Guidance Clinic," *Social Work* (July, 1970), 15 (3):33–48; William J. Reid and Ann W. Shyne, *Brief and Extended Casework.*

55. See Alice Overton and Katherine Tinker, *Casework Notebook;* Dorthea Lane, "Psychiatric Patients Learn a New Way of Life," in National Association of Social Workers, *New Perspectives on Services to Groups,* pp. 114–23; Neighborhood Youth Association, *Changing the Behavior of Hostile Delinquency-prone Adolescents,* I. 1960 and Follow-up Study, 1962; Edith Tufts, *Group Work with Young School Girls.*

56. Alfred Kadushin, *The Social Work Interview,* p. 106.

57. Briar and Miller, *Problems and Issues in Social Casework,* p. 110; see also Beulah Roberts Compton and Burt Galaway, *Social Work Processes;* Pincus and Minahan, *Social Work Practice.*

58. Allen P. Webb and Patrick V. Riley, "Effectiveness of Casework with Young Female Probationers," *Social Casework* (November, 1970) 51 (9):566–72.

59. Briar and Miller, *Problems and Issues in Social Casework,* p. 98; Siporin, *Introduction to Social Work Practice,* ch. 8.

60. Rachel A. Levine, "A Short Story on the Long Waiting List," *Social Work* (January, 1963), 8 (1):20–22; Dorothy Fahs Beck, *Patterns in Use of Family Agency*

Services; Martha Lake and George Levinger, "Continuance Beyond Application Interviews at a Child Guidance Clinic," *Social Casework* (June, 1960), 4 (6):303–9; George H. Wolkon, "Effecting a Continuum of Care," *Community Mental Health Journal* (February, 1968), 4 (1):63–72; and Serapio R. Zalba, "Discontinuance during Social Service Intake."

6. THE INITIAL PHASE

1. Alfred Kadushin, *The Social Work Interview,* p. 118.

2. William Schwartz, "Between Client and System," in Robert W. Roberts and Helen Northen, eds., *Theories of Social Work with Groups,* pp. 186–88.

3. Kadushin, *The Social Work Interview,* p. 123.

4. For the use of groups in intake see: Albertina Mabley, "Group Application Interviews in a Family Agency," *Social Casework* (March, 1966), 47 (3):158–64; Harris B. Peck, "An Application of Group Therapy to the Intake Process," *American Journal of Orthopsychiatry* (April, 1953), 23 (2):338–49; Herbert L. Rooney and Alan D. Miller, "A Mental Health Clinic Intake Policy Project," *Mental Hygiene* (July, 1955), 39 (3):391–405; F. H. Cameron, "The Use of Pre-intake Group Meetings for Prospective ANC Applicants," in Norman Fenton, ed., *Group Methods in the Public Welfare Program,* pp. 51–58; Miriam Jolesch, "Strengthening Intake Practice through Group Discussion," *Social Casework* (November, 1959), 40 (9):504–10.

5. Several similar principles are set forth by Max Siporin, *Introduction to Social Work Practice,* pp. 198–206.

6. Phyllis R. Silverman, "The Influence of Racial Differences on the Negro Patient Dropping Out of Psychiatric Treatment," *Psychiatric Opinion* (January, 1971), 8 (1):29–36; D. Corydon Hammond, "Cross-cultural Rehabilitation," *Journal of Rehabilitation* (September–October, 1971), 37 (5):34–36.

7. Shirley A. Cooper, "A Look at the Effect of Racism on Clinical Work," *Social Casework* (February, 1973), 54 (2):76.

8. Alfred Kadushin, "The Racial Factor in the Interview," *Social Work* (May, 1972), 17 (3):88–98; see also Crawford E. Burns, "White Staff, Black Children: Is There a Problem?" *Child Welfare* (February, 1971), 50 (2):90–96.

9. Leon W. Chestang, "The Issue of Race in Casework Practice," in *Social Work Practice, 1972,* pp. 114–26.

10. For a discussion of racial barriers in the social work relationship, see Evelyn Stiles et al., "Hear It Like It Is," *Social Casework* (May, 1972), 53 (5):292–99.

11. Joan Velasquez et al., "A Framework for Establishing Social Work Relationships Across Racial Ethnic Lines," in Beulah Roberts Compton and Burt Galaway, eds., *Social Work Processes,* pp. 197–203.

12. *Ibid.,* pp. 200–201.

13. Ignacio Aguilar, "Initial Contacts with Mexican-American Families," *Social Work* (May, 1972), 17 (3):66–70.

14. D. Corydon Hammond, "Cross-cultural Rehabilitation," pp. 34–36.

15. George Nakama, "Japanese Americans' Expectations of Counseling."

16. Barbara Bryant Solomon, *Black Empowerment*, p. 211.

17. Man Keung Ho and Eunice McDowell, "The Black Worker–White Client Relationship," *Clinical Social Work Journal* (Fall, 1973), 1 (3):161–67.

18. Maynard Calnek, "Racial Factors in the Countertransference," *American Journal of Orthopsychiatry* (January, 1970), 40 (1):39–46.

19. Kadushin, "The Racial Factor in the Interview," p. 94.

20. Morris B. Parloff, Irene E. Waskow, and Barry E. Wolfe, "Research on Therapist Variables in Relation to Process and Outcome," in Sol Garfield and Allen E. Bergin, eds., *Handbook of Psychotherapy and Behavior Change*, p. 262.

21. *Ibid.*, p. 272.

22. Mildred M. Reynolds, "Threats to Confidentiality," *Social Work* (April, 1976), 21 (2):110, and Suanne J. Wilson, *Confidentiality in Social Work*.

23. Solomon, *Black Empowerment*, pp. 324–25.

24. For a good discussion of work with clients who do not initially want help, see Alice Overton and Katherine Tinker, *Casework Notebook*.

25. Lilian Ripple, "Factors Associated with Continuance in Casework Service," *Social Work* (January, 1957), 2 (1):87–94.

26. David Fanshel, "A Study of Caseworkers' Perceptions of Their Clients," *Social Casework* (December, 1958), 39 (10):543–51.

27. Serapio R. Zalba, "Discontinuance during Social Service Intake."

28. Frances L. Boatman, "Caseworkers' Judgments of Clients' Hope."

29. For a good discussion, see Overton and Tinker, *Casework Notebook*.

30. Gordon Hamilton, *Psychotherapy in Child Guidance*, pp. 134–36.

31. Baruch Levine, *Group Psychotherapy*.

32. Ronald C. Bounous, "A Study of Client and Worker Perceptions in the Initial Phase of Casework Marital Counseling," pp. 94–95.

33. Max Siporin, *Introduction to Social Work Practice*, p. 208.

34. Helen Harris Perlman, *Social Casework*, pp. 149–52.

35. Anthony N. Maluccio and Wilma D. Marlow, "The Case for the Contract," *Social Work* (January, 1974), 19 (1):28–36.

36. Lynette Beall, "The Corrupt Contract," *American Journal of Orthopsychiatry* (January, 1972), 42 (1):77–81.

37. John Dewey, *Democracy and Education*, p. 104.

38. Donald E. Wallens, "Congruence," *American Journal of Psychotherapy* (January, 1969), 23 (1):207–16.

39. Dewey, *Democracy and Education*, p. 110.

40. *Ibid.*, pp. 102–3.

41. Genevieve B. Oxley, "The Caseworker's Expectations and Client Motivation," *Social Casework* (July, 1966). 47 (7):432–37.

42. David S. Freeman, "Phases of Family Treatment," *The Family Coordinator* (July, 1976), 25 (3):265–70.

43. Julianna Schmidt, "The Use of Purpose in Casework Practice," *Social Work* (January, 1969), 4 (1):77–84.

44. Gerald Raschella, "An Evaluation of the Effect of Goal Congruence between Client and Therapist on Premature Client Dropout from Therapy."

45. Helen M. Levinson, "Use and Misuse of Groups," *Social Work* (January, 1973), 18 (1):66–73.

46. Norman A. Polansky, *Ego Psychology and Communication,* p. 187.

47. See, for example, Grace Ganter, Margaret Yeakel, and Norman A. Polansky, *Retrieval from Limbo;* Dorthea Lane, "Psychiatric Patients Learn a New Way of Life," in National Association of Social Workers, *New Perspectives on Services to Groups,* pp. 114–23.

48. Nakama, "Japanese Americans' Expectations of Counseling."

49. Florence Clemenger, "Congruence between Members and Workers on Selected Behaviors of the Role of the Social Group Worker."

50. Leonard N. Brown, "Social Workers' Verbal Acts and the Development of Mutual Expectations with Beginning Client Groups."

51. Aaron Rosen and Dina Lieberman, "The Experimental Evaluation of Interview Performance of Social Workers," *Social Service Review* (September, 1972), 46 (3):395–412.

52. Martha Gentry, "Initial Group Meetings: Member Expectations and Information Distribution Process."

53. Lilian Ripple, Ernestina Alexander, and Bernice W. Polemis, *Motivation, Capacity, and Opportunity.*

54. Deborah Ann Farber, "A Study of Clients' Reactions to Initial Contacts with a Community Mental Health Center," *Smith College Studies in Social Work* (November, 1975), 46 (1):44–45; John E. Mayer and Noel Timms, "Clash in Perspective between Worker and Client," *Social Casework* (January, 1969), 50 (1):32–40; Helen Harris Perlman, "Intake and Some Role Considerations," in *Persona,* pp. 162–76; Phyllis R. Silverman, "A Reexamination of the Intake Procedure," *Social Casework* (December, 1970), 51 (10):625–34; Ann W. Shyne, "What Research Tells Us about Short-term Cases in Family Agencies," *Social Casework* (May, 1957), 38 (5):223–31.

55. Scott Briar, "Family Services," in Henry Maas, ed., *Five Fields of Social Service,* pp. 14–15, 21–27.

56. Charles D. Garvin, "Complementarity of Role Expectations in Groups," in *Social Work Practice, 1969,* pp. 127–45.

7. The Core Phase: System Maintenance and Development

1. See Florence Hollis, *Casework,* pp. 228–42; Helen Northen, *Social Work with Groups,* pp. 156–61, 192–95; Helen Harris Perlman, *Relationship;* Katherine Wood, "The Contribution of Psychoanalysis and Ego Psychology to Social Casework," in Herbert S. Strean, ed., *Social Casework,* pp. 45–122.

2. Perlman, *Relationship,* pp. 74–84.

3. Baruch Levine, *Group Psychotherapy*, pp. 160–64, 257–80; Saul Scheidlinger, *Psychoanalysis and Group Behavior*, pp. 80–85; Irvin D. Yalom, *The Theory and Practice of Group Psychotherapy*, pp. 200–202.

4. Sidney Wasserman, "Ego Psychology," in Francis J. Turner, ed., *Social Work Treatment*, p. 42.

5. Domenic N. Gareffa and Stanley A. Neff, "Management of the Client's Seductive Behavior," *Smith College Studies in Social Work* (February, 1974), 44 (2):110–24.

6. Noel K. Hunnybun, "David and His Mother," in Eileen Younghusband, ed., *Social Work with Families*, pp. 80–86.

7. For a good analysis of scapegoating, see James A. Garland and Ralph Kolodny, "Characteristics and Resolution of Scapegoating," in Saul Bernstein, ed., *Further Explorations in Group Work*, pp. 55–74.

8. For further information about this role and other ones, see Margaret E. Hartford, *Groups in Social Work*, pp. 216–18 and Helen Northen, *Social Work with Groups*, pp. 161–69.

9. Barbara Bryant Solomon, *Black Empowerment*, p. 236.

10. Janice Perley, Carolyn Winget, and Carlos Placci, "Hope and Discomfort as Factors Influencing Treatment Continuance," *Comprehensive Psychiatry* (November, 1971), 12 (6):557–63.

11. In Allen Pincus and Anne Minahan, *Social Work Practice*, pp. 146–51 and 184–93, there is the most complete presentation of resistance, but it is focused primarily on task-centered systems.

12. Nathan Ackerman, *Treating the Troubled Family*, p. 88.

13. P. R. Balgopal and R. F. Hull, "Keeping Secrets: Group Resistance for Patients and Therapists," *Psychotherapy: Theory, Research and Practice*, (Winter, 1973), 10 (4):334–36.

14. Warren G. Bennis, "Personal Change through Interpersonal Relations," in Warren G. Bennis et al, eds., *Interpersonal Dynamics*, pp. 357–94.

15. For a fuller presentation of evaluation of communication, see Jules Riskin and Elaine E. Faunce, "An Evaluative Review of Family Interaction Research," *Family Process* (December, 1972), 11 (4):365–455. See also Shirley Luthman with Martin Kirschenbaum, *The Dynamic Family*, pp. 35–43, 65–80.

16. See, for example, Grace Ganter, Margaret Yeakel, and Norman A. Polansky, *Retrieval from Limbo;* Dorthea Lane, "Psychiatric Patients Learn a New Way of Life," in National Association of Social Workers, *New Perspectives in Services to Groups*, pp. 114–23.

17. Salvador Minuchin et al., *Families of the Slums*.

18. Virginia M. Satir, *Conjoint Family Therapy*.

19. Charles D. Garvin, "Group Process: Usage and Uses in Social Work Practice," in Paul H. Glasser, Rosemary Sarri, and Robert Vinter, eds., *Individual Change through Small Groups*, p. 210.

8. THE CORE PHASE: ACHIEVEMENT OF GOALS

1. Barbara Bryant Solomon, *Black Empowerment*, pp. 299–304.

2. *Ibid.*, p. 301.

3. Warren G. Bennis, et al., eds., *Interpersonal Dynamics*, Part II: Introduction, pp. 207–11.

4. Florence Hollis, "The Psychosocial Approach to the Practice of Casework," in Robert W. Roberts and Robert H. Nee, eds., *Theories of Social Casework*, p. 66.

5. Florence Hollis, *ibid.*, pp. 48–49; Grace L. Coyle, "Social Group Work: an Aspect of Social Work Practice," *Journal of Social Issues* (1952) 8 (1):29.

6. Robert A. Brown, "The Technique of Ascription." For an article based on this research see Robert A. Brown, "Feedback in Family Interviewing," *Social Work* (September, 1973), 18 (5):52–59.

7. Gisela Konopka, *Social Group Work*, p. 128.

8. Solomon, *Black Empowerment*, p. 348.

9. This unpublished study was reported in Patricia L. Ewalt, "A Psychoanalytically Oriented Child Guidance Center," in William J. Reid and Laura Epstein, eds., *Task-centered Practice*, p. 34.

10. William J. Reid, "Process and Outcome in Treatment of Family Problems," in *ibid.*, pp. 58–77.

11. The first major book on problem solving in social work was Helen Harris Perlman, *Social Casework*. Others who have used problem solving as the major construct in their books are: Beulah Roberts Compton and Burt Galaway, *Social Work Processes;* Howard Goldstein, *Social Work Practice;* Irving A. Spergel, *Community Problem Solving*. In an historical review of social work with groups, Somers found that problem solving is a theme that has cut across other theoretical differences among writers. See Mary Louise Somers, "Problem-solving in Small Groups," in Robert W. Roberts and Helen Northen, eds., *Theories of Social Work with Groups*, pp. 331–67.

12. Compton and Galaway, Social Work Processes, p. 236.

13. John Dewey, *How We Think*.

14. Perlman, *Social Casework*, p. 91.

15. Gertrude Wilson and Gladys Ryland, *Social Group Work Practice*, p. 52.

16. Somers, "Problem-solving in Small Groups," p. 365.

17. Goldstein, *Social Work Practice*, p. 101.

18. William J. Reid, *The Task-centered System;* Elliot Studt, "Social Work Theory and Implications for the Practice of Methods," *Social Work Education Reporter* (June, 1968), 16 (2):22–46.

19. Fritz Redl and David Wineman, *Controls from Within*.

20. Quentin A. F. Rae-Grant, Thomas Gladwin, and Eli M. Bower, "Mental Health, Social Competence, and the War on Poverty," *American Journal of Orthopsychiatry* (July, 1966), 36 (4):660. See also: Thomas Gladwin, *Poverty, USA*.

21. Julianne L. Wayne and Barbara B. Feinstein, "Group Work Outreach to Parents by School Social Workers," *Social Casework* (June, 1978), 59 (6):345–51.

22. Audrey Oppenheimer, "Triumph over Trauma in the Treatment of Child Abuse," *Social Casework* (June, 1978), 59 (6):356.

23. James K. Whittaker, "A Developmental-educational Approach to Child Treatment," in Francine Sobey, ed., *Changing Roles in Social Work Practice*, p. 180.

24. Lydia Rapoport and Leah Potts, "Abortion of Unwanted Pregnancy as a Potential Life Crisis," in Florence Haselkorn, ed., *Family Planning*, pp. 249–66.

25. Gisela Konopka, *Young Girls*, p. 57.

26. Lola Elizabeth Buckley, "The Use of the Small Group at a Time of Crisis: Transition of Girls from Elementary to High School."

27. Salvador Minuchin et al., *Families of the Slums*, p. 269.

28. The following writers have given considerable attention to the influence of environment on individual and group functioning: Carel B. Germain, ed., *Social Work Practice;* Richard M. Grinnell, "Environmental Modification: Factors Associated with Its Use in Casework Practice"; Ann Hartman, "To Think about the Unthinkable," *Social Casework* (October, 1970), 51 (8):467–74; Carol H. Meyer, *Social Work Practice* (1976), pp. 42–88; Bertha C. Reynolds, *Social Work and Social Living*.

29. Grinnell, "Environmental Modification," p. 38.

30. Bertha C. Reynolds, "Can Social Case Work Be Interpreted to a Community as a Basic Approach to Human Problems?" *The Family* (February, 1933), 13 (1):337.

31. Martin Rein, "Social Work in Search of a Radical Profession," *Social Work* (April, 1970), 15 (2):15–19.

32. Martin Davies, "The Assessment of Environment in Social Work Research," *Social Casework* (January, 1974), 55 (1):3–12.

33. Lilian Ripple, Ernestina Alexander, and Bernice W. Polemis, *Motivation, Capacity, and Opportunity*, pp. 203–20.

34. Gerald Caplan, *Support Systems and Community Mental Health*, pp. 216–17.

35. See Alan S. Gartner and Frank Riessman, *Self-Help in the Human Services* and Alfred H. Katz and Eugene Bender, *The Strength in Us*.

36. Solomon, *Black Empowerment*, p. 347.

37. For references on referrals, see Nicholas Long, "Information and Referral Services," *Social Service Review* (March, 1973), 47 (1):49–62; Sherman Barr, "The Social Agency as a Disseminatory of Information," in Harold H. Weissman, ed., *Individual and Group Services in the Mobilization for Youth Experience*, pp. 54–61; Max Siporin, *Introduction to Social Work Practice*, pp. 311–15.

38. Harold H. Weissman and Marie Weil, "Success and Failure in Integrating Services and Helping Families," in Harold H. Weissman, ed., *Integrating Services for Troubled Families*, ch. 7. On advocacy, see Compton and Galaway, *Social Work Processes*, pp. 348–49; David Hallowitz, "Advocacy in the Context of Treatment," *Social Casework* (July, 1974), 55 (7):416–20; Allen Pincus and Anne Minahan, *Social Work Practice*, pp. 342–43.

39. National Association of Social Workers, "Ad Hoc Committee on Advocacy Report," *Social Work* (April, 1969) 14 (2):16–22.

40. For a good discussion of collaboration, see Compton and Galaway, *Social Work Processes,* pp. 451–58, and Naomi Brill, *Team Work.*

41. See Charlotte L. Towle, "Social Work: Cause and Function, 1961," *Social Casework* (October, 1961), 42 (8): 385–96; Leonard Schneiderman, "A Social Action Model for the Social Work Practitioner," *Social Casework* (October, 1965), 46 (8):490–93.

42. Ruth R. Middleman and Gale Goldberg, *Social Service Delivery,* pp. 17–24.

43. Solomon, *Black Empowerment,* pp. 352–54.

44. Francis P. Purcell and Harry Specht, "The House on Sixth Street," *Social Work* (October, 1965), 10 (4):69–76.

9. Termination and Transition

1. Only a few articles on termination were available a decade ago. By 1978, Beit-Hallahmi located twenty-eight articles or chapters of books that dealt with the subject—twelve with individuals, ten with groups, four with individuals and groups, and only two with families. See Mary Beit-Hallahmi, "Termination: The Crucial Stage of Social Work," D.S.W. diss., University of Southern California, 1981.

2. Gordon Hamilton, *Theory and Practice of Social Case Work,* p. 236.

3. Lydia Rapoport, "Crisis Intervention as a Mode of Brief Treatment," in Robert W. Roberts and Robert H. Nee, eds., *Theories of Social Casework,* p. 236.

4. Margaret E. Hartford, *Groups in Social Work,* p. 53.

5. See Erik H. Erikson, *Identity, Youth, and Crisis,* pp. 99–141; Constance Hoenk Shapiro, "Termination: a Neglected Concept in the Social Work Curriculum," *Journal of Education for Social Work* (Summer, 1980), 16 (2):13–19.

6. For a similar statement on worker goals during termination, see Beulah Roberts Compton and Burt Galaway, *Social Work Processes,* pp. 429–30.

7. Anthony N. Maluccio, *Learning from Clients,* pp. 180–86.

8. Jane K. Bolen, "Easing the Pain of Termination for Adolescents," *Social Casework* (November, 1972), 53 (9):519–27.

9. Evelyn Fox, Marion Nelson, and William Bolman, "The Termination Process," *Social Work* (October, 1969) 14 (4):55.

10. Sheldon K. Schiff, "Termination of Therapy," *Archives of General Psychiatry* (January, 1962), 6 (1):80.

11. Phyllis Blanchard, "Tommy Nolan," in Helen Witmer, ed., *Psychiatric Interviews with Children,* p. 92.

12. James A. Garland, Hubert E. Jones, and Ralph Kolodny, "A Model for Stages of Development in Social Work Groups," in Saul Bernstein, ed., *Explorations in Group Work,* p. 57; Benjamin Stempler, "A Group Work Approach to Family Group Treatment," *Social Casework* (March, 1977), 58 (3):143–52.

13. Schiff, "Termination of Therapy," p. 80.

14. Paul Bywaters, "Ending Casework Relationships (2)," *Social Work Today* (September, 1975), 6 (11):337.

15. John Bowlby, "Separation Anxiety," *International Journal of Psychoanalysis* (March–June, 1960), 41:102; David Peretz, "Reaction to Loss," in Bernard Schoenberg et al., eds., *Loss and Grief*, pp. 20–35.

16. Rose Green, "Terminating the Relationship in Social Casework," p. 11.

17. Bolen, "Easing the Pain of Termination for Adolescents."

18. Fox, Nelson, and Bolman, "The Termination Process," 63.

19. Hartford, *Groups in Social Work*, p. 89.

20. William Schwartz, "Between Client and System," in Robert W. Roberts and Helen Northen, eds., *Theories of Social Work with Groups*, p. 192.

21. Sidney Z. Moss and Miriam S. Moss, "When a Caseworker Leaves an Agency," *Social Casework* (July, 1967), 48 (7):437.

22. Rapoport, "Crisis Intervention as a Mode of Brief Treatment, p. 302.

23. Beryce W. MacLennan and Naomi Felsenfeld, *Group Counseling and Psychotherapy with Adolescents*, pp. 108–9.

24. Margaret E. Hartford, "Group Methods and Generic Practice," in Roberts and Northen, eds., *Theories of Social Work with Groups*, p. 70; Saul Scheidlinger and Marjorie A. Holden, "Group Therapy of Women with Severe Character Disorders," *International Journal of Group Psychotherapy* (April, 1966), 16 (2):174–89.

25. This section is adapted from Helen Northen, *Social Work with Groups*, pp. 224–26.

26. Robert Chin, "Evaluating Group Movement and Individual Change," in National Association of Social Workers, *Use of Groups in the Psychiatric Setting*, p. 42.

27. Maluccio, *Learning from Clients*, pp. 181–93.

28. See Compton and Galaway, *Social Work Processes*, pp. 404–12.

29. This example is paraphrased from one in Shirley Luthman with Martin Kirschenbaum, *The Dynamic Family*, p. 137.

30. Fox, Nelson, and Bolman, "The Termination Process," p. 53.

31. Hamilton, *Theory and Practice of Social Case Work*, p. 81.

32. Max Siporin, *Introduction to Social Work Practice*, p. 341.

33. *Ibid.*, pp. 339–40.

10. SUMMARY

1. Jerome Cohen, "Nature of Clinical Social Work," in Patricia L. Ewalt, ed., *Toward a Definition of Clinical Social Work*, p. 30.

2. *Ibid.*, p. 24.

3. Gordon Hearn, *Theory Building in Social Work*, p. 1.

BIBLIOGRAPHY

Ackerman, Nathan. *Treating the Troubled Family*. New York: Basic Books, 1966.

Addams, Jane. *Twenty Years at Hull House*. New York: Macmillan, 1910.

Aguilar, Ignacio. "Initial Contacts with Mexican-American Families." *Social Work* (May, 1972) 17 (3):66–70.

Albee, George W. and Justin M. Jaffe, eds. *Primary Prevention of Psychopathology*, vol. 1. Hanover, N.H.: University Press of New England, 1977.

Allport, Gordon W. *The Nature of Prejudice*, Garden City, N.Y.: Doubleday Anchor, 1958.

Allport, Gordon W. "The Open System in Personality Theory." In Walter Buckley, ed., *Modern Systems Research for the Behavioral Scientist*, pp. 343–50. Chicago: Aldine, 1968.

American Association of Social Workers. *Social Case Work: Generic and Specific: a Report of the Milford Conference*. New York: the Association, 1929.

Arieti, Silvano, ed. *American Handbook of Psychiatry*. Rev. ed. New York: Basic Books, 1976.

Auerswald, Edgar H. "Interdisciplinary versus Ecological Approach." *Family Process* (September, 1968), 9 (3):202-15.

Austin, Lucille N. "Some Psychoanalytic Principles Underlying Casework with Children." In Eleanor Clifton and Florence Hollis, eds., *Child Therapy: a Casework Symposium*, pp. 3–25. New York: Family Service Association of America, 1948.

Bakalinsky, Rosalie. "Teaching Generic Practice." D.S.W. diss., University of Southern California, 1980.

Baker, Ron. "The Multirole Practitioner in the Generic Orientation to Social Work Practice." *British Journal of Social Work* (Autumn, 1976), 6 (3):327-52.

Baker, Ron. "Toward Generic Social Work Practice—a Review and Some Innovations." *British Journal of Social Work* (Summer, 1975), 5 (2):193–215.

Balgopal, P. R. and R. F. Hull. "Keeping Secrets: Group Resistance for Patients and Therapists." *Psychotherapy: Theory, Research, and Practice* (Winter, 1973), 10 (4):334–36.

Bardill, Donald R. and Joseph J. Bevilacqua. "Family Interviewing by Two Caseworkers." *Social Casework* (May, 1964), 45 (5):278–82.

Barr, Sherman. "The Social Agency as a Disseminatory of Information." In Harold H. Weisman, ed., *Individual and Group Services in the Mobilization for Youth Experience*, pp. 54–61. New York: Association Press, 1969.

Bartlett, Harriet M. *Analyzing Social Work Practice by Fields.* New York: National Association of Social Workers, 1961.

Bartlett, Harriet M. *The Common Base of Social Work Practice.* New York: National Association of Social Workers, 1970.

Bartlett, Harriet M. "Toward Clarification and Improvement of Social Work Practice: the Working Definition." *Social Work* (April, 1958), 3 (2):3–9.

Beall, Lynette. "The Corrupt Contract: Problems in Conjoint Therapy with Parents and Children." *American Journal of Orthopsychiatry* (January, 1972), 42 (1):77–81.

Beck, Dorothy Fahs. *Patterns in Use of Family Agency Services.* New York: Family Service Association of America, 1962.

Beck, Dorothy Fahs. "Research Findings on the Outcomes of Marital Counseling." In David H. Olson, ed., *Treating Relationships*, pp. 431–74. Lake Mills, Iowa: Graphic, 1976.

Beck, Dorothy Fahs and Mary Ann Jones. *Progress on Family Problems.* New York: Family Service Association of America, 1973.

Beisser, Arnold with Rose Green. *Mental Health Consultation and Education.* Palo Alto, Calif.: National Press Books, 1972.

Beit-Hallahmi, Mary. "Termination: the Crucial Stage of Social Work." D.S.W. diss., University of Southern California, 1981.

Bell, Norman W. and Ezra Vogel, eds. *A Modern Introduction to the Family.* Glencoe, Ill.: Free Press, 1960.

Benne, Kenneth D. "The Uses of Fraternity." In Warren G. Bennis et al., eds., *Interpersonal Dynamics*, pp. 301–03. Homewood, Ill.: Dorsey Press, 1968.

Bennis, Warren G. "Personal Change through Interpersonal Relations." In Warren G. Bennis et al., eds. *Interpersonal Dynamics.* pp. 357–94. Homewood, Ill.: Dorsey Press, 1968.

Bennis, Warren G. et al., eds. *Interpersonal Dynamics: Essays and Readings on Human Interaction.* Homewood, Ill.: Dorsey Press, 1968.

Bennis, Warren G., Kenneth D. Benne, and Robert Chin. *The Planning of Change.* New York: Holt, Rinehart & Winston, 1962.

Bernstein, Saul. "Self-Determination—Citizen or King in the Realm of Values?" *Social Work* (January, 1970), 5 (1):3–8.

Bernstein, Saul, ed. *Explorations in Group Work.* Boston: Milford House, 1973.

Bernstein, Saul, ed. *Further Explorations in Group Work.* Boston: Milford House, 1973.

Bertcher, Harvey and Frank Maple. *Creating Groups.* Beverly Hills, Calif.: Sage Publications, 1978.

Biddle, Bruce and Edwin J. Thomas, eds. *Role Theory: Concepts and Research.* New York: Wiley, 1966.

Blanchard, Phyllis. "Tommy Dolan." In Helen Witmer, ed., *Psychiatric Interviews with Children,* pp. 59–92. New York: Commonwealth Fund, 1946.

Blanck, Gertrude and Rubin Blanck. *Ego Psychology: Theory and Practice.* New York: Columbia University Press, 1974.

Bloom, Martin. *The Paradox of Helping: Introduction to the Philosophy of Scientific Practice.* New York: Wiley, 1975.

Blum, Arthur. "The 'Aha' Response as a Therapeutic Goal." In Henry W. Maier, ed., *Group Work as Part of Residential Treatment,* pp. 47–56. New York: National Association of Social Workers, 1965.

Boatman, Frances L. "Caseworkers' Judgments of Clients' Hope: Some Correlates among Client-Situation Characteristics and among Workers' Communication Patterns." D.S.W. diss., Columbia University, 1975.

Boehm, Werner W. "The Nature of Social Work." *Social Work* (April, 1958), 3 (2):10–18.

Boehm, Werner W. *The Social Casework Method in Social Work Education: a Project Report of the Curriculum Study.* vol. 10. New York: Council on Social Work Education, 1959.

Boer, Annette K. and James E. Lantz. "Adolescent Group Therapy Membership Selection." *Clinical Social Work Journal* (Fall, 1974), 2 (3):172–81.

Bolen, Jane K. "Easing the Pain of Termination for Adolescents." *Social Casework* (November, 1972), 53 (9):519–27.

Bott, Elizabeth. *Family and Social Networks: Roles, Norms, and Extended Relationships in Ordinary Urban Families.* 2d ed. New York: Free Press, 1971.

Bounous, Ronald C. "A Study of Client and Worker Perceptions in the Initial Phase of Casework Marital Counseling." Ph.D. diss., University of Minnesota, 1965.

Bowlby, John. "Separation Anxiety." *International Journal of Psychoanalysis* (March–June 1960): 41:89–113.

Bradford, Leland, ed. *Group Development*. Washington, D.C.: National Training Laboratory, National Education Association, 1961.

Bradford, Leland, Dorothy Stock, and Murray Horowitz. "How to Diagnose Group Problems." In Leland Bradford, ed., *Group Development*, pp. 37–50. Washington, D.C.: National Training Laboratory, National Education Association, 1961.

Brenner, Charles. *An Elementary Textbook of Psychoanalysis*. Rev. ed. Garden City, N.Y.: International Universities Press, 1973.

Briar, Scott. "Family Services." In Henry S. Maas, ed., *Five Fields of Social Service: Reviews of Research*, pp. 9–50. New York: National Association of Social Workers, 1966.

Briar, Scott and Henry Miller. *Problems and Issues in Social Casework*. New York: Columbia University Press, 1971.

Brill, Naomi. *Team Work: Working Together in the Human Services*. Philadelphia: Lippincott, 1976.

British Association of Social Workers. *The Social Work Task: Working Party Report*. Newcastle: Trafford Press, 1977.

Brown, Emily M. "Divorce Counseling," In David H. Olson, ed., *Treating Relationships*, pp. 399–429. Lake Mills, Iowa: Graphic, 1976.

Brown, June H. "Social Services and Third World Communities." *Social Work Papers* (1974) 12:23–36.

Brown, Leonard N. "Social Workers' Verbal Acts and the Development of Mutual Expectations with Beginning Client Groups." D.S.W. diss., Columbia University, 1971.

Brown, Robert A. "Feedback in Family Interviewing." *Social Work* (September, 1973), 18 (5):52–59.

Brown, Robert A. "The Technique of Ascription." D.S.W. diss., University of Southern California, 1971.

Brown, William. "Communication Theory and Social Casework." In Herbert S. Strean, ed., *Social Casework: Theories in Action*, pp. 246–66. Metuchen, N.J.: Scarecrow Press, 1971.

Buckley, Lola Elizabeth. "The Use of the Small Group at a Time of Crisis: Transition of Girls from Elementary to Junior High School." D.S.W. diss., University of Southern California, 1970.

Buckley, Walter. *Sociology and Modern Systems Theory*. Englewood Cliffs, N.J.: Prentice-Hall, 1967.

Buckley, Walter, ed. *Modern Systems Research for the Behavioral Scientist.* Chicago: Aldine, 1968.

Burns, Crawford E. "White Staff, Black Children: Is There a Problem?" *Child Welfare* (February, 1971), 50 (2):90–96.

Burns, Eveline M. "Tomorrow's Social Needs and Social Work Education." *Journal of Education for Social Work* (Winter, 1966), 2 (1):10–20.

Burns, Mary E. and Paul H. Glasser. "Similarities and Differences in Casework and Group Work Practice." *Social Service Review* (December, 1963), 37 (4):416–28.

Bywaters, Paul. "Ending Casework Relationships (1)." *Social Work Today* (August, 1975), 6 (10):301–04.

Bywaters, Paul. "Ending Casework Relationships (2)." *Social Work Today* (September, 1975), 6 (11):336–38.

Cameron, F. H. "The Use of Pre-intake Group Meetings for Prospective ANC Applicants." In Norman Fenton, ed., *Group Methods in the Public Welfare Program,* pp. 51–58. Palo Alto, Calif.: Pacific Books, 1963.

Calnek, Maynard. "Racial Factors in the Countertransference: the Black Therapist and the Black Client." *American Journal of Orthopsychiatry* (January, 1970), 40 (1):39–46.

Caplan, Gerald. *Principles of Preventive Psychiatry.* New York: Basic Books, 1964.

Caplan, Gerald. *Support Systems and Community Mental Health.* New York: Behavioral Publications, 1974.

Case, Lois P. and Neverlyn B. Lingerfelt. "Name-Calling: the Labeling Process in the Social Work Interview." *Social Service Review* (March, 1974) 48 (1):75–86.

Chestang, Leon W. "The Issue of Race in Casework Practice." In *Social Work Practice, 1972,* pp. 114–26. New York: Columbia University Press, 1972.

Chin, Robert. "Evaluating Group Movement and Individual Change." In National Association of Social Workers, *Use of Groups in the Psychiatric Setting,* pp. 34–45. New York: the Association, 1960.

Chin, Robert. "The Utility of Systems Models and Developmental Models for Practitioners." In Warren G. Bennis, Kenneth D. Benne, and Robert Chin, eds., *The Planning of Change,* pp. 201–14. New York: Holt, Rinehart & Winston, 1962.

Churchill, Sallie R. "Social Group Work: a Diagnostic Tool in Child Guidance." *American Journal of Orthopsychiatry* (April, 1965), 35 (3):581–88.

Class, Norris E. "Child Care Licensing as a Preventive Welfare Service." *Children* (September–October, 1968), 15 (5):188–92.

Clemenger, Florence. "Congruence between Members and Workers on Selected Behaviors of the Role of the Social Group Worker." D.S.W. diss., University of Southern California, 1965.

Clement, Robert G. "Factors Associated with Continuance and Discontinuance in Cases Involving Problems in Parent-Child Relationships." Ph.D. diss., University of Chicago, 1964.

Clifton, Eleanor and Florence Hollis, eds. *Child Therapy: a Casework Symposium.* New York: Family Service Association of America, 1948.

Cohen, Jerome. "Nature of Clinical Social Work." In Patricia L. Ewalt, ed., *Toward a Definition of Clinical Social Work,* pp. 23–31. Washington, D.C.: National Association of Social Workers, 1980.

Cohen, Jerome. "Social Work and the Culture of Poverty." *Social Work* (January, 1964), 9 (1):3–11.

Collins, Alice H. and Diane L. Pancoast. *Natural Helping Networks: a Strategy for Prevention.* Washington, D.C.: National Association of Social Workers, 1976.

Community Service Society of New York. *Dynamic Approaches to Serving Families.* New York: the Society, 1970.

Compton, Beulah Roberts and Burt Galaway, eds. *Social Work Processes.* 2d ed. Homewood, Ill.: Dorsey Press, 1979.

Cooper, Shirley A. "A Look at the Effect of Racism on Clinical Work." *Social Casework* (February, 1973), 54(2):76–84.

Couch, Elsbeth Herzstein. *Joint and Family Interviews in the Treatment of Marital Problems.* New York: Family Service Association of America, 1969.

Council on Social Work Education. *Educational Developments in Social Group Work.* New York: the Council, 1962.

Council on Social Work Education. *Public Health Concepts in Social Work Education.* New York: the Council, 1962.

Council on Social Work Education. *Statistics on Social Work Education in the United States.* New York: the Council, 1979.

Council on Social Work Education. *Teaching for Competence in the Delivery of Direct Services.* New York: the Council, 1976.

Coyle, Grace L. "Concepts Relevant to Helping the Family as a Group." *Social Casework* (March, 1962), 43 (3):347–54.

Coyle, Grace L. "Social Group Work: an Aspect of Social Work Practice." *Journal of Social Issues* (1952), 8 (1):21–35.

Coyle, Grace L. *Social Process in Organized Groups.* New York: Smith, 1930.

Coyle, Grace L. "Some Basic Assumptions about Social Group Work." In Marjorie Murphy, ed., *The Social Group Work Method in Social Work Education*, pp. 88–105. New York: Council on Social Work Education, 1959.

Davies, Bernard. *The Use of Groups in Social Work Practice.* London: Routledge & Kegan Paul, 1975.

Davies, Martin. "The Assessment of Environment in Social Work Research." *Social Casework* (January, 1974), 55 (1):3–12.

Davis, Inger P. "Advice-giving in Parent Counseling." *Social Casework* (June, 1975), 56 (6):343–47.

Davis, L. Jeannette. "Human Communication Concepts and Constructs: Tools for Change as Applied to Social Work Practice Theory." D.S.W. diss., University of Southern California, 1976.

Dewey, John. *Democracy and Education.* New York: Free Press (paperback ed.), 1966.

Dewey, John. *How We Think.* Boston: Heath, 1910.

Dixon, William G., ed. *Social Welfare and the Preservation of Human Values.* Montreal: Dent, 1957.

Douglas, Tom. *Groupwork Practice.* New York: International Universities Press, 1976.

Duehn, Wayne O. and Enola K. Proctor. "Initial Clinical Interaction and Premature Discontinuance in Treatment." *American Journal of Orthopsychiatry* (March, 1977), 40 (2):284–90.

Duvall, Evelyn M. *Family Development.* Rev. ed. Philadelphia: Lippincott, 1971.

Epstein, Norman. "Brief Group Therapy in a Child Guidance Clinic." *Social Work* (July, 1970), 15 (3):33–48.

Erikson, Erik H. *Childhood and Society.* 2d ed. New York: Norton, 1963.

Erikson, Erik H. "Identity and the Life Cycle." In *Psychological Issues,* pp. 18–164. New York: International Universities Press, 1959.

Erikson, Erik H. *Identity, Youth, and Crisis.* New York: Norton, 1968.

Ernst, Theodore D. "Ego Assessment in Social Casework." D.S.W. diss., Columbia University, 1968.

Ewalt, Patricia L. "A Psychoanalytically Oriented Child Guidance Center." In William J. Reid and Laura Epstein, eds., *Task-centered Practice,* pp. 27–49. New York: Columbia University Press, 1977.

Ewalt, Patricia L., ed. *Toward a Definition of Clinical Social Work; Conference Proceedings.* Washington, D.C.: National Association of Social Workers, 1980.

Ewalt, Patricia L. and Janice Kutz. "An Examination of Advice-giving as a Therapeutic Intervention." *Smith College Studies in Social Work* (November, 1976), 47 (1):3–9.

Fanshel, David. "A Study of Caseworkers' Perceptions of Their Clients." *Social Casework* (December, 1958), 39 (10):543–51.

Farber, Deborah Ann. "A Study of Clients' Reactions to Initial Contacts with a Community Mental Health Center: Another Look." *Smith College Studies in Social Work* (November, 1975), 46 (1):44–45.

Fatout, Marian F. "A Comparative Analysis of Practice Concepts Described in Selected Social Work Literature." D.S.W. diss., University of Southern California, 1975.

Feldman, Frances Lomas. *The Family in Today's Money World.* New York: Family Service Association of America, 1977.

Feldman, Frances Lomas and Frances H. Scherz. *Family Social Welfare: Helping Troubled Families.* New York: Atherton Press, 1967.

Feldman, Ronald A. *et al.* "Treating Delinquents in Traditional Agencies." *Social Work* (September, 1972), 17 (5):71–78.

Fenton, Norman, ed. *Group Methods in the Public Welfare Program.* Palo Alto, Calif.: Pacific Books, 1963.

Fischer, Joel. *Effective Casework Practice; an Eclectic Approach.* New York: McGraw-Hill, 1978.

Flanzer, Jerry. "Conintegration: the Concurrent Integration of Treatment Modalities in Social Work Practice." D.S.W. diss., University of Southern California, 1973.

Fong, Stanley L. M. "Assimilation and Changing Social Roles of Chinese Americans," *Journal of Social Issues* (1973) 29 (2):115–27.

Forgays, Donald G., ed. *Primary Prevention of Psychopathology.* vol. 2: *Environmental Influences.* Hanover, N.H.: University Press of New England, 1978.

Fox, Evelyn, Marion Nelson, and William Bolman. "The Termination Process: a Neglected Dimension in Social Work." *Social Work* (October, 1969), 14 (4):53–63.

Freed, Anne O. "Social Casework: More than a Modality," *Social Casework* (April, 1977), 58 (4):214–22.

Freeman, David S. "Phases of Family Treatment." *The Family Coordinator* (July, 1976), 25 (3):265–70.

Freeman, David S. "Social Work with Families: a Systems Approach to a Unified Theoretical Model." D.S.W. diss., University of Southern California, 1973.

Freud, Anna. *The Ego and the Mechanisms of Defense.* New York: International Universities Press, 1946.

Freud, Sigmund. *An Outline of Psychoanalysis*. Rev. ed. New York: Norton, 1949.

Frey, Louise A. "Support and the Group: Generic Treatment Form." *Social Work* (October, 1962), 7 (3):35–42.

Friedlander, Walter A., ed. *Concepts and Methods of Social Work*. Englewood Cliffs. N.J.: Prentice-Hall, 1958.

Ganter, Grace, Margaret Yeakel, and Norman A. Polansky. *Retrieval from Limbo—the Intermediary Group Treatment of Inaccessible Children*. New York: Child Welfare League of America, 1967.

Gareffa, Domenic N. and Stanley A. Neff. "Management of the Client's Seductive Behavior." *Smith College Studies in Social Work* (February, 1974) 44 (2):110–24.

Garfield, Sol and Allen E. Bergin, eds. *Handbook of Psychotherapy and Behavior Change*. New York: John Wiley, 1978.

Garland, James A., Hubert E. Jones, and Ralph Kolodny. "A Model for Stages of Development in Social Work Groups." In Saul Bernstein, ed., *Explorations in Group Work*, pp. 17–71. Boston: Milford House, 1973.

Garland, James A. and Ralph Kolodny. "Characteristics and Resolution of Scapegoating." In Saul Bernstein, ed., *Further Explorations in Group Work*, pp. 55–74. Boston: Milford House, 1973.

Gartner, Alan S. and Frank Riessman. *Self-Help in the Human Services*. San Francisco: Jossey-Bass, 1977.

Garvin, Charles D. "Complementarity of Role Expectations in Groups: the Member-Worker Contract." In *Social Work Practice, 1969*, pp. 127–45. New York: Columbia University Press, 1969.

Garvin, Charles D. "Group Process: Usage and Uses in Social Work Practice." In Paul H. Glasser, Rosemary Sarri, and Robert Vinter, eds., *Individual Change through Small Groups*, pp. 209–32. New York: Free Press, 1974.

Garvin, Charles D. and Paul H. Glasser. "The Bases of Social Treatment." In *Social Work Practice, 1970*, pp. 149–77. New York: Columbia University Press, 1969.

Gentry, Martha. "Initial Group Meetings: Member Expectations and Information Distribution Process." Ph.D. diss., Washington University, 1974.

Germain, Carel B. "General Systems Theory and Ego Psychology; an Ecological Perspective." *Social Service Review* (December, 1978), 52 (4):535–50.

Germain, Carel B. "Social Context of Clinical Social Work." In Patricia

L. Ewalt, ed., *Toward a Definition of Clinical Social Work,* pp. 54–65. Washington, D.C.: American Association of Social Workers, 1980.

Germain, Carel B. "Social Study: Past and Future." *Social Casework* (July, 1968), 49 (7):403–09.

Germain, Carel B. "Teaching an Ecological Perspective for Social Work Practice." In Council on Social Work Education, *Teaching for Competence in the Delivery of Direct Services,* pp. 31–39. New York: the Council, 1976.

Germain, Carel B., ed. *Social Work Practice: People and Environments; an Ecological Perspective.* New York: Columbia University Press, 1979.

Germain, Carel B. and Alex Gitterman. *The Life Model of Social Work Practice.* New York: Columbia University Press, 1980.

Gilbert, Neil and Harry Specht. "The Incomplete Profession." *Social Work* (November, 1974), 19 (6):665–74.

Gladwin, Thomas. *Poverty USA.* Boston: Little, Brown, 1967.

Glasser, Paul H. and Charles D. Garvin. "An Organizational Model." In Robert W. Roberts and Helen Northen, eds., *Theories of Social Work with Groups,* pp. 75–115. New York: Columbia University Press, 1976.

Glasser, Paul H., Rosemary Sarri, and Robert Vinter, eds. *Individual Change through Small Groups.* New York: Free Press, 1974.

Golan, Naomi. *Treatment in Crisis Situations.* New York: Free Press, 1978.

Goldberg, E. "The Normal Family: Myth and Reality." In Eileen Younghusband, ed., *Social Work with Families,* pp. 11–27. London: Allen & Unwin, 1965.

Goldstein, Howard. *Social Work Practice: a Unitary Approach.* Columbia, S.C.: University of South Carolina Press, 1973.

Green, Joseph M., Frank Trenhim, and Nelba Chavez. "Therapeutic Intervention with Mexican-American Children." *Psychiatric Annals* (May, 1976), 6 (5):68–75.

Green, Rose. "Terminating the Relationship in Social Casework." Unpublished paper, School of Social Work, University of Southern California.

Greer, Colin, ed. *Divided Society: the Ethnic Experience in America.* New York: Basic Books, 1974.

Grinnell, Richard M. "Environmental Modification; Factors Associated with Its Use in Casework Practice." Ph.D. diss., University of Wisconsin, 1974.

Grinnell, Richard M. and Nancy S. Kyte. "Environmental Modification: a Study." *Social Work* (May, 1974), 20 (3):313–18.

Group for the Advancement of Psychiatry. Report # 78. *The Field of Family Therapy* (March, 1970), 7:531–644.

Gullerud, Ernest N. and Virginia Lee Harlan. "Four-Way Joint Interviewing in Marital Counseling." *Social Casework* (December, 1962), 43 (10):532–37.

Gurin, Gerald, Joseph Veroff, and Sheila Field. *Americans View Their Mental Health.* New York: Basic Books, 1960.

Gurman, Alan S. "The Effects and Effectiveness of Marital Therapy: a Review of Outcome Research." *Family Process* (June, 1973), 12 (2):145–70.

Hall, Edward T. *The Hidden Dimension.* Garden City, N.Y.: Doubleday, 1966.

Hallowitz, David. "Advocacy in the Context of Treatment." *Social Casework* (July, 1974), 55 (7):416–20.

Hallowitz, David et al. "The Assertive Counseling Component of Therapy." *Social Casework* (November, 1967), 48 (9):543–48.

Hamilton, Gordon. *Psychotherapy in Child Guidance.* New York: Columbia University Press, 1947.

Hamilton, Gordon. *Theory and Practice of Social Case Work.* 2d ed. New York: Columbia University Press, 1951.

Hammond, D. Corydon. "Cross-cultural Rehabilitation." *Journal of Rehabilitation* (September–October, 1971), 37 (5):34–36.

Hartford, Margaret E. "Group Methods and Generic Practice." In Robert W. Roberts and Helen Northen, eds., *Theories of Social Work with Groups,* pp. 45–74. New York: Columbia University Press, 1976.

Hartford, Margaret E. *Groups in Social Work.* New York: Columbia University Press, 1971.

Hartford, Margaret E., ed. *Working Papers toward a Frame of Reference for Social Group Work.* New York: National Association of Social Workers, 1964.

Hartman, Ann. "The Generic Stance and the Family Agency." *Social Casework* (April, 1974) 55 (4):199–208.

Hartman, Ann. "To Think about the Unthinkable." *Social Casework* (October, 1970), 51 (8):467–74.

Hartmann, Heinz. *Ego Psychology and the Problem of Adaptation.* New York: International Universities Press, 1958.

Haselkorn, Florence, ed. *Family Planning.* New York: Council on Social Work Education, 1971.

Hathway, Marion E. "Twenty-five Years of Professional Education for Social Work—and a Look Ahead." *The Compass* (June, 1946), 27 (5):13–18.

Hearn, Gordon. *Theory Building in Social Work.* Toronto: University of Toronto Press, 1958.

Hearn, Gordon, ed. *The General Systems Approach: Contributions toward an Holistic Conception of Social Work.* New York: Council on Social Work Education, 1968.

Heine, R. W. "A Comparison of Patients' Reports on Psychotherapeutic Experience with Psychoanalytic, Nondirective, and Adlerian Therapists." Ph.D. diss., University of Chicago, 1950.

Herzog, Elizabeth et al. *Families for Black Children: the Search for Adoptive Parents.* (Washington, D.C.: Children's Bureau, Department of Health, Education, and Welfare, 1971.

Hinchman, Madison. "Social Work Practice with Children and Youth: a Content Analysis of Social Work Practice Literature 1947–1973." D.S.W. diss., University of Southern California, 1977.

Ho, Man Keung and Eunice McDowell. "The Black Worker-White Client Relationship." *Clinical Social Work Journal* (Fall, 1973), 1 (3):161–67.

Hobbs, Nicholas. *The Futures of Children: Categories, Labels, and Their Consequences.* San Francisco: Jossey-Bass, 1975.

Hobbs, Nicholas. "Sources of Gain in Psychotherapy." *American Psychologist* (October, 1962), 17 (10):741–47.

Hollis, Florence. *Casework: a Psychosocial Therapy.* 2d ed. New York: Random House, 1972.

Hollis, Florence. "The Psychosocial Approach in the Practice of Casework." In Robert W. Roberts and Robert H. Nee, eds., *Theories of Social Casework,* pp. 33–76. Chicago: University of Chicago Press, 1970.

Hunnybun, Noel K. "David and His Mother." In Eileen Younghusband, ed., *Social Work with Families,* pp. 80–86. London: Allen & Unwin, 1965.

Hutten, Joan M. "Short-Term Contracts IV. Techniques: How and Why to Use Them." *Social Work Today* (August, 1976), 6 (20):614–18.

Hutten, Joan M. *Short-Term Contracts in Social Work.* London: Routledge & Kegan Paul, 1977.

Janchill, Sister Mary Paul. "Systems Concepts in Casework Theory and Practice." *Social Casework* (February, 1969), 50 (2):74–82.

Jenkins, Shirley and Elaine Norman. *Filial Deprivation and Foster Care.* New York: Columbia University Press, 1972.

Johnson, Arlien. "Development of Basic Methods of Social Work Practice and Education." *Social Work Journal* (July, 1955), 36 (3):109–13.

Joint Commission on Mental Health of Children. *Crisis in Child Mental Health: Challenge for the 1970s.* New York: Harper & Row, 1970.

Jolesch, Miriam. "Strengthening Intake Practice through Group Discussion." *Social Casework* (November, 1959), 40 (9):504–10.

Kadushin, Alfred. The Racial Factor in the Interview." *Social Work* (May, 1972), 17 (3):88–98.

Kadushin, Alfred. *The Social Work Interview.* New York: Columbia University Press, 1972.

Kahn, Alfred J. "Therapy, Prevention and Developmental Provision: a Social Work Strategy." In Council on Social Work Education, *Public Health Concepts in Social Work Education,* pp. 132–48. New York: the Council, 1962.

Kahn, Alfred J., ed. *Issues in American Social Work.* New York: Columbia University Press, 1959.

Kahn, Alfred J., ed. *Shaping the New Social Work.* New York: Columbia University Press, 1973.

Kaiser, Clara A. "Current Frontiers in Social Group Work." in *Proceedings, National Conference of Social Work, 1947,* pp. 418–28. New York: Columbia University Press, 1947.

Kamerman, Sheila B. et al. "Knowledge for Practice: Social Science in Social Work." In Alfred J. Kahn, ed., *Shaping the New Social Work,* pp. 97–146. New York: Columbia University Press, 1973.

Kaplan, Jerome. "The Social Worker in the Long-Term Facility." *Hospital Progress* (May, 1970), 51 (5):116–32.

Kasius, Cora, ed. *A Comparison of Diagnostic and Functional Casework.* New York: Family Service Association of America, 1950.

Katz, Alfred H. and Eugene Bender. *The Strength in Us: Self-Help Groups in the Modern World.* New York: New Viewpoints, 1976.

Keefe, Thomas. "Empathy: the Critical Skill." *Social Work* (January, 1976), 21 (1):10–15.

Kerns, Elizabeth. "Planned Short-term Treatment: a New Service to Adolescents." *Social Casework* (June, 1970), 51 (6):340–46.

King, B. L. "Diagnostic Activity Group for Latency Age Children." In Community Service Society of New York, *Dynamic Approaches to Serving Families,* pp. 55–67. New York: the Society, 1970.

Kitano, Harry and Stanley Sue. "The Model Minorities." *Journal of Social Issues* (1973), 29 (2):1–9.

Klein, Alan F. *Effective Group Work.* New York: Association Press, 1972.

Kluckhohn, Florence. "Family Diagnosis: Variations in the Basic Values of Family Systems." *Social Casework* (February, 1958), 39 (2):66–69.

Kogan, Leonard S., J. McVicker Hunt, and Phyllis F. Bartelme. *A Follow-up Study of the Results of Social Casework*. New York: Family Service Association of America, 1953.

Kolodny, Ralph. *Peer-oriented Group Work for the Physically Handicapped Child*. Boston: Charles Rivers Books, 1974.

Konopka, Gisela. *Social Group Work: a Helping Process*. Englewood Cliffs, N.J.: Prentice-Hall, 1963.

Konopka, Gisela. *Young Girls*. Minneapolis: University of Minnesota Press, 1976.

Kurland, Roselle. "Planning: the Neglected Component of Group Development." *Social Work with Groups* (Summer, 1978), 1 (2):173–78.

Lake, Martha and George Levinger. "Continuance Beyond Application Interviews at a Child Guidance Clinic." *Social Casework* (June, 1960), 41 (6):303–09.

Lane, Dorthea. "Psychiatric Patients Learn a New Way of Life." In National Association of Social Workers, *New Perspectives on Services to Groups,* pp. 114–23. New York: the Association, 1961.

Lathrope, Donald E. "The General Systems Approach in Social Work Practice." In Gordon Hearn, ed., *The General Systems Approach,* pp. 45–61. New York: Council on Social Work Education, 1968.

Leichter, Elsa and Gerda Schulman. "The Family Interview as an Integrative Device in Group Therapy with Families." *International Journal of Group Psychotherapy* (July, 1963), 13(3):335–45.

Levine, Baruch. *Group Psychotherapy. Practice and Development*. Englewood Cliffs, N.J.: Prentice-Hall, 1979.

Levine, Rachel. "A Short Story on the Long Waiting List." *Social Work* (January, 1963), 8(1):20–22.

Levinson, Helen M. "Use and Misuse of Groups." *Social Work* (January, 1973), 18 (1):66–73.

Levinson, Hilliard L. "Termination of Psychotherapy: Some Salient Issues." *Social Casework* (October, 1977), 48 (8):480–89.

Levy, Charles S. *Social Work Ethics*. New York: Human Sciences Press, 1976.

Lewis, Harold. "Reasoning in Practice." *Smith College Studies in Social Work* (November, 1975), 46 (1):1–12.

Lieberman, Florence. "Clients' Expectations, Preferences and Experiences of Initial Interviews in Voluntary Social Agencies." D.S.W. diss., Columbia University, 1968.

Lieberman, Florence. *Social Work with Children*. New York: Human Sciences Press, 1979.

Lieberman, Morton A. "The Implications of Total Group Phenomena Analysis for Patients and Therapists." *International Journal of Group Psychotherapy* (January, 1967), 17 (1):71–81.

Lieberman, Morton A., Irvin D. Yalom, and Matthew B. Miles. *Encounter Groups: First Facts.* New York: Basic Books, 1973.

Lindzey, Gardner and Elliott Aronson, eds. *Handbook of Social Psychology.* Reading, Mass.: Addison-Wesley, 1968.

Lippitt, Ronald, Jeanne Watson, and Bruce Westley. *The Dynamics of Planned Change.* New York: Harcourt Brace, 1958.

Locklear, Herbert H. "American Indian Myths." *Social Work* (May, 1972), 17 (3):72–80.

Loevinger, Jane. *Ego Development.* San Francisco: Jossey-Bass, 1976.

Long, Nicholas. "Information and Referral Services." *Social Service Review* (March, 1973), 47 (1):49–62.

Luthman, Shirley with Martin Kirschenbaum. *The Dynamic Family.* Palo Alto, Calif.: Science and Behavior Books, 1974.

Maas, Henry S. "Children's Environments and Child Welfare." *Child Welfare* (March, 1971), 50 (3):132–42.

Mabley, Albertina. "Group Application Interviews in a Family Agency." *Social Casework* (March, 1966), 47 (3):158–64.

McBroom, Elizabeth. "Individual, Group, and Community in the Behavior Sequence." *Journal of Education for Social Work* (Spring, 1965), 1 (2):27–34.

McBroom, Elizabeth. "Socialization through Small Groups." In Robert W. Roberts and Helen Northen, eds., *Theories of Social Work with Groups,* pp. 268–303. New York: Columbia University Press, 1976.

McGriff, Dorothy. "A Coordinated Approach to Discharge Planning." *Social Work* (January, 1965), 10 (1):45–50.

MacLennan, Beryce W. and Naomi Felsenfeld. *Group Counseling and Psychotherapy with Adolescents.* New York: Columbia University Press, 1968.

Macon, Lilian. "A Comparative Study of Two Approaches to the Treatment of Marital Dysfunction." D.S.W. diss., University of Southern California, 1975.

Maier, Henry W., ed. *Group Work as Part of Residential Treatment.* New York: National Association of Social Workers, 1965.

Main, Marjorie White. "Selected Aspects of the Beginning Phase of Social Group Work." Ph.D. diss., University of Chicago, 1964.

Maluccio, Anthony N. *Learning from Clients: Interpersonal Helping as Viewed by Clients and Their Workers.* New York: Free Press, 1979.

Maluccio, Anthony N. and Wilma D. Marlow. "The Case for the Contract." *Social Work* (January, 1974), 19 (1):28–36.

Martinez, Cervando. "Community Mental Health and the Chicano Movement." *American Journal of Orthopsychiatry* (July, 1973), 43 (4):595–610.

Mayer, John E. and Noel Timms. "Clash in Perspective between Worker and Client." *Social Casework* (January, 1969), 50 (1):32–40.

Mendes, Helen. *Some Religious Values Held by Blacks, Chicanos, and Japanese Americans; Their Implications for Casework Practice.* Monograph #4. Boulder, Colo.: Western Interstate Commission for Higher Education, 1974.

Merton, Robert K. *Social Theory and Social Structure.* Glencoe, Ill.: Free Press, 1949.

Meyer, Carol H. "The Relationship of Licensing to Child Welfare Concepts and Principles." *Social Service Review* (September, 1968), 42 (3):344–54.

Meyer, Carol H. *Social Work Practice: the Changing Landscape.* New York: Free Press, 1976.

Meyer, Carol H. *Social Work Practice: the Urban Crisis.* New York: Free Press, 1970.

Meyer, Carol H. ed. *Preventive Intervention in Social Work.* New York: National Association of Social Workers, 1974.

Middleman, Ruth R. and Gale Goldberg. *Social Service Delivery; a Structural Approach to Social Work Practice.* New York: Columbia University Press, 1974.

Milner, John G. "Ethnic and Cultural Considerations in Child Placement." Unpublished paper, School of Social Work, University of Southern California, 1976.

Minuchin, Salvador et al. *Families of the Slums.* New York: Basic Books, 1967.

Moos, Rudolph, ed. *Human Adaptation.* London: Heath, 1976.

Moss, Sidney Z. and Miriam S. Moss. "When a Caseworker Leaves an Agency: the Impact on Worker and Client." *Social Casework* (July, 1967), 48 (7):433–37.

Mullen, Edward J. "Casework Treatment Procedures as a Function of Client-diagnostic Variables." D.S.W. diss., Columbia University, 1968.

Murphy, Marjorie, ed. *The Social Group Work Method in Social Work Education: a Project Report of the Curriculum Study.* Vol. 11. New York: Council on Social Work Education, 1959.

Nadel, Robert M. "Interviewing Style and Foster Parents' Verbal Accessibility." *Child Welfare* (April, 1967), 46 (4):207–11.

Nakama, George. "Japanese Americans' Expectations of Counseling: an Exploratory Survey." D.S.W. diss., University of Southern California, 1980.

National Association of Social Workers. "Ad Hoc Committee on Advocacy Report." *Social Work* (April, 1969), 14 (2):16–22.

National Association of Social Workers. *Building Social Work Knowledge.* New York: the Association, 1964.

National Association of Social Workers. *Code of Ethics,* 1980.

National Association of Social Workers. *New Perspectives on Services to Groups.* New York: the Association, 1961.

National Association of Social Workers. *Social Work with Groups, 1959.* New York: the Association, 1959.

National Association of Social Workers. *The Family is the Patient: the Group Approach to the Treatment of Family Health Problems.* Monograph VII. New York: the Association, 1965.

National Association of Social Workers. *The Psychiatric Social Worker as Leader of a Group.* New York: the Association, 1959.

National Association of Social Workers. *Use of Groups in the Psychiatric Setting.* New York: the Association, 1960.

Neighborhood Youth Association. *Changing the Behavior of Hostile Delinquency-prone Adolescents, I* (1960) and *Follow-up Study* (1962).

Nelsen, Judith. *Communication Theory and Social Work Practice.* Chicago: University of Chicago Press, 1980.

Northen, Helen. "Psychosocial Practice in Small Groups." In Robert W. Roberts and Helen Northen, eds., *Theories of Social Work with Groups,* pp. 116–52. New York: Columbia University Press, 1976.

Northen, Helen. *Social Work with Groups.* New York: Columbia University Press, 1969.

Olson, David H., ed. *Treating Relationships.* Lake Mills, Iowa: Graphic, 1976.

Oppenheimer, Audrey. "Triumph over Trauma in the Treatment of Child Abuse." *Social Casework* (June, 1978), 59 (6):352–58.

Orcutt, Ben A., ed. *Poverty and Social Casework Services; Selected Papers.* New York: Scarecrow Press, 1974.

Ormont, Louis R. and Herbert S. Strean. *The Practice of Conjoint Therapy.* New York: Human Sciences Press, 1978.

Overton, Alice. "The Issue of Integration of Casework and Group Work." *Social Work Education Reporter* (June, 1968), 16 (2):25–27.

Overton, Alice and Katherine Tinker. *Casework Notebook.* St. Paul, Minn.: Greater St. Paul Community Chests and Councils, 1957.

Oxley, Genevieve G. "The Caseworker's Expectations and Client Motivation." *Social Casework* (July, 1966), 47 (7):432–37.

Parad, Howard J. "Preventive Casework: Problems and Implications." In *The Social Welfare Forum, 1961,* pp. 178–93. New York: Columbia University Press, 1961.

Parad, Howard J., ed. *Crisis Intervention: Selected Readings.* New York: Family Service Association of America, 1965.

Parad, Howard J. and Roger R. Miller, eds. *Ego-oriented Casework: Problems and Perspectives.* New York: Family Service Association of America, 1963.

Parad, Howard J., Lola G. Selby, and James Quinlan. "Crisis Intervention with Families and Groups," in Robert W. Roberts and Helen Northen, eds., *Theories of Social Work with Groups,* pp. 304–30. New York: Columbia University Press, 1976.

Parloff, Morris B., Irene E. Waskow, and Barry E. Wolfe. "Research on Therapist Variables in Relation to Process and Outcome." In Sol Garfield and Allen Bergin, eds., *Handbook of Psychotherapy and Behavior Change,* pp. 233–82. New York: Wiley, 1978.

Peck, Harris B. "An Application of Group Therapy to the Intake Process." *American Journal of Orthopsychiatry* (April, 1953), 23 (2):338–49.

Peretz, David. "Reactions to Loss." In Bernard Schoenberg et al., eds., *Loss and Grief,* pp. 20–35. New York: Columbia University Press, 1970.

Perley, Janice, Carolyn Winget, and Carlos Placci. "Hope and Discomfort as Factors Influencing Treatment Continuance." *Comprehensive Psychiatry* (November, 1971), 12 (6):557–63.

Perlman, Helen Harris. "Identity Problems, Role, and Casework Treatment." *Social Service Review* (September, 1963), 37 (3):307–18.

Perlman, Helen Harris. "Intake and Some Role Considerations." In Helen Harris Perlman, *Persona,* pp. 162–76. Chicago: University of Chicago Press, 1968.

Perlman, Helen Harris. *Persona. Social Role and Personality.* Chicago: University of Chicago Press, 1968.

Perlman, Helen Harris. "The Problem-solving Model in Social Casework." In Robert W. Roberts and Robert H. Nee, eds., *Theories of Social Casework,* pp. 162–76. Chicago: University of Chicago Press, 1970.

Perlman, Helen Harris. *Relationship, the Heart of Helping People.* Chicago: University of Chicago Press, 1979.

Perlman, Helen Harris. *Social Casework: a Problem-solving Process*. Chicago: University of Chicago Press, 1957.

Perlman, Helen Harris. "Social Work Method: a Review of the Past Decade." *Social Work* (October, 1965), 10 (4):166–78.

Pernell, Ruby B. "Identifying and Teaching the Skill Components of Social Group Work." In Council on Social Work Education, *Educational Developments in Social Group Work*, pp. 18–36. New York: the Council, 1962.

Peters, Edward N., Muriel W. Pumphrey, and Norman Flax. "Comparison of Retarded and Nonretarded Children on the Dimensions of Behavior in Recreation Groups." *American Journal of Mental Deficiency* (July, 1974), 79 (1):87–89.

Pinamonti, Guido. "Caseworkers' Use of Groups in Direct Practice." D.S.W. diss., University of Southern California, 1961.

Pincus, Allen and Anne Minahan. *Social Work Practice: Model and Method*. Itasca, Ill.: Peacock, 1973.

Pinkus, Helen et al. "Education for the Practice of Clinical Social Work at the Master's Level: a Position Paper." *Clinical Social Work Journal* (Winter, 1977), 5 (4):251–68.

Polansky, Norman A. *Ego Psychology and Communication: Theory for the Interview*. New York: Atherton Press, 1971.

Pollak, Otto. "Disturbed Families and Conjoint Family Counseling." *Child Welfare* (March, 1967), 46 (3):143–49.

Pollak, Otto. "Social Determinants of Family Behavior." *Social Work* (July, 1963), 8 (3):95–101.

Pray, Kenneth L. M. *Social Work in a Revolutionary Age*. Philadelphia: University of Pennsylvania Press, 1949.

Preininger, David. "Reactions of Normal Children to Retardates in Integrated Groups." *Social Work* (April, 1968), 13 (2):75–78.

Pumphrey, Muriel W. *The Teaching of Values and Ethics in Social Work Education*. Vol. 13. A Project Report of the Curriculum Study. New York: Council on Social Work Education, 1959.

Purcell, Francis P. and Harry Specht. "The House on Sixth Street." *Social Work* (October, 1965), 10 (4):69–76.

Rae-Grant, Quentin A. F., Thomas Gladwin, and Eli M. Bower. "Mental Health, Social Competence, and the War on Poverty." *American Journal of Orthopsychiatry* (July, 1966), 36 (4):652–64.

Rapoport, Lydia. "Crisis Intervention as a Mode of Brief Treatment." In Robert W. Roberts and Robert H. Nee, *Theories of Social Casework*, pp. 267–311. Chicago: University of Chicago Press, 1970.

Rapoport, Lydia and Leah Potts. "Abortion of Unwanted Pregnancy as a Potential Life Crisis." In Florence Haselkorn, ed., *Family Planning*, pp. 249–66. New York: Council on Social Work Education, 1971.

Raschella, Gerald. "An Evaluation of the Effect of Goal Congruence between Client and Therapist on Premature Client Dropout from Therapy." Ph.D. diss., University of Pittsburgh, 1975.

Redl, Fritz. "The Art of Group Composition." In Suzanne Schulze, ed., *Creative Group Living in a Children's Institution*, pp. 76–96. New York: Association Press, 1951.

Redl, Fritz, "The Concept of a Therapeutic Milieu." *American Journal of Orthopsychiatry* (July, 1959), 29 (4): 721–36.

Redl, Fritz and David Wineman. *Controls from Within*. Glencoe, Ill.: Free Press, 1952.

Regensburg, Jeanette. *Toward Education for Health Professions*. New York: Harper & Row, 1978.

Reid, William J. "Process and Outcome in Treatment of Family Problems." In William J. Reid and Laura Epstein, eds., *Task-centered Practice*, pp. 58–77. New York: Columbia University Press, 1977.

Reid, William J. and Laura Epstein. *Task-centered Casework*. New York: Columbia University Press, 1972.

Reid, William J. and Laura Epstein, eds. *Task-centered Practice*. New York: Columbia University Press, 1977.

Reid, William J. and Barbara L. Shapiro. "Client Reactions to Advice." *Social Service Review* (June, 1969), 43 (2):165–73.

Reid, William J. and Ann W. Shyne. *Brief and Extended Casework*. New York: Columbia University Press, 1969.

Rein, Martin. "Social Work in Search of a Radical Profession." *Social Work* (April, 1970), 15 (2):15–19.

Reynolds, Bertha C. "Can Social Case Work be Interpreted to a Community as a Basic Approach to Human Problems?" *The Family* (February, 1933), 13 (10):336–42.

Reynolds, Bertha C. *Learning and Teaching in the Practice of Social Work*. New York: Farrar & Rinehart, 1942.

Reynolds, Bertha C. *Social Work and Social Living*. New York: Citadel Press, 1951.

Reynolds, Mildred M. "Threats to Confidentiality." *Social Work* (April, 1976), 21 (2):108–13.

Rice, David G., William F. Fey, and Joseph G. Kepecs. "Therapist Experience and Style as Factors in Co-therapy." *Family Process* (March, 1972), 11 (1):1–12.

Rich, John. *Interviewing Children and Adolescents*. New York: St. Martin's Press, 1968.

Richmond, Mary E. *Social Diagnosis*. New York: Russell Sage Foundation, 1917.

Richmond, Mary E. "The Social Case Worker's Task." In *Proceedings, National Conference of Social Work, 1917*, pp. 112–15. Chicago: National Conference of Social Work, 1917.

Richmond, Mary E. *What Is Social Case Work?* New York: Russell Sage Foundation, 1922.

Ripple, Lilian. "Factors Associated with Continuance in Casework Service." *Social Work* (January, 1957), 2 (1):87–94.

Ripple, Lilian, Ernestina Alexander, and Bernice W. Polemis. *Motivation, Capacity, and Opportunity: Studies in Casework Theory and Practice*. Chicago: School of Social Service Administration, University of Chicago, 1964.

Riskin, Jules and Elaine E. Faunce. "An Evaluative Review of Family Interaction Research." *Family Process* (December, 1972), 11 (4):365–455.

Roberts, Robert W. and Robert H. Nee, eds. *Theories of Social Casework*. Chicago: University of Chicago Press, 1970.

Roberts, Robert W. and Helen Northen, eds. *Theories of Social Work with Groups*. New York: Columbia University Press, 1976.

Rogers, Carl R. "The Necessary and Sufficient Conditions for Therapeutic Personality Change." *Journal of Consulting Psychology* (1957) 21 (1):95–103.

Rokeach, Milton. *The Nature of Human Values*. New York: Free Press, 1973.

Rooney, Herbert L. and Alan D. Millèr. "A Mental Health Clinic Intake Policy Project." *Mental Hygiene* (July, 1955), 39 (3):391–405.

Rosen, Aaron and Dina Lieberman. "The Experimental Evaluation of Interview Performance of Social Workers." *Social Service Review* (September, 1972), 46 (3):395–412.

Rothman, Jack, ed. *Issues in Race and Ethnic Relations*. Itasca, Ill.: Peacock, 1977.

Rubin, Gerald K. "General Systems Theory: an Organismic Conception for Teaching Modalities of Social Work Intervention." *Smith College Studies in Social Work* (June, 1973), 43 (3):206–19.

Rutter, Michael. *Helping Troubled Children*. New York: Plenum Press, 1975.

Ryder, Claire F. "The Five Faces of Prevention." In Council on Social Work Education, *Public Health Concepts in Social Work Education*, pp. 107–15. New York: the Council, 1962.

Sainsbury, Eric. *Social Work with Families.* London: Routledge & Kegan Paul, 1975.

Sarbin, Theodore and Vernon Allen. "Role Theory." In Gardner Lindzey and Elliott Aronson, eds., *Handbook of Social Psychology,* pp. 488–567. Reading, Mass.: Addison-Wesley, 1968.

Satir, Virginia M. *Conjoint Family Therapy; a Guide to Theory and Technique.* Palo Alto, Calif.: Science and Behavior Books, 1964.

Scheidlinger, Saul. "The Concept of Empathy in Group Psychotherapy." *International Journal of Group Psychotherapy* (October, 1966), 16 (4):413–24.

Scheidlinger, Saul. *Psychoanalysis and Group Behavior.* New York: Norton, 1952.

Scheidlinger, Saul and Marjorie A. Holden. "Group Therapy of Women with Severe Character Disorders: the Middle and Final Phases." *International Journal of Group Psychotherapy* (April, 1966), 16 (2):174–89.

Scherz, Frances H. "Family Therapy." In Robert W. Roberts and Robert H. Nee, eds., *Theories of Social Casework,* pp. 219–64. Chicago: University of Chicago Press, 1970.

Scherz, Frances H. "Maturational Crises and Parent-Child Interaction." *Social Casework* (June, 1971), 52 (6):362–69.

Schiff, Sheldon K. "Termination of Therapy: Problems in a Community Psychiatric Outpatient Clinic." *Archives of General Psychiatry* (January, 1962), 6 (1):77–82.

Schmidt, Julianna. "The Use of Purpose in Casework Practice." *Social Work* (January, 1969), 4 (1): 77–84.

Schneiderman, Leonard. "A Social Action Model for the Social Work Practitioner." *Social Casework* (October, 1965), 46 (8):490–93.

Schoenberg, Bernard et al. eds. *Loss and Grief.* New York: Columbia University Press, 1970.

Schulze, Susanne, ed. *Creative Group Living in a Children's Institution.* New York: Association Press, 1951.

Schwartz, Edward. "Macro Social Work: a Practice in Search of Some Theory." *Social Service Review* (June, 1977), 51 (2):207–27.

Schwartz, William. "Between Client and System: the Mediating Function." In Robert W. Roberts and Helen Northen, eds., *Theories of Social Work with Groups,* pp. 171–97. New York: Columbia University Press, 1976.

Schwartz, William. "Group Work and the Social Scene." In Alfred J. Kahn, ed., *Issues in American Social Work,* pp. 110–37. New York: Columbia University Press, 1959.

Schwartz, William. "Private Troubles and Public Issues: One Social Work Job or Two?" In *The Social Welfare Forum, 1969*, pp. 22–43. New York: Columbia University Press, 1969.

Schwartz, William. "The Social Worker in the Group." In *The Social Welfare Forum, 1961*, pp. 146–71. New York: Columbia University Press, 1961.

Seabury, Brett A. "Arrangement of Physical Space in Social Work Settings." *Social Work* (October, 1971), 16 (4):43–49.

Selby, Lola G. "Supportive Treatment: the Development of a Concept and a Helping Method." *Social Service Review* (December, 1956), 30 (4):400–414.

Selby, Lola G. "Support Revisited." *Social Service Review* (December, 1979), 53 (4):573–85.

Sereno, Kenneth K. and C. David Mortensen. *Foundations of Communication Theory*. New York: Harper & Row, 1970.

Shapiro, Constance Hoenk. "Termination: a Neglected Concept in the Social Work Curriculum." *Journal of Education for Social Work* (Summer, 1980), 16 (2):13–19.

Shaw, Lulie A. "Impressions of Life in a London Suburb." *Sociological Review* (December, 1954), 2 (2):177–94.

Sherman, Sanford N. "Family Therapy." In Francis J. Turner, ed., *Social Work Treatment: Interlocking Theoretical Approaches*, pp. 457–94. New York: Free Press, 1974.

Sherman, Sanford N. "The Choice of Group Therapy for Casework Clients." In *Social Work Practice, 1962*, pp. 174–86. New York: Columbia University Press, 1962.

Shulman, Lawrence. *The Skills of Helping Individuals and Groups*. Itasca, Ill.: Peacock. 1979.

Shyne, Ann W. "What Research Tells Us about Short-Term Cases in Family Agencies." *Social Casework* (May, 1957) 38 (5):223–31.

Silverman, Phyllis R. "A Reexamination of the Intake Procedure." *Social Casework* (December, 1970), 51 (10):625–34.

Silverman, Phyllis R. "The Influence of Racial Differences on the Negro Patient Dropping Out of Psychiatric Treatment." *Psychiatric Opinion* (January, 1971), 8 (1):29–36.

Simon, Bernece K. *Relation between Theory and Practice in Social Casework*. New York: National Association of Social Workers, 1960.

Simon, Bernece K. "Social Casework Theory: an Overview." In Robert W. Roberts and Robert H. Nee, eds., *Theories of Social Casework*, pp. 355–95. Chicago: University of Chicago Press, 1970.

Siporin, Max. *Introduction to Social Work Practice.* New York: Macmillan, 1975.

Smith, Larry. *Crisis Intervention: Theory and Practice.* Washington, D.C.: University Press of America, 1976.

Sobey, Francine, ed. *Changing Roles in Social Work Practice.* Philadelphia: Temple University Press, 1977.

Solomon, Barbara Bryant. *Black Empowerment: Social Work in Oppressed Communities.* New York: Columbia University Press, 1976.

Somers, Mary Louise. "Group Process within the Family Unit." In National Association of Social Workers, *The Family Is the Patient: the Group Approach to the Treatment of Family Health Problems,* pp. 22–39. Monograph VII. New York: the Association, 1965.

Somers, Mary Louise. "Problem-solving in Small Groups." In Robert W. Roberts and Helen Northen, eds., *Theories of Social Work with Groups,* pp. 331–67. New York: Columbia University Press, 1976.

Sorenson, Roy. Case Work and Group Work Integration: Its Implications for Community Planning." In *Proceedings, National Conference of Social Work, 1935,* pp. 311–22. Chicago: University of Chicago Press, 1935.

Sotomayor, Marta. "Mexican-American Interaction with Social Systems." *Social Casework* (May, 1971), 52 (5):316–22.

Spergel, Irving A. *Community Problem Solving: the Delinquency Example.* Chicago: University of Chicago Press, 1969.

Spitzer, Kurt and Betty Welsh. "A Problem-focused Model of Practice." *Social Casework* (June, 1969), 50 (6):323–29.

Stark, Frances B. "Barriers to Client-Worker Communication at Intake." *Social Casework* (April, 1959), 40 (4):177–83.

Startz, Morton R. and Helen F. Cohen. "The Impact of Social Change on the Practitioner." *Social Casework* (September, 1980), 61 (7):400–406.

Stein, Herman D. "The Concept of Environment in Social Work Practice." In Howard J. Parad and Rober R. Miller, eds., *Ego-oriented Casework; Problems and Perspectives,* pp. 65–72. New York: Family Service Association of America, 1963.

Stein, Irma L. *Systems Theory, Science, and Social Work.* Metuchen, N.J.: Scarecrow Press, 1974.

Stein, Irma L. "The Systems Model and Social Systems Theory." In Herbert S. Strean, ed., *Social Casework: Theories in Action,* pp. 123–95. Metuchen, N.J.: Scarecrow Press, 1971.

Stempler, Benjamin. "A Group Work Approach to Family Group Treatment." *Social Casework* (March, 1977), 58 (3):143–52.

Stiles, Evelyn et al. "Hear It Like It Is." *Social Casework* (May, 1972), 53 (5):292–99.

Strean, Herbert S. *Crucial Issues in Psychotherapy*. Metuchen, N.J. Scarecrow Press, 1976.

Strean, Herbert S., ed. *Social Casework: Theories in Action*. Metuchen, N.J.: Scarecrow Press, 1971.

Studt, Elliot. "Social Work Theory and Implications for the Practice of Methods." *Social Work Education Reporter* (June, 1968), 16 (2):22–24.

Sundel, Martin, Norma Radin, and Sallie R. Churchill. "Diagnosis in Group Work." In Paul Glasser, Roxemary Sarri, and Robert Vinter, eds., *Individual Change through Small Groups*, pp. 105–25. New York: Free Press, 1974.

Taber, Richard H. "A Systems Approach to the Delivery of Mental Health Services in Black Ghettos." *American Journal of Orthopsychiatry* (July, 1970), 40 (3):702–9.

Tennant, Violet. "The Caseworker's Experience in Working with Groups." D.S.W. diss., University of Pennsylvania, 1968.

Thomas, Edwin, ed. *Behavioral Science for Social Workers*. New York: Free Press, 1967.

Tilbury, Derek. "The Selection of Method in Social Work." *Social Work Today* (April, 1971), 2 (2):9–12.

Toch, Hans. "The Care and Feeding of Typologies and Labels." *Federal Probation* (September, 1970), 34 (3):15–19.

Towle, Charlotte. "Social Casework in Modern Society." *Social Service Review* (June, 1946), 20 (2):65–79.

Towle, Charlotte. "Social Work: Cause and Function, 1961." *Social Casework* (October, 1961), 42 (8):385–96.

Tropp, Emanuel. "A Developmental Theory." In Robert W. Roberts and Helen Northen, eds., *Theories of Social Work with Groups*, pp. 198–237. New York: Columbia University Press, 1976.

Truax, Charles B. and Robert R. Carkhuff. *Toward Effective Counseling and Psychotherapy: Training and Practice*. Chicago: Aldine, 1967.

Tufts, Edith. *Group Work with Young School Girls*. Los Angeles: Los Angeles Area Council, Camp Fire Girls, 1968.

Turner, Francis J. *Psychosocial Therapy; a Social Work Perspective*. New York: Free Press, 1978.

Turner, Francis J., ed. *Social Work Treatment: Interlocking Theoretical Approaches*. New York: Free Press, 1974.

Velasquez, Joan et al. "A Framework for Establishing Social Work Relationships across Racial Ethnic Lines." In Beulah Roberts Compton and

Burt Galaway, eds., *Social Work Processes*, pp. 197–203. Homewood, Ill.: Dorsey Press, 1979.

von Bertalanffy, Ludwig. *A General Systems Theory*. New York: Braziller, 1968.

von Bertalanffy, Ludwig. "General Systems Theory and Psychiatry." In Silvano Arieti, ed., *American Handbook of Psychiatry*, pp. 1095–1117. New York: Basic Books, 1976.

Wallens, Donald E. "Congruence." *American Journal of Psychotherapy* (January, 1969), 23 (1):207–16.

Wanamaker, Claudia. "The Integration of Group Work and Case Work." In *Proceedings, National Conference of Social Work, 1935*, pp. 300–310. Chicago: University of Chicago Press, 1935.

Wasserman, Sidney. "Ego Psychology." In Francis J. Turner, ed., *Social Work Treatment: Interlocking Theoretical Approaches*, pp. 42–83. New York: Free Press, 1974.

Wayne, Julianne L. and Nancy Avery. "Activities as a Tool for Group Termination." *Social Work* (January, 1979), 24 (1):58–62.

Wayne, Julianne L. and Barbara B. Feinstein. "Group Work Outreach to Parents by School Social Workers." *Social Casework* (June, 1978), 59 (6):345–51.

Webb, Allen P. and Patrick V. Riley. "Effectiveness of Casework with Young Female Probationers." *Social Casework* (November, 1970), 51 (9):566–72.

Weissman, Harold H., ed. *Individual and Group Services in the Mobilization for Youth Experience*. New York: Association Press, 1969.

Weissman, Harold H., ed. *Integrating Services for Troubled Families*. San Francisco: Jossey-Bass, 1978.

Weissman, Harold H. and Marie Weil. "Success and Failure in Integrating Services and Helping Families." In Harold H. Weissman, ed., *Integrating Services for Troubled Families*, ch. 7. San Francisco: Jossey-Bass, 1978.

White, Robert W. "Ego and Reality in Psychoanalytic Theory." *Psychological Issues* (1963), 3 (11):entire issue.

Whittaker, James K. "A Developmental-educational Approach to Child Treatment." In Francine Sobey, ed., *Changing Roles in Social Work Practice*, pp. 176–96. Philadelphia: Temple University Press, 1977.

Whittaker, James K. "Causes of Childhood Disorders: New Findings." *Social Work* (March, 1976), 21 (2):91–96.

Whittaker, James K. *Social Treatment: an Approach to Interpersonal Helping*. Chicago: Aldine, 1974.

Wiener, Norbert. *The Human Use of Human Beings*. New York: Doubleday, 1954.

Wilensky, Harold L. and Charles N. Lebeaux. *Industrial Society and Social Welfare*. New York: Russell Sage Foundation, 1958.

Williamson, Margaretta. *The Social Worker in Group Work*. New York: Harper, 1929.

Wilmott, Peter. *Family and Kinship Ties in East London*. London: Routledge & Kegan Paul, 1957.

Wilson, Gertrude. *Group Work and Case Work: Their Relationship and Practice*. New York: Family Welfare Association of America, 1941.

Wilson, Gertrude and Gladys Ryland. *Social Group Work Practice*. Boston: Houghton-Mifflin, 1949.

Wilson, Suanne J. *Confidentiality in Social Work*. New York: Free Press, 1978.

Winnicott, Clare. "Casework Techniques in the Child Care Service." In Eileen Younghusband, ed., *New Developments in Casework*, pp. 135–54. London: Allen & Unwin, 1966.

Witmer, Helen, ed. *Psychiatric Interviews with Children*. New York: Commonwealth Fund, 1946.

Wittman, Milton. "Application of Knowledge about Prevention in Social Work Education and Practice." *Social Work in Health Care* (Spring, 1977), 3 (1):37–47.

Wittman, Milton. "Preventive Social Work: a Goal for Practice and Education." *Social Work* (January, 1961), 6 (1):19–28.

Wolins, Martin. "Licensing and Recent Developments in Foster Care." *Child Welfare* (December, 1968), 47 (10):570–82.

Wolkon, George H. "Effecting a Continuum of Care." *Community Mental Health Journal* (February, 1968), 4 (1):63–72.

Wood, Katherine. "The Contribution of Psychoanalysis and Ego Psychology to Social Casework." In Herbert S. Strean, ed., *Social Casework: Theories in Action*, pp. 45–122. Metuchen, N.J.: Scarecrow Press, 1971.

Yalom, Irvin D. *The Theory and Practice of Group Psychotherapy*. New York: Basic Books, 1975.

Yalom, Irvin D. et al. "Preparation of Patients for Group Therapy." *Archives of General Psychiatry* (1967), 17 (4):416–27.

Young, Michael and Peter Wilmott. *Family and Kinship Ties in East London*. London: Routledge & Kegan Paul, 1957.

Younghusband, Eileen. *Social Work and Social Change*. London: Allen & Unwin, 1964.

Younghusband, Eileen. "Social Work Education in the World Today." In William G. Dixon, ed., *Social Welfare and the Preservation of Human Values,* pp. 3–13. Montreal: Dent, 1957.

Younghusband, Eileen, ed. *New Developments in Casework.* London: Allen & Unwin, 1966.

Younghusband, Eileen, ed. *Social Work with Families.* London: Allen & Unwin, 1965.

Zalba, Serapio R. "Discontinuance during Social Service Intake." Ph.D. diss., Western Reserve University, 1971.

INDEX